HOLT *Traditions*
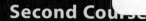
Second Course

Language and Sentence Skills Practice
Support for *Warriner's Handbook*

► **Lesson Worksheets**
► **Chapter Reviews**
► **"Choices" Activities**
► **Literary Models**
► **Proofreading Applications**

FOR
■ **Grammar**
■ **Usage**
■ **Mechanics**
■ **Sentences**

HOLT, RINEHART AND WINSTON

ISBN 978-0-03-099703-7
ISBN 0-03-099703-8

10 11 12 1689 15 14 13
4500421327

Contents

Contents

Contents

Contents

Contents

Chapter 14

PUNCTUATION:
END MARKS, COMMAS, SEMICOLONS, AND COLONS

Chapter 15

PUNCTUATION:
UNDERLINING (ITALICS), QUOTATION MARKS, APOSTROPHES, HYPHENS, PARENTHESES, BRACKETS, DASHES

Contents

Contents

Using This Workbook

The worksheets in this workbook provide practice, reinforcement, and extension for *Warriner's Handbook*.

Most of the worksheets you will find in this workbook are **traditional worksheets** providing practice and reinforcement activities on every rule and on all major instructional topics in the grammar, usage, and mechanics chapters in *Warriner's Handbook*.

You will also find in the workbook several kinds of **Language in Context worksheets**, which have been developed to expand the exploration and study of grammar, usage, and mechanics. The Language in Context worksheets include Choices worksheets, Proofreading Applications, Literary Model worksheets, and Writing Applications.

- **Choices** worksheets offer up to ten activities that provide new ways of approaching grammar, usage, and mechanics. Students can choose and complete one independent or group activity per worksheet. Choices activities stimulate learning through research, creative writing, nonfiction writing, discussion, drama, art, games, interviews, music, cross-curricular activities, technology, and other kinds of projects, including some designed entirely by students.

- **Proofreading Application** worksheets help students apply what they learn in class to contexts in the real world. Students use proofreading symbols to correct errors in grammar, usage, and mechanics in practical documents such as letters, applications, brochures, and reports. A chart of proofreading symbols is provided on page 396 of this workbook.

- **Literary Model** worksheets provide literary models that demonstrate how published authors use various grammatical forms to create style or meaning. Students identify and analyze each author's linguistic choices and then use grammatical forms to create style or meaning in their own literary creations. Students are asked to reflect on their own linguistic choices and to draw connections between the choices they make and the style or meaning of their work.

- **Writing Application** worksheets are similar to the Writing Application activities in the grammar, usage, and mechanics chapters in *Warriner's Handbook*. Following the writing process, students use specific grammatical forms as they create a publishable document such as a letter, report, script, or pamphlet.

The Teaching Resources include the **Answer Key** in a separate booklet titled *Language and Sentence Skills Practice Answer Key*.

Choices: Examining the Sentence

Here's your chance to step out of the grammar book and into the real world. You may not notice sentences, but you and the people around you use them every day. The following activities challenge you to find a connection between sentences and the world around you. Do the activity below that suits your personality best, and then share your discoveries with your class. Have fun!

DISCUSSION

Natural Habitats

Some places provide natural habitats for different sentence types. For instance, you can hear plenty of imperative sentences in the kitchen of a restaurant. Discuss other places where you might find examples of declarative, imperative, interrogative, and exclamatory sentences. Create a list of natural habitats for each of the four kinds of sentences. Pass out copies of your list.

BUILDING BACKGROUND KNOWLEDGE

"Give Me Liberty or Give Me Death!"

Exclamatory and strong imperative sentences can play a big part in our lives, but most writers seldom use them. Such sentences are generally out of place in nonfiction writing. In history and in literature, though, many exclamatory and imperative sentences have become known as famous quotations. What are some of these well-known exclamatory or imperative sentences? Get together with a group of friends and come up with a list of ten or more quotations. Then, write the quotations in large print on large pieces of paper and post them in the classroom. Under each quotation, write the speaker's name, the time period, and the situation that inspired the quotation. Remember to identify the sentence as either exclamatory or imperative.

RESEARCH/ETYMOLOGY

What's in a Name?

Investigate the origin of the word *sentence*. What is its history? When was the word first used? Does it have more than one meaning? What are these meanings? Let your classmates know what you have discovered.

WRITING

Order Your World

Take a look around you. How would you change your classroom if you had the opportunity? Think about it. Then, write a series of orders (imperative sentences, of course) to an architect or interior designer. Pretend that money is no object. Order anything at all. What will your dream classroom include—computers for everyone? more comfortable chairs? a well-stocked refrigerator? a television set? Be sure to include at least ten imperative sentences.

MEDIA

Extra! Extra! Read All About It!

Journalists, novelists, and advertisers vary their sentences according to the purpose at hand. Browse through newspapers, magazines, and books to see if you can find examples of the four types of sentences classified by purpose (declarative, imperative, interrogative, and exclamatory). On poster board, write out (or cut out and paste) at least two examples of each type.

DISCUSSION

Fifth Wheel

Now that you've learned about the four kinds of sentences classified by purpose (declarative, imperative, interrogative, and exclamatory), ask yourself if these categories are accurate. Should there be another kind of sentence? If so, what kind of sentence would you create? What would you name this new category? How would you punctuate the kind of sentence? Present your written proposal to the class for approval.

GRAMMAR

Sentences and Sentence Fragments A

1a. A *sentence* is a word group that contains a subject and a verb and that expresses a complete thought.

A *sentence fragment* is a word group that looks like a sentence but does not contain both a subject and a verb or does not express a complete thought.

SENTENCE FRAGMENT Those on board the sailboat. [no verb]

Shouted to the swimmers near the shore. [no subject]

SENTENCE Those on board the sailboat shouted to the swimmers near the shore.

EXERCISE Identify each of the following word groups as a sentence or a sentence fragment. On the line provided, write *S* for *sentence* or *F* for *sentence fragment*.

Examples __*S*__ **1.** Last Saturday, Antonio and his friends went to the beach.

__*F*__ **2.** A day that they will not soon forget.

_____ **1.** Antonio and his friends in the bay.

_____ **2.** They spotted a shark swimming toward a sailboat.

_____ **3.** One of the sailboats nearby.

_____ **4.** Efforts to distract the shark.

_____ **5.** The people on the shore shouted at the swimmers.

_____ **6.** The shark opened its huge jaws.

_____ **7.** As close to the shore as this shark was.

_____ **8.** The fast-moving shark swam under one of the sailboats.

_____ **9.** On its way toward shore.

_____ **10.** Slicing the surface of the water.

_____ **11.** The swimmers could see only the fin on the shark's back.

_____ **12.** Everyone on the beach continued to wave and shout.

_____ **13.** Swam toward shore with all their strength.

_____ **14.** With much help from the lifeguards.

_____ **15.** When they reached the shore.

_____ **16.** The swimmers were trembling.

_____ **17.** After they realized that they were safe.

_____ **18.** Later, the swimmers spoke to news reporters and photographers.

_____ **19.** The lifeguards closed the beach.

_____ **20.** And sent everyone away.

Sentences and Sentence Fragments B

1a.	A ***sentence*** is a word group that contains a subject and a verb and that expresses a complete thought.

A *sentence fragment* is a word group that looks like a sentence but does not contain both a subject and a verb or does not express a complete thought.

SENTENCE FRAGMENT	Shirley Chisholm, the first African American congresswoman.
SENTENCE	Shirley Chisholm, the first African American congresswoman, was elected to the U.S. House of Representatives in 1968.

EXERCISE Identify each of the following word groups as a sentence or a sentence fragment. On the line provided, write *S* for *sentence* or *F* for *sentence fragment*.

Example __*F*__ **1.** One clear night in the middle of summer.

_____ **1.** Several teenagers went camping one clear night in the middle of summer.

_____ **2.** The campers sat around a campfire.

_____ **3.** Which kept them warm.

_____ **4.** Someone suggested that they tell stories.

_____ **5.** Camila told an interesting story.

_____ **6.** About a man who lived on a houseboat near a village.

_____ **7.** Never spoke to the villagers.

_____ **8.** People thought he was a thief.

_____ **9.** And blamed him when things were lost.

_____ **10.** One day the man left the boat.

_____ **11.** And walked far away.

_____ **12.** A curious villager entered the boat.

_____ **13.** To see what was inside.

_____ **14.** Very surprised by what he found inside.

_____ **15.** There were all kinds of wooden toys.

_____ **16.** That the mysterious man had built.

_____ **17.** Each toy was carefully painted.

_____ **18.** The toys were gifts for the village children.

_____ **19.** The villagers had misjudged the man.

_____ **20.** Realized that the man was very kind and felt sorry.

Sentences and Sentence Fragments C

1a. A *sentence* is a word group that contains a subject and a verb and that expresses a complete thought.

A *sentence fragment* is a word group that looks like a sentence but does not contain both a subject and a verb or does not express a complete thought.

SENTENCE FRAGMENT   As we carved the ice sculpture.

SENTENCE   My cousin and I carved an ice sculpture of a unicorn.

EXERCISE Each of the following groups of words is a sentence fragment because it is missing either a subject or a verb. On the line provided, write *S* if the incomplete sentence is missing a subject or *V* if it is missing a verb. Then, rewrite the word group to make it a complete sentence.

Example ___*S*___ **1.** Played for hours in the park.

Daniel and I played for hours in the park.

_____ **1.** The two energetic boys and their little sister. _____

_____

_____ **2.** The man with the small dog on a leash. _____

_____

_____ **3.** Ran through the trails. _____

_____

_____ **4.** Played until it was too dark to see. _____

_____

_____ **5.** The people near the large oak trees. _____

_____

_____ **6.** A small group of sparrows or wrens. _____

_____

_____ **7.** Flew rapidly from tree to tree. _____

_____

_____ **8.** Perched on a high branch of a hackberry tree. _____

_____

_____ **9.** The smallest squirrel in the group. _____

_____

_____ **10.** Hid in the hollow of an old log. _____

_____

for **CHAPTER 1: THE SENTENCE**   pages 7–10

Subjects and Predicates

1b. A *subject* tells *whom* or *what* the sentence is about.

To find the subject, ask *who* or *what* is doing something or *about whom* or *what* something is being said.

1d. The *predicate* of a sentence tells something about the subject.

In the following examples, the subjects are underlined once and the predicates are underlined twice.

EXAMPLES   The construction of the White House began in 1792.

Not until 1800 did the presidential residence have its first occupants.

EXERCISE A   Identify the underlined part or parts of each of the following sentences as the subject or the predicate. On the line provided, write *S* for *subject* or *P* for *predicate*.

Example ___*P*___ **1.** Has the White House been the home of every United States president except George Washington?

_____ **1.** The White House was originally called the President's House.

_____ **2.** Later, it was called the Executive Mansion.

_____ **3.** The building's design was chosen after a contest in 1791.

_____ **4.** The Irish American architect James Hoban won five hundred dollars for his design.

_____ **5.** The original structure was built of white-gray sandstone.

_____ **6.** British forces attacked the capital in 1814 and burned the President's House.

_____ **7.** After the fire, painters whitewashed the new mansion.

_____ **8.** Covering smoke stains were several coats of white paint.

_____ **9.** People commonly called the building the White House.

_____ **10.** During his presidency, Theodore Roosevelt authorized the popular name.

EXERCISE B   Identify the underlined part or parts of each of the following sentences as the subject or the predicate. On the line provided, write *S* for *subject* or *P* for *predicate*.

Example ___*P*___ **1.** One symbol of United States independence is the Liberty Bell.

_____ **11.** A picture of the Liberty Bell appears in our social studies textbook.

_____ **12.** Does the Liberty Bell really weigh over two thousand pounds?

_____ **13.** The nation's flag also symbolizes independence.

_____ **14.** The flag's thirteen stripes stand for the nation's original thirteen colonies.

_____ **15.** Can any of you explain the symbolic meaning of the flag's fifty stars?

Simple and Complete Subjects

1c. The *simple subject* is the main word or word group that tells *whom* or *what* the sentence is about.

The simple subject is part of the *complete subject*, which consists of all the words that tell *whom* or *what* the sentence is about.

SENTENCE	The Kabuki dancers' costumes are beautiful.
COMPLETE SUBJECT	The Kabuki dancers' costumes
SIMPLE SUBJECT	costumes

EXERCISE A In each of the following sentences, the complete subject is underlined. Circle the word or word group that is the simple subject.

Example 1. The long (journey) would have been impossible without these boots.

1. Traditional Inuit dress includes the parka and mukluks.

2. People in snowy climates wear snowshoes for a variety of purposes.

3. North American Indians developed moccasins centuries ago.

4. The upper part of this comfortable footwear is often adorned with colorful beads.

5. A simple piece of leather with rawhide lacings was the first kind of shoe.

EXERCISE B In each of the following sentences, underline the complete subject and circle the simple subject.

Example 1. Traditional (cowboys) in the American West wore boots with spurs.

6. Most of the ancient Egyptians went barefoot.

7. Some kinds of sandals can be laced almost to the knee.

8. Have you ever worn a plastic shoe?

9. At one time, some shoes in Japan were attached to stilts as high as six inches.

10. The Romans shaped shoes to fit the left foot and the right foot.

11. In ancient Rome, shoe style depended on social class.

12. During the 1300s in England, shoes with pointed toes eighteen inches long were popular.

13. The people of some mountainous areas wear shoes with an upturned toe and a high heel.

14. Decorations of gold, silver, and gems adorned some eighteenth-century shoes.

15. The first shoe factory appeared in Massachusetts in 1760.

Simple and Complete Predicates

1e. The *simple predicate,* or *verb,* is the main word or word group that tells something about the subject.

The simple predicate is part of the *complete predicate,* which consists of a verb and all the words that describe the verb and complete its meaning.

> **SENTENCE** The party for my grandparents' fiftieth anniversary ended with a grand display of fireworks.
>
> **COMPLETE PREDICATE** ended with a grand display of fireworks
>
> **SIMPLE PREDICATE** ended

EXERCISE In each of the following sentences, underline the complete predicate and circle the simple predicate.

Example 1. The musician ⟨played⟩ a twelve-string guitar.

1. The guitarist put new strings on her guitar.

2. The new strings sounded much better.

3. She tuned her guitar several times.

4. The guitarist played the first string with the help of a pitch pipe.

5. She then tuned all the strings to the first string.

6. Strings in tune are important to the musician.

7. The guitarist has a good ear for pitch.

8. She tried several chords on her guitar.

9. Then she made some adjustments to the tuning.

10. The new strings stretched a bit.

11. Some strings are lighter than others.

12. Do many guitarists prefer the lightest strings?

13. Sometimes the guitarist uses a thumb pick.

14. She plays the low notes with the thumb pick.

15. The guitarist often sings her own lyrics with the chords.

16. She uses a capo for some songs.

17. Capos change the pitch of the strings.

18. Capos fit around the neck of the guitar.

19. The musician plays in a different key with a capo.

20. Have you ever played a guitar?

Verb Phrases

A *verb phrase* consists of a main verb and one or more helping verbs.

EXAMPLES   **Did** you **see** the meteor shower last night?

One of my cousins in South Carolina **has been training** for the U.S. Olympic wrestling team.

EXERCISE   In each of the following sentences, underline the complete verb phrase.

Example 1. Jillian <u>has been swimming</u> for four years.

1. Jillian's swim team is practicing for a meet.

2. Her team will be competing next month.

3. Jillian will be swimming freestyle.

4. The coach has been teaching new drills.

5. Some of the swimmers are training for the backstroke competition.

6. Jillian has competed in two other meets.

7. She was practicing each morning before school.

8. Now she will be practicing twice a day.

9. The team members are feeling more confident.

10. The coach has helped everyone on the team.

11. Years ago, Jillian could not swim a whole lap.

12. Now she can swim long distances.

13. Her little sister Rebecca has joined the team.

14. Rebecca is improving quickly.

15. She can do the butterfly stroke already.

16. Next year, Rebecca will compete in Jillian's age group.

17. Jillian and Rebecca have never raced one another at a meet.

18. They do race for fun quite often.

19. Swimming is recognized as a very healthful form of exercise.

20. Rebecca and Jillian are enjoying the sport.

Complete and Simple Subjects and Predicates A

1c. | The *simple subject* is the main word or word group that tells *whom* or *what* the sentence is about.

The simple subject is part of the *complete subject*, which consists of all the words that tell *whom* or *what* the sentence is about.

1e. | The *simple predicate,* or *verb,* is the main word or word group that tells something about the subject.

The simple predicate is part of the *complete predicate*, which consists of a verb and all the words that describe the verb and complete its meaning.

EXERCISE A   In each of the following sentences, underline the complete subject and circle the simple subject.

Example 1. Examples of amphibians include salamanders, frogs, and toads.

1. Many types of amphibians can be found in the United States.

2. Several kinds of salamanders inhabit forest areas.

3. The largest salamander on land is the Pacific giant salamander.

4. The Pacific giant salamander can grow to nearly one foot in length.

5. A small mouse might be a meal to this salamander.

6. The main predator in a small stream might be this large salamander.

7. A smaller salamander is the Olympic salamander.

8. Logs provide shady spots for the Olympic salamander.

9. To these salamanders, moisture from the forest floor is extremely important.

10. These smaller salamanders live on land but need to be near moisture.

EXERCISE B   In each of the following sentences, underline the complete predicate and circle the simple predicate.

Example 1. Ancient forests are extremely valuable to many life-forms.

11. Many mammals, amphibians, and reptiles live in ancient forests.

12. Animals can make nests in dead trees.

13. Logs in streams and along the forest floor become part of an ancient forest.

14. These logs are beneficial for the soil and for animals.

15. All of the elements of an ancient forest work together.

GRAMMAR

Complete and Simple Subjects and Predicates B

1c.   The *simple subject* is the main word or word group that tells *whom* or *what* the sentence is about.

The simple subject is part of the *complete subject*, which consists of all the words that tell *whom* or *what* the sentence is about.

1e.   The *simple predicate,* or *verb,* is the main word or word group that tells something about the subject.

The simple predicate is part of the *complete predicate*, which consists of a verb and all the words that describe the verb and complete its meaning.

EXERCISE A   In each of the following sentences, underline the complete subject and circle the simple subject.

Example 1. More and more people are learning to use the Internet.

1. Use of the Internet is becoming increasingly common.

2. The World Wide Web is an excellent research tool.

3. Different search engines are available to users.

4. The purpose of a search engine is to help users find information.

5. The person looking for information types key words into a search engine.

6. The search engine looks for Web sites containing the key words.

7. The results of the search then appear in a list.

8. The user clicks on any Web site.

9. Very specific key words are sometimes necessary.

10. A search engine can be easy to use and fast.

EXERCISE B   In each of the following sentences, underline the complete predicate and circle the simple predicate.

Example 1. Finding information on the Internet may seem difficult at first.

11. A wealth of information is available on the Internet.

12. People can find ZIP Codes on the Internet.

13. Telephone directories are available on the Internet.

14. Students can find tutorials on the World Wide Web.

15. Can drivers find maps to their destinations?

Compound Subjects

1f. A *compound subject* consists of two or more connected subjects that have the same verb.

The most common connecting words are *and* and *or*.

COMPOUND SUBJECT   The **doorbell** and the **telephone** rang at the same time.

EXERCISE A   Each of the following sentences contains a compound subject. Underline the parts of the subject in each sentence.

Example 1. <u>Pepper</u> and <u>Salty</u> are our pet cats.

1. Kelly and I found two kittens.

2. My sister and Kelly named them Pepper and Salty.

3. The cats and our dog get along well.

4. My classmates and neighbors often come to visit.

5. Jacqui or Danielle will bring a leash for our dog.

6. Will the other dogs and my dog play together?

7. My sister or I will feed all the dogs.

8. Pepper and Salty sometimes wake up the dogs in the morning.

9. My aunts and uncles all have pets.

10. Parakeets, poodles, and goldfish are my grandmother's favorite pets.

EXERCISE B   For each of the following sentences, underline all parts of the compound subject.

Example 1. <u>Glenn</u> and his <u>brother</u> visited Knoxville, Tennessee.

11. The brothers and their father went to the lake.

12. Ducks, geese, and other birds gathered around the lake.

13. Several picnic tables and benches were lined up on one side of the lake.

14. Are the sandwiches and drinks in the ice chest?

15. The brothers, their father, and several other tourists played a game of kickball.

16. Did Glenn or his father bring the kickball to the lake?

17. Glenn's brother and a duck got into a tug of war over a slice of bread.

18. Were the sandwiches, drinks, and fresh fruit enough to feed everyone?

19. Glenn's brother and father cleared the table after the meal.

20. Glenn, his brother, and his father had a splendid time at the lake.

Compound Verbs

1g.   A *compound verb* consists of two or more verbs that have the same subject.

A connecting word—usually *and, or,* or *but*—is used between the verbs.

COMPOUND VERB   The Tigers **won** the first game of the double-header but **did** not **win** the second.

EXERCISE A Each of the following sentences contains a compound verb. Underline the parts of the verb in each sentence.

Example 1. Megan <u>loves</u> music and <u>enjoys</u> classical concerts.

1. Megan will learn viola, study music theory, and take piano lessons.

2. Her school music teacher gives her lessons and shows her new tunes.

3. Megan reads music but doesn't sight-read fast.

4. The study of rhythm requires patience and takes time.

5. A music staff has five lines and can look complex at first.

6. Notes may sit on the lines or occupy the spaces between the lines.

7. The notes correspond to the first seven letters of the alphabet and stand for certain tones.

8. Megan reads the note and bows the appropriate string.

9. Megan practices viola often and is improving day by day.

10. Should Megan practice for another hour or start her homework now?

EXERCISE B Underline the parts of the compound verb in each of the following sentences.

Example 1. Ted <u>stood</u>, <u>slipped</u> on the grass, and <u>fell</u> into the pond.

11. The cattle slipped and slid in the muddy creek bed.

12. Will Mara come to the party or stay home?

13. Close the hood, wipe the oil off your hands, and start the engine again.

14. Carlie shot the final picture on the roll and rewound the film.

15. Did the outfielder drop the ball or make the catch?

Compound Subjects and Verbs

1f.   A *compound subject* consists of two or more connected subjects that have the same verb.

     EXAMPLE   **Gloria** and **Susan** are good singers.

1g.   A *compound verb* consists of two or more verbs that have the same subject.

     EXAMPLE   Rita Moreno **sings** and **dances** beautifully.

EXERCISE A   Underline the compound subject or compound verb in each of the following sentences. Then, on the line provided, identify the compound part by writing *CS* for *compound subject* or *CV* for *compound verb*.

Example   _CS_   **1.** Vegetables and whole grains are good for your heart.

_____ **1.** According to scientists, too much fat and cholesterol in the diet are harmful.

_____ **2.** Cheeseburgers and milkshakes contain large amounts of both.

_____ **3.** Therefore, you should not eat or drink such fatty snacks too often.

_____ **4.** Did you and your sister have apples or carrot sticks as a snack today?

_____ **5.** In the future, stop and think about the health effects of your meals.

EXERCISE B   On the lines provided, combine each of the following pairs of sentences by writing one sentence with a compound subject or a compound verb. Hint: When you create a sentence with a compound subject, you may also need to change other words in the sentence.

Example   **1.**   Gettysburg is a Civil War battle site. Fredericksburg is, too.

     Gettysburg and Fredericksburg are Civil War battle sites.

6. Maples grow well in this area. Birches grow well, too. _____

_____

7. Sabrina runs every other day. Sabrina swims every other day. _____

_____

8. The emu is a flightless bird. So is the kiwi. _____

_____

9. Kwanita designed a new kind of kite. Then she built the kite. _____

_____

10. When was Sandra Day O'Connor confirmed to the U.S. Supreme Court? When was Ruth

Bader Ginsburg confirmed? _____

_____

GRAMMAR

Subjects and Verbs A

1b. A *subject* tells *whom* or *what* the sentence is about.

>   **EXAMPLES**   Did **everyone** in your class enjoy the field trip?
>   **Ross** and **Roger** will report on it tomorrow.

1e. The *simple predicate,* or **verb,** is the main word or word group that tells something about the subject.

>   **EXAMPLES**   Did everyone in your class **enjoy** the field trip?
>   Ross and Roger **will report** on it tomorrow.

EXERCISE A   For the following sentences, underline the subjects and circle the verbs.

Example 1. Katya and her younger sister [play] basketball for our school.

1. Rogelio and Martin are brothers and best friends.

2. Every morning before school, the two brothers practice tennis.

3. Rogelio and his coach will play tennis this afternoon.

4. After lunch, Martin will go to his science class in the portable building outside.

5. The teacher and some visitors were talking in the loud, busy hallway.

6. At seven this evening, Katya and her best friend will study geometry together.

7. Algebra and geometry can be fun.

8. A scientist should know math and enjoy methodical research.

9. Next year, Rogelio will study trigonometry.

10. Ever since the sixth grade, Katya has dreamed of a career as a marine biologist.

EXERCISE B   For the following sentences, underline the subjects and circle the verbs.

Example 1. Engineers [must know] math and [understand] science.

11. Engineering is a specialized field and requires a lot of study.

12. A civil engineer might plan roadways or design bridges.

13. Most engineers study their fields carefully and develop new ideas.

14. The field of engineering requires creativity and demands attention to detail.

15. Engineers often specialize in one area and focus their attention on that subject.

Subjects and Verbs B

1b. A *subject* tells *whom* or *what* the sentence is about.

> EXAMPLES Did **Harry** and **Sally** leave or just go outside?
>
> In the morning, **we** will go.

1e. The *simple predicate,* or **verb,** is the main word or word group that tells something about the subject.

> EXAMPLES **Did** Harry and Sally **leave** or just **go** outside?
>
> In the morning, we **will go.**

EXERCISE For the following sentences, underline the subjects and circle the verbs.

Example 1. Rosa and Marta are on the volleyball team.

1. Venus and Mars are Earth's nearest planetary neighbors.

2. Gilbert will create a short film or write a one-act play.

3. Her three-year-old brother does a silly dance and gives us all a good laugh.

4. Jamal and Tina carried the boxes of books up three flights of stairs.

5. The best movie of the summer created suspense and frightened the audience.

6. Especially during this close game, the team members and the coach must work together.

7. Last weekend, Aunt Sally went to the neighborhood pool and read for hours.

8. When will we see our relatives and exchange the gifts?

9. Both Hannah and Chuck worked hard on the science project.

10. In her spare time, Elena studies art books, finds interesting ideas, and creates new projects.

11. Push-ups and chin-ups require strength in the arms and shoulders.

12. Every evening before dark, the athlete and her coach jog three miles together.

13. Among those with perfect attendance for the year were Joey, Dannika, and Steig.

14. On the hike up the mountain, I stumbled over a log and bruised my knee.

15. Either the baseball team or the softball team should win the state championship this year.

16. To our surprise, neither Mom nor Grandpa particularly liked the salsa.

17. The amateur photographer takes pictures regularly but never develops her own photographs.

18. My neighbor writes short films but usually doesn't produce them.

19. Will lettuce and tomatoes be crops in our backyard garden this year?

20. During a funny scene, that actor skipped a line and confused the star of the show.

Classifying Sentences by Purpose A

1h.	A *declarative sentence* makes a statement and ends with a period.
1i.	An *imperative sentence* gives a command or makes a request.
1j.	An *interrogative sentence* asks a question and ends with a question mark.
1k.	An *exclamatory sentence* shows excitement or strong feeling and ends with an exclamation point.

DECLARATIVE	I asked the librarian for help.
IMPERATIVE	Help me. *or* Help me!
INTERROGATIVE	What is the Trail of Tears?
EXCLAMATORY	What a sad part of American history it is!

EXERCISE A   Classify each of the following sentences by purpose. On the line provided, write *DEC* for *declarative, IMP* for *imperative, INT* for *interrogative,* or *EXC* for *exclamatory.*

Example __DEC__ **1.** The Cherokee were forced from their homeland in the Southeast.

_____ **1.** This forced migration became known as the Trail of Tears.

_____ **2.** Look at this map.

_____ **3.** Many migrated west to what is now Oklahoma.

_____ **4.** How many Cherokee escaped the Trail of Tears?

_____ **5.** How tragic the story is!

EXERCISE B   Rewrite each of the sentences below using the instructions given in brackets.

Example 1. George Catlin began painting professionally in the 1820s. *[Ask a question.]*

When did George Catlin begin painting professionally?

6. George Catlin painted portraits of many of the Plains Indians. *[Ask a question.]*

_____

7. Have you seen Catlin's picture of the Seminole chief Osceola? *[Make a statement.]*

_____

8. Osceola looks handsome and grand in that picture. *[Express strong feeling.]*

_____

9. Catlin created more than five hundred pictures showing American Indian life. *[Ask a question.]*

_____

10. For more information about Catlin, you may want to read this book. *[Give a command.]*

_____

NAME _____ CLASS _____ DATE _____

GRAMMAR

for **CHAPTER 1: THE SENTENCE** page 19

Classifying Sentences by Purpose B

1h. A *declarative sentence* makes a statement and ends with a period.

1i. An *imperative sentence* gives a command or makes a request.

1j. An *interrogative sentence* asks a question and ends with a question mark.

1k. An *exclamatory sentence* shows excitement or strong feeling and ends with an exclamation point.

DECLARATIVE	One of my hobbies is stargazing.
IMPERATIVE	Please look through this telescope.
IMPERATIVE	Look now!
INTERROGATIVE	Do all stars give off light?
EXCLAMATORY	How magnificent the sky looks tonight!

EXERCISE A Classify each of the following sentences by purpose. On the line provided, write *DEC* for *declarative, IMP* for *imperative, INT* for *interrogative,* or *EXC* for *exclamatory*.

Example _INT_ **1.** Did you go to the concert?

_____ **1.** The orchestra played magnificent Argentine tango music.

_____ **2.** Did you hear the violin solos?

_____ **3.** What an amazing arrangement that was!

_____ **4.** Please find out who the composer is.

_____ **5.** The composer's name is Diego Sanchez.

EXERCISE B Classify each of the following sentences by purpose. On the line provided, write *DEC* for *declarative, IMP* for *imperative, INT* for *interrogative,* or *EXC* for *exclamatory*. Then, write an appropriate end mark at the end of each sentence.

Example _EXC_ **1.** What a lovely tune that was /

_____ **6.** Have you ever heard this type of music before

_____ **7.** The cello contributed to the haunting and beautiful melody

_____ **8.** Did you notice how the accordion blends perfectly with the violins

_____ **9.** The compositions are brilliantly designed to showcase each instrument

_____ **10.** What a talented composer we have discovered

Review A: Sentences and Sentence Fragments

EXERCISE Identify each of the following groups of words as a sentence or a sentence fragment. On the line provided, write *S* for *sentence* or *F* for *sentence fragment*.

Examples __*S*__ **1.** Here are the photographs of my visit to Assateague Island.

__*F*__ **2.** An island along the Maryland and Virginia coasts.

_____ **1.** In a place called Assateague Island.

_____ **2.** Wild horses live on the island.

_____ **3.** Not on the mainland, though.

_____ **4.** Where it is slightly above sea level at the highest point.

_____ **5.** There is no shelter there from hurricanes.

_____ **6.** Except sand dunes and a few trees.

_____ **7.** However, the horses have survived for centuries.

_____ **8.** No one knows how they got there.

_____ **9.** According to legend, a great Spanish sailing ship.

_____ **10.** They may be descendants of horses taken to the island in the 1600s.

_____ **11.** Wow, there are herds running wild!

_____ **12.** Thoroughly enjoyed watching them run.

_____ **13.** Have you ever seen a wild horse?

_____ **14.** The island is also home to a great variety of birds.

_____ **15.** How many species?

_____ **16.** Three kinds of egrets on the island.

_____ **17.** Some ducks, swans, and geese migrate to the island.

_____ **18.** Sika elk, which are originally from Japan, Korea, and China.

_____ **19.** If you have an opportunity to visit this beautiful island refuge.

_____ **20.** Take your camera along.

for **CHAPTER 1: THE SENTENCE** pages 7–17

Review B: **Subjects and Predicates**

EXERCISE In each of the following sentences, draw one line under the complete subject and two lines under the complete predicate. Then, circle each simple subject and verb.

Example 1. Does Guido's little brother collect rocks?

1. The party for Victor is tomorrow.

2. The soundtrack of that movie features several jazz standards.

3. Every club in our school is building a float for the parade.

4. The huge mirror in the hall is a valuable antique.

5. Our entire family attended the commencement exercises.

6. In front of the garage lay three bicycles.

7. My younger brother sat in the back seat with the dogs.

8. Is this vacation plan the least expensive?

9. Our neighbor helped us with the clothesline.

10. Will the members of the committee be making the decisions?

11. Our team finally won its first game.

12. With the help of her teammates, the young woman limped off the soccer field.

13. Would any of you listen to this music by Igor Stravinsky?

14. The science teacher gave us an interesting assignment.

15. What a celebration our class had!

16. Does Mr. Wong give you cello lessons?

17. My English teacher gave me a copy of the book *Little Women*.

18. At the Japanese restaurant, both of us ordered tempura.

19. Neither of these answers is correct.

20. On opening night of the World Series, the ten-year-old girl beamed with excitement.

Review C: Compound Subjects and Compound Verbs

EXERCISE A For each of the following sentences, underline each part of the compound subject.

Example 1. <u>Tools</u> and <u>materials</u> are necessary for home repair.

1. Wood and paint are useful materials for home repair.

2. Aren't hammers and nails usually necessary for repair?

3. Plumbers or electricians might help with more serious problems.

4. Saws, chisels, and planes are important tools for woodworking.

5. A chisel or gouge helps a carpenter work with wood.

6. Sanders and planes are tools for leveling wood surfaces.

7. Windows and doors require special care.

8. For many projects, measuring tapes or rulers are useful.

9. The height, width, and depth of the windows are important measurements.

10. The weight and thickness of the doors determine the type of hinges necessary.

EXERCISE B For each of the following sentences, underline each part of the compound verb.

Example 1. Frank and Edwina <u>will buy</u> and <u>restore</u> an old house.

11. Frank examined the house and noticed several problems.

12. To Frank's dismay, parts of the roof leaked or were damaged.

13. Frank removed the old shingles near the chimney and added new ones.

14. Edwina cleaned the leaves out of the gutters and then repaired the one rusty gutter.

15. Did that same windowpane slip and crack again?

16. Edwina cut some glass, shaped its edges, and then replaced the old pane.

17. Next she bought some fabric and made new curtains.

18. The door in the front hallway squeaked and dragged on the floor.

19. After dinner, Frank cleaned and oiled the hinges.

20. Frank removed the door but hasn't sanded the bottom of it yet.

Review D: **Classifying Sentences by Purpose**

EXERCISE Classify each of the following sentences by purpose. On the line provided, write *DEC* for *declarative*, *IMP* for *imperative*, *INT* for *interrogative*, or *EXC* for *exclamatory*.

Example _DEC_ **1.** A laser produces an intense beam of light.

_____ **1.** What kinds of operations can a laser perform?

_____ **2.** Look at this list of operations.

_____ **3.** A laser can drill through a diamond, carry information, or measure the distance to the moon.

_____ **4.** Don't eye surgeons use lasers?

_____ **5.** How extremely bright the light from a laser is!

_____ **6.** Scientists are studying the power of the laser.

_____ **7.** Even a tiny beam produces an enormous amount of power!

_____ **8.** Perhaps in this mysterious beam lies the answer to an alternative power source.

_____ **9.** What new machines would you like to see in the near future?

_____ **10.** Class, please make a list of your ideas.

_____ **11.** Jackie wishes for cars that do not rely on fossil fuels.

_____ **12.** Will computer-controlled robots become commonplace?

_____ **13.** Study this sketch of a future space colony.

_____ **14.** What courage it would take to live there!

_____ **15.** Perhaps someday we will all be able to travel in space.

_____ **16.** Do you think the future holds unlimited potential?

_____ **17.** The way we treat our planet today affects the way we will live in the future.

_____ **18.** Make smart choices or pay the price.

_____ **19.** Have you ever wondered what future generations will think of us?

_____ **20.** I am willing to do what I can to make the world a better place.

Literary Model: Dialogue

"Mama, I'm hungry," I complained one afternoon.
"Jump up and catch a kungry," she said, trying to make me laugh and forget.
"What's a kungry?"
"It's what little boys eat when they get hungry," she said.
"What does it taste like?"
"I don't know."
"Then why do you tell me to catch one?"
"Because you said that you were hungry," she said, smiling....
"But I want to eat," I said, beginning to cry.
"You'll just have to wait," she said again.
"But why?"
"For God to send some food."
"When is He going to send it?"
"I don't know."
"But I'm hungry!"

—from *Black Boy* by Richard Wright

EXERCISE A   Each line in the preceding excerpt contains a direct quotation. The numbers below correspond to each line of the story. On each blank line that follows, write *S* if the direct quotation is a
complete sentence or *F* if the direct quotation is a sentence fragment. Then, for each complete sentence,
write *DEC* for *declarative*, *IMP* for *imperative*, *INT* for *interrogative*, or *EXC* for *exclamatory*. The first line,
which corresponds to the first line of the excerpt, has been filled in for you.

1. *S–DEC*   6. _____   11. _____

2. _____   7. _____   12. _____

3. _____   8. _____   13. _____

4. _____   9. _____   14. _____

5. _____   10. _____   15. _____

EXERCISE B   Why do you think the author included fragments and a variety of kinds of sentences in this
dialogue? How would the dialogue sound if it contained only complete sentences? How would it sound
if all the sentences were the same kind?

_____

_____

_____

Literary Model (continued)

EXERCISE C Write a dialogue between a child and an adult. Be sure to include both complete sentences and sentence fragments as well as at least one of each of the four kinds of sentences: declarative, imperative, interrogative, and exclamatory. When you have finished, read your dialogue and decide whether each line sounds realistic and natural. Make any changes necessary to make the dialogue seem real.

_____

_____

_____

_____

_____

_____

_____

_____

EXERCISE D Could you have expressed everything in your dialogue if you had used only complete sentences? only fragments? Would the dialogue have sounded the same if you had used only one or two kinds of sentences? Explain your answers.

_____

_____

_____

_____

_____

_____

_____

_____

_____

_____

Language and Sentence Skills Practice

Writing Application: Brochure

Exclamatory sentences are powerful, but they lose their punch when writers overuse them. When you want to create a sense of excitement in your writing, using needless exclamation points is rarely as effective as making the right word choices.

INEFFECTIVE   Wow!! This roller coaster is so scary!!!!

EFFECTIVE   Wow! The high-speed drops and steep banks of the roller coaster add up to one scary ride!

WRITING ACTIVITY

You have been hired to create a brochure for a campaign to attract tourists to your city or town. Your job is to combine words and images that will convince people that your hometown is worth a visit. Use several different sentence types to make your brochure more varied and interesting.

PREWRITING   Make a list of your favorite aspects of your hometown. Your list can include restaurants, parks, sports attractions, festivals, museums, and shops; or, your list can include qualities that make your hometown a comfortable or interesting place to be. Be thinking about the shape and size of your brochure, as well as the best ways to portray the items on your list.

WRITING   Choose two or three items that best represent your town. Then, write a description of each item you've chosen. Feel free to use exclamation points, but remember to create enthusiasm by combining the four sentence types in an interesting, effective way.

REVISING   Ask a classmate to read your descriptions and give you feedback about your use of sentence variety. Incorporate any suggestions that make your writing more clear or interesting. Check to make sure your brochure contains at least one example of each sentence type.

PUBLISHING   Check your descriptions for errors in grammar, usage, spelling, and punctuation. Then, determine the shape and size of your brochure. Design your brochure, using a pencil for your first draft. When you are ready, use bold text and colorful illustrations to create your final version.

EXTENDING YOUR WRITING

If you enjoyed this exercise, you could develop it into a longer writing project. Get together with one or two classmates, and develop an ad campaign. Create three advertisements for your hometown: a TV ad, a magazine ad, and a radio ad.

Choices: Exploring Nouns, Pronouns, and Adjectives

Here's your chance to step out of the grammar book and into the real world. You may not always notice parts of speech, but you and the people around you use them every day. The following activities challenge you to find a connection between nouns, pronouns, and adjectives and the world around you. Do the activity below that suits your personality best, and then share your discoveries with your class. Have fun!

MATHEMATICS

Tools of the Trade

What are the tools that a mathematician uses? Make a list of these nouns, and draw an illustration of each tool. Start with a compass, and, if you like, include computer programs. Then, create an illustrated poster of these terms. Remember to check a dictionary for the proper spelling and hyphenation of compound nouns.

GEOGRAPHY

National or International

Lots of countries, states, and towns have compound nouns for names. Get a map of your state, the United States, or the world. Then, make a copy of the map. On your copy, write twenty compound nouns in the correct locations. Show your map to the class, and point out each compound noun. Be sure to capitalize each one correctly.

BUILDING BACKGROUND KNOWLEDGE

Chicks and Ducks and Geese

Do you know what a group of several geese is called? There are dozens of specific names for different groups of animals (and people!). What are they? Find out. Then, give your classmates an alphabetized list of these collective nouns and their definitions. Create a visual display of the collective nouns you discover. With your teacher's permission, post your display in class.

ORGANIZING INFORMATION

Expert Testimony

There certainly are a lot of different types of pronouns, aren't there? On a piece of poster board, create a chart of all the pronouns, each grouped by category. Then, make copies of the chart for your classmates. Look out! You may become the class expert.

USING RESOURCES

Opt for Options

You'll be needing lots of nouns, verbs, and adjectives for your writing assignments. A thesaurus is an excellent resource for expanding your vocabulary. Did you know that there is more than one type of thesaurus? There's more than one way to use a thesaurus, too. Ask the librarian to show you at least three different thesauruses. Learn how to use them. Then, show them to your classmates and explain how to find words in each one.

WRITING

With One Exception

Write a page about what you did after school last week. You can use any parts of speech you like with one exception: Don't use any nouns. That's right—no nouns. You can use every other part of speech except nouns. When you're done, read your paragraph to the class. If you want to have some fun, hand out copies of your page and let your classmates replace your pronouns with their own nouns.

ETYMOLOGY

The Family Tree

Look in a dictionary to find out the root words for *noun, pronoun,* and *adjective.* Brainstorm a list of other words that come from these roots. On poster board, draw a tree with a branch for each word. On each branch, write the word and its meaning. Get your teacher's permission to display your poster in the classroom. If you do this project with friends, you'll have a forest. If you are working alone, you'll have one spectacular tree.

Nouns

2a. A **noun** is a word or word group that is used to name a person, a place, a thing, or an idea.

PERSONS	Maya Angelou, Mr. Johnson, firefighters, audience
PLACES	hospital, library, classroom, New Zealand
THINGS	dolphin, burritos, 1776, Big Dipper
IDEAS	joy, faith, freedom, destiny

EXERCISE A   Underline the nouns in each of the following sentences. Hint: The number in parentheses indicates the number of nouns in each sentence.

Example 1. (3) Thomas Hooker has been called the father of American democracy.

1. (4) Thomas Hooker immigrated to the Massachusetts Bay Colony in 1633 to find religious freedom.

2. (3) Disagreements with the religious leaders of the colony soon developed.

3. (5) Hooker and several followers carved out a new, independent settlement nearby, which eventually became Hartford, Connecticut.

4. (5) He supported the right of the people—not just the members of the church—to vote for their judges.

5. (3) He explained his beliefs in a book published in 1648.

EXERCISE B   Underline the nouns in the following sentences.

Example 1. This past summer, Joey and his sister Dawn took a photography class.

6. On the first day, Mr. Armstrong went around and demonstrated how to use the various cameras.

7. Each camera had at least one mysterious button that had to be explained.

8. After this first lesson, the class learned about composition.

9. Mr. Armstrong displayed his best photos, and Dawn was impressed and inspired.

10. The next class was a field trip to the San Diego Zoo.

11. Joey got a great shot of a howler monkey showing its teeth.

12. Dawn, who adores koalas, was determined to get a picture to put on her wall.

13. Waiting patiently, Dawn finally caught a koala that was looking in her direction.

14. Joey wanted to see the photos right away, so his dad dropped off the film at the drugstore.

15. Dawn bought a shiny silver frame for the koala picture that now hangs over her desk.

Compound Nouns

2b. A *compound noun* is made up of two or more words used together as a single noun.

EXAMPLES   backpack, Haleakala National Park, brother-in-law

EXERCISE   Underline the compound nouns in the following sentences. There may be more than one compound noun in a sentence.

Example 1. The <u>Marx Brothers</u> were a family of comedians.

1. They were born in New York City and began working as children.

2. Originally, five of the brothers were in show business.

3. Their given names were Leonard, Adolph, Julius, Milton, and Herbert.

4. Thousands of theatergoers, however, knew them as Chico, Harpo, Groucho, Gummo, and Zeppo.

5. Their first successful play on Broadway was *I'll Say She Is* in 1924.

6. One of their films was a version of their stage play *The Cocoanuts,* which was written by George S. Kaufman.

7. This film was followed by *Animal Crackers*, *Monkey Business*, and *Duck Soup*.

8. Every film was a whirlwind of hilarity, with nonstop jokes and physical comedy.

9. The three best-known Marx Brothers were Groucho, Chico, and Harpo.

10. Groucho was known for his eyebrows, his moustache, and his constant wisecracks.

11. He often played characters with funny names, such as Rufus T. Firefly in *Duck Soup*.

12. Chico Marx spoke with an accent, mispronounced words, and excelled as a pianist.

13. Harpo never spoke, so he specialized in sight gags and slapstick.

14. His harp playing was a highlight of every film.

15. The actress Margaret Dumont was often the target of Groucho's jokes.

16. One of the brothers' later films was *A Night in Casablanca.*

17. Warner Brothers, a rival studio, threatened to sue the Marx Brothers because of the film.

18. They felt its name was too similar to a film starring Humphrey Bogart and Ingrid Bergman.

19. Groucho Marx sent the studio a humorous letter.

20. "I'll sue you," wrote Groucho Marx, "for using the word 'Brothers.'"

Common and Proper Nouns

2c. A *common noun* names any one of a group of persons, places, things, or ideas.

2d. A *proper noun* names a particular person, place, thing, or idea.

COMMON NOUNS	doctor, planet, contest, religion
PROPER NOUNS	Dr. Hopkins, Neptune, Special Olympics, Shinto

EXERCISE Identify the nouns in the following sentences. Underline the common nouns once and the proper nouns twice.

Example 1. Mark Twain is my favorite author.

1. The fish in the tank are a variety of colors.

2. Mr. Townsend has the *Detroit Free Press* delivered daily to his house.

3. Of all the people in my class, Amy is probably the funniest person.

4. The calendar over my desk has a picture of a lighthouse in Maine.

5. The first day that the doctor is available is Thursday.

6. The two ships just docked at the port.

7. My brother showed me an article about archaeology in *The New Yorker*.

8. Two of the most memorable characters in the novel *Moby-Dick* by Herman Melville are Ahab,
   a one-legged whaling captain, and the whale itself.

9. The facial expressions of the actor caused a great deal of laughter.

10. A picture of the actor Sidney Poitier was pinned to the bulletin board by thumbtacks.

11. Can Uncle Tim take us to the beach?

12. Guadalupe Street runs along the west side of the University of Texas in Austin.

13. My father and my uncle grew up near the Muskegon River in Big Rapids, Michigan.

14. My grandfather taught for many years at Ferris State University.

15. There are several types of hammers, including the claw hammer, the ball-peen hammer, and
    the sledgehammer.

16. Please take this copy of the book back to the library.

17. In the backyard of our house, I can still find old arrowheads occasionally.

18. The photography in that film is superb.

19. Will Professor Ondaatje be lecturing later?

20. The Reverend Jane Wilcox will be coming to dinner soon.

Concrete, Abstract, and Collective Nouns

2e. A *concrete noun* names a person, place, or thing that can be perceived by one or more of the senses (sight, hearing, taste, touch, and smell).

2f. An *abstract noun* names an idea, a feeling, a quality, or a characteristic.

CONCRETE NOUNS   friend, restaurant, garlic, *The Sound of Music*
ABSTRACT NOUNS   friendship, danger, loyalty, Judaism

2g. A *collective noun* is a word that names a group.

EXAMPLES   orchestra, herd, bunch, Ecology Club

EXERCISE A In the following sentences, underline the concrete nouns once and the abstract nouns twice.

Example 1. Victor is an expert on Zen Buddhism.

1. Christa read a book about increasing her self-confidence.

2. Please bring me a box of pencils from the closet.

3. Time moves slowly for people caught in a traffic jam.

4. An editorial is an essay, usually in a newspaper, in which the writer expresses his or her opinion.

5. Tito, do you believe his story is the truth?

6. Professor Said is writing a book about art history.

7. Jennifer learned to overcome her fear of dogs.

8. Dr. Melfi is a specialist in the treatment of certain illnesses.

9. My brother, the playwright, is working on a new play.

10. He likes to talk about what he calls the principles of comedy.

EXERCISE B Underline the collective nouns in the following sentences.

Example 1. We picked Sam from a litter of black and white kittens.

11. My sister Sandra received a set of drums and a collection of stamps for her tenth birthday.

12. The fleet left the harbor under full steam, followed by a flock of seagulls.

13. The faculty voted to change the requirements for graduation.

14. As the magazine photographer came over the ridge, he saw a herd of water buffalo that stretched to the horizon.

15. The audience applauded so fervently that the band and the chorus returned to the stage for an encore.

Kinds of Nouns

2c. A *common noun* names any one of a group of persons, places, things, or ideas.

2d. A *proper noun* names a particular person, place, thing, or idea.

> **COMMON** books   **PROPER** Library of Congress

2e. A *concrete noun* names a person, place, or thing that can be perceived by one or more of the senses (sight, hearing, taste, touch, and smell).

2f. An *abstract noun* names an idea, a feeling, a quality, or a characteristic.

> **CONCRETE** money   **ABSTRACT** generosity

2g. A *collective noun* is a word that names a group.

2b. A *compound noun* is made up of two or more words used together as a single noun.

> **COLLECTIVE** flock, crew, Congress   **COMPOUND** baseball, World Series

EXERCISE A Identify each of the following nouns. On the line provided, write *COM* for *common noun* or *PRO* for *proper noun*. Then, write *CON* for *concrete noun* or *ABS* for *abstract noun*.

Example _COM, ABS_ **1.** honesty

_____ **1.** Philadelphia   _____ **6.** Thomas Jefferson

_____ **2.** wisdom   _____ **7.** federalism

_____ **3.** Potomac River   _____ **8.** eagle

_____ **4.** freedom   _____ **9.** First Continental Congress

_____ **5.** airport   _____ **10.** independence

EXERCISE B Identify each of the following nouns. On the line provided, write *COLL* for *collective noun* or *COMP* for *compound noun*. Hint: One noun is both collective and compound.

Example _COMP_ **1.** space shuttle

_____ **11.** sister-in-law   _____ **16.** Super Bowl

_____ **12.** family   _____ **17.** Gulf of Mexico

_____ **13.** Lake Ontario   _____ **18.** self-respect

_____ **14.** houseboat   _____ **19.** audience

_____ **15.** team   _____ **20.** Boston Pops Orchestra

for **CHAPTER 2: PARTS OF SPEECH OVERVIEW**   `page 31`

Pronouns and Antecedents

2h. | A *pronoun* is a word used in place of one or more nouns or pronouns.

The word that a pronoun stands for is called its *antecedent*.

    EXAMPLE   **Arlon** wanted snapshots, but **he** did not have **his** camera handy. [The pronouns *he* and *his* refer to the antecedent *Arlon*.]

Sometimes a pronoun's antecedent is not stated.

    EXAMPLE   The teacher asked **everyone** to bring in art supplies for the project. [The pronoun *everyone* has no stated antecedent.]

EXERCISE   For each of the following sentences, identify each pronoun and its antecedent. Underline every pronoun once and its antecedent twice. Some of the pronouns do not have stated antecedents. If a pronoun has no stated antecedent, write *NSA* above the pronoun.

Example 1. Parker brought her tap shoes to the party, but she did not dance.

1. The gazelles came down to the stream, but they did not drink.

2. Dean and Jim decided to pool their resources and buy a video camera.

3. Debra set up an easel and a palette, and then she began to paint.

4. Don't play the piano; it needs tuning.

5. Are you going to the library?

6. After seeing three more movies, Paula decided that she liked that actor after all.

7. The crowd lifted their voices in song as the team took the field.

8. Somebody answer the phone, please.

9. Mariella posted a Stephen Crane poem on her Web site.

10. George told Mary that he would love to see the film.

11. On his trip to India, Steve Decker was attacked by a cow.

12. Sandrine signed her name inside the book's front cover.

13. No one knew who brought the banana bread to the potluck dinner.

14. Carla called out, "The red bass guitar is mine!"

15. The day Dave didn't use his sunblock, he got badly sunburned.

16. "See that painting on the far wall? Jane knows the woman who painted it."

17. As the cattle came through the gate, some headed for the barn, but most stayed in the yard.

18. If Randy wants the pen, why doesn't Brad buy it?

19. Steve invited us to his house to watch his favorite show on television.

20. I bought fresh flowers yesterday; aren't they beautiful?

Personal, Reflexive, and Intensive Pronouns

2i. A *personal pronoun* refers to the one speaking *(first person)*, the one spoken to *(second person)*, or the one spoken about *(third person)*.

EXAMPLES   **They** asked **me** to give **you** this message and to wait for **your** reply. [*They* is third person, *me* is first person, and *you* and *your* are second person.]

2j. A *reflexive pronoun* refers to the subject and functions as a complement or an object of a preposition.

2k. An *intensive pronoun* emphasizes a noun or another pronoun.

All reflexive and intensive pronouns end in *–self* or *–selves.*

REFLEXIVE   The explorers had promised **themselves** that one day they would scale Mount McKinley. [*Themselves*, an indirect object, refers to the subject *explorers*.]

INTENSIVE   Mark had prepared the entire dinner **himself.** [*Himself* emphasizes the noun *Mark*.]

EXERCISE   In each of the following sentences, underline the pronoun or pronouns. Above each pronoun, write *P* for *personal,* *R* for *reflexive,* or *I* for *intensive.*

Example 1. Mimi finally gave up looking, and she told herself that the missing book would turn up eventually.

1. Hari bought the bicycle himself, with his own money.

2. As soon as the students decided to write and perform a play, they created an outline of the story.

3. After waiting an hour for Jesse to stop talking on the phone, the kids filled the wading pool themselves.

4. Did you leave the cup on the counter?

5. When Mr. and Mrs. Britt sold their house, it was on the market for only a week.

6. I bought the sandwich for you, Al, and the salad for myself.

7. "We should not be too hard on ourselves," the coach told the team. "We worked hard and did the best we could."

8. Gwen, you need to ask yourself some tough questions about the future.

9. The Wahrmans painted their new house themselves.

10. Dr. Connolly himself cooked the main course for us.

Demonstrative and Relative Pronouns

2l. | A *demonstrative pronoun* points out a person, a place, a thing, or an idea.

EXAMPLE   **That** is a photograph of the space shuttle *Atlantis*. [*That* points out *photograph*.]

2n. | A *relative pronoun* introduces a subordinate clause.

EXAMPLE   Is this the book **that** describes the Hopi Snake Dance? [*That* introduces the subordinate clause *that describes the Hopi Snake Dance*.]

EXERCISE   Identify the demonstrative and the relative pronouns in the following sentences. Underline each demonstrative pronoun once and each relative pronoun twice.

Example 1. This is the best banana bread that I have ever tasted!

1. Last night we watched *The Searchers*, which is my father's favorite movie.

2. That is the book assigned for class for next week.

3. This is not the sweater that I want to wear.

4. Ms. Garson offered a ride to Dr. Conrad, whose car was being repaired.

5. Dinesh, who is in the chess club, showed me how the pieces on a chessboard move.

6. The sonata, which is usually played on the harpsichord, can also be played on the piano.

7. This is the roll-top desk that my mother refinished.

8. Please tell me the names of those who are willing to work on Saturday.

9. Mr. Cotten, whose book we are reading in English class, is coming to speak to us.

10. That is the ugliest painting that I have ever seen, but this is quite lovely.

11. The apple on the plate was picked yesterday, but those that are on the counter were picked two days ago.

12. My older sister, whose dog is named Padgett, is very fond of all animals.

13. Why don't we ask Mimi, to whom the package was addressed?

14. This is the best time to speak to Professor Kinbote, who might know the answer to the question.

15. If you follow the directions that Alice gave you, you will find the house with no problem.

16. This is the best-looking pecan pie in the competition, but that tastes better.

17. Are these the kittens that you found under the bridge?

18. These seem to be the shoes that I left in the locker room yesterday.

19. The book, which has two authors, should be filed under the first author's name.

20. The artist who did the mural in the library probably did this as well.

Indefinite Pronouns and Interrogative Pronouns

2m. An *interrogative pronoun* introduces a question.

2o. An *indefinite pronoun* refers to a person, a place, a thing, or an idea that may or may not be specifically named.

EXERCISE A In the following sentences, underline each indefinite pronoun once and each interrogative pronoun twice.

Example 1. Who told everyone to meet at my house?

1. Which is the restaurant you would like to try?

2. I found a red jacket! Whose is it?

3. Most of the job was finished by the time Allan arrived.

4. Several of the buildings were damaged by the tornado.

5. Which of the films at the festival did you see?

6. To whom did the broken coffee cup belong?

7. Neither of the dogs was willing to try two types of dog food.

8. What did they think of the last movement of the symphony?

9. Nobody answered the phone when I called.

10. Each car comes with everything a driver could need.

EXERCISE B Write an indefinite pronoun in the blank in each of the following sentences. Use a different pronoun for each sentence.

Example 1. _____Each_____ of the brothers decided on his own to enter the science fair.

11. Could _____ please give me a hand with this table?

12. Jamal and Karen gave _____ the same present for Christmas.

13. _____ of the delicate plants outside survived the first frost of the season.

14. We used _____ of the flour baking bread for the reunion banquet.

15. Do you know _____ about the Civil War?

16. _____ have ever claimed to have seen that bird in the wild.

17. Brenda told _____ at school about her new job at the pharmacy.

18. _____ of the guests at the wedding enjoyed the music, but _____ did not.

19. Please don't tell _____ about the surprise party.

20. _____ of the band members can read music.

Kinds of Pronouns

2h. A *pronoun* is a word used in place of one or more nouns or pronouns.

EXAMPLES   By studying **this, you** can teach **yourself** how to make origami figures. [*This* is a demonstrative pronoun, *you* is a personal pronoun, and *yourself* is a reflexive pronoun.]

Who composed the music **that** Jacob played at the recital? [*Who* is an interrogative pronoun, and *that* is a relative pronoun.]

The students did **all** of the research **themselves.** [*All* is an indefinite pronoun, and *themselves* is an intensive pronoun.]

EXERCISE   Underline the pronoun in each of the following sentences. Then, identify the pronoun by writing above it one of these abbreviations: *PER* for *personal, REF* for *reflexive, INTEN* for *intensive, DEM* for *demonstrative, INTER* for *interrogative, IND* for *indefinite,* or *REL* for *relative.*

Example 1. The managers of the company gave themselves raises. *[REF]*

1. My uncle does not like snow-skiing, but he loves water-skiing.

2. Is that the World Trade Center?

3. Everyone here has read the book.

4. Who discovered DNA?

5. "We are not amused," said the queen to the ambassador.

6. The new student, who is from Iran, is named Darob.

7. Mr. Kilkerney retired in April, and the school gave him a going-away party.

8. Are these the oldest rocks on earth?

9. Whom did the filmmakers cast in the role of King Arthur?

10. The film, which contains extraordinary special effects, will become a blockbuster.

11. The governor herself spoke to the graduating class.

12. Is something burning?

13. The band members worked hard to buy themselves new uniforms.

14. Did Paul write the short story himself?

15. The teacher assigned each of the students a poem to read aloud in class.

16. Which of the planets is farthest from the sun?

17. Mr. Wu and she left nearly an hour ago.

18. Are the gloves on the desk yours?

19. The only U.S. president who served more than two terms is Franklin D. Roosevelt.

20. Dad went to the mall by himself to shop for holiday gifts.

Language and Sentence Skills Practice

GRAMMAR

Adjectives and Articles

2p. An *adjective* is a word used to modify a noun or a pronoun.

An adjective modifies a word by telling *what kind, which one, how much,* or *how many.*

> **EXAMPLES**   Mr. Cruz collects **Egyptian** art. [What kind of art?]
>
> Sara won **first** prize. [Which prize?]
>
> Do you have **enough** money for the tickets? [How much money?]
>
> Our computer club has **fifty-seven** members. [How many members?]

An adjective may come before or after the word it modifies.

> **EXAMPLES**   The **soccer** players, **confident** and **enthusiastic,** were **ready** to begin the game.

The most frequently used adjectives are the *articles a, an,* and *the.*

EXERCISE A   In each sentence below, underline all of the adjectives, including the articles *a, an,* and *the.*

Example 1. Jenny Lind was a popular Swedish singer with a beautiful voice.

1. Jenny Lind starred in several operas and gained great renown in European cities.

2. At the absolute height of a brilliant career, she stopped performing in operas.

3. In 1849, the talented diva gave up an operatic career and began planning a concert tour.

4. From 1850 to 1851, Lind gave ninety-three concerts for the American public.

5. This extraordinary performer delighted audiences for fifty-three years.

EXERCISE B   In each of the following sentences, underline all the adjectives except the articles *a, an,* and *the.* Then, draw an arrow from each adjective to the word it modifies.

Example 1. President Thomas Jefferson gave two American explorers a difficult assignment.

6. These bold explorers were Meriwether Lewis and William Clark.

7. They were to explore the uncharted, western lands.

8. The long and arduous expedition began in St. Louis, Missouri, in 1804.

9. They made their winter camp in what is now North Dakota.

10. During that winter a Shoshone woman, Sacagawea, joined the expedition.

11. Her name translates into the English language as "Bird Woman."

12. Sacagawea and her husband, a French-Canadian trader, accompanied the explorers through a

large portion of the West.

13. As an interpreter of native languages, Sacagawea was helpful to the expedition.

14. The group, daring and resourceful, surmounted many obstacles.

15. The two-year journey was successful.

Demonstrative Adjectives

This, *that*, *these*, and *those* can be used both as adjectives and as pronouns. When they modify nouns or pronouns, they are called *demonstrative adjectives*. When they take the place of nouns or pronouns, they are called *demonstrative pronouns*.

EXAMPLES   Look at **that** pumpkin! [demonstrative adjective]

That is the biggest pumpkin I have ever seen! [demonstrative pronoun]

EXERCISE In the following sentences, underline the demonstrative adjectives once and the demonstrative pronouns twice.

Example 1. That building is much taller than this.

1. These stories are the best I've ever read.

2. Do you want this CD or that one?

3. That was the song Rashid has been humming all afternoon.

4. Those cats have been resting on the windowsill for two hours.

5. These are the funniest jokes I've ever heard!

6. This is the moment all those fans of the singer have been anticipating.

7. Joseph will be recycling those tomorrow, so he put them in the garage.

8. These parts will need to be cleaned before we can use them.

9. Wasn't that the worst movie you've ever seen?

10. Those grapes were tastier than these are.

11. I'll purchase this, and you can keep that one.

12. That is not what I meant to say.

13. Those comments of yours were right on target.

14. If you'll put away those toys, I'll take care of these.

15. Is that all you have to say?

16. That Norman Rockwell painting has always been Tera's favorite.

17. After reading descriptions of both books, Malcolm has decided to buy this.

18. Would you mind explaining how to solve this equation?

19. I have been needing a new pair of glasses, so I am happy to have these.

20. This photograph of Yvonne's fifth birthday party makes me laugh.

Proper Adjectives

Unlike a common adjective, a *proper adjective* is formed from a proper noun and begins with a capital letter.

EXAMPLES Does **every** play by William Shakespeare have **five** acts? [common adjectives]

Does every **Shakespearean** play have five acts? [proper adjective]

EXERCISE In the following sentences, underline each proper adjective once and underline twice the word it modifies.

Example 1. Mark Twain is one of the most popular American authors.

1. I have a CD of the singer Frank Sinatra performing Cole Porter songs.

2. The French novelist Jules Verne predicted such inventions as the submarine and the television.

3. A Norwegian expedition reached the South Pole a month before a British expedition arrived.

4. Akira Kurosawa, the Japanese filmmaker, directed many entertaining films.

5. Today, the prime minister issued a statement about the Northern Ireland peace talks.

6. I really enjoy the Spanish dish paella; my sister prefers the North African dish couscous.

7. I enjoy Georgia peaches almost as much as I like Michigan cherries.

8. Giuseppe Verdi, the composer of *Rigoletto*, was one of the leading figures of Italian opera.

9. Did you know that Mordecai Richler, who is a novelist, is Canadian?

10. The most famous British rock-and-roll songwriters may be John Lennon and Paul McCartney.

11. Candy skulls are a tradition during the Mexican holiday called the Day of the Dead.

12. My father, who likes spicy food, enjoys eating Indian curry and Thai green curry.

13. Ms. Henderson prefers Chinese food over Vietnamese cuisine.

14. Grandmother Adams was born during the Roosevelt administration.

15. The Inca ruins at Machu Picchu are located high in the Peruvian Andes.

16. Cassie will study Italian architecture at the University of Washington next semester.

17. Nicola's favorite restaurant in New Orleans often has Cajun music.

18. Uncle Shawn is bringing his specialty, chicken Caesar salad, to the picnic.

19. Joel's mother told us that the college years pass by in a New York minute.

20. What is Reverend Bowman's opinion of this Biblical passage?

Noun, Pronoun, or Adjective?

The way that a word is used in a sentence determines what part of speech the word is. Some words may be used as nouns or as adjectives. Other words may be used as pronouns or as adjectives.

NOUN	May I have an **apple**?
ADJECTIVE	May I have some **apple** juice?
PRONOUN	**This** is a painting by Mary Cassatt.
ADJECTIVE	**This** painting is by Mary Cassatt.

EXERCISE In each sentence below, identify the part of speech of the underlined word. Above each, write *N* for *noun*, *P* for *pronoun*, or *A* for *adjective*.

Examples 1. J. R. R. Tolkien is my favorite <u>fantasy</u> writer. *A*

        2. John Crowley's novel *Little, Big* is an intriguing <u>fantasy</u>. *N*

1. <u>Some</u> people like their salsa hot.

2. <u>Some</u> prefer salsa that is mild.

3. The rookie hit the <u>baseball</u> over the outfield fence.

4. Did you see the <u>baseball</u> game on television last night?

5. <u>Which</u> way did the dog go?

6. <u>Which</u> of the cats is the oldest?

7. In <u>astronomy</u> class we learned which stars are likely to become supernovas.

8. Antonio plans to study <u>astronomy</u> in college.

9. The <u>lighthouse</u> remained in operation until 1983.

10. The morning after the storm, the <u>lighthouse</u> keeper slept in late.

11. <u>That</u> telephone is not working properly.

12. Is <u>that</u> a real duck or a decoy?

13. We heard the tornado warning on the <u>radio</u>.

14. Audra got a job as an intern at the local <u>radio</u> station.

15. Do you have <u>any</u> apples this morning?

16. Ted claimed he had not received <u>any</u> of my messages.

17. Are you happy with your <u>Internet</u> provider?

18. Let's see if we can find the information we need on the <u>Internet</u>.

19. Nicci saw a very enjoyable movie at the <u>film</u> festival.

20. The action <u>film</u> was three weeks behind its schedule.

Review A: **Nouns**

EXERCISE A Identify the underlined noun in each of the following sentences. On the line provided, write *COM* for *common noun* or *PRO* for *proper noun*. Then, write *CON* for *concrete noun* or *ABS* for *abstract noun*.

Example __*COM, CON*__ **1.** Dorothy Parker was a famous critic and writer.

_____ **1.** Parker is especially remembered for her sharp humor.

_____ **2.** As a critic, she often used sarcasm in her evaluations.

_____ **3.** Once, Parker felt that an actress had given a very stiff performance.

_____ **4.** She wrote that the actress had shown a full range of emotion, from A to B.

_____ **5.** Parker regularly met with other writers at the Algonquin Hotel in New York City.

EXERCISE B Above the underlined noun in each of the following sentences, write *COMP* if the noun is compound or *COLL* if it is collective. Hint: One noun is both compound and collective.

Example 1. A large crowd gathered outside the theater.
                      COLL

6. Vermont is known as the Green Mountain State.

7. The tour group enjoyed visiting the Alamo in San Antonio, Texas.

8. Did you know that Abraham Lincoln was primarily self-educated?

9. The United States Senate contains two members from each state.

10. South Carolina produces many fruits and vegetables.

EXERCISE C Identify the part of speech of the underlined word in each of the following sentences. Above the word, write *N* for *noun* or *A* for *adjective*. Then, write *P* if the word is a proper noun or proper adjective.

Example 1. Who were the first European explorers in Australia?
                              A, P.

11. Australia is an island continent.

12. In 1770, Captain James Cook sailed to the island.

13. Cook claimed it for the British.

14. British convicts were sent there from the beginning of colonization.

15. Much of the continent's animal life is unique.

16. One animal unique to Australia is the duck-billed platypus.

17. What is the capital city of Australia?

18. The capital of Australia is Canberra.

19. Do most of the people in Australia speak the English language?

20. Yes, English is the primary language spoken in Australia.

Review B: **Pronouns**

EXERCISE A Identify each underlined word by writing above it *PRO* for *pronoun* or *ADJ* for *adjective*.

         PRO
Example 1. This is the funniest part of the movie.

1. I have seen this movie three times.

2. Many of my friends helped me search for my missing kitten.

3. Many years passed before his grandparents visited their homeland.

4. Which book do you want to read next?

5. Which of the computer games do you want to play first?

EXERCISE B Underline the pronoun in each of the following sentences. Then, draw an arrow from the pronoun to its antecedent(s). If the pronoun has no antecedent, write *NA* above the pronoun.

Example 1. Joan and Mary wanted to paint the room by themselves.

6. Carleen bought four tickets to the concert but then misplaced them.

7. Which of the English kings signed the Magna Carta?

8. Mother thanked Barbara and Tim for their thoughtful note.

9. Can anyone here play the piano?

10. Mark Twain, who was a great writer, once worked on a riverboat.

EXERCISE C Underline the pronoun in each of the following sentences. Then, identify the pronoun by writing above it one of these abbreviations: *PER* for *personal,* *REF* for *reflexive,* *INTEN* for *intensive,* *DEM* for *demonstrative,* *INTER* for *interrogative,* *IND* for *indefinite,* and *REL* for *relative.*

         DEM
Example 1. This is an excellent movie about South Africa.

11. Why did she miss the soccer banquet?

12. The record album was signed by Garth Brooks himself.

13. That is a beautiful cathedral!

14. For Hank's birthday, which is next Tuesday, Odessa will bake a cake.

15. Someone on the faculty wrote the school song.

16. Ms. Wang reminded herself to order tickets as soon as possible.

17. Most of Shika's neighbors were extremely friendly.

18. Whom did Selena invite to the dance?

19. Sean washed and dried the dishes and stacked them in the cabinet.

20. The sailors spotted a squid that was thirty feet long.

Review C: **Nouns and Adjectives**

EXERCISE A In the following sentences, underline each adjective once. Then, draw an arrow from each adjective to the word it modifies. Do not include the articles *a, an,* and *the*.

Example 1. After he bought the old house, Mr. Blandings repaired the stone wall that surrounded the overgrown garden.

1. The bright banner hung from the underside of the wooden bridge.

2. Our old cat, once energetic, now sleeps all day.

3. The red light on the video camera means that the camera is recording.

4. Dora prefers Chinese soup that is extremely spicy.

5. The quick brown fox jumped over the lazy dog.

6. That book with the blue cover was written by a good friend of ours.

7. Each member of the marching band brought something to sell at the bake sale.

8. Eight boxes of adhesive tape arrived at the central office.

9. The ambitious swimmer hoped to win a gold medal for an Olympic event.

10. The little car is often overshadowed by giant trucks on the highway.

EXERCISE B In each of the following sentences, identify each underlined word by writing above it *N* for *noun* or *A* for *adjective*.

Examples 1. I'm looking forward to the Fourth of July celebrations this year.
        2. I'm looking forward to the Fourth of July this year.

11. Would you like to go to the movies Wednesday night?

12. Wednesday is the least crowded night at the theater.

13. Thelonius Monk performed playfully on the piano.

14. Ask the piano player if he knows "As Time Goes By."

15. Please tell the actor that we enjoyed his comedy performance.

16. My brother is writing a comedy for his playwriting class.

17. The chalk broke in two as the teacher wrote on the chalkboard.

18. The children drew a chalk circle on the driveway.

19. The space exhibit was the fair's most popular attraction.

20. The satellite was lost in space and never heard from again.

Literary Model: Description

> Nonno Frankie and Nonno Mamie had made the best meal I had ever seen or eaten on earth. Mom, Betty, me, and the twins sat around the big kitchen table while Connie and her mother and father put a breathtaking Sicilian gourmet feast before us. After the eel appetizer came large hot plates of spaghetti with shimmering lakes of tomato sauce ladled out from a ten-gallon pot bubbling on top of the stove. Nonno Frankie ran around with a big slab of Parmesan cheese, rubbing it like crazy against a metal-toothed rack. I had never seen fresh-grated cheese before.
>
> "Ho! Ho! Ho! What's a ghost's favorite food?" he quizzed.
> None of us knew.
> "Spookghetti!" he howled. *"Spookghetti!"*
>
> —from *The Pigman and Me* by Paul Zindel

EXERCISE A   On the appropriate lines below, write the adjectives that appear in the above passage. Do not write the same adjective more than once, and do not include articles. (Hint: Circling all the adjectives in the passage before filling in the chart may be helpful.)

Nouns used as adjectives _____

_____

Proper adjectives _____

Other adjectives _____

_____

EXERCISE B

1. In this passage, the description of a meal includes several adjectives that relate to the senses of touch, hearing, and sight. Which adjectives relate to these senses?

_____

_____

_____

2. How does the author make you, the reader, feel as if you were in the scene being described?

_____

_____

GRAMMAR | Language in Context: Literary Model

Literary Model (continued)

EXERCISE C Using Zindel's passage as a model, write a vivid paragraph in which you describe a meal you have actually experienced or one that you can imagine. Use many adjectives that relate to all the senses.

_____

_____

_____

_____

_____

_____

_____

_____

_____

_____

_____

_____

EXERCISE D Write down the one word that best describes the overall tone of your paragraph. Then, choose three adjectives from your paragraph and explain how each adjective demonstrates the tone you named.

_____

_____

_____

_____

_____

_____

_____

_____

_____

_____

_____

_____

for **CHAPTER 2: PARTS OF SPEECH OVERVIEW**   *pages 38–42*

Writing Application: Job Application

Writers and speakers use adjectives to make language more exact and interesting. Well-chosen adjectives help readers and listeners understand *what kind, how much, how many,* and *which one.* In doing so, they bring bland writing to life by providing sensory details.

NEEDS DETAIL   The girl bought the book.

HAS DETAIL   The stylishly dressed girl bought the old, leather-bound book.

In the second sentence, readers can "see" what kind of girl bought what sort of book.

WRITING ACTIVITY

When students reach middle school, they often have the chance to spend part of their day working as an office aide or library assistant. They begin to learn about daily activities in an office setting. Write a brief letter of application for such a position at your school. Your letter should have four parts: a greeting, a paragraph explaining why you want the position, a paragraph stating what you hope to learn from the position, and a closing. In the body of the letter, use carefully chosen adjectives to describe yourself as the right person for the position.

PREWRITING   Find out which office aide positions are available in your school. You can ask teachers or inquire at the main office or library. Then, decide on the position for which you would like to apply. You will want to address your letter to the right person, so find that information, too. Finally, list the skills and character traits that make you the best student for the position, and jot down your thoughts on what you might learn as an aide. If there are no positions available at your school, write a job description for a similar type of job that interests you.

WRITING   Letters of application should be brief and to the point. Write each of the two body paragraphs several times, trying to express yourself briefly but clearly. Do not settle for "any old" adjective as you describe yourself. Use a dictionary to check meanings so that you select the very best adjectives.

REVISING   Once you are satisfied with the content of your letter, turn your attention to its tone, which should be both polite and confident. Strike a balance between polite respect for the letter's recipient and confidence that you can handle the job of aide. Read your letter to a trusted adult, and consider any suggestions for making the letter stronger.

PUBLISHING   Check your letter for errors in spelling and punctuation. Follow the correct format for a business letter, and write neatly or type your letter. Then, get together with a partner and hold two mock interviews. Determine who will be the first interviewer. Have the interviewer look over the interviewee's application letter and write three interview questions. Do the first mock interview, and then trade roles.

EXTENDING YOUR WRITING

If you enjoyed this exercise, you could develop it into a longer writing project. Some people argue that all of a student's day should be spent in the classroom, while others think that getting work experience during school also benefits students. For a speech class, choose one side of this argument and debate it with other students.

Language and Sentence Skills Practice   **45**

GRAMMAR | Language in Context: Choices

Choices: Exploring Parts of Speech

Here's your chance to step out of the grammar book and into the real world. You may not notice parts of speech, but you and the people around you use them every day. The following activities challenge you to find a connection between parts of speech and the world around you. Do the activity below that suits your personality best, and then share your discoveries with your class. Have fun!

GAMES

Anyone for POS?

Invent a game that involves identifying the parts of speech. For instance, you could design a maze made of words. Only by following the path of a specific part of speech could a player escape the maze. Use your imagination! Just be sure to write down all the rules, and give your classmates copies.

MATHEMATICS

By the Numbers

Now that you know all the parts of speech, choose a page or two that you have already written. Then, count the number of each part of speech that you use. If you can't identify a word's part of speech, ask your teacher or a classmate for help. Transfer your tallies to a chart. Then, compare your chart with your classmates'. What parts of speech do you favor? Which do you seem to avoid? How does your usage compare with your classmates'? with your textbook's? with your favorite writer's?

TECHNOLOGY

Brave New World

The last few decades have seen amazing technological advances. With these advances have come new verbs and new ways of using old verbs. Brainstorm a list of these new verbs and new meanings. Start with *e-mail*. Looking through a computer magazine will give you lots of ideas. Cut out pictures from the magazine to illustrate a poster of your list. Then, with your teacher's permission, hang your poster in the classroom. Be ready to answer questions about these new verbs.

ETYMOLOGY

Plant Trees

Make family tree posters for *verb, adverb, preposition, conjunction,* and *interjection.* Look up the root word of each of these words for the parts of speech. Then, make a list of other words that use this same root. Pay particular attention to *verb* because it has some very interesting relatives, such as *verbalize.* With your teacher's permission, hang your completed posters where the rest of the class can read them.

TEACHING

The Buddy System

Do you remember when you were first learning about adverbs and adjectives? You'd think you knew the difference, and then you'd see a word that totally confused you. There are a lot of younger kids in that same fix today. Be a buddy and help them out. Design an activity that helps younger kids learn about the parts of speech. Then, put your idea to the test! Find a class of younger students, and present your activity.

REPRESENTING

4-D, 3-D, or 2-D

Words have many dimensions. They have a history. They have multiple meanings. They may function as different parts of speech. They may have emotional, historical, or legal connotations. Use your artistic abilities to express these many dimensions of a single word. You might consider using a computer program to create a three-dimensional representation of a word, or you could do a cutaway drawing or some other type of representation. Whatever you do, choose your word carefully. Page through a dictionary, and look for a long, but not too long, entry. Be sure to share your artwork with the class.

The Verb

3a. A *verb* is a word used to express action or a state of being.

> **EXAMPLES** We **looked** through the telescope and **observed** the comet.
> The night sky **was** cloudy, so we **were** unable to see the comet clearly.

EXERCISE A Underline the verb in each of the following sentences.

Example 1. The ducks <u>swam</u> in the lake.

1. A lady threw bread to the ducks.
2. Several birds flew by.
3. The sky was bright blue.
4. We saw a beautiful sea gull.
5. One of the ducks made a strange noise.
6. She called her ducklings to her.
7. We took a photograph of the ducks and birds.
8. My sister identified the duck.
9. This one is a Muscovy.
10. We learned the names of all the ducks.

EXERCISE B Underline the verb in each of the following sentences.

Example 1. Mary Ellen <u>has</u> three cats.

11. My father traveled to Easter Island last year.
12. She sliced an onion for the stew.
13. Bring your beach towel with you on the picnic.
14. Is that a sandhill crane?
15. Lyle and Hector walked across the village.
16. Michele is a very good singer.
17. The fox watched the chickens from the other side of the fence.
18. Michael spread the blanket over the bed.
19. These horses are the prettiest in the herd.
20. Orange juice dripped all over the floor.

Helping Verbs and Main Verbs

A *helping verb* helps the *main verb* express action or a state of being. Together, a main verb and at least one helping verb (also called an *auxiliary verb*) make up a *verb phrase*.

> **EXAMPLES**   I **have read** many of Ernesto Galarza's poems.
>
>   **Have** you **read** any of his poems?

EXERCISE   In each of the following sentences, draw one line under the helping verb(s) and two lines under the main verb.

Example 1. Ernesto Galarza was born in Mexico.

1. When did the Galarza family move to Sacramento, California?

2. Other Mexican families had also immigrated to the United States.

3. Many of them had come to the United States for economic reasons.

4. In what year did Galarza publish his first book?

5. Many people have been enjoying his works for years.

6. Many are reading his works in the original Spanish.

7. Galarza has written about the struggles of farmworkers.

8. You have probably read some of his poetry.

9. Did you read the poetry in Spanish or in English?

10. You may like his poem about Mother Nature.

11. It is translated as "Copy from an Old Master."

12. Most young readers do enjoy his poem about the traffic light.

13. Will we be reading any of his poems in class this year?

14. Your teacher may recommend his book *Short Poems for Youngsters*.

15. This collection was published in 1971.

16. You will learn valuable lessons from these poems.

17. Galarza has been called the Father Goose of Mexican children.

18. Which poem should we read first?

19. Galarza's autobiographical work is titled *Barrio Boy*.

20. Does your literature book contain excerpts from *Barrio Boy*?

Action Verbs

An *action verb* is a verb that expresses either physical or mental activity.

EXAMPLES   Carlos **painted** this picture from a snapshot he **had taken.** [physical activities]

His friends **think** that he **should consider** a career in art. [mental activities]

EXERCISE A   In each of the following sentences, underline the action verb.

Example 1. The tourists <u>visited</u> the large wildlife preserve.

1. Dmitri liked the cougar exhibit at the wildlife preserve.

2. A rescue team found two young cougars in the mountains.

3. The team treated the cougars for injuries.

4. They brought the young cougars to the wildlife preserve.

5. The wildlife preserve staff members raised the cougars to adulthood.

6. They named the cougars Wolfgang and Julianna.

7. Next year the wildlife preserve will provide mates for the brother and sister pair.

8. The cougars enjoy healthy lives with good care.

9. Dmitri took a few photographs of the magnificent cats.

10. Months later, Dmitri often remembered the cougar pair.

EXERCISE B   On the line provided, write an appropriate action verb to complete each sentence.

Example 1. Kim _____ *mowed* _____ the lawn to earn her allowance.

11. Steve _____ the new song on the radio.

12. A runner from Nigeria _____ the marathon this weekend.

13. Neither of the boys _____ the answer to the question.

14. The secretary _____ a bag lunch to work.

15. Another meteor _____ across the sky.

Linking Verbs

A *linking verb* connects the subject to a word or word group that identifies or describes the subject. The noun, pronoun, or adjective that is connected to the subject by a linking verb completes the meaning of the verb.

> **EXAMPLES** Judy Blume **is** a writer. [Judy Blume = writer]
>
> Her books **remain** popular among young readers. [popular books]
>
> Some verbs may be used as linking verbs or as action verbs.
>
> **LINKING** The room **smelled** smoky.
>
> **ACTION** We **smelled** smoke in the room.

EXERCISE A In each of the following sentences, draw one line under the linking verb and two lines under the words that the verb connects.

Example 1. The pilot remained calm.

1. Beryl Markham was a famous pilot.

2. She stayed alert on many difficult and long flights.

3. Her accomplishments seem remarkable to many people.

4. Markham became the first woman to fly nonstop from England to America.

5. The task was difficult because of strong opposing winds.

6. A new club in 1929 was the Ninety-Nines.

7. Ninety-nine was the number of its original members.

8. Members were female pilots only.

9. The club remains active today.

10. Female pilots are more common now than many years ago.

EXERCISE B In each of the following sentences, identify the underlined verb by writing above it *LV* for *linking verb* or *AV* for *action verb*.

Examples 1. Mr. Singh <u>looked</u> in the cabinet for a serving dish. *(AV)*

  2. The vegetable curry <u>looked</u> tasty. *(LV)*

11. Mr. Singh <u>tasted</u> the vegetable curry.

12. The stew <u>tasted</u> deliciously spicy.

13. Mr. Singh <u>grew</u> many of the vegetables in his backyard.

14. He <u>grew</u> fond of curry dishes when he lived in India.

15. Mr. Singh's recipe for vegetable curry <u>remains</u> his secret.

Transitive and Intransitive Verbs

A *transitive verb* is a verb that expresses an action directed toward a person, place, thing, or idea. Words that receive the action of transitive verbs are called *objects*. An *intransitive verb* expresses action (or tells something about the subject) without the action passing to a receiver.

> **TRANSITIVE**   She **began** her speech. [The object of the transitive verb *began* is *speech*.]
>
> **INTRANSITIVE**   The train **arrived** on time.

A verb may be transitive in one sentence and intransitive in another.

> **TRANSITIVE**   Marcia **sings** two solos in the play. [The object is *solos*.]
>
> **INTRANSITIVE**   Marcia **sings** in the school's chorus. [no object]

EXERCISE   In each of the following sentences, identify the underlined verb by writing above it *TR* for *transitive* or *IN* for *intransitive*. Then, for each transitive verb, circle its object.

Example 1. No one in the accident suffered any injuries.

1. My watch stopped at 8:22.

2. Marguerite called a meeting on Wednesday.

3. The trainer slowly walked toward the tiger.

4. The trainer slowly approached the tiger.

5. Bradley and Chloe successfully flew the box kite.

6. During winter break we traveled to Orlando, Florida.

7. By the time we arrived, the concert had already begun.

8. By the time we arrived, the band had already begun the concert.

9. After a few minutes, the teakettle whistled.

10. Yolanda whistled a tune from the early 1990s.

11. The family gave its fair share to the charity.

12. The family gave generously to the charity.

13. For a long while the tree did not grow.

14. Did Marvin grow a mustache?

15. Some of the guests left early.

16. Some of the guests left the party early.

17. The nation's economy has improved in recent years.

18. What has improved the nation's economy?

19. Franklin Roosevelt served as President of the United States for more than twelve years.

20. President Franklin Roosevelt served more terms than any other President.

Identifying Kinds of Verbs/Verb Phrases A

3a.   A **verb** is a word used to express action or a state of being.

Verbs may be classified as (1) helping or main verbs, (2) action or linking verbs, and (3) transitive or intransitive verbs.

EXAMPLES   The USS *Nautilus*, the first nuclear-powered submarine, **had been cruising** the seas for many years. [*Had* and *been* are helping verbs, and *cruising* is the main verb. *Had been cruising* is both an action verb and a transitive verb.]

Before its retirement, it **had traveled** around the world. [*Had* is a helping verb, and *traveled* is the main verb. *Had traveled* is both an action verb and an intransitive verb.]

For how long **had** the submarine **been** operational? [*Had* is a helping verb, and *been* is the main verb. *Had been* is both a linking verb and an intransitive verb.]

EXERCISE A   In each of the following sentences, draw one line under the helping verb(s) and two lines under the main verb. Then, on the line to the left of each sentence, write *TR* if the verb is *transitive* or *IN* if the verb is *intransitive*.

Example   _TR_   **1.** A band <u>will perform</u> German music at the cafe tonight.

_____ **1.** The couple had visited the German cafe several times.

_____ **2.** Katerina had heard a few bands there.

_____ **3.** Tonight a new band will perform.

_____ **4.** Boris will be listening carefully.

_____ **5.** Boris might sing with the band.

_____ **6.** The band will be playing popular German songs.

_____ **7.** All last week, Boris had been practicing the songs.

_____ **8.** Boris will be learning new German music.

_____ **9.** He has been studying the German language for two years.

_____ **10.** Katerina will play accordion with the band.

EXERCISE B   For each of the following sentences, underline the verb. Then, on the line before each sentence, write *AV* if the verb is an *action verb* or *LV* if the verb is a *linking verb*.

Example   _LV_   **1.** We <u>grew</u> tired after several hours.

_____ **11.** The soup tasted salty.

_____ **12.** The chef tasted the soup.

_____ **13.** Martin grew roses in his garden.

_____ **14.** She became a police officer.

_____ **15.** The daisy smelled sweet.

Identifying Kinds of Verbs/Verb Phrases B

3a. A **verb** is a word used to express action or a state of being.

EXAMPLES We **have been making** piñatas for the fiesta. [*Have* and *been* are helping verbs, and *making* is the main verb. *Have been making* is both an action verb and a transitive verb.]

You certainly **have been** busy! [*Have* is a helping verb, and *been* is the main verb. *Have been* is both a linking verb and an intransitive verb.]

EXERCISE In each of the following sentences, draw one line under any helping verb(s) and two lines under the main verb. Then, on the line to the left of each sentence, write *AV* if the verb is an *action verb* or *LV* if the verb is a *linking verb*. Also, on the line, write *TR* if the verb is *transitive* or *IN* if the verb is *intransitive*.

Example *AV, IN* **1.** Will you dance at the talent show?

_____ **1.** I will dance a reel.

_____ **2.** Our costumes look beautiful.

_____ **3.** How will they look?

_____ **4.** We have sewn them ourselves.

_____ **5.** Mine is purple and black.

_____ **6.** Hillary will wear blue.

_____ **7.** Both of us will be leaping.

_____ **8.** Have you thought about tomorrow's performance?

_____ **9.** You gave a good show last year.

_____ **10.** Have you learned improvisational dance?

_____ **11.** Improvisation requires creativity.

_____ **12.** The dancer remains very aware.

_____ **13.** Each movement flows into the next.

_____ **14.** Duets are especially difficult.

_____ **15.** Partners turn somersaults together.

_____ **16.** This has turned too difficult for me.

_____ **17.** Actually, everyone can dance.

_____ **18.** Many have grown more self-confident.

_____ **19.** Dance class has made me more agile.

_____ **20.** Will you come to the class next week?

The Adverb

3b. An *adverb* is a word that modifies a verb, an adjective, or another adverb.

An adverb tells *where*, *when*, *how*, or *to what extent* (*how much* or *how long*).

EXAMPLES The popularity of television grew **slowly.** [*Slowly* modifies the verb *grew*, telling *how*.]

Some people were **rather** pessimistic about the future of television. [*Rather* modifies the adjective *pessimistic*, telling *to what extent*.]

Others had believed **quite strongly** in its potential. [*Quite* modifies the adverb *strongly*, telling *to what extent*. *Strongly* modifies the verb *had believed*, telling *how*.]

EXERCISE For each of the following sentences, underline the adverb(s).

Example 1. The contestants arrived <u>surprisingly</u> <u>early</u>.

1. Each skater practiced nearby.

2. The fans waited impatiently.

3. The skaters moved quite gracefully.

4. One skater seemed very nervous.

5. She stopped practicing rather early.

6. She sat silently and waited.

7. Her coach came quickly to see her.

8. He calmly encouraged her.

9. She began to skate quite skillfully.

10. Another skater moved somewhat reluctantly.

11. He timidly approached his coach.

12. His coach whispered softly to him.

13. The skater nodded enthusiastically.

14. He began to feel surprisingly confident.

15. He performed exceedingly well.

16. Then several other skaters danced.

17. Other skaters spun extremely well.

18. The fans applauded approvingly.

19. The judges decided the scores quickly.

20. The competition was unusually successful.

Adverbs and the Words They Modify

3b.   An *adverb* is a word that modifies a verb, an adjective, or another adverb.

An adverb tells *where, when, how,* or *to what extent (how much* or *how long).*

EXAMPLES   **Soon** many birds will be flying **south** for the winter. [The adverb *soon,* telling *when,* and the adverb *south,* telling *where,* modify the verb *will be flying.*]

Amelia appears **thoroughly** confident on the stage. [The adverb *thoroughly,* telling *to what extent,* modifies the adjective *confident.*]

Luis left the room **quite suddenly.** [The adverb *quite,* telling *to what extent,* modifies the adverb *suddenly. Suddenly,* telling *how,* modifies the verb *left.*]

EXERCISE   Circle the adverbs in the following sentences. Then, draw an arrow from each adverb to the word it modifies.

Example 1. In the Arctic Circle, the cold winds can cut very quickly to the bone.

1. Only lichens and a few other hardy plants can actually grow in the Arctic Circle.

2. Lichens can be easily seen in a light dusting of snow.

3. Sometimes caribou feed on the lichens.

4. Would wolves be closely following the caribou?

5. Most people never experience the harsh environment of the tundra.

6. Is the blimp somewhat risky for passenger travel?

7. Thuan really liked the airships.

8. Airships are an extremely effective means of advertising.

9. They float magically among the clouds.

10. Current designs seem much safer than those of the past.

11. The submarine descended rather slowly.

12. No bird flies more swiftly than the peregrine falcon.

13. Janine's unusual invention works quite effectively.

14. For a beginner, Eugene plays chess extraordinarily well.

15. The team is playing much better.

16. The qualifying exam for a pilot's license is extremely difficult.

17. The song ended rather abruptly, I thought.

18. Turn left at the stop sign and proceed slowly.

19. If you come early to the concert, you can easily find a seat.

20. Amin took the news calmly.

GRAMMAR

Adverb or Adjective?

Many adverbs end in *–ly*. However, some words ending in *–ly* can be used as adjectives. Remember: An *adverb* modifies a verb, an adjective, or another adverb by telling *where, when, how,* or *to what extent (how much* or *how long).* An *adjective* modifies a noun or a pronoun by telling *what kind, which one, how many,* or *how much.*

> **EXAMPLES**   Melissa writes **daily** in her journal. [The adverb *daily* modifies the verb *writes,* telling *when.*]
>
> Her journal is a **daily** record of events in her life. [The adjective *daily* modifies the noun *record,* telling *what kind.*]

EXERCISE A Above each underlined word in the following sentences, write *ADJ* if the underlined word is an *adjective* or write *ADV* if the underlined word is an *adverb.*

Example 1. Comets <u>sometimes</u> produce meteors.   *[ADV]*

1. Comets often contain <u>large</u> rocks.

2. The rocks inside comets are held together by <u>icy</u> material.

3. A comet that passes by the sun enough times <u>steadily</u> loses its icy material.

4. <u>Rocky</u> material and grains of dust remain near the head of the comet and in its orbit.

5. These rocks and dust grains <u>sometimes</u> enter the earth's atmosphere.

6. These particles in the earth's atmosphere can cause a <u>spectacular</u> shower.

7. Meteors don't come <u>only</u> from comets.

8. In fact, meteors resulting from other sources in space are <u>quite</u> common.

9. The <u>only</u> meteor I've ever seen was an awe-inspiring sight.

10. If you gaze into the night sky, it is <u>likely</u> that you will see one.

EXERCISE B Above each underlined word in the following sentences, write *ADJ* if the underlined word is an *adjective* or write *ADV* if the underlined word is an *adverb.*

Example 1. A new moon occurs <u>monthly</u>.   *[ADV]*

11. The <u>monthly</u> appearance of the full moon is always welcome.

12. Padgett is a very <u>friendly</u> dog.

13. Our cat always seems <u>lonely</u>.

14. Mom gave me a <u>timely</u> reminder to visit the dentist.

15. The newspaper arrives <u>daily</u> at 8 A.M.

The Preposition

3c.   A *preposition* is a word that shows the relationship of a noun or pronoun, called the *object of the preposition,* to another word.

A preposition that consists of more than one word is called a *compound preposition*.

EXAMPLES   The leader **of** the scout troop led the scouts **out of** the woods. [*Troop* is the object of the preposition *of*, and *woods* is the object of the compound preposition *out of*.]

EXERCISE A   Underline the prepositions in the following sentences.

Example 1. Before the hike, the scouts checked the supplies in their backpacks.

1. The scout troop went on a hike.

2. They climbed to the top of Mount Milligan.

3. The climb up the mountain was long and difficult.

4. They crossed over a stream and under fallen trees.

5. During the hike a few scouts went off the trail.

6. Boulders had fallen on the trail from a cliff.

7. They went either around the fallen rocks or between them.

8. There is a great deal of wildlife on the ground and under the brush.

9. On account of snakes, hikers should stay on the trail at all times.

10. The climb down the mountain took them in front of the lodge.

EXERCISE B   Underline the compound preposition in each of the following sentences. Then, circle the object of the preposition.

Example 1. Lars and I decided to go to the library instead of the bookstore.

11. We found the biographies next to the mysteries.

12. The seasonal books were in front of them.

13. According to Mr. Wu, some books were not seasonal.

14. They were there because of a space problem.

15. I borrowed the Sue Grafton mystery in spite of its torn cover.

16. A bird book was the only book I liked aside from that.

17. I did not check out the World Series history on account of Lars.

18. Lars checked out that sports book along with a poetry collection.

19. As of last Friday, I had read ten books this month alone.

20. I read Richard Peck's latest novel in addition to Barbara Kingsolver's first book.

Language and Sentence Skills Practice   **57**

GRAMMAR

Prepositional Phrases

3c. A *preposition* is a word that shows the relationship of a noun or pronoun, called the ***object of the preposition,*** to another word.

All together, the preposition, its object, and any modifiers of the object are called a *prepositional phrase*.

   EXAMPLE   Which flowers grow best **in this sandy soil?** [The prepositional phrase consists of the preposition *in*, the object *soil*, and the adjectives *this* and *sandy*.]

Do not confuse a prepositional phrase that begins with *to* (*to the game, to me*) with an infinitive that begins with *to* (*to read, to be heard*).

EXERCISE A For each of the following sentences, underline the prepositional phrase.

Example 1. Maya Angelou was born in St. Louis, Missouri.

1. Maya Angelou grew up in rural Arkansas.

2. Her career began with dance and drama.

3. Dr. Angelou is fluent in several languages.

4. Audiences throughout the United States have enjoyed Dr. Angelou's lectures.

5. Maya Angelou has also lectured in several foreign countries.

6. Dr. Angelou lived in Cairo, Egypt.

7. Dr. Angelou has also lived and taught in Ghana.

8. In 1969, Maya Angelou wrote an autobiographical novel.

9. She has made several appearances on television.

10. Dr. Maya Angelou's great works are respected around the world.

EXERCISE B For each of the following sentences, circle the preposition and underline the object of the preposition.

Example 1. Please don't run (in) the hallway.

11. This film takes place during the Depression.

12. I found my baseball glove underneath the bed.

13. In spite of the rain the band continued playing.

14. Everybody ran five laps around the track.

15. Is Santa Monica near the beach?

Preposition or Adverb?

Some words may be used as both prepositions and adverbs. To tell a preposition from an adverb, remember that a preposition always has a noun or pronoun as an object.

PREPOSITION	We walked **around** the new civic center for several hours. [*Center* is the object of *around*.]
ADVERB	As we walked **around,** we saw many unique exhibits. [*Around* modifies the verb *walked*, telling *where*.]

EXERCISE Above the underlined word in each sentence, write *PREP* if the underlined word is a *preposition* or write *ADV* if the underlined word is an *adverb*.

Example 1. Would you like to come <u>inside</u>?   *ADV*

1. From atop the mountain, we looked <u>below</u> and saw the green fields.

2. The cat was sleeping <u>under</u> the blanket.

3. She crawled <u>inside</u> the box.

4. When they heard the noise, they began to look <u>about</u>.

5. Will the children be playing <u>outside</u> today?

6. The family lives <u>near</u> the lake.

7. The squirrel was frightened and ran <u>off</u>.

8. He wants to travel <u>around</u> the world.

9. We will wait until the prices go <u>down</u>.

10. Did you see the robin perched <u>on</u> the branch?

11. Come <u>along</u>, children.

12. Tobias ran <u>down</u> the stairs.

13. I fed the ducks that were crowded <u>along</u> the shore.

14. As soon as we reached the boat, we climbed <u>aboard</u>.

15. I had never traveled <u>aboard</u> a spaceship before.

16. <u>Besides</u> the time I went to New Delhi, I hadn't ever flown.

17. The airplane made a humming sound as it zoomed <u>off</u> the runway.

18. <u>During</u> the flight, I was served fruit.

19. A cluster of restless creatures murmured <u>nearby</u>.

20. <u>Below</u>, my classmates were probably doing grammar exercises.

The Conjunction A

| **3d.** | A *conjunction* is a word used to join words or groups of words. |

Coordinating conjunctions—*and, but, for, nor, or, so,* and *yet*—join words or groups of words that are used in the same way.

> **EXAMPLE** Would you rather have shrimp **or** salmon for dinner?

Correlative conjunctions are pairs of conjunctions that join words or word groups that are used in the same way. The correlative conjunctions are *both . . . and, either . . . or, neither . . . nor, not only . . . but also,* and *whether . . . or.*

> **EXAMPLE** **Both** Zina **and** Jada can play the mandolin.

EXERCISE A Underline the coordinating conjunction in each of the following sentences.

Example 1. The river flows through several states <u>and</u> empties into the Gulf of Mexico.

1. She didn't stay up too late, nor did she watch too much television.

2. The sun had risen, yet it was still too foggy to drive.

3. Arguments soon broke out, for the players had not agreed upon the rules beforehand.

4. The baby cried, so her mother comforted her.

5. Will you be taking the bus or riding your bike?

6. Terri picked the basketball, and Nikki picked the football.

7. I wanted to see the previews, but the movie had already started.

8. Rocco didn't think the joke was funny, yet he pretended to laugh.

9. He lifted the vase carefully, for he didn't want to break it.

10. Karin ordered a salad and a baked potato.

EXERCISE B For each of the following sentences, underline the correlative conjunctions.

Example 1. The child wanted <u>neither</u> food <u>nor</u> water.

11. They took vacations not only in July, but also in December.

12. She will neither take a cab nor ride the bus.

13. The team couldn't decide whether to practice more or take a break.

14. Both the team captain and the coach thought that the competition went well.

15. We will see either the new French film or the popular German film.

The Conjunction B

3d. A *conjunction* is a word used to join words or groups of words.

Coordinating conjunctions—*and*, *but*, *for*, *nor*, *or*, *so*, and *yet*—join words or groups of words that are used in the same way.

EXAMPLE   Birthdays **and** wedding anniversaries are among the events we celebrate.

Correlative conjunctions are pairs of conjunctions that join words or word groups that are used in the same way. The correlative conjunctions are *both . . . and*, *either . . . or*, *neither . . . nor*, *not only . . . but also*, and *whether . . . or*.

EXAMPLE   Their family celebrates **not only** birthdays **but also** name days.

EXERCISE A   Circle the coordinating conjunction in each of the following sentences. Then, underline the words or word groups that the conjunction joins.

Example 1. All around the world people hold parties, (and) they have festive celebrations.

1. Many African American families celebrate Juneteenth and Kwanzaa.

2. At an African coming-of-age party, there are music and dancing.

3. At a Jewish bar mitzvah or bat mitzvah, there is prayer.

4. At a Polish or Mexican wedding, the bride collects money during a special dance.

5. For some, weddings are held in houses of worship, for they are religious ceremonies.

6. Some wedding ceremonies are not religious, so they are held at home.

7. Nearly all people welcome the new year, yet not everyone celebrates it on January 1.

8. New Year's Day is the same date each year in Sweden, but it falls on different dates

   in Vietnam.

9. The Chinese celebrate January 1 and their lunar new year.

10. Name a holiday or festival that is important to your family.

EXERCISE B   Circle the correlative conjunctions in each of the following sentences. Then, underline the words or word groups that the conjunctions join.

Example 1. Unique species of (both) plants (and) animals exist in rain forests.

11. Not only parrots but also hornbills can be seen in some rain forests.

12. Both eagles and monkeys live in rain forests, too.

13. Either people take steps to save the rain forests now, or these habitats will be lost.

14. The question is not whether the rich nations or the poor ones are at fault.

15. Neither one group nor another is solely to blame for the destruction of the rain forests.

GRAMMAR

The Interjection

| **3e.** | An *interjection* is a word used to express emotion. |

An interjection has no grammatical relation to other words in the sentence. Usually an interjection is followed by an exclamation point. Sometimes an interjection is set off by a comma or commas.

EXAMPLES   **Hey!** Did you see those deer?

Well, we played hard and did our best.

We could, **oh,** have a picnic.

EXERCISE A   Underline the interjection in each of the following sentences.

Example 1. <u>Wow!</u> That movie was outstanding!

1. Ah, now I understand what to do.

2. Ouch! Another mosquito bit me.

3. Oh! What beautiful flowers those are!

4. Hey, we need to get ready, or we will be late.

5. Excellent! Let's go right away.

6. I like playing this computer game, but, gee, it is complicated.

7. Ugh! I should have caught that ball.

8. The team finally won a game. Hooray!

9. Well, Guido, what did you learn from the field trip to the aquarium?

10. What a spectacular fireworks display that was! Wow!

EXERCISE B   In the blank provided in each of the following sentences, write an appropriate interjection and mark(s) of punctuation.

Example 1. _____*Whew!*_____ I am tired.

11. _____ Let's go to the park.

12. _____ That is an excellent idea!

13. I should practice _____ for at least another hour.

14. _____ I forgot to return those library books.

15. What a cold day it is! _____

Determining Parts of Speech

| **3f.** | The way a word is used in a sentence determines what part of speech it is. |

The same word may be used as different parts of speech.

PRONOUN	**Some** of these baseball cards are quite valuable.
ADJECTIVE	**Some** baseball cards are quite valuable.
ADVERB	Let's go **outside** and pass the football.
PREPOSITION	We will meet you **outside** the main entrance to the stadium.
NOUN	Please turn off the **light.**
VERB	Alex, will you **light** the candles?
INTERJECTION	**Good!** I'm glad you agree.
ADJECTIVE	Everyone agreed the plan was a **good** one.

EXERCISE In each of the following sentences, identify the part of speech of the underlined word by writing above it *NOUN* for *noun,* *PRO* for *pronoun,* *VERB* for *verb,* *PREP* for *preposition,* *ADJ* for *adjective,* *ADV* for *adverb,* or *INT* for *interjection.*

             PRO
Example 1. <u>All</u> of the students were in the classroom.

1. The worried young man wandered <u>about</u>.

2. The article is <u>about</u> the ancient rain forests.

3. The <u>dark</u> night felt quiet and empty.

4. She strolled around in the <u>dark</u>.

5. The startled deer ran <u>fast</u>.

6. She worked at an astonishingly <u>fast</u> rate.

7. I <u>run</u> every morning.

8. The sprinter had an excellent <u>run</u> in this morning's competition.

9. You got tickets to the show? <u>Great</u>!

10. It should be a <u>great</u> show.

Review A: **Parts of Speech**

EXERCISE A Underline the verb or verb phrase in each of the following sentences. Then, circle any help-ing verbs. On the line provided, write *AV* for *action verb* or *LV* for *linking verb*. Then, write *TR* for *transitive verb* or *IN* for *intransitive verb*.

Example _LV, IN_ **1.** The car (will) appear unlike any other car on the road.

_____ **1.** The car of the future might use batteries as its main source of power.

_____ **2.** Computers in the car monitor everything.

_____ **3.** The car will not operate by itself, however.

_____ **4.** A driver must program his or her destination.

_____ **5.** To me the car looks extremely small.

_____ **6.** Today's cars seem huge by comparison.

_____ **7.** The exterior appears sleek and shiny.

_____ **8.** The design, though, is practical and efficient.

_____ **9.** Today's designers have been very creative.

_____ **10.** Their imaginations have soared!

EXERCISE B Identify the underlined word(s) in each of the following sentences by writing above them *ADV* for *adverb*, *PREP* for *preposition*, *CONJ* for *conjunction*, or *INT* for *interjection*.

Example 1. At first, we thought we would go <u>either</u> to the Everglades in Florida <u>or</u> to the Rocky Mountains in Colorado.

11. Before we took the trip, we read <u>extensively</u> about each place.

12. We decided to go to <u>both</u> the Everglades <u>and</u> the Rockies.

13. The climate of the Everglades is <u>exceptionally</u> hot and humid.

14. <u>Wow!</u> Did you see any alligators while you were there?

15. Yes, we did, and we also saw some <u>rather</u> unusual birds.

16. We took an ambitious hike <u>in</u> the Rockies.

17. For several hours we climbed <u>steadily</u> upward.

18. <u>Not only</u> the wildflowers <u>but also</u> the alpine vegetation fascinated us.

19. On the hike <u>around</u> the mountains, we saw several mountain goats.

20. In addition to mountain goats, we saw two species of deer running <u>around</u>.

Review B: **Parts of Speech**

EXERCISE A   In each of the following sentences, identify the part of speech of the underlined word by writing above it *NOUN* for *noun, PRO* for *pronoun, VERB* for *verb, PREP* for *preposition, ADJ* for *adjective, ADV* for *adverb, CONJ* for *conjunction,* or *INT* for *interjection.*

                                                              PREP
Example 1. Connie and Aunt Jessica learned to row <u>in</u> a nearby lake.

1. Jessica was <u>quite</u> interested in sweep rowing.

2. In sweep rowing, <u>each</u> rower uses only one oar.

3. In sculling, however, <u>each</u> uses two oars simultaneously.

4. Recreational boats are <u>usually</u> wider than racing boats.

5. A narrow, lightweight boat can glide faster <u>through</u> the water.

6. Jessica and Connie are rowing <u>through</u>.

7. <u>Wow</u>! Their arms, legs, and backs generate amazing power.

8. The <u>seats</u> slide on a track to allow them to push with their legs.

9. This boat <u>seats</u> several.

10. They will train <u>hard</u> and begin racing next season.

EXERCISE B   Underline the verb or verb phrase in each of the following sentences. Circle any helping verbs. Then, identify each on the line provided by writing *AV* for *action verb* or *LV* for *linking verb* and *TR* for *transitive verb* or *IN* for *intransitive verb.*

Example *AV, TR* **1.** People ⟨have⟩ long celebrated Valentine's Day.

_____ **11.** Opinions vary as to the origins of Valentine's Day.

_____ **12.** It might have begun as early as the 1400s.

_____ **13.** According to an old English belief, birds choose their mates on February 14.

_____ **14.** The exchange of romantic messages became customary in the 1700s.

_____ **15.** Have you sent anyone a valentine?

Review C: **Parts of Speech**

EXERCISE In each of the following sentences, identify the part of speech of each underlined word by writing above it *NOUN* for *noun*, *PRO* for *pronoun*, *VERB* for *verb*, *PREP* for *preposition*, *ADJ* for *adjective*, *ADV* for *adverb*, *CONJ* for *conjunction*, or *INT* for *interjection*.

CONJ
Example 1. She left early, but didn't tell anyone.

1. Whew! We finally finished this chess game!

2. After lunch, we walked around.

3. I can't decide whether to write about the short story or the poem.

4. The injured patient made rapid progress in learning to walk again.

5. We thought that they would have arrived by now.

6. Whoops! I dropped the cup of juice.

7. The workers were tired, for they had worked hard all day.

8. I can hardly see the top of that building.

9. The team scored a safety toward the end of the game.

10. I enjoyed the movie, but I was disappointed with the ending.

11. I forgot to bring the book you wanted to borrow.

12. You will find the tools behind the lawn mower.

13. We looked above and saw the constellations.

14. Wow! I can't believe we're finally here!

15. The children were hungry, so they ate lunch.

16. The roses smell lovely.

17. The roses have a lovely smell.

18. I couldn't see beyond the trees.

19. We asked to see both the new painting and the sculptures.

20. The girl's mother sewed her a blue blouse.

for **CHAPTER 3: PARTS OF SPEECH OVERVIEW**   *pages 51–60*

Literary Model: Dialogue

> The dogs sprang against the breastbands, strained hard for a few moments, then relaxed. They were unable to move the sled.
>
> "The lazy brutes, I'll show them," he cried, preparing to lash out at them with the whip.
>
> But Mercedes interfered, crying, "Oh, Hal, you mustn't," as she caught hold of the whip and wrenched it from him. "The poor dears! Now you must promise you won't be harsh with them for the rest of the trip, or I won't go a step."
>
> "Precious lot you know about dogs," her brother sneered; "and I wish you'd leave me alone, ..."
>
> —from *The Call of the Wild*, by Jack London

EXERCISE A

1. Write the verbs the author uses instead of a form of *to say* in expressions, called dialogue tags, that identify the speaker.

   _____

2. Name at least three additional verbs that a writer could use instead of *to say* in expressions that identify the speaker.

   _____

EXERCISE B

1. Why do you think authors might use verbs other than forms of *to say* to identify speakers in dialogue?

   _____

   _____

   _____

2. How would the excerpt above be different if its author, Jack London, had used only *said* in the dialogue tags?

   _____

   _____

   _____

Literary Model (continued)

EXERCISE C Write a brief narrative that includes several lines of dialogue. Do not use a form of *to say* more than once to identify the speakers.

_____

_____

_____

_____

_____

_____

_____

_____

_____

_____

_____

_____

_____

_____

EXERCISE D How does your use, in dialogue tags, of verbs other than *to say* affect your narrative?

_____

_____

_____

_____

_____

for **CHAPTER 3: PARTS OF SPEECH OVERVIEW**   **pages 61–64**

Writing Application: Travel Narrative

The right adverb can add helpful detail to a sentence and catch readers' interest by telling *where, when, how,* or *to what extent* an action takes place or a quality exists. On the other hand, overused adverbs like *very, really,* and *quite* can weaken a sentence.

STALE ADVERB	The students **really** enjoyed the April Fools' Magic Show.
PRECISE ADVERB	The students **noisily** enjoyed the April Fools' Magic Show.

WRITING ACTIVITY

From Marco Polo to Barry Lopez, people have written about their travels. Become a travel writer yourself by writing a brief account of a trip you have taken. You might write about a trip to a distant land or about a trip to a neighboring town. Either way, use at least five adverbs in your account to describe your journey.

PREWRITING After you have decided on a trip to describe, brainstorm as many details about the trip as possible. *Where* and *when* did you go? *How* did you get there? *What* was the place like? Brainstorm narrative details, or details that describe actions and events, as well as descriptive details, or details that describe people, places, and things.

WRITING Once you have brainstormed a wealth of details, arrange those details in a logical order. You might describe your journey chronologically (in the order that it happened), or you might use spatial order (the way things are arranged in space). Be sure to include plenty of adverbs to tell *where, when, how,* and *to what extent.*

REVISING In addition to revising your account for content and organization, revise it for style by making sure you haven't used any stale adverbs, such as *very* and *really.* Replace any such adverbs with fresh, precise adverbs.

PUBLISHING After you have corrected any errors in punctuation, spelling, grammar, or usage, publish your travel writing as widely as possible. You might collaborate with classmates to compile a booklet of travel accounts that people can read when choosing vacation spots. Such a booklet might also include photographs and drawings of travel destinations.

EXTENDING YOUR WRITING

If you enjoyed this exercise, you might develop it into a longer travel narrative and submit it to the travel section of your local newspaper.

Choices: Investigating Complements

Here's your chance to step out of the grammar book and into the real world. You may not notice complements, but you and the people around you use them every day. The following activities challenge you to find a connection between complements and the world around you. Do the activity below that suits your personality best, and then share your discoveries with your class. Have fun!

POETRY

Happiness Is . . .

What people, places, situations, events, or objects make you happy? Write a short poem that uses predicate nominatives to name a few sources of happiness. Rhyming isn't necessary, but your poem should be at least ten lines long.

WRITING

All About You

Have you ever filled out sheets that asked you to name your favorite song, color, and other things? Design a sheet of ten fill-in-the-blank sentences for your class. Each of your sentences should require a complement. Appropriate sentences might include statements such as *My favorite class is* _____ or *If I had a million dollars, I would give* _____ *half.* For each blank, specify which of the four types of complements should be supplied: direct object, indirect object, predicate nominative, and predicate adjective. Make copies and give one to everyone in the class.

MATHEMATICS

180°

What does the word *complement* mean to a mathematician? Prepare a diagram that clearly illustrates mathematical complements. Then, with your teacher's permission, present your definition and your diagram to the class.

MUSIC

Intervals and Octaves

If you've been studying music, here's a project for you. What does the word *complement* mean to a musician? Prepare illustrations, both visual and musical. Then, get permission to present your definition and your examples to the class. You may either give a short presentation or prepare handouts for your class.

ART

Moody Faces

How are you feeling? Are you happy or sad? Answering these questions will probably lead you to use a predicate adjective. Become aware of your feelings by making a list of a dozen different emotions. Then, draw cartoon faces illustrating a number of these emotions. Under each face, write a sentence with the appropriate predicate adjective. Make a poster out of your illustrations and sentences. Then, ask to show your work to the class.

LINGUISTICS

The Object of the Game

Wait until you see the number of meanings in a dictionary for the word *object*! Check out these definitions for yourself. Then, make a chart of the different meanings. Include a sentence for each meaning. Your chart could be simply geometrical, or your chart could be more pictorial, such as a tree or an octopus, with each branch or arm representing a meaning. Pass out copies of your chart or make a poster so everyone can get a good look at it. Be sure to ask your teacher before you hang up anything in the classroom.

DRAMA

One of Each

Write a dialogue for four people in which each character uses only one type of complement. For instance, one character will include a predicate adjective in each of his or her sentences, another character will include a direct object in each of his or her sentences, and so on. With your teacher's approval, perform your dialogue for the class. At the end of your dialogue, ask audience members to identify each character by the type of complement he or she used.

Complements

4a. A *complement* is a word or a word group that completes the meaning of a verb.

EXAMPLES Fran told **him** the good **news.** [*Him* and *news* complete the meaning of the verb *told*.]

Paco was **happy** about the news. [*Happy* completes the meaning of the verb *was*.]

EXERCISE A Underline the complement(s) in each of the following sentences.

Example 1. Mia and I visited Mr. Merkenson's plant nursery.

1. Mr. Merkenson is a horticulturist.

2. He grows many different kinds of plants at the nursery.

3. Mr. Merkenson showed us some lovely ferns.

4. All of the ferns looked extremely healthy.

5. Do ferns require any special care?

6. Ferns are rather hardy plants.

7. Mr. Merkenson handed me a booklet about ferns.

8. I read the part about plant care.

9. Mia and I bought our mother a beautiful Boston fern.

10. Our mother seemed appreciative of the gift.

EXERCISE B In each of the following sentences, identify the underlined word by writing above it *COMP* for *complement,* *ADV* for *adverb,* or *OP* for *object of a preposition.*

Example 1. I met with my school <u>counselor</u> today. *[OP]*

11. The eighth-graders are forming a recycling <u>campaign</u> at the school.

12. Because of the rainy weather, we stayed <u>indoors</u> all day.

13. Are all of these cards and letters for <u>me</u>?

14. The guest speaker spoke to the <u>class</u> about fire prevention.

15. The Nineteenth Amendment gave <u>women</u> the right to vote.

16. My little brother grew <u>restless</u> toward the end of the movie.

17. The president of the company addressed her audience <u>eloquently</u>.

18. Do all bears hibernate during the winter <u>months</u>?

19. Claudio had bought a new suit especially for the <u>occasion</u>.

20. Aunt Epatha is a <u>collector</u> of rare books.

for **CHAPTER 4: COMPLEMENTS** pages 81–82

Direct Objects

4b. | A *direct object* is a noun, pronoun, or word group that tells who or what receives the action of the verb.

EXAMPLES   Ms. Damon arranged the **desks** into a circle.
She bought a **sofa** and a **chair**. [compound direct object]

EXERCISE   In the following sentences, circle the verb and underline the direct object. Some sentences do not have a direct object.

Example 1. Tonight I (will read) the last <u>chapter</u> of this book.

1. Ms. McCourt manages her business carefully.

2. Our tabby cat, Mr. Alp, stalked the mouse through the garden.

3. Please bring me a salad from the sandwich shop on the corner.

4. At first, she put the dog and the cat in separate rooms.

5. Jada and Whitney attended their ten-year high school reunion last week.

6. He could have talked about African history for hours.

7. Has the detective reached a conclusion about the burglary yet?

8. The mathematician thought about the unusual proof for several days.

9. The final scene of that movie completely surprised me.

10. After the final performance of the play, Ms. Marrazzo congratulated the cast and crew.

11. At his concert last night, Taj Mahal played "Think," a blues song.

12. Did you rent any videos last week?

13. The author finally published the article.

14. Conchata practices piano three times a week.

15. I'll be waiting for your call.

16. Mr. Pinkett gave his old books, a computer, and a mattress to the Salvation Army.

17. Did you hear the president on the radio this morning?

18. For my birthday, my sister gave me the latest book in the series.

19. Mr. Miyasaki is an expert on bonsai trees.

20. In a seat at the back of the theater, the playwright watched her play.

Indirect Objects

| **4c.** | An *indirect object* is a noun, pronoun, or word group that sometimes appears in sentences containing direct objects. |

An indirect object tells *to whom* or *to what* or *for whom* or *for what* the action of the verb is done.

EXAMPLES Aunt Aretha bought **herself** a terrarium. [Note: *Terrarium* is the direct object.]

Later she gave **Theo** and **me** the terrarium. [compound indirect object]

An indirect object is never part of a prepositional phrase.

EXAMPLE Later she gave the terrarium to **Theo** and **me**. [objects of the preposition *to*]

EXERCISE In each of the following sentences, underline the indirect object. If a sentence does not have an indirect object, write *None* after it.

Example 1. In 1993, the Swedish Academy gave Toni Morrison the Nobel Prize for Literature.

1. Iola sent her brother a gift certificate for his birthday.

2. Miriam, Judy, and Roberto taught themselves three-part harmony.

3. Tell me the answer.

4. Ms. Ankers found her glasses on the floor under her bed.

5. The tall man gave us directions to the film festival.

6. Gregory bought himself a burrito for lunch.

7. At the American Museum of Natural History, Mr. Hsing showed James the hall of dinosaurs.

8. Kendall offered Jason his congratulations for winning the bicycle race.

9. At the wedding reception Chang sang Meg and Gordon their favorite song.

10. What gave you the idea for your story?

11. Mr. Linson took us on a field trip to the art museum.

12. After pondering the problem for a long time, Dean revealed his solution to us.

13. Very carefully, Annie offered the cat a piece of tuna fish.

14. The coach gave Vic, Bob, and Dan their varsity sweaters.

15. Carter returned the broken CD player to the manufacturer.

16. Our neighborhood grocery store provided the food for our annual charity picnic.

17. When you come back to the table, please bring me the mustard.

18. Jed told the class a story about his trip to Vermont.

19. The company will give you whatever you need to finish the job.

20. The little girl's story won the hearts of the nation.

Language and Sentence Skills Practice

Direct Objects and Indirect Objects A

4b.   A *direct object* is a noun, pronoun, or word group that tells who or what receives the action of the verb.

   EXAMPLE   The Bavarian king Ludwig II built **Neuschwanstein Castle.**

4c.   An *indirect object* is a noun, pronoun, or word group that sometimes appears in sentences containing direct objects.

An indirect object tells *to whom* or *to what* or *for whom* or *for what* the action of the verb is done.

   EXAMPLE   Ludwig II built **himself** many other castles. [Note: *Castles* is a direct object.]

EXERCISE A   In each of the following sentences, identify the underlined word by writing above it *DO* for *direct object,* IO for *indirect object,* or OP for *object of a preposition.*

Example 1. Robert Louis Stevenson wrote <u>Kidnapped</u>. *DO*

1. The novel offers <u>readers</u> a great adventure.

2. In the novel a poor boy finds himself a captive on a <u>ship</u>.

3. The captain of the ship forces the young prisoner to work for <u>him</u>.

4. He brings the <u>captain</u> food and other supplies.

5. Eventually, the boy and another passenger secretly make <u>plans</u> to escape.

EXERCISE B   In the following sentences, draw one line under each direct object and two lines under each indirect object. Not every sentence contains an indirect object. (Hint: At least one sentence contains a compound direct object or a compound indirect object.)

Example 1. Carlos bought his <u><u>brother</u></u> a birthday <u>gift</u>.

6. Charlotte and I gave our Dalmatian puppy a bath.

7. Eartha told Kim and me a secret.

8. Pass me the ball!

9. After dinner last night, Dad told us a hilarious story.

10. The explorers found the valuable treasure in a cave.

11. At soccer practice, we ran ten laps around the field.

12. At the request of the teacher, each student made a list of his or her goals.

13. Did Karen accept your invitation to the fiesta?

14. Gail gave her story a one-word title.

15. At the beginning of the tour, the museum guide handed each of us a name tag and a brochure.

Direct Objects and Indirect Objects B

4b. A *direct object* is a noun, pronoun, or word group that tells who or what receives the action of the verb.

   EXAMPLE   Terence framed a **photograph** for his grandmother.

4c. An *indirect object* is a noun, pronoun, or word group that sometimes appears in sentences containing direct objects.

An indirect object tells *to whom* or *to what* or *for whom* or *for what* the action of the verb is done.
   EXAMPLE   Terence sent **her** the card for Grandparents Day. [Note: *Card* is a direct object.]

EXERCISE A   In each of the following sentences, identify the underlined word by writing above it *DO* for *direct object,* *IO* for *indirect object,* or *OP* for *object of a preposition.*

Example 1. My uncle gave *me* [IO] a guitar for my birthday.

1. He also gave me a <u>book</u> of easy-to-play Beatles songs.

2. The book shows the reader the hand positions for each <u>song</u>.

3. So far, I have taught <u>myself</u> three songs.

4. I have learned "<u>Yesterday</u>," "<u>Hey Jude</u>," and "<u>Yellow Submarine</u>."

5. After he heard me play, my uncle praised me for my <u>talent</u>.

EXERCISE B   In the following sentences, draw one line under each direct object and two lines under each indirect object. Not every sentence contains an indirect object.

Example 1. The coach offered us a chance to play.

6. Ms. Wong wrote the store a check for the groceries.

7. Sophie told Carmen the complete story.

8. Carl proposed a title for the film.

9. Offer our guest some soup, Cedric.

10. The newspaper article gave Cody an idea for a story.

11. Just in case, the purser issued every passenger a life vest.

12. Give yourselves a nice round of applause.

13. The avalanche carried away the empty cabin.

14. Mother gave Tim and me some money for lunch at school.

15. Helen gave a tour of the studio to Tonya and Peter.

Subject Complements

| **4d.** | A *subject complement* is a word or word group that completes the meaning of a linking verb and that identifies or describes the subject. |

EXAMPLES The horse seemed exhausted. [The adjective *exhausted* completes the meaning of the linking verb *seemed* and describes the subject *horse*.]

Roberto became a teacher. [The noun *teacher* completes the meaning of the linking verb *became* and identifies the subject *Roberto*.]

EXERCISE A In the following sentences, circle the linking verb and underline the subject complement.

Example 1. Jeremiah (is) a friend of mine.

1. Joyce certainly seemed busy this afternoon.

2. Over the years, the song became an anthem for a generation.

3. The tall man at the back of the photograph is my grandfather.

4. Are the pies ready yet?

5. The bad weather in Minnesota this time of year is a good reason to stay home.

6. The cat seems friendly.

7. Jake is the winner of this week's prize.

8. Dr. Morbius appears happy about the results of his experiment.

9. Irene was the last person out of the pool.

10. Carey was the most improved player.

EXERCISE B In the blank in each of the following sentences, write a subject complement that will complete the meaning of the linking verb.

Example 1. Kyle felt _____*excited*_____ after he heard the news.

11. Gail became a respected _____ after she graduated from college.

12. Michael appeared _____ as he played his guitar and sang for us.

13. The squirrel seemed _____ when we walked past it.

14. Does the soup taste too _____ to you?

15. We all thought that the movie was very _____.

Predicate Nominatives

4e. A *predicate nominative* is a word or word group that is in the predicate and that identifies the subject or refers to it.

EXAMPLES   The protagonist of *The Call of the Wild* is a **dog** named Buck.

Buck becomes a hard-working **sled dog** and a devoted **companion** of John Thornton. [compound predicate nominative]

EXERCISE   In the following sentences, circle the linking verb and underline the predicate nominative. (Hint: Some sentences contain a compound predicate nominative.)

Example   1.   The leader (will be) Maria.

1. My partner for biology lab is Penelope.

2. Jason will be the next student council president.

3. Mrs. Furillo's favorite song is still "Night and Day."

4. Rocky Marciano was the world heavyweight boxing champion from 1952 to 1956.

5. My coat is the red one.

6. Leon would have been my first choice for the part.

7. Michelle Kwan has become an inspiration to us all.

8. Is Sara the runner in the blue T-shirt?

9. I could have been a contender.

10. The winner of the spelling bee was Tracy.

11. The next speaker will be Mr. Gonzalez.

12. Who was the fourteenth president of the United States?

13. My favorite memory of the trip is our day at the Grand Canyon.

14. At the age of eighteen, my father became the first person in his family to go to college.

15. Were the stars of that movie Lauren Bacall and Humphrey Bogart?

16. The winner is Terry!

17. Did Sheila become an accountant?

18. Grace's preferences for lunch are sandwiches or soup.

19. The next contestant on the show is Mr. Hynes.

20. Ginger should have become an actress.

Predicate Adjectives

| **4f.** | A *predicate adjective* is an adjective that is in the predicate and that describes the subject. |

EXAMPLES Those enchiladas look **delicious.**

The sauce is **spicy** and uncommonly **sweet.** [compound predicate adjective]

EXERCISE In each of the following sentences, circle each linking verb and underline all predicate adjectives.

Example 1. (Was) the new airplane <u>smaller</u> and <u>faster</u> than the older planes?

1. Our cat Conrad is small for his age.

2. The boiled potatoes tasted a little too bland for me.

3. Belinda sounded optimistic about the outcome of the student council election.

4. Parker looks very nice in that hat.

5. Sales of the new school calendar appear brisk.

6. The llama's fur felt soft to Marcia's touch.

7. The door to the basement is squeaky.

8. After his feeding, the baby remained quiet for the rest of the night.

9. The crowd at the championship game was energetic and enthusiastic.

10. Michael's new wool coat felt rough and scratchy against his skin.

11. Lance didn't become tired until the final lap of the race.

12. The maze can be frustrating and tiring.

13. The moon appeared big and bright in the evening sky.

14. The bittersweet comedy seemed both funny and sad.

15. The soup may be too hot to eat right now.

16. Have you ever been afraid of the dark?

17. The trail of the meteor appeared blue, green, and red.

18. Every day, Taylor grew more confident about riding her new unicycle.

19. Is your new dog brown and white?

20. The slope of the mountainside is quite steep.

Predicate Nominatives and Predicate Adjectives A

4e. A *predicate nominative* is a word or word group that is in the predicate and that identifies the subject or refers to it.

EXAMPLES   Leonardo da Vinci was a great **artist.**
   He was not only an **artist** but also an **inventor**. [compound predicate nominative]

4f. A *predicate adjective* is an adjective that is in the predicate and that describes the subject.

EXAMPLES   Leonardo da Vinci was highly **competent** in many fields.
   How **talented** and **creative** this versatile man was! [compound predicate adjective]

EXERCISE A   In the following sentences, circle the linking verb and underline each subject complement. Then, on the line provided, identify each subject complement as *PN* for *predicate nominative* or *PA* for *predicate adjective*.

Example ___*PN*___ **1.** (Was) Enrico Caruso a famous tenor?

_____ **1.** The bag with the bowling ball in it felt heavy.

_____ **2.** Mrs. Kaufman is my favorite teacher.

_____ **3.** The dog seemed eager to see us.

_____ **4.** The best vegetable, in my opinion, is spinach.

_____ **5.** Our next-door neighbor is a teacher at the local high school and the coach of the

   football team.

_____ **6.** Even after a week, the cat remained aloof from the other pets in the house.

_____ **7.** That casserole certainly smells delicious!

_____ **8.** Isn't Sonya the lead singer for the band?

_____ **9.** Some Asian dishes are perhaps too hot and spicy for some people.

_____ **10.** Toni Morrison is the author of several novels, including *Beloved* and *Song of Solomon.*

EXERCISE B   Each of the following sentences contains at least one subject complement. Underline each predicate nominative once and each predicate adjective twice.

Example 1. The test did not seem very difficult to us.

11. Robert is the fastest runner on the team.

12. Does the pattern on this shirt seem faded to you?

13. The author Joseph Heller was a famous novelist.

14. Jorge's two favorite composers are Beethoven and Holst.

15. Will this energetic puppy ever become a calm pet?

Language and Sentence Skills Practice

Predicate Nominatives and Predicate Adjectives B

4e. A **predicate nominative** is a word or word group that is in the predicate and that identifies the subject or refers to it.

> **EXAMPLE** Faith Ringgold is a talented **artist.**

A predicate nominative is never part of a prepositional phrase.

> **EXAMPLE** That quilt is **one** of her creations. [*One,* not *creations,* is the predicate nominative. *Creations* is the object of the preposition *of.*]

4f. A **predicate adjective** is an adjective that is in the predicate and that describes the subject.

> **EXAMPLE** Faith Ringgold is extremely **talented.**

EXERCISE A In each of the following sentences, identify the underlined word or word group by writing above it *PN* for *predicate nominative,* *PA* for *predicate adjective,* or *OP* for *object of a preposition.*

Example 1. Ms. Juarez is my English <u>teacher</u>. *(PN)*

1. Ms. Juarez is also an imaginative <u>playwright</u>.

2. "A Dog's Life" is <u>one</u> of her humorous one-act plays.

3. In this play a man becomes a full-grown <u>Labrador retriever</u>.

4. The man's children seem pleased with their new <u>pet</u>.

5. As the play unfolds, the dog's behavior grows comically <u>strange</u>.

EXERCISE B In the following sentences, identify each predicate nominative or predicate adjective by writing above it *PN* for *predicate nominative* or *PA* for *predicate adjective.* (Hint: At least one sentence contains a compound predicate nominative or a compound predicate adjective.)

Example 1. Did Randy seem *(PA)* angry and *(PA)* frustrated to you?

6. The dachshund is a highly intelligent breed of dog.

7. Does the water in the swimming pool feel too cold to you?

8. Broccoli is one of my favorite vegetables.

9. The finalists in the eighth-grade geography bee are Kim Chun and she.

10. The action in this movie may be too violent for some viewers.

11. The photographer seemed quite pleased with his pictures.

12. Una was certainly happy about the contest results.

13. All of the scouts appeared tired and hungry after their long hike.

14. My mother is a skilled carpenter.

15. Is Rufino Tamayo the Mexican artist who painted *Homage to Juárez*?

Review A: **Complements**

EXERCISE A In each of the following sentences, identify the underlined word by writing above it *COMP* for *complement*, *ADV* for *adverb*, or *OP* for *object of a preposition*.

Examples 1. Who invented the <u>telephone</u>?   *COMP*

　　　　　2. Who was the inventor of the <u>telephone</u>?   *OP*

1. Alexander Graham Bell is the name of the <u>inventor</u> of the telephone.

2. For many years, telephones did not have <u>dials</u> or push buttons.

3. Telephone operators would place calls for <u>people</u>.

4. A caller would tell an <u>operator</u> the telephone number to call.

5. Telephones with dials became <u>popular</u> in the 1930s.

6. Callers would turn the dials with their <u>fingers</u>.

7. With dial phones people could place their calls more <u>readily</u> than before.

8. Today's touch-tone phones are an <u>improvement</u> over dial phones.

9. With touch-tone phones people can place their calls <u>quickly</u>.

10. Today, callers can telephone nearly anyone in the <u>world</u> in a few seconds.

EXERCISE B Underline every complement that appears in each of the following sentences. Then, identify each complement by writing above it *DO* for *direct object*, *IO* for *indirect object*, *PN* for *predicate nominative*, or *PA* for *predicate adjective*.

Example 1. Nearly every day, my pen pal sends <u>me</u> an e-mail <u>message</u>.   *IO*   *DO*

11. Celine, my e-mail pal, is Canadian.

12. Montreal, Quebec, is her hometown.

13. Celine and I are both excited about our correspondence.

14. Like me, she speaks both English and French fluently.

15. We have the same tastes in music.

16. She e-mailed me a long letter yesterday.

17. In her letter she thanked me for the birthday gift.

18. I had given her the latest CD by her favorite country singer.

19. We are great fans of the last song on the CD.

20. Celine sent my family and me tickets to a concert in New York City.

Review B: **Complements**

EXERCISE A In each of the following sentences, identify the underlined word by writing above it *COMP* for *complement*, *ADV* for *adverb*, or *OP* for *object of a preposition*.

Examples 1. Baseball is my favorite <u>sport</u>. *COMP*

2. Have you ever been to a professional baseball <u>game</u>? *OP*

1. My uncle Mark took my entire <u>family</u> to a baseball game yesterday.

2. It was a beautiful day for the <u>game</u>.

3. The weather was <u>sunny</u> and warm.

4. The weather, however, suddenly changed on our way to the <u>stadium</u>.

5. The sun disappeared, and storm clouds gathered directly <u>overhead</u>.

6. By the time of our arrival, though, the sky was once again <u>clear</u>.

7. Everyone in my family, even my sister, enjoyed the <u>game</u>.

8. One player gave my <u>sister</u> his autograph.

9. Naturally, we cheered <u>enthusiastically</u> during each of his turns at bat.

10. Like me, my sister is now an avid baseball <u>fan</u>.

EXERCISE B Underline every complement that appears in each of the following sentences. Then, identify each complement by writing above it *DO* for *direct object*, *IO* for *indirect object*, *PN* for *predicate nominative*, or *PA* for *predicate adjective*.

Example 1. People ask <u>me</u> many <u>questions</u> about my hobby. *IO DO*

11. People are curious about my unusual collection.

12. I started the collection at my old house in Michigan.

13. My mother had hired a crew of carpenters.

14. Each carpenter was a skilled roofer.

15. They carefully pulled the old shingles off the roof.

16. The nails in the boards under the shingles were old and unusually large.

17. One of the carpenters noticed my interest in the nails.

18. I handed her an empty box.

19. She gave me some of the nails.

20. Those were the first ones in my collection of handmade nails.

Review C: **Complements**

EXERCISE In each of the following sentences, identify each of the underlined words or word groups by writing above it *DO* for *direct object,* *IO* for *indirect object,* *PN* for *predicate nominative,* or *PA* for *predicate adjective.*

Examples 1. Please bring <u>me</u> a <u>towel</u>.
                        IO   *DO*

          2. Don't worry; this recipe is <u>easy</u>.
                                          PA

1. Now that the election is over, Mr. Danton will be our new <u>representative</u> in Congress.

2. The English author Charles Dickens offers modern <u>readers</u> a vivid look at city life in the nineteenth century.

3. That seedling will eventually become a <u>tree</u>.

4. Marcia, read the <u>class</u> and <u>me</u> your essay.

5. We all use our <u>backpacks</u> to carry our books to and from school.

6. Jenna, my best friend, is the tallest <u>person</u> on our volleyball team.

7. This music is pretty <u>exotic</u>, don't you think?

8. Some people buy older <u>homes</u> and restore them.

9. Doesn't the new stereo sound <u>wonderful</u>?

10. Call the <u>switchboard</u> and ask for Jill.

11. The millionaire provided the <u>scientist</u> with the money to finish his research.

12. Did you give the dog his <u>medicine</u> and a <u>treat</u> this morning?

13. The aspiring writer gave the <u>editor</u> several chapters from his book.

14. Everyone in our family is a good <u>diver</u> and a good <u>swimmer</u>.

15. Nelson is <u>curious</u> about marine archaeology.

16. Please tell your <u>sister</u> and <u>me</u> the truth.

17. The ice on the lake seemed <u>thicker</u> the day after the temperature dropped.

18. Who is the <u>person</u> who left the beautiful flowers on my desk?

19. I think I look <u>good</u> in my new shirt.

20. Freddie brought a <u>bat</u> and a baseball <u>glove</u> to the first day of practice.

Literary Model: Predicate Nominatives in Poetry

On the Vanity of Earthly Greatness
by Arthur Guiterman

The tusks that clashed in mighty brawls
Of mastodons, are billiard balls.

The sword of Charlemagne the Just
Is ferric oxide, known as rust.

The grizzly bear whose potent hug
Was feared by all, is now a rug.

Great Caesar's bust is on the shelf,
And I don't feel so well myself.

EXERCISE A   Make a list of the predicate nominatives that appear in the above poem. After each one, write the subject that the predicate nominative describes or identifies.

_____
_____
_____
_____
_____
_____

EXERCISE B   Why do predicate nominatives work well in this poem?

_____
_____
_____
_____
_____
_____

Literary Model (continued)

EXERCISE C   Guiterman's poem uses predicate nominatives to give us a humorous look at the way things change. Now, write a few stanzas of your own. Using Guiterman's poem as a model, write at least three stanzas that tell about things that used to be one way, but now exist in new forms. Rhyming is optional, but be sure to use a predicate nominative in each stanza. You can extend Guiterman's theme of uselessness, or you can show how some things change for the better. (Hint: In addition to the verb *be,* you can use other linking verbs such as *appear, become, remain,* and *seem.*)

_____

_____

_____

_____

_____

_____

_____

_____

EXERCISE D

1. Make a list of the predicate nominatives that appear in your stanzas. After each one, write the subject that the predicate nominative describes or identifies.

_____

_____

_____

_____

_____

_____

_____

2. Would your stanzas have worked better without predicate nominatives? Explain your answer.

_____

_____

_____

_____

Writing Application: Description

Writers and speakers often use linking verbs and subject complements to describe the senses—taste, smell, touch, hearing, and sight. Predicate adjectives and predicate nominatives complete the meaning of a linking verb, while at the same time making a sentence interesting or memorable.

PREDICATE ADJECTIVES	The soup tastes **spicy.** Cold water is **refreshing.** Sandpaper feels **rough.**
PREDICATE NOMINATIVES	Hot cider is a tasty **drink** in winter weather, but cold water is the best **beverage** on a scorching day.

WRITING ACTIVITY

In art class, you are about to design a picture of some place that was special to you in the past. To prepare for the sketch, write several brief paragraphs about the place. Use linking verbs and complements as you recall every detail you can about the place—its sights, sounds, aromas, even textures. Your description will serve as a written companion piece for your drawing.

PREWRITING   After you have chosen the special place, close your eyes and return to it in memory. Recall as many details about it as you can, and then open your eyes and write them down. Repeat this process until you generate enough details to write a vivid description of the place. Then, decide how you will organize your writing. Writers often use spatial organization when describing a place.

WRITING   With your details and plan of organization in front of you, write reflectively about the special place. Describe the place, tell who shared the place with you, and explain why it is special to you. You may write rather dreamily at first—later, you can revise any vague sentences. Use linking verbs and complements as you re-create the sensory experience of the place you've chosen.

REVISING   Ask several friends to close their eyes and listen as you read aloud. Ask them what they can see, hear, smell, feel—even taste—about the memory. They will let you know if you forgot to write about the sounds or smells of the place. Finally, re-read the paragraphs, asking yourself if they are detailed enough to guide you as you draw or paint. Place additional sensory details in an appropriate place in your description.

PUBLISHING   Check your paragraphs for errors in spelling and punctuation. Using the details you have written, illustrate your special place. Then, tape your illustration beside your paragraphs; you may use poster board or construction paper. With your teacher's permission, display your description and picture in the classroom.

EXTENDING YOUR WRITING

If you enjoyed this exercise, you could develop it into a longer writing project. For an English class, you could write a personal narrative about an event that happened in this special place and how the event continues to affect you today. Alternatively, you could write a poem about the place and its importance to you.

Choices: Investigating Phrases

Here's your chance to step out of the grammar book and into the real world. You may not realize it, but examples of phrases appear in your life every day. The following activities challenge you to find a connection between phrases and the world around you. Do the activity below that suits your personality best, and then share your discoveries with your class. Have fun!

VISUAL

Spring Training

Write the word *sports* in large open letters. (An open letter is one that is merely outlined so that the inside is empty.) In the empty space inside each letter, write gerunds naming sports, such as *fishing* and *running*. Don't forget to label your graphic *Sports Gerunds*.

BUILDING BACKGROUND KNOWLEDGE

Betwixt and Between

Using a variety of prepositions can help readers visualize a writer's words as well as add precision to writing. Do your classmates a favor: Make an alphabetized list of all the prepositions you can find. Make copies of your list, and give one to each of your friends.

MUSIC

The Impossible Dream

A few years back, a musical called *Man of La Mancha* made the song "The Impossible Dream" famous. Find a copy of this song's lyrics, and write them down. Underline each infinitive and infinitive phrase. Then, tell whether each infinitive phrase is used as a noun, adjective, or adverb. Play the song for your class, explaining how infinitive phrases drive the song.

GROUP PROJECT

Are Two Heads Better Than One?

With your teacher's help, divide your class into groups of four. Starting with yourself as number one, number off the members of your group. In the middle of a sheet of paper, write a noun. Hand the paper to person two, who will add a vivid verb to your noun. Person three goes next, adding a descriptive phrase. Finally, person four gets to add another phrase. Be creative. When your sentence is complete, read it aloud. Is the sentence funny? boring? interesting? confusing?

MOVIES

At the Theater

Prepositional phrases can show up in all kinds of unexpected places—even at the movie theater. Have you ever noticed that many movie titles contain prepositional phrases? In fact, many movie titles *are* prepositional phrases. In a group or by yourself, brainstorm to come up with at least ten of these movie titles—five that contain prepositional phrases and five that are prepositional phrases. (*Hint:* An Internet movie database or book that contains movie reviews can help you get ideas.)

WORD ORDER

Arranging the Pieces

Find out how different a sentence can sound when you add, delete, or move phrases within it. First, write a sentence that contains a subject, a verb, and at least two phrases. Then, get your scissors and cut out each phrase. Next, see how many ways you can combine the separate pieces of your sentence. (Don't forget that punctuation often changes when you rearrange a sentence.) When you move a certain phrase from, say, the middle of the sentence to the beginning, does the new sentence sound more powerful? more confusing? more interesting? Explain. The next time you write a letter or a story, remember what a difference phrases can make.

ART

A Challenging Illustration

Illustrate a scene that allows your classmates to see these terms—a participle, a gerund, or both—in action. Draw a running cheetah, or create a jumping Olympian. Paint a picture of a favorite hobby, such as fishing. Place a caption under your artwork, and be sure to identify the caption's participle or gerund.

Phrases

5a. A *phrase* is a group of related words that is used as a single part of speech and that does not contain both a verb and its subject.

EXAMPLES Colors can influence the way we feel **about a place or thing.** [prepositional phrase]

A room **painted white** often seems larger than it is. [participial phrase]

Painting something orange draws people's attention to it. [gerund phrase]

Studies show that more women than men seem **to prefer red.** [infinitive phrase]

Green, **the color of many things in nature,** relaxes people. [appositive phrase]

A group of words that has both a verb and its subject is called a *clause*.

EXAMPLES The class has been conducting a survey. [*Class* is the subject of the verb *has been conducting*.]

after I completed my research [*I* is the subject of the verb *completed*.]

EXERCISE Determine whether the underlined word group in each of the following sentences is a phrase or not. If the word group is a phrase, write *phrase*. If the word group is not a phrase, write *not a phrase*.

Example _____*phrase*_____ **1.** The cup slipped from her hands and shattered <u>on the floor</u>.

_____ **1.** Please place the keys <u>on the table</u>.

_____ **2.** They decided <u>to watch a movie</u>.

_____ **3.** The glasses are <u>on the shelf</u>.

_____ **4.** Enrique became excited <u>when he heard the news</u>.

_____ **5.** Jimmy, <u>fearing a low score</u>, studied diligently for his exam.

_____ **6.** <u>In 1934</u>, my grandfather came to the United States.

_____ **7.** The clothes <u>in the corner</u> should be donated to charity.

_____ **8.** Casper, <u>a master of the violin</u>, is learning to play the guitar.

_____ **9.** <u>To repair a car</u>, you need to have tools and experience.

_____ **10.** <u>Before she left home</u>, Helena ate breakfast and read a magazine.

The Prepositional Phrase

5b.   A *prepositional phrase* includes a preposition, a noun or pronoun called *the object of the preposition,* and any modifiers of that object.

EXAMPLES   up the Amazon River   on a memorable trip
                     by themselves   along with my family and me

EXERCISE A   Underline the prepositional phrase(s) in each of the following sentences.

Example 1. For several years farmers in England found strange patterns throughout their grain fields.

1. The first reports about the cause of these mysterious patterns appeared in 1978.

2. In the middle of a field, the grain would be flattened in huge circles.

3. Some people believed the circles in the fields were made by extraterrestrials.

4. Many others throughout the country attributed the designs to rare weather conditions.

5. Instead of circles, more elaborate designs appeared in 1990.

6. Investigators said that no one had actually seen any of the patterns being formed.

7. In 1991, the mystery may have been solved.

8. The strange patterns could have been made by two pranksters as a practical joke.

9. Since these two hoaxers' confessions, the number of occurrences of these strange patterns has declined significantly.

10. Several books about the mysterious phenomenon were written during the 1980s and 1990s.

EXERCISE B   Complete each of the following sentences by writing in the blank an appropriate prepositional phrase.

Example 1. The birthday gift _____*from his parents*_____ surprised Mateo.

11. _____ Mateo's parents bought him a pony.

12. The pony had black patches _____.

13. So Mateo said _____, "Let's call the pony Salt and Pepper."

14. Mateo's father helped his son into the saddle, and Mateo rode _____.

15. Then they led the pony _____ and gave it some fresh hay and water.

The Adjective Phrase

5c. A prepositional phrase that modifies a noun or a pronoun is called an *adjective phrase.*

An *adjective phrase* tells *what kind* or *which one.*

> **EXAMPLES** My favorite writer **for young readers** is Beverly Cleary. [The adjective phrase modifies the noun *writer,* telling *what kind.*]
>
> I have read most **of Beverly Cleary's books.** [The adjective phrase modifies the pronoun *most,* telling *which one.*]

An adjective phrase usually follows the word it modifies. That word may be the object of another prepositional phrase.

> **EXAMPLE** Jane read a book **about the fall of Rome.** [The adjective phrase *of Rome* modifies *fall,* which is the object of the preposition *about.* The adjective phrase *about the fall* modifies *book.*]

More than one adjective phrase may modify the same word.

> **EXAMPLE** The bowl **of fruit salad in the refrigerator** is for the party. [The adjective phrases *of fruit salad* and *in the refrigerator* modify the noun *bowl.*]

EXERCISE In each of the following sentences, underline the adjective phrase or phrases. Then, circle the word that each adjective phrase modifies.

Example 1. The (town) beyond those (mountains) to the east is no longer inhabited.

1. My favorite writer of science fiction is Ray Bradbury.

2. The recipe needs four cups of fruit.

3. A student from Mr. Levy's class won first prize.

4. The loud crash of the cymbal was deafening.

5. The directions for the assignment confused Gilbert.

6. The glass of water on the table is mine.

7. The play of the sunlight on the water was a beautiful sight.

8. Somebody with feet of large proportions has scuffed the gym floor.

9. Susie mowed the area around the trunk of the tree.

10. The house on the corner of Main and Elm has been abandoned.

The Adverb Phrase

5d.   A prepositional phrase that modifies a verb, an adjective, or an adverb is called an *adverb phrase.*

An *adverb phrase* tells *how, when, where, why,* or *to what extent* (*how long, how many, how much,* or *how far*).

EXAMPLES   We completed the science project **before the deadline.** [The adverb phrase modifies the verb *completed,* telling *when.*]

                We were happy **with the results.** [The adverb phrase modifies the adjective *happy,* telling *how.*]

                We had worked diligently **for a week.** [The adverb phrase modifies the adverb *diligently,* telling *to what extent.*]

An adverb phrase may come before or after the word it modifies. In each of the following examples, the adverb phrase modifies the verb *learned.*

EXAMPLES   **From our research** we learned many facts about the solar system.

                We learned **from our research** many facts about the solar system.

More than one adverb phrase may modify the same word.

EXAMPLE   **On Friday** we presented our work **to our teacher.** [Both adverb phrases modify the verb *presented.*]

EXERCISE   In each of the following sentences, underline the adverb phrase or phrases. Then, circle the word or words that each adverb phrase modifies.

Example 1. During the summer, Carlie (went) to Italy and Spain.

1. Terra walked across the street.

2. Throughout next month, the band will perform at the fair.

3. Before Sunday, please clean your room.

4. Mr. Monroe has lived on Mason Street for twenty-two years.

5. Jason was pleased with his grades.

6. For several hours, a cool wind blew from the east.

7. Mrs. Green teaches history through books, magazines, and videos.

8. The boys dipped their feet into the cool, soothing water.

9. Please complete your project by Friday.

10. A quiet stillness reigned at the school throughout spring break.

GRAMMAR

Adjective and Adverb Phrases A

| **5c.** | A prepositional phrase that modifies a noun or a pronoun is called an ***adjective phrase.*** |

An *adjective phrase* tells *what kind* or *which one.*

> **EXAMPLE** What do you think influences the changes **in hairstyles**? [The adjective phrase modifies the noun *changes,* telling *what kind.*]

| **5d.** | A prepositional phrase that modifies a verb, an adjective, or an adverb is called an ***adverb phrase.*** |

An *adverb phrase* tells *how, when, where, why,* or *to what extent.*

> **EXAMPLE** Why do you think some hairstyles remain popular **for only a short time**? [The adverb phrase modifies the adjective *popular,* telling *to what extent.*]

EXERCISE A In each of the following sentences, circle the word or words that the underlined prepositional phrase modifies. Then, identify the phrase by writing above it *ADJ* for *adjective phrase* or *ADV* for *adverb phrase.*

Example 1. Throughout the night, water from the ceiling annoyingly (dripped) into the bucket. [*ADV* above "Throughout the night"]

1. Sonya is good at soccer.

2. Raphael enjoys reading articles about early space exploration.

3. Throughout the spring, Archimedes spent much time fishing.

4. The young cheetah quietly crouched behind the tall, yellow grass.

5. Herbert watched an informative video on the air battles of World War II.

EXERCISE B In each of the following sentences, underline each prepositional phrase. Then, identify the phrase by writing above it *ADJ* for *adjective phrase* or *ADV* for *adverb phrase.*

Example 1. The store on the corner was damaged during a severe hailstorm. [*ADJ* above "on the corner"; *ADV* above "during a severe hailstorm"]

6. The day before Memorial Day, Henry visited his grandfather for two hours.

7. With great skill, the doctor removed several tiny shards of glass.

8. Elizabeth's essay about Victorian customs in England earned her an A.

9. During the celebration of Mom's birthday, Uncle Jimmy told hilarious jokes for a whole hour.

10. Helga's cousin from New Orleans waited in the living room.

11. The cost of the new bridge went beyond the previous estimate.

12. The skateboard was too expensive for Li.

13. Before an evening of relaxation, Erin likes jogging for an hour.

14. That boy with a broken leg had been injured during a soccer game.

15. On the beach of the tiny island, the castaways constructed a hut of leaves and grass.

Adjective and Adverb Phrases B

5c. A prepositional phrase that modifies a noun or a pronoun is called an *adjective phrase.*

An *adjective phrase* tells *what kind* or *which one.*

> **EXAMPLE** A glider is an aircraft **with no engine.** [The adjective phrase modifies the noun *aircraft*, telling *what kind*.]

5d. A prepositional phrase that modifies a verb, an adjective, or an adverb is called an *adverb phrase.*

An *adverb phrase* tells *how, when, where, why,* or *to what extent.*

> **EXAMPLE** The chef seasoned the casserole **with garlic, pepper, and thyme.** [The adverb phrase modifies the verb *seasoned*, telling *how*.]

EXERCISE A In each of the following sentences, circle the word or words that the underlined prepositional phrase modifies. Then, identify the underlined phrase by writing above it *ADJ* for *adjective phrase* or *ADV* for *adverb phrase.*

Example 1. Elaine was (unhappy) with the predictable movie plot. [ADV]

1. The house beyond that hill belongs to Mrs. Wilton.

2. The woman in the business suit is giving out free tickets.

3. Carl plays piano well for a beginner.

4. The most exciting game of the season occurred last night.

5. Before noon, please complete your projects.

EXERCISE B Underline each prepositional phrase in the following sentences. Then, identify each phrase by writing above it *ADJ* for *adjective phrase* or *ADV* for *adverb phrase.*

Example 1. With a mighty toss [ADV], Philip launched the paper airplane into the sky [ADV].

6. The scientists watched with satisfaction as the probe flew into space.

7. On October 21, the mayor of the city spoke at the convention center.

8. The tower behind the temple was constructed over a ten-year period .

9. At malls, people with clipboards sometimes give shoppers surveys.

10. Frank rode his bike over the rough trails and hills of Pete's Peak.

11. On Friday, Lisa watched a show about the Maya.

12. A Spanish galleon from the sixteenth century was discovered off the coast.

13. Over the weekend, Adele enjoyed the crisp air of the Rocky Mountains.

14. Mr. James is good at basketball.

15. For his birthday, José wants a red convertible with a black top.

Language and Sentence Skills Practice

The Participle

5e.   A *participle* is a verb form that can be used as an adjective.

(1) Present participles end in *–ing*.

EXAMPLES   Our soccer team had a **winning** season. [*Winning* modifies *season*.]
Shivering with cold, we decided to go indoors. [*Shivering* modifies *we*.]
I found three kittens **sleeping** in the flower bed. [*Sleeping* modifies *kittens*.]

(2) Most past participles end in *–d* or *–ed*. Some are irregularly formed.

EXAMPLES   We visited a Spanish mission **established** in the 1600s. [*Established* modifies *mission*.]
The **swollen** river overflowed its banks. [*Swollen* modifies *river*.]

Do not confuse a participle used as an adjective with a participle used as part of a verb phrase.
ADJECTIVE   We found Ms. Jacobs **working** in her garden.
VERB PHRASE   Ms. Jacobs **was working** in her garden.

EXERCISE A   In each of the following sentences, circle the noun or pronoun that the underlined participle modifies. Then, above the participle, write *present* for *present participle* or *past* for *past participle*.

Example 1. The broken (glass) is on the floor.
(above "broken": past)

1. Clara likes to eat canned peaches.

2. Clapping wildly, the fans welcomed the band.

3. Theresa watered the blossoming flowers.

4. The child's forgotten toys lined the bottom of the toy chest.

5. Decorated with care, the float was popular at the parade.

EXERCISE B   Underline the participle in each of the following sentences. Then, above the participle, write *present* for *present participle* or *past* for *past participle*.

Example 1. The painting, purchased at a garage sale, was worth one million dollars.
(above "purchased": past)

6. The book, chosen for its unusual characters, was a class favorite.

7. Feeling confident, Larry volunteered to list all of the state capitals.

8. Dale watched the kitten playing with his shoe.

9. The students planning the field trip decided to take a trip to Washington, D.C.

10. Janet discovered a treasure map on the piece of yellowed paper.

The Participial Phrase

5f.	A *participial phrase* consists of a participle and any modifiers or complements the participle has. The entire phrase is used as an adjective.

> **EXAMPLES**   **Reaching for a bagel,** she knocked over her glass of milk. [The participial phrase modifies the pronoun *she.*]
>
> Aunt Molly sent me a baseball glove **autographed by Sammy Sosa.** [The participial phrase modifies the noun *glove.*]

A participial phrase should be placed as close as possible to the word it modifies. Otherwise, the phrase may appear to modify another word, and the sentence may not make sense.

MISPLACED   Many holiday decorations adorned the gift shop made of papier mâché.

CORRECTED   Many holiday decorations **made of papier mâché** adorned the gift shop.

EXERCISE A   Underline the participial phrase in each of the following sentences. Then, circle the noun or pronoun that the participial phrase modifies.

Example 1. Appreciated for his contribution, (Alfred) was awarded a trip to Paris.

1. The mascot, known to the students as Sparky, entertained the crowd.

2. Walter, running with speed and purpose, passed the other joggers.

3. Seeing the bump in the road, Nell swerved to avoid it.

4. Dressed in style, Blake left his house and headed for the school dance.

5. The mayor has a building named in her honor.

EXERCISE B   Use each of the following participial phrases in a sentence. Be sure to place each phrase as close as possible to the noun or pronoun it modifies.

Example 1. looking down at his shoes

    Looking down at his shoes, Bart noticed that they were untied.

6. feeling tired

_____

7. dressed in shorts and a T-shirt

_____

8. hiding under the bed

_____

9. damaged by the rain

_____

10. signed by President Abraham Lincoln

_____

Participles and Participial Phrases A

| **5e.** | A *participle* is a verb form that can be used as an adjective. |

(1) Present participles end in *–ing*.

> **EXAMPLE**   The **threatening** weather caused us to delay our trip. [*Threatening* modifies *weather*.]

(2) Most past participles end in *–d* or *–ed*. Some are irregularly formed.

> **EXAMPLE**   The **worried** meteorologist issued a weather alert. [*Worried* modifies *meteorologist*.]

| **5f.** | A *participial phrase* consists of a participle and any modifiers or complements the participle has. The entire phrase is used as an adjective. |

> **EXAMPLE**   We heeded the warning **given by the reporter.** [The participial phrase modifies the noun *warning*.]

EXERCISE A   In each of the following sentences, draw one line under the participle used as an adjective and two lines under the word it modifies.

Example   1. A storm named Hurricane Albert had formed.

1. The roaring wind came first.

2. A concerned look was on my father's face.

3. The emergency instructions prepared by my mother came in handy.

4. In a few hours, our house had taped windows.

5. Candles brought by my mother were ready on the table.

6. My parents had also bought a large supply of bottled water.

7. The pouring rain beat against the windows.

8. The flickering lights prompted us to light the candles.

9. Huddled around the radio, we listened for weather updates.

10. Finally, the storm passed, leaving behind considerable damage.

EXERCISE B   In each of the following sentences, draw one line under the participial phrase and two lines under the word or words it modifies.

Example   1. I saw a picture of a woolly mammoth lifting its hairy trunk.

11. Born during the Ice Age, woolly mammoths needed a great deal of hair.

12. The land, covered with ice, was a difficult place to survive.

13. Even a big beast protected by hair had trouble.

14. Searching for food, the woolly mammoths roamed the land.

15. Looking at pictures of these animals, I wonder how they survived at all.

Participles and Participial Phrases B

5e. | A *participle* is a verb form that can be used as an adjective.

(1) Present participles end in –*ing*.

> **EXAMPLE** The mascot of the **opposing** team is a cougar. [*Opposing* modifies *team*.]

(2) Most past participles end in –*d* or –*ed*. Some are irregularly formed.

> **EXAMPLE** At the cookout, they served **grilled** salmon. [*Grilled* modifies *salmon*.]

5f. | A *participial phrase* consists of a participle and any modifiers or complements the participle has. The entire phrase is used as an adjective.

> **EXAMPLE** The Akashi-Kaiko Bridge, **located in Kobe-Naruto, Japan,** is the world's largest suspension bridge. [The participial phrase modifies the noun *Akashi-Kaiko Bridge*.]

EXERCISE A In each of the following sentences, underline the participle. Then, circle the word or words that the participle modifies.

Example 1. Pepe admired the darkening sky.

1. The battered ship was anchored off the coast of Florida.

2. The hikers took plenty of bottled beverages on their journey.

3. José bought ten used magazines.

4. The beaten team did not advance to the playoffs.

5. The running child almost slipped and fell.

EXERCISE B In each of the following sentences, underline the participial phrase. Then, circle the word or words that the participial phrase modifies.

Example 1. Preparing for the winter storm, Jimmy took his plants inside.

6. The tools used by professional mechanics are usually very expensive.

7. Covered with snow for weeks, the ground was now hard.

8. The basement, filled with old boxes, was damp and musty.

9. Simple jewelry left behind by ancient Egyptians can be very valuable today.

10. Wanting to make a good impression, Harry wore his favorite shirt to the game.

11. The dogs, barking noisily throughout the night, kept the neighbors awake.

12. Jeff wanted to buy an antique desk used by a famous writer.

13. Feeling exhausted after a day of hard work, Ellen decided to go to sleep early.

14. The boys playing in the park found an arrowhead and the fragments of a necklace.

15. Torn and tattered, the clothes looked as if they had been worn for a long time.

The Gerund

5g.   A *gerund* is a verb form ending in *–ing* that is used as a noun.

EXAMPLES   **Skiing** is my favorite sport. [subject of the verb *is*]
My hobby is **fishing.** [predicate nominative identifying the subject *hobby*]
Sam enjoys rock **climbing.** [direct object of the verb *enjoy*]
We should give **snorkeling** a try. [indirect object of the verb *should give*]
Saul has shown great interest in **skating.** [object of the preposition *in*]

Do not confuse a gerund with a present participle used as part of a verb phrase or as an adjective.

EXAMPLES   The rabbit was sitting by the edge of the running stream. [*Sitting* is part of the verb phrase *was sitting. Running* is a participle modifying *stream.*]

EXERCISE A   Underline the gerund in each of the following sentences.

Example 1. The key to <u>playing</u> guitar is finger dexterity.

1. Becoming a doctor takes years of serious study.

2. Kino's specialty is cooking mushrooms and onions.

3. The subtle squeaking of the door hinges told Mira that her sister was home.

4. Carla decided on writing about famous women in history.

5. Mr. Riley enjoys the crackling of a campfire on a winter's evening.

EXERCISE B   Underline the gerund in each of the following sentences. Then, above each gerund, write *S* for *subject, PN* for *predicate nominative, DO* for *direct object, IO* for *indirect object,* or *OP* for *object of a preposition.* If a sentence does not contain a gerund, write *none* after the sentence.

Example 1. Laurie loves <u>running</u> early in the morning.   *DO*

6. Traveling to new and interesting places is fun.

7. The smiling child amused his parents.

8. Give playing golf another chance.

9. The powerful writing made the novel exciting to read.

10. Carla was talking in a low whisper to her best friend.

11. Cecil's favorite hobby is building scale models of World War II airplanes.

12. The key to fishing is patience.

13. Fielding a pop fly on a sunny day can be a tricky play.

14. Pam is studying for her French exam.

15. Marie's favorite event is swimming.

The Gerund Phrase

5h. | A *gerund phrase* consists of a gerund and any modifiers or complements the gerund has. The entire phrase is used as a noun.

EXAMPLES **Holding a class election** taught us much about politics. [subject of the verb *taught*]

When did the candidates begin **campaigning for the class offices**? [direct object of the verb *did begin*]

Carrie's passion is **rock climbing.** [predicate nominative identifying the subject *passion*]

Javier gave **fishing for bass** another chance. [indirect object of the verb *gave*]

Election officials made an error in **counting the votes.** [object of the preposition *in*]

EXERCISE A Underline the gerund phrase in each of the following sentences.

Example 1. Jim's tiny handwriting is sometimes difficult to read.

1. The vibrating of the tire caused the car to shake.

2. The noise you heard is the soft chirping of a baby bird.

3. Sally is an expert at identifying Grecian artifacts.

4. Playing the piano well is a difficult skill to learn.

5. Jason's method of fly-fishing for trout is unique but effective.

EXERCISE B Underline the gerund phrase in each of the following sentences. Then, above each gerund phrase, write *S* for *subject,* *PN* for *predicate nominative,* *DO* for *direct object,* *IO* for *indirect object,* or *OP* for *object of a preposition.* If a sentence does not contain a gerund phrase, write *none* after the sentence.

Example 1. The slow rocking of the boat made Daniel seasick.

6. Javier wants to write an essay about the art of playing video games.

7. The swerving car avoided the fallen tree lying in the road.

8. Julie's favorite pastime is running along the trails near the park.

9. Having defined goals will help you plan your future.

10. Katy's favorite weekend activity is sleeping late on Saturday mornings.

11. The class used up half an hour by asking the guest speaker questions about comets.

12. The chef gave cooking the stew the attention it deserved.

13. Try flying the kite one more time before the wind dies down.

14. Terra dreams of flying a helicopter for a television news station.

15. Our baseball team is playing out of town this week.

Language and Sentence Skills Practice

Gerunds and Gerund Phrases A

5g. A *gerund* is a verb form ending in –*ing* that is used as a noun.

EXAMPLES **Spelunking** is a wonderful adventure. [subject of the verb *is*]

We could hear the distant **rumbling** of thunder. [direct object of the verb *could hear*]

We should give **rafting** another try. [indirect object of the verb *should give*]

5h. A *gerund phrase* consists of a gerund and any modifiers or complements the gerund has. The entire phrase is used as a noun.

EXAMPLES One of the president's duties is **serving as commander in chief.** [predicate nominative identifying one of the president's duties]

The settlers cleared part of the land by **burning down the forest.** [object of the preposition *by*]

EXERCISE A Underline the gerund in each of the following sentences.

Example 1. The sharp <u>clanging</u> of the bell alerted the students.

1. Jackie saved money for the trip by grooming horses at a local stable.

2. Training a pet to obey simple commands can be difficult.

3. Jerry's phobia is speaking to large crowds.

4. Sarah believes in saving money for the future.

5. The annoying rooster enjoys crowing outside my window.

EXERCISE B Underline the gerund phrase in each of the following sentences. Then, above each gerund phrase, write *S* for *subject, PN* for *predicate nominative, DO* for *direct object, IO* for *indirect object,* or *OP* for *object of a preposition.* If a sentence does not contain a gerund phrase, write *none* after the sentence.

Example 1. <u>Traveling to distant places</u> is easier today than it was two hundred years ago. [*S* written above]

6. Flying in an airplane sounds dangerous, but it is actually quite safe.

7. A far more dangerous activity is driving a car.

8. Some drivers endanger others as well as themselves by recklessly disobeying traffic laws.

9. David's family is taking a train to New York this summer.

10. For our next vacation we may give riding on a train a try.

11. Watching the countryside roll by from the window of a train would be fun.

12. My sister votes for driving to Seattle, Washington, in an RV.

13. Preston heard the crashing of the surf.

14. Traveling across the country takes a lot of time.

15. Wherever we go on our vacation, my aunt is coming with us.

Gerunds and Gerund Phrases B

5g.　A *gerund* is a verb form ending in *–ing* that is used as a noun.

EXAMPLES　**Playing** chess well requires concentration. [subject of the verb *requires*]

My sister Tyra has started **collecting** rocks. [direct object of the verb *has started*]

5h.　A *gerund phrase* consists of a gerund and any modifiers or complements the gerund has. The entire phrase is used as a noun.

EXAMPLES　Before Martin became a journalist, he had given **becoming an English teacher** serious thought. [indirect object of the verb *had given*]

When did Tori Murden fulfill her dream of **rowing solo across the Atlantic Ocean**? [object of the preposition *of*]

EXERCISE A　Underline the gerund in each of the following sentences.

Example　1. The rumbling of Joe's stomach told us it was time to eat.

1. Larry was intent on watching every movie in our video collection in one weekend.

2. My sister is responsible for cleaning the garage.

3. Deanna's powerful speaking caused the audience to erupt in applause.

4. The difficult aspect of the workout program is getting up at four in the morning.

5. The cacophonous clanking of the car's engine could be heard from blocks away.

EXERCISE B　Underline the gerund phrase in each of the following sentences. Then, above each gerund, write *S* for *subject, PN* for *predicate nominative, DO* for *direct object, IO* for *indirect object,* or *OP* for *object of a preposition.* If a sentence does not contain a gerund phrase, write *none* after the sentence.

Example　1. The barking of the menacing dog caused the cat to flee from the yard.

6. Theresa began her report on Medieval Europe with an interesting question.

7. When he was five, the musical prodigy started playing the piano.

8. Plato gave fishing for rainbow trout another chance.

9. Jack's parents supported his dream of winning a gold medal.

10. The charging rhinoceros on the video frightened the kindergartners.

11. Among other sports, Li enjoys snorkeling in the ocean.

12. The teacher noted that Paul has a love of reading poems and writing them.

13. His strongest event in the track meet was running hurdles.

14. At sunrise the girls began raking the golden leaves.

15. One popular hobby is collecting baseball cards.

Language and Sentence Skills Practice

Participle or Gerund?

Both present participles and gerunds end in *–ing*. To avoid confusing these two verb forms, remember that a present participle functions as an adjective or as part of a verb phrase and that a gerund functions as a noun.

EXAMPLES   Brian is in his room, **writing** in his journal. [present participle modifying the noun *Brian*.]

Brian is **writing** in his journal. [part of the verb phrase *is writing*.]

Brian enjoys **writing** in his journal. [gerund used as the direct object of the verb *enjoys*.]

EXERCISE A   In each of the following sentences, identify the underlined word as a *participle* or *gerund*. If the underlined word is part of the verb phrase, write *verb* on the line provided.

Example   _participle_   **1.** The <u>dancing</u> duo amazed the audience with their flawless routine.

_____   **1.** <u>Planning</u> ahead, David carried an umbrella to school.

_____   **2.** The <u>zoning</u> committee would not allow a strip mall to be built next to the park.

_____   **3.** The tireless beavers were <u>building</u> a dam across the stream.

_____   **4.** Brian likes <u>racing</u> remote-controlled cars.

_____   **5.** The restless boy was <u>fidgeting</u> throughout the entire movie.

EXERCISE B   Use each of the following words as a gerund or a participle. The gerund or participle may be a single word or part of a phrase.

Example 1. writing (gerund)   _Ben enjoys writing to his pen pal in Italy._

6. jumping (participle) _____

_____

7. swimming (gerund) _____

_____

8. feeling (participle) _____

_____

9. seeing (participle) _____

_____

10. tasting (gerund) _____

_____

The Infinitive

| **5i.** | An *infinitive* is a verb form that can be used as a noun, an adjective, or an adverb. Most infinitives begin with *to*. |

NOUN I have always wanted **to visit** the Egyptian pyramids. [direct object of the verb *have wanted*]

ADJECTIVE I may soon have the opportunity **to visit** the Egyptian pyramids. [modifying the noun *opportunity*]

ADVERB I may travel to Egypt next summer **to visit** the pyramids. [modifying the verb phrase *may travel*]

Do not confuse an infinitive with a prepositional phrase beginning with *to*. A prepositional phrase always has an object that is a noun or a pronoun. An infinitive is a verb form.

INFINITIVE to travel

PREPOSITIONAL PHRASE to Japan

EXERCISE Underline the infinitive in each of the following sentences. If the sentence does not have an infinitive, write *none* after the sentence.

Example 1. To visit the pyramids in Egypt would be exciting.

1. Laurie said that the best place to go on Friday is the roller rink.

2. Elaine wants to be a writer after she graduates.

3. The idea to remember is that an infinitive is a verb form.

4. The clerk gave the sack of groceries to him.

5. The neatly chopped tomatoes were ready to go into the salad.

6. Emile read the article to find information about Korea.

7. To learn facts, some people use mnemonics, or memory devices.

8. Eddie came to school late on Wednesday.

9. She wanted her guest to be comfortable.

10. A person needs coordination to dance well.

The Infinitive Phrase

5j. An *infinitive phrase* consists of an infinitive and any modifiers or complements the infinitive has. The entire phrase may be used as a noun, an adjective, or an adverb.

NOUN	**To climb Mount Everest** is one of Ann's goals. [subject of the verb *is*]
ADJECTIVE	Any time is a great time **to be in New Orleans.** [modifying the noun *time*]
ADVERB	We displayed posters **to remind everyone of the Earth Day festivities.** [modifying the verb *displayed*]

EXERCISE Underline the infinitive phrase in each of the following sentences. Then, above the infinitive phrase, write *N* for *noun, ADJ* for *adjective,* or *ADV* for *adverb.* If a sentence does not have a infinitive phrase, write *none* after the sentence.

Example 1. Sarah took the time to decorate her notebooks. [ADJ, underlined "to decorate her notebooks"]

1. To fix a flat bicycle tire you may need a tire patch and some glue.

2. Alex was ready to begin his new class on Monday.

3. The campers went to a campsite near the mountains.

4. The ability to play a musical instrument comes from talent and practice.

5. Henry's little brother always wants to play hide-and-seek.

6. The team went to the stadium to practice the new plays.

7. The purpose of a persuasive speech is to convince others.

8. The salesperson measured Roy's arm to determine his sleeve size.

9. Please hand your science project to the person behind you.

10. Yori wants to eat Italian food for lunch.

11. To study a foreign language is a worthwhile pursuit.

12. We were told to put the food away.

13. Please tell them to be quiet.

14. Saturday is a good day to mow the lawn.

15. Are you prepared to answer the question?

16. Martina sent the results to her father.

17. The president asked her advisers to propose a solution.

18. My chief goal in college is to earn my degree.

19. To remember a conversation from three years ago is quite a trick.

20. Don't forget to return the basketball to the equipment room.

Infinitives and Infinitive Phrases A

5i. | An *infinitive* is a verb form that can be used as a noun, an adjective, or an adverb. Most infinitives begin with *to*.

NOUN	Would you like **to dance**? [direct object of the verb *would like*]
ADJECTIVE	A relatively simple dance **to perform** is the waltz. [modifying the noun *dance*]
ADVERB	Are all of the dancers ready **to rehearse**? [modifying the adjective *ready*]

5j. | An *infinitive phrase* consists of an infinitive and any modifiers or complements the infinitive has. The entire phrase may be used as a noun, an adjective, or an adverb.

NOUN	**To become a singer** requires talent and desire. [subject of the verb *requires*]
ADJECTIVE	Do you have the desire **to become a singer**? [modifying the noun *desire*]
ADVERB	You seem eager **to become a singer.** [modifying the adjective *eager*]

EXERCISE A   Underline the infinitive phrase in each of the following sentences. Then, identify the use of the phrase by writing above it *N* for *noun*, *ADJ* for *adjective*, or *ADV* for *adverb*.

Example 1. Do you like to make things out of paper? [N]

1. An easy thing to form out of paper is an envelope.

2. To make a paper airplane takes little time.

3. Some children were eager to fold paper into shapes of animal figures.

4. One child's goal was to create a paper jacket.

5. Others were content to design paper baskets.

EXERCISE B   Use each of the following infinitives in a sentence. The part of speech is indicated in parentheses.

Example 1. to build (noun)   *Katy said she wanted to build a treehouse in the back yard.*

6. to feel (noun) _____

_____

7. to become (adverb) _____

_____

8. to believe (adverb) _____

_____

9. to fill (adjective) _____

_____

10. to decide (noun) _____

_____

Infinitives and Infinitive Phrases B

5i. An *infinitive* is a verb form that can be used as a noun, an adjective, or an adverb. Most infinitives begin with *to.*

NOUN	At an early age the child learned **to sign.** [direct object of the verb *learned*]
ADJECTIVE	Raisins and other dried fruit would be good snacks **to serve.** [modifying the noun *snacks*]
ADVERB	This jigsaw puzzle will be difficult **to work.** [modifying the adjective *difficult*]

5j. An *infinitive phrase* consists of an infinitive and any modifiers or complements the infinitive has. The entire phrase may be used as a noun, an adjective, or an adverb.

NOUN	Two of my classmates are trying **to build a computer.** [direct object of the verb *are trying*]
ADJECTIVE	Who was the first woman **to command a space shuttle**? [modifying the noun *woman*]
ADVERB	We gathered outside **to observe the meteor shower.** [modifying the verb *gathered*]

EXERCISE Underline the infinitive or infinitive phrase in each of the following sentences. Then, write above the infinitive or infinitive phrase *N* for *noun, ADJ* for *adjective,* or *ADV* for *adverb.*

Example 1. Jacob was the first student to volunteer for the cleanup crew.

1. Francis wrapped the sandwich in cellophane to keep the sandwich fresh.

2. The assignment was not difficult to complete.

3. At four o'clock, Charles began to paint the garage a dazzling shade of pink.

4. Lee and his buddies got together to design a video game.

5. Fruits and vegetables are good, nutritious foods to eat.

6. The teacher asked the class not to talk.

7. Terry used the World Wide Web to find information about lemurs.

8. We tried to capture the runaway dog, but it was too fast and wily for us.

9. To climb that colossal rock will take skill and concentration.

10. They used nails and ropes to fasten the boards to the tree.

Verbals and Verbal Phrases

A *verbal* is a word that is formed from a verb but is used as a noun, an adjective, or an adverb. There are three kinds of verbals: the *participle*, the *gerund*, and the *infinitive*. A verbal that has modifiers or complements is called a *verbal phrase*. Below are some examples of verbal phrases.

PARTICIPIAL PHRASE	The language **spoken by the greatest number of people** is Mandarin. [The past participle *spoken* begins a phrase that modifies the noun *language*.]
GERUND PHRASE	For some people, **learning a foreign language** can be a challenge. [The gerund *learning* begins a phrase used as the subject of the verb *can be*.]
INFINITIVE PHRASE	I am learning **to speak Japanese.** [The infinitive *to speak* begins a phrase used as the direct object of the verb *am learning*.]

EXERCISE A   Underline the verbal or verbal phrase in each of the following sentences. Above each verbal or verbal phrase, write *gerund, gerund phrase, participle, participial phrase, infinitive,* or *infinitive phrase.*

                                             gerund phrase

Example 1. Kevin researched different methods of <u>measuring time</u>.

1. The plan accepted by the mayor involved a tax cut.

2. Paula expected the paper airplane to fly.

3. Feeling dizzy, Helena stopped and took a break.

4. The weight of the sack made it difficult to carry.

5. My uncle from Michigan enjoys canoeing.

6. The squeaking wheel alerted the mechanic to a potential problem.

7. Getting up early in the morning is sometimes a challenge.

8. We bought a new wrench to fix the leaky faucet.

9. The forgotten treasure lay at the bottom of the sea for three hundred years.

10. Fascinated, Pepe stood and admired the mural for several hours.

EXERCISE B   Decide how the underlined word groups are used in each of the following sentences. Options for each sentence are given in parentheses. Circle the correct option.

Example 1. <u>Coughing and sneezing,</u> Doug stayed home from band practice. (*adjective* or *noun*)

11. The easiest part of the project is <u>cutting out the pattern</u>. (*direct object* or *predicate nominative*)

12. The tools <u>used by some ancient cultures</u> are impressive. (*adverb* or *adjective*)

13. <u>Running five miles per week</u> is Joanna's goal. (*subject* or *direct object*)

14. They went to the park <u>to have a picnic</u>. (*adverb* or *adjective*)

15. The coach's philosophy is <u>to practice every day</u>. (*predicate nominative* or *direct object*)

Appositives

5k. An *appositive* is a noun or a pronoun placed beside another noun or pronoun to identify or describe it.

> **EXAMPLES** The Drama Club will be performing a play about the mythological hero **Perseus.** [The appositive identifies the noun *hero*.]
>
> Only two eighth-graders, **Saul** and **I,** auditioned for the lead role. [The compound appositive identifies the noun *eighth-graders*.]

EXERCISE A Underline the appositive in each of the following sentences.

Example 1. Charles Dickens is known for his novel <u>Great Expectations</u>.

1. The scientist Marie Curie was born in 1867.

2. Her husband, Pierre Curie, was also a scientist.

3. The novelist Jack London wrote *Call of the Wild*.

4. Nathan studied the explorer Vasco da Gama.

5. Karen's brother, Darren, plays the flute.

EXERCISE B Underline the appositive in each of the following sentences. Then, circle the noun or pronoun that the appositive identifies or describes.

Example 1. The (character) <u>Tom</u> appears in Chapter One.

6. His cousin Ellen has a magnificent geode collection.

7. The famous baseball player Hank Aaron hit 755 home runs.

8. The book *Sounder* is John's favorite novel.

9. Harry told his sister Lana that he would take her to the carnival.

10. My mom, Regina, volunteers at the city library.

Appositive Phrases

| **5l.** | An *appositive phrase* consists of an appositive and its modifiers. |

> **EXAMPLES** The restaurant's specialty is paella, **a Spanish dish of rice and various meats and spices.** [The appositive phrase identifies the noun *paella*.]
>
> Paella, **one of the restaurant's specialties,** is a Spanish dish of rice and various meats and spices. [The appositive phrase identifies the noun *paella*.]

EXERCISE A Underline the appositive phrase in each of the following sentences.

Example 1. Pedro, <u>a tall and slender man</u>, rescued the kitten from the tree.

1. Vasco da Gama, a Portuguese explorer, was the first European to reach India by sea.

2. Last week, Freddie witnessed an odd event, a pig and a cat taking a nap together.

3. The professor, a woman of keen insight, explained her interpretation of the story.

4. Charles Dickens, author of *A Christmas Carol*, had to work in a shoe polish factory as a boy.

5. The band played "Panther Pride," the school's fight song, during the graduation ceremony.

EXERCISE B Underline the appositive phrase in each of the following sentences. Then, circle the noun or pronoun that the appositive phrase identifies or describes.

Example 1. The (meteor shower) <u>an unpredicted event</u>, caught the scientists by surprise.

6. Hank Aaron, the right fielder from Alabama, broke Babe Ruth's record for home runs.

7. Make sure that you bring the most important item, your permission slip.

8. Paul, his cousin from St. Louis, could juggle six tennis balls at once.

9. The Mexican food, a delicious change of pace, spiced things up in the cafeteria.

10. Leslie's cat, an amazingly smart animal, learned to sit up and roll over on command.

Appositives and Appositive Phrases A

5k. An *appositive* is a noun or a pronoun placed beside another noun or pronoun to identify or describe it.

> **EXAMPLE** The patriot **Andrew Jackson** became president in 1829. [The appositive identifies the noun *patriot*.]

5l. An *appositive phrase* consists of an appositive and its modifiers.

> **EXAMPLE** Jackson wanted a new American Indian policy, **one with a guarantee of separate lands for native peoples.** [The appositive phrase identifies the noun *policy*.]

EXERCISE Underline the appositives and appositive phrases in the following sentences. Then, circle the noun or pronoun that the appositive identifies or describes.

Example 1. James Monroe an earlier president, had hoped to establish a similar policy.

1. The Battle of Bad Axe River, a struggle between a band of American Indians and the United States government, occurred in 1832.

2. Black Hawk, a member of the Sauk nation, led the American Indian forces.

3. Many Mesquakies, allies of the Sauks, followed Black Hawk into battle.

4. This battle, the last skirmish of Black Hawk's War, resulted in the removal of the Sauks and Mesquakies from their homelands.

5. Other Indian leaders, Chief Joseph, Crazy Horse, and Sitting Bull, fought in battles to protect their homelands and cultures.

6. The Nez Perce leader, Chief Joseph, and his followers fought heroically.

7. Chief Joseph and his forces, a band of fewer than five hundred warriors, defended themselves against a force of five thousand U.S. government troops.

8. After a 1,300-mile trek to Canada, a long and difficult journey, the U.S. troops attacked.

9. After a five-month siege, the Nez Perce were relocated to Indian Territory, a region that is now part of Oklahoma.

10. Crazy Horse and Sitting Bull, two leaders of the Sioux, also fought bravely in their battles against U.S. government forces.

for **CHAPTER 5: THE PHRASE**   *pages 112–113*

Appositives and Appositive Phrases B

5k. An *appositive* is a noun or a pronoun placed beside another noun or pronoun to identify or describe it.

    EXAMPLE Yellowstone National Park extends into three states, **Wyoming, Montana,** and **Idaho.** [The appositives identify the noun *states*.]

5l. An *appositive phrase* consists of an appositive and its modifiers.

    EXAMPLE The Channel Tunnel, **the underwater tunnel connecting England and France,** was completed in 1994. [The appositive phrase identifies the noun *Channel Tunnel*.]

EXERCISE Underline the appositives and appositive phrases in the following sentences. Then, circle the noun or pronoun that the appositive identifies or describes.

Example **1.** (Shelby) the winner of the spelling bee, was mentioned in the newspaper.

1. The pillow was made of an extremely soft material, goose feathers.

2. Gena's favorite comic strip, *Peanuts*, is a constant source of amusement to her.

3. We listened to beautiful piano sonatas by Beethoven, the famous composer.

4. Kevin gave his sister, Valerie, his old catcher's mitt as a gift.

5. The skateboarder, an expert at negotiating the half pipe, dazzled the crowd.

6. A single clue, a torn-up slipper, alerted Kim to the fact that her dog had been in the closet.

7. The impressive flag, a symbol of national pride, fluttered softly in the wind.

8. Berkeley has watched the movie *Babe* twelve times.

9. For the afternoon hike, Gino packed an orange, one of his favorite fruits.

10. Ricky chose to study the artist Picasso for his art project.

11. Uncle Mike, my father's younger brother, is an art director in Hollywood.

12. In New York we saw the musical *Cats*.

13. My grandmother went to high school with the famous film director Stanley Kubrick.

14. *West Side Story*, a retelling of *Romeo and Juliet*, was first a Broadway play.

15. My favorite book is *Lord of the Rings*, an epic fantasy in three volumes.

16. Ms. Hong, my math teacher, is retiring this year.

17. *A Prairie Home Companion*, Helen's favorite radio show, plays every Saturday night.

18. Jason, the last person you would expect, volunteered to cook.

19. Lara's hometown, Big Rapids, is in Michigan.

20. Roger has lived in three countries, England, Switzerland, and the United States.

GRAMMAR

Review A: **Verbal Phrases**

EXERCISE A Underline the verbal phrase in each of the following sentences. Above each verbal or verbal phrase, write *gerund, gerund phrase, participle, participial phrase, infinitive,* or *infinitive phrase.*

                  participial phrase
Example 1. Feeling proud, Enrique walked down the hall with a confident swagger.

1. Heloise wants to be an airline pilot.

2. The meowing cat slunk out of the room.

3. Jonathan went to the store to buy the latest magazine.

4. Standing on its hind legs, the cute Chihuahua walked around the room.

5. One of Jane's favorite pastimes is flying kites.

6. Beth said that the most convenient time to study is at three o'clock.

7. Ruth listened to the pleasant strumming of the Spanish guitar.

8. Charles, seeing the clouds in the sky, proclaimed that it would soon rain.

9. You can save some time by removing the shells first.

10. The artifacts buried beneath layers of dirt and rock were important finds.

EXERCISE B Write a sentence using the specified verbal as indicated in each of the following items. If needed, you may add words to the verbal.

Example 1. owning (gerund as a subject)   *Owning a pet is a great responsibility.*

11. sailing (gerund phrase as a direct object) _____

_____

12. to become (infinitive phrase as a predicate nominative) _____

_____

13. agreeing (participial phrase) _____

_____

14. sailing (gerund phrase as subject) _____

_____

15. seeing (participial phrase) _____

_____

Review B: **Phrases**

EXERCISE A Underline the prepositional phrase in each of the following sentences. Then, above each phrase, write *adjective phrase* or *adverb phrase*. Some sentences contain more than one prepositional phrase.

     ADV   ADJ   ADJ
Example 1. In what year did the settlement of North America by Europeans begin?

1. In the East the Europeans built houses, roads, and cities.

2. Areas of wilderness lay to the west.

3. The land of the open prairie beckoned to them.

4. Cattle could be raised throughout these wide-open ranges.

5. There they could roam freely over large areas.

6. On these ranges most of the beef eaten in cities would be raised.

7. The hides of the cattle were branded to show ownership.

8. A single cow was valuable to a rancher.

9. Cattle that strayed were caught with a lasso.

10. The pioneer spirit of most of the early settlers remained high in spite of the hardship.

EXERCISE B Underline the phrases in each of the following sentences. Then, above each phrase, write *participial phrase, gerund phrase, infinitive phrase, appositive phrase,* or *prepositional phrase.* Hint: Ignore any prepositional phrases within appositive phrases.

      prepositional phrases   *infinitive phrase*
Example 1. For thousands of years, farmers have used plows to till the soil.

11. Before the invention of the tractor, farmers used oxen or other animals to pull the plows.

12. One farmworker, the plowman, would walk behind the plow to guide it.

13. Another worker would stand in front of the oxen to guide them.

14. Raising a crop was a strenuous job.

15. One part of the job was plowing the soil, a difficult task.

16. Fertilizer, an important ingredient for a productive crop, was added to the soil.

17. A farmer would walk across the field, spreading the fertilizer.

18. To nourish the ground, the farmer would work the fertilizer into the ground.

19. Sowing the seeds was the next step.

20. Unfortunately, some of the seeds would be eaten by birds.

Review C: **Phrases**

EXERCISE A   In each of the following sentences, identify the underlined phrase by writing above it *prepositional phrase, participial phrase, gerund phrase, infinitive phrase,* or *appositive phrase.* Hint: Ignore any prepositional phrases within a verbal phrase.

infinitive phrase
Example 1. In an effort to protect seeds, farmers would often place scarecrows in the fields.

1. Scarecrows seemed to scare away at least some of the birds.

2. The weather, of course, plays a significant role in the growing of a crop.

3. A crop ripening in the sun can look beautiful.

4. Have you ever stood in a sunlit field to watch the wheat or some other crop sway in the wind?

5. Corn, a plant that has several thousands of varieties, is an important crop.

6. A stalk of corn can grow up to twenty feet tall.

7. A field of corn glimmering in the sun is a beautiful sight.

8. Many varieties of corn from the United States are grown in the Corn Belt.

9. Eating corn on the cob is a common activity at some picnics.

10. The planting and harvesting of crops such as corn is a demanding job.

EXERCISE B   Underline the phrases in each of the following sentences. Then, above each phrase, write *participial phrase, gerund phrase, infinitive phrase, appositive phrase,* or *prepositional phrase.* Hint: Ignore any prepositional phrases within verbal or appositive phrases.

participial phrase   *participial phrase*
Example 1. Glistening in the summer sun, the yogurt topped with fruit looked delicious.

11. The building towering ten stories tall is a treasured landmark.

12. Watching the driveway intently, Janet waited for David.

13. Kelly, wanting a treat, walked to the grocery store to buy a fresh watermelon.

14. The tree, a tall pine with a thick trunk, was over a century old.

15. This lesson's objective is to learn about phrases in action.

16. Helena, one of the girls from our school, received a blue ribbon.

17. The class heard the soft whimpering of a puppy.

18. The girl standing on the stage is Celia.

19. Sally's favorite hobby is learning about her family's history.

20. Swooping down from the sky, the bird buzzed over Tim's head.

Literary Model: Using Prepositional Phrases

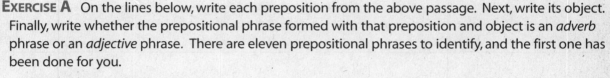

> Just before dusk in the late afternoon of June 16, 1832, I found myself walking along the crowded docks of Liverpool, England, following a man by the name of Grummage. Though a business associate of my father, Mr. Grummage was, like my father, a gentleman. It was he my father delegated to make the final arrangements for my passage to America. (p. 7)
>
> —from *The True Confessions of Charlotte Doyle* by Avi

EXERCISE A On the lines below, write each preposition from the above passage. Next, write its object. Finally, write whether the prepositional phrase formed with that preposition and object is an *adverb* phrase or an *adjective* phrase. There are eleven prepositional phrases to identify, and the first one has been done for you.

before/dusk—adverb

_____

_____

_____

_____

_____

EXERCISE B What is your reaction as a reader to so many prepositional phrases being used in three sentences of a novel? Do you think each phrase is necessary? Give examples from the passage to support your response.

_____

_____

_____

_____

_____

_____

_____

_____

Literary Model (continued)

EXERCISE C   Rewrite the passage, replacing each prepositional phrase you identified in Exercise A with a prepositional phrase of your own invention. Your phrases may modify different words, but they should function as they did in the original passage. For example, an adverbial prepositional phrase from the original passage should be replaced with a different adverbial prepositional phrase. You may change any other words necessary to make your new phrases make sense.

_____

_____

_____

_____

_____

_____

_____

_____

_____

_____

_____

EXERCISE D

1. Did your prepositional phrases affect the setting and tone of the original passage? If so, how? If not, could the setting and tone have been changed if you had used other phrases? Explain.

_____

_____

_____

_____

2. Given the choice, do you generally prefer to use many prepositional phrases in your writing? Why or why not? Give examples to support your response.

_____

_____

_____

_____

_____

Writing Application: Using Infinitive Phrases

In writing and speaking, we often use infinitive phrases to speak of the future and our role in it. Consider these famous examples: In some marriage ceremonies, the couple is asked, "Do you promise *to love and to cherish this person,* today and always?" The President of the United States pledges *"to uphold and defend the Constitution"* when he or she is inaugurated. Witnesses on the stand swear *"to tell the truth and nothing but the truth."* Many people resolve each January *"to read good books"* or *"to contact old friends."* In fact, many vows—statements about what someone plans to do in the future—use infinitive phrases.

WRITING ACTIVITY

Marriage and inaugural vows mark major, life-changing events. However, many less momentous occasions call for vows, too, including joining school groups. For a group in which you participate or in which you would like to participate, write a short vow for members to repeat. The vow should remind members of what the group stands for and hopes to accomplish. It should use infinitives and infinitive phrases to help members focus on their role in making the group's future successful.

PREWRITING If you have never paid much attention to vows, you may wish to look at a few before beginning your prewriting. Organizations such as the Thespians and the National Junior Honor Society would provide models to imitate. Then, consider the group whose vow you are composing. What sets the group apart from other groups? What are its goals for participants, the school, and the community? Why do students join the group? Answering these questions will provide material for shaping a fitting vow.

WRITING The bulk of the work in this exercise is the prewriting. Once you complete the prewriting, arrange the infinitives and infinitive phrases of the vow in the order that strikes you as most effective. Many vows work from the least difficult goal to the most difficult one, or from least to most important. Most vows save the most sweeping and critical goal for last. For example, the mission statement for a popular science fiction program ends with "to boldly go where no one has gone before." The beginning is also important: Will students say "I promise" or "I pledge" or some other variation?

REVISING Vows are serious promises that we make about the future, so a serious tone and formal diction, or word choice, fit this writing occasion. Read the vow to other students in the group and to teachers who sponsor it. Would they add or change anything? Consider their suggestions.

PUBLISHING Pledge right now to check your vow for errors in spelling and punctuation. Then, make copies of the vow so that each student has one to read. With the group's sponsor's permission, post a nicely printed copy of the vow in the room where the group meets.

EXTENDING YOUR WRITING

If you enjoyed this exercise, you could develop it into a longer writing project. Taking a vow is one way to set goals for the future, and setting goals is the first step toward achieving them. For a speech class, write a speech in which you explain to your audience how goals can direct our actions and how to set realistic, achievable goals.

Choices: Creating with Clauses

Here's your chance to step out of the grammar book and into the real world. You may not notice parts of speech, but you and the people around you use them every day. The following activities challenge you to find a connection between parts of speech and the world around you. Do you the activity below that suits your personality best, and then share your discoveries with your class. Have fun!

VISUAL DEMONSTRATION

Cut It Out

Ask for permission to prepare a demonstration that will help your classmates understand independent and subordinate clauses. Cut out strips of paper that are about a foot long. In large print on these strips, write sentences that each have a subordinate clause. Include examples of adverb, adjective, and noun clauses. Then, give your demonstration. Use scissors to cut the subordinate clause out of each strip. Ask someone to read each clause, and point out that the independent clauses can stand alone but the subordinate clauses cannot. Have about two dozen extra strips of paper available so that students can write down their own sentences, and cut and read the clauses.

ETYMOLOGY

Between the Lines

Look up the word *subordinate*. What is its root? What are its meanings? As what parts of speech can it function? Then, look up the word *independent*—its root, its meanings, and its use as different parts of speech. When you're finished with your research, present your findings to your class in the form of a brief oral report.

STUDY AIDS

How and Why?

Do you know the questions that adverbs answer? No? Look up these questions. Then, make a chart that has each question heading a column. Write appropriate subordinating conjunctions under each column. You could either make a poster of your chart for the classroom or simply make copies for everyone to put in his or her notebook.

DEMONSTRATION

5W-How?

Some subordinate clauses, especially those that include the words *who, what, where, when, why,* and *how*, can easily be turned into questions. Show your classmates how this change takes place. Create a diagram or some other visual to represent the transformation from subordinate clause to question. Make sure that the class can identify the parts of speech of the words *(who, what, when, where, why, how)* as they are used in the questions.

REVISING

From Little Acorns

Show your classmates how to grow a clause from a word. Write three sentences. The first sentence should contain a word that will be expanded into a phrase in the second sentence. In the third sentence, expand the phrase into a clause. When you have finished, use your sentences as examples to demonstrate to classmates how these expansions can be made. Then, with your teacher's approval, lead a discussion comparing and contrasting the three versions.

ANALYSIS

Point by Point

An adjective clause acts as an adjective, but is it the same as an adjective? How does an adjective clause differ from an adjective? For instance, an adjective can be modified by an adverb. Can an adjective clause be modified the same way? What can an adjective do that a clause can't? Think about these questions. Think, too, about the ways that an adjective clause is like an adjective. Then, make a chart that shows the similarities and differences between the two. Ask for permission to present your chart to the class.

Identifying Clauses

6a.   A *clause* is a word group that contains a verb and its subject and that is used as a sentence or as part of a sentence.

Every clause has a subject and a verb, but not every clause expresses a complete thought.

SENTENCE	While the bear crossed the road, the tourists stayed inside their cars.

                S   V

CLAUSE	While the bear crossed the road [incomplete thought]

              S   V

CLAUSE	the tourists stayed inside their cars [complete thought]

Do not mistake a phrase for a clause. A phrase does not contain both a verb and its subject.

PHRASE	**After the soccer game,** the coach took us out for pizza.
CLAUSE	**After we won the soccer game,** the coach took us out for pizza.

EXERCISE A   For the underlined clause in each of the following sentences, identify the subject and verb by writing *S* above the subject and *V* above the verb.

                    S   V

Example 1. After Jim woke, he watched a Japanese monster movie on television.

1. Antonio told her that he had not planned on coming to the party.

2. I have no idea when the mechanic finished the repairs on the car.

3. Before the storm struck, the sky turned an odd shade of green.

4. When she arrived at the dock, the ferry had already left for the island.

5. At last Gretchen met Conrad and Padgett, who were the pets of her friend Mimi.

6. Grabbing his hat, Robb dashed out into the snow.

7. Even though they invited her, Joie decided not to come along on the field trip.

8. Vince decided to read the book before he saw the movie.

9. You may come with us if you want.

10. Teddy stopped the dryer when he heard his boots clunking around inside it.

EXERCISE B   On the line provided, identify the underlined word group in each of the following sentences as a *clause* or a *phrase*.

Example *clause* **1.** Before I met you, I had never heard of the jazz musician Miles Davis.

_____ **11.** After the game, the winning team shook hands with the losing team.

_____ **12.** While they waited for sunset, the crowd sang songs.

_____ **13.** During the broadcast, the singer kept her eye on the camera.

_____ **14.** Unfortunately for us, Warren did not bring enough food for everybody.

_____ **15.** Sometimes the Santos family likes to eat popcorn while they watch a video.

GRAMMAR

The Independent Clause

6b. An *independent* (or *main*) *clause* expresses a complete thought and can stand by itself as a complete sentence.

EXAMPLES **People from many parts of Europe have immigrated to the United States.** [one independent clause]

In the mid-1800s, a famine hit Ireland, and **many Irish citizens moved to the United States.** [two independent clauses]

Although the immigrants left many of their belongings behind, **they brought with them their traditions.** [one subordinate clause and one independent clause]

EXERCISE A In each of the following sentences, draw one line under the subject and two lines under the verb in the independent clause.

Example 1. The United States is known as a country of immigrants.

1. In the nineteenth century, Scotch-Irish immigrants came to the United States.

2. They brought with them their music and their way of speaking.

3. Many settled in the south-central part of the United States.

4. In some places you can still hear some of the Scotch-Irish songs.

5. One singer of those old ballads is Jean Ritchie.

6. Audiences love Ritchie's version of "Barbara Allan."

7. Ritchie can play the dulcimer as well as the guitar.

8. The dulcimer, which is an oval-shaped stringed instrument, is especially popular among the people of the southern Appalachians.

9. Before her solo career, Ritchie sang with her family.

10. Every group of immigrants brings its own special treasures to our shores.

EXERCISE B For each of the following sentences, decide whether the underlined clause is or is not an independent clause. On the line provided, write *Yes* if it is or *No* if it is not.

Example ___No___ **1.** The campers fished until they were exhausted.

_____ **11.** Alex sang, and Lani played the harpsichord.

_____ **12.** Have you met our new next-door neighbors?

_____ **13.** We cannot leave because the work has not been completed.

_____ **14.** If I were president, I would send an environmental bill to Congress.

_____ **15.** Some cobras squirt poison when they are attacked.

120

The Subordinate Clause

6c. A *subordinate* (or *dependent*) *clause* does not express a complete thought and cannot stand by itself as a complete sentence.

    EXAMPLE   **if wishes were horses**

The meaning of a subordinate clause is complete only when the clause is attached to an independent clause.

    EXAMPLE   **If wishes were horses,** then beggars would ride.

Sometimes the word that begins the subordinate clause is the subject of the clause.

    EXAMPLE   This is a line **that comes from a Mother Goose rhyme.**

EXERCISE A Underline the subordinate clause in each of the following sentences. Then, write *S* above the subject and *V* above the verb of each subordinate clause.

Example 1. When my grandmother was young, many children were learning Mother Goose rhymes.

1. England is the country where Mother Goose rhymes originated.

2. The people who composed the rhymes lived hundreds of years ago.

3. These rhymes became popular because they were fun and easy to learn.

4. If a rhyme was especially funny or interesting, children would sing it.

5. One rhyme that children enjoyed was "Baa, Baa Black Sheep."

6. Some people think that this rhyme is actually a protest against taxes.

7. In the rhyme, the three bags of wool that the sheep produces are given away.

8. Since the sheep has only three bags of wool, it is left with nothing.

9. So, "Baa, Baa Black Sheep" may be a rhyme that protests high taxes.

10. Mother Goose rhymes, which are always fun to read, may or may not have political meanings.

EXERCISE B On the line provided, expand each of the following sentences by adding a subordinate clause that begins with the word given in parentheses.

Example 1. *(that)* This is the trophy *that our soccer team won* .

11. *(if)* On Friday we will go on a picnic _____ .

12. *(who)* Do you know _____ ?

13. *(that)* Is the story _____ true?

14. *(Whenever)* _____ , our dogs bark.

15. *(because)* The band canceled its performance _____ .

Independent and Subordinate Clauses

6b. An *independent* (or *main*) *clause* expresses a complete thought and can stand by itself as a complete sentence.

                      S V   S   V

    EXAMPLE   **I left Trina a message on her voice mail,** but **she never returned my call.**

6c. A *subordinate* (or *dependent*) *clause* does not express a complete thought and cannot stand by itself as a complete sentence.

                                S   V

    EXAMPLES   **When the pot boiled over,** the oatmeal spilled onto the stove.

                                   S   V

                         One bird **that travels long distances in the spring and fall** is the osprey.

EXERCISE A On the line provided, identify each of the following word groups as an *independent* clause or a *subordinate* clause.

Example   __*subordinate*__   **1.** whenever she chops onions

_____ **1.** as she leaned across the table

_____ **2.** they voted for a new chairperson

_____ **3.** the bottle was broken

_____ **4.** which they all said

_____ **5.** if someone can help me

_____ **6.** that the car was already in the garage

_____ **7.** my birthday comes in August

_____ **8.** that photograph is striking

_____ **9.** is the cup full

_____ **10.** since Keeley is not going

EXERCISE B Draw one line under each independent clause and two lines under each subordinate clause in the following sentences.

Example 1. When she had finished skating, the judges awarded the French skater, who was my favorite, the gold medal.

11. Dr. Zamora left the dinner party before the main course was served.

12. Before we begin the meeting, let me introduce the newest member of our team.

13. The last singer on the program is the one who can hit the high notes.

14. When the conductor tapped her baton, the orchestra fell silent.

15. One planet that has often excited the imaginations of science fiction writers is Mars, which is sometimes called the red planet.

The Adjective Clause A

6d. An *adjective clause* is a subordinate clause that modifies a noun or a pronoun.

An adjective clause usually follows the word or words it modifies and tells *which one* or *what kind*.

    EXAMPLES   There are some insects **that can survive inside blocks of ice all winter.** [The adjective clause modifies the noun *insects*, telling *what kind*.]

          Is Samantha the one **who helped you?** [The adjective clause modifies the pronoun *one*, telling *which one*.]

          That book, **which tells the story of an orphan,** is one of my favorites. [The adjective clause modifies the noun *book*, telling *which one*.]

EXERCISE A For each of the following sentences, underline the adjective clause.

Example 1. One entertainer <u>whom we saw backstage</u> was Italian.

1. The music that you have just heard was composed by Wolfgang Amadeus Mozart.

2. Mr. Cohen, who conducts the school chorus, collects songbooks.

3. Denver, which is situated 5,280 feet above sea level, is called the Mile High City.

4. Is Florida the place where Ponce de León sought the Fountain of Youth?

5. Ed White, whom NASA chose for the first spacewalk, was born in San Antonio.

EXERCISE B Underline the adjective clause in each of the following sentences. Then, circle the word or words that the clause modifies.

Example 1. The (pteranodon,) <u>which was a flying reptile,</u> had a wingspan of thirty-six feet.

6. The fourteenth century was a time when many people died of the bubonic plague.

7. Mollusks, which have either one shell or two, are classified as either univalves or bivalves.

8. How many of the written records that were kept during the Middle Ages have survived?

9. Antonia Novello, who was Surgeon General of the United States in 1990, is Puerto Rican.

10. The lightning that flashes during a rainstorm is hotter than the surface of the sun.

11. President Harry Truman was one of those people whose middle name is a single letter.

12. Marian Anderson, who was one of the greatest opera singers, often struggled against racial discrimination.

13. Nyos, in Cameroon, is a lake that sometimes releases huge bursts of carbon dioxide from its floor.

14. Saving the tiger, which is an endangered species, may depend upon preserving its habitat.

15. My sister spends much time working with my aunt, who is president of the local Red Cross.

The Adjective Clause B

6d. An *adjective clause* is a subordinate clause that modifies a noun or a pronoun.

An adjective clause usually follows the word or words it modifies and tells *which one* or *what kind*.

EXAMPLES   Gary Soto is the writer **whom I selected for my report.** [The adjective clause modifies the noun *writer*.]

The principal told us everything **that we needed to know.** [The adjective clause modifies the pronoun *everything*.]

Jaime showed us the place **where the accident had occurred.** [The adjective clause modifies the noun *place*.]

EXERCISE A   Underline the adjective clause in each of the following sentences.

Example 1. The speaker brought slides, <u>which she showed to the class.</u>

1. My aunt Becky, who is an editor for a university press, showed me her office.

2. The soldier with whom my grandmother corresponded during World War II eventually came home and became her husband.

3. *The Chocolate War* is the book that I read for my book report.

4. The project is called SETI, which stands for "Search for Extraterrestrial Intelligence."

5. The road that leads to the old mill has been washed out by the flood.

6. She served in the administration of Bill Clinton, who was the forty-second president of the United States.

7. My little brother is a kid whom you can really love.

8. She was the player whose skill at jump shots became legendary.

9. The corn bread that Tish brought to the party was gone within twenty minutes.

10. Dean gave his results to the scientist, who incorporated them into his report.

EXERCISE B   Underline the adjective clause in each of the following sentences. Then, circle the word it modifies.

Example 1. I took my brother to the ⬭place⬭ where I first saw the stray dog.

11. The model whose face appears on so many magazine covers is a Rhodes scholar.

12. The pictures that we took on our vacation are missing.

13. The church where my sister was married is closed now for renovations.

14. This is the spot where President Kennedy announced the creation of the Peace Corps.

15. Was Ed Bradley the correspondent who reported the story?

124

Relative Pronouns and Relative Adverbs

A *relative pronoun* or *relative adverb* relates an adjective clause to the word or words the clause modifies.

EXAMPLE   One of the slides **that we saw** showed the hospital **where I was born.** [*That* relates *we saw* to *slides*. *Where* relates *I was born* to *hospital*.]

EXERCISE A   Underline each adjective clause, and circle each relative pronoun or relative adverb.

Example   1.   Last night was the first time (that) she conducted the orchestra.

1. Is Rafael the one who wrote the poem about trees in winter?

2. Starr Auditorium is the place where I first heard *English Folk Song Suite*.

3. The river that was polluted by the factory has been restored to its natural state.

4. Ms. Pollard is the teacher for whom I wrote my history report about the Gulf War.

5. He won't be able to come until Saturday, when he has a day off from his job.

6. The famous author, whose novel I read, visited our school.

7. Gettysburg, where a famous battle was fought in the Civil War, is in southern Pennsylvania.

8. I was awake at dawn, which is too early.

9. The newspaper printed a picture of the old barn in which the stolen money was found.

10. I know a few lines of the poem that Kerry quoted on television.

EXERCISE B   On the lines provided, add an adjective clause to each of the following sentences. Then, circle the relative pronoun or relative adverb in each adjective clause.

Example   1.   The student has a cold. *The student (who) left early has a cold.*

11. The director will present his new film at the film festival. _____

_____

12. A cat is rolling in the grass. _____

_____

13. My aunt and uncle drove through New Mexico. _____

_____

14. The band will play at the dance. _____

_____

15. Clare and Ruben wrote the class song. _____

_____

The Adverb Clause A

6e. An *adverb clause* is a subordinate clause that modifies a verb, an adjective, or an adverb.

An adverb clause tells *where, when, how, why, to what extent*, or *under what condition*. Unlike an adverb or an adverb phrase, an adverb clause has a subject and a verb.

> **EXAMPLES** Did you see the manatee exhibit **when you visited the aquarium?** [The adverb clause modifies the verb *Did see*, telling *when*.]
>
> The dolphin show was just as entertaining **as it was before.** [The adverb clause modifies the adjective *entertaining*, telling *to what extent*.]

EXERCISE A In each of the following sentences, underline the adverb clause and circle the word or words it modifies.

Example 1. Before I left the aquarium, I (had learned) many facts about some of our most

common sea animals.

1. A lobster fears few enemies because it has a hard, protective shell.

2. A shark can swim faster than a human can.

3. The life expectancy of a sea turtle is not as long as it once was.

4. When an octopus is attacked, it can spray a jet of inky fluid at its opponent.

5. Up close at night, a coral reef is more beautiful than you can imagine.

6. When a moray eel feels threatened, it withdraws into its hiding place.

7. A sea cow can swim faster than you might think.

8. The sting of most jellyfish can be dangerous unless it is treated.

9. A puffer inflates itself like a balloon until its attacker swims away.

10. Ice fish live where temperatures sometimes drop below freezing.

EXERCISE B On the lines provided, complete the adverb clauses in each of the following sentences.

Example 1. No one has broken the shot put record since *Alex set it in 1995* _____.

11. While _____, Bert took the bread out of the oven.

12. The salsa dancers were upset because _____.

13. The spy hid the documents where _____.

14. As soon as _____, people swarmed into the Amazon jungle.

15. Kim can throw a football farther than _____.

The Adverb Clause B

6e. An *adverb clause* is a subordinate clause that modifies a verb, an adjective, or an adverb.

An adverb clause tells *where, when, how, why, to what extent,* or *under what condition.* An adverb clause is introduced by a *subordinating conjunction*—a word or word group that shows the relationship between the adverb clause and the word or words the clause modifies. Common subordinating conjunctions include *although, as, because, if, since, so that, than, unless, until, when, where,* and *while.*

EXAMPLES **As the storm clouds gathered,** a waterspout formed over the bay. [The adverb clause modifies the verb *formed*, telling *when*.]

Brad can run faster **than anyone else on the track team can.** [The adverb clause modifies the adverb *faster*, telling *to what extent*.]

EXERCISE A In each of the following sentences, underline the adverb clause and circle the word or words it modifies.

Example 1. After I had locked the door behind me, I realized I had left my keys inside the house.

1. Please read whenever you like.

2. Regis looked as though he had been caught in a rainstorm.

3. None of you should build a campfire until you have learned the proper technique.

4. If your uncle comes to the reunion tomorrow, ask him about his experiences in Indonesia.

5. Paolo mixed the pancake batter carefully so that there wouldn't be any lumps.

6. Ever since James hiked the Appalachian Trail, he has been in better shape.

7. We traveled slowly unless we were forced to go faster.

8. Although she wrote a book set in the Galápagos Islands, she has never been there.

9. After the rainstorm ended, the droplets on the leaves of the trees sparkled like diamonds.

10. I recited the poem more dramatically than she did.

EXERCISE B Underline the adverb clause in each of the following sentences. Then, circle the subordinating conjunction.

Example 1. The cat won't do tricks unless you give it treats.

11. Until Maya brings the eggplant, we won't be able to start dinner.

12. Clarence is a much better bicycle mechanic than I am.

13. The cat batted its toy mouse under the refrigerator so that no one could reach it.

14. Vladimir played the piano as though his life depended on it.

15. Because the sky is clear, we will have a good view of the meteor shower.

Subordinating Conjunctions

An adverb clause is introduced by a *subordinating conjunction*—a word or word group that shows the relationship between the adverb clause and the word or words the clause modifies. Common subordinating conjunctions include *although, as if, because, if, so that, than, unless, when, where,* and *while.*

> **EXAMPLES** The aroma of shrimp gumbo greeted Mother **when she arrived home from work.**
> [*When* shows the relationship between the adverb clause and the verb *greeted*.]

EXERCISE A In each of the following sentences, draw a line under the adverb clause and circle the subordinating conjunction.

Example 1. (Before) she left for work, Keiko remembered to pack a lunch.

1. Though I did not enjoy the first page, I finished the story.

2. Oscar can swim much farther than I can.

3. You may watch television after dinner as long as you finish your homework first.

4. The post office is closed because today is Presidents' Day.

5. Unless the track team wins its next two meets, it will not go to the state finals.

6. There are footnotes at the bottom of each page so that the reader can immediately see the meaning of old or obscure words.

7. If the weather stays nice, we can go biking this afternoon.

8. Susannah sounds as though she has a bad cold.

9. Although the salad usually came with olives, Gretchen asked the cook not to put olives on hers.

10. Jan's kite soared higher than Mimi's model airplane flew.

EXERCISE B On the line provided, identify the underlined word group as *AC* for *adverb clause* or *PP* for *prepositional phrase.*

Example __PP__ **1.** Until Saturday, the folk singer will be appearing nightly at the pizza parlor.

_____ **11.** Until I was born, my family lived in St. Louis, Missouri.

_____ **12.** We left the campsite a few minutes before dawn.

_____ **13.** Since breakfast, we have seen eight blue jays.

_____ **14.** Hilary spoke to Steve and Judy after she spoke to me.

_____ **15.** Try to finish those dishes before you leave.

The Noun Clause

6f.	A *noun clause* is a subordinate clause that is used as a noun.

> **EXAMPLES**   **That life exists on other planets** seems possible. [subject of the verb *seems*]
>
> A new computer is **what Matthew needs.** [predicate nominative identifying the subject *computer*]
>
> A good salesperson knows **what customers want.** [direct object of the verb *knows*]
>
> I will pay **whoever finds the gerbil** a reward. [indirect object of the verb *will pay*]
>
> Are you particular about **what you watch on television?** [object of the preposition *about*]

EXERCISE A   In each of the following sentences, underline the noun clause.

Example 1. You may take <u>whomever you wish</u> to the dance.

1. The film told us about what we should do in the case of an earthquake.

2. That some tapeworms grow to lengths of more than one hundred feet seems incredible.

3. No one could explain what had happened to all of the treasure.

4. Leuwana sent whoever asked her for one a postcard from Puerto Rico.

5. The ending of the book is not what I had expected.

EXERCISE B   Underline the noun clause in each of the following sentences. Then, identify the use of the clause by writing above it one of these abbreviations: *S* for *subject, PN* for *predicate nominative, DO* for *direct object, IO* for *indirect object,* or *OP* for *object of a preposition.*

Example 1. No one knows <u>who first set foot in America</u>.   [*DO* above "who first set foot in America"]

6. That the referee called a technical foul caused an uproar among the fans.

7. The guest speaker told us what could be done about acid rain.

8. The number of commercials during a television program is what annoys me most.

9. The cafeteria worker gave whoever asked for more pasta another generous helping.

10. Whatever happens at the Super Bowl will be seen by millions of people.

11. Please do not tell me how the movie ends.

12. That the storm caused some damage is an understatement.

13. The ship's captain offered whoever spotted a whale three gold coins.

14. Whatever happened to Amelia Earhart's airplane remains a mystery.

15. Tsang Ying is reading a book about what happened to the bison of North America.

Adjective, Adverb, and Noun Clauses A

6d.   An *adjective clause* is a subordinate clause that modifies a noun or a pronoun.

   EXAMPLE   *Hannah,* **which is spelled the same way backward and forward,** is an example of a palindrome. [The adjective clause modifies the noun *Hannah*.]

6e.   An *adverb clause* is a subordinate clause that modifies a verb, an adjective, or an adverb.

   EXAMPLE   **Whenever the Moscow Circus performs,** it draws a large crowd. [The adverb clause modifies the verb *draws*.]

6f.   A *noun clause* is a subordinate clause that is used as a noun.

   EXAMPLE   **What they saw on the treasure map** confused the explorers at first. [The noun clause is the subject of verb *confused*.]

EXERCISE   Underline each subordinate clause in the following sentences. Then, write over the clause *ADJ* if it is an adjective clause, *ADV* if it is an adverb clause, or *N* if it is a noun clause.

Example   1. Whenever the weather was nice, Jackie and Nicci played in the backyard.
                          ADV

1. Jeri, who learned to dance from his grandmother, taught us the Charleston.

2. Because her favorite program was on, Stacy wanted to stay home.

3. Any author whose books make the bestseller list is likely to make a lot of money.

4. Whoever spilled the mustard all over the floor should clean it up.

5. Esai rode his bicycle whenever he had errands to run.

6. This is the garden where we grow tomatoes.

7. He told his story to whoever would listen.

8. Mother explained why we should change the oil in the car.

9. If we want to get to the game on time, we should leave now.

10. The play on which the film is based is quite good.

Adjective, Adverb, and Noun Clauses B

6d.	An *adjective clause* is a subordinate clause that modifies a noun or a pronoun.

> **EXAMPLE** The panda, **which is an endangered species,** eats mainly bamboo plants. [The adjective clause modifies the noun *panda*.]

6e.	An *adverb clause* is a subordinate clause that modifies a verb, an adjective, or an adverb.

> **EXAMPLE** After the game, the pitcher felt **as if she had strained a muscle in her right arm.** [The adverb clause modifies the verb *felt*.]

6f.	A *noun clause* is a subordinate clause that is used as a noun.

> **EXAMPLE** My parents strongly suggested **that I clean my room.** [The noun clause is the direct object of the verb *suggested*.]

EXERCISE Underline each subordinate clause in the following sentences. Then, write above the clause *ADJ* if it is an adjective clause, *ADV* if it is an adverb clause, or *N* if it is a noun clause.

                                                           ADV

Example 1. Brigitte has read more of the assignment than Sven has read.

1. He rode his bicycle wherever he wanted to go.

2. The poet to whom she is referring is Robert Frost.

3. Whatever you want to do tonight is okay with me.

4. He is the artist whose sculptures are placed in the courtyard.

5. As soon as she got home from the library, she started the book.

6. Ernesto studied hard so that he could pass the sergeant's exam.

7. We often visited Dr. Ito on Sunday evenings, when he usually cooked a traditional Japanese meal.

8. At last, Carla remembered what she had meant to say before.

9. Because he had a cold that evening, Stevie missed the premiere of the film.

10. The hostess gave whoever came to the party a paper hat and a noisemaker.

Review A: The Clause

EXERCISE A   For each of the following sentences, identify the underlined clause by writing above it *IND* for *independent clause* or *SUB* for *subordinate clause*.

Example 1. Edward Jenner became famous <u>when he introduced the smallpox vaccination</u>. *SUB*

1. The dog acted <u>as if it understood French</u>.

2. <u>As the others watched the parade on television</u>, Jim went into the bedroom and took a nap.

3. The athlete <u>whose face is on the cover of the magazine</u> retired from the game recently.

4. We should ask Peter <u>whether he knows Mr. Mugabe</u>.

5. <u>This year the town was prepared for tornado season</u> because of the disaster last year.

6. Dario folded the towels <u>so that they would fit in the cupboard</u>.

7. Bob, <u>who is my favorite cousin</u>, will be attending West Point in the fall.

8. <u>We were surprised</u> when we found the cat playing happily with the dog.

9. Bring <u>whoever asks</u> a napkin.

10. After the explorers arrived at the top of the mountain, <u>they took each other's picture</u>.

EXERCISE B   Underline the subordinate clause in each of the following sentences. Then, identify the subordinate clause by writing above it *N* for *noun clause*, *ADJ* for *adjective clause*, or *ADV* for *adverb clause*.

Example 1. It has been raining <u>since I arrived</u>. *ADV*

11. The relatives whom Christopher visited last week are friendly and generous.

12. Divers wear masks so that they can see underwater.

13. The traveler was grateful to whoever put up the road sign.

14. A person whose temperature rises above 102° Fahrenheit should see a doctor.

15. Is this the time when you usually go to lunch?

16. Until the pool is cleaned, no one is allowed to swim in it.

17. No one has proved the existence of the Loch Ness monster, although many people believe in its existence.

18. You can send whomever you choose a card for Valentine's Day.

19. If the earth's climate grows warmer, sea levels will rise, and crops will fail.

20. What actually happened to my baseball glove is anyone's guess.

Review B: The Clause

EXERCISE A In each of the following sentences, identify the underlined clause by writing on the line provided *I* for *independent clause* or *S* for *subordinate clause*. Then, identify the use of each subordinate clause by also writing on the line *N* for *noun*, *ADJ* for *adjective*, or *ADV* for *adverb*.

Example <u>S-ADJ</u> **1.** In 1859, there lived in Australia an Englishman <u>whose name was

Thomas Austin.</u>

_____ **1.** Two thousand dollars was <u>what the owner was asking for the old Volkswagen.</u>

_____ **2.** The general, <u>who served in the North African and Italian campaigns during

World War II,</u> died in 1967.

_____ **3.** John Ford was a filmmaker <u>who was known for making westerns.</u>

_____ **4.** <u>Even though it was raining,</u> the race continued as planned.

_____ **5.** <u>If we leave now,</u> we can beat the traffic to the stadium.

_____ **6.** Tell them <u>whatever they need to know.</u>

_____ **7.** <u>Whenever she is painting or sculpting,</u> she listens to the radio.

_____ **8.** That is the island <u>where the ship ran aground.</u>

_____ **9.** The eulogy brought tears to the eyes of <u>whoever knew Mr. Muñoz.</u>

_____ **10.** Lance warmed up with some stretches <u>before the marathon began.</u>

EXERCISE B Underline the subordinate clause in each of the following sentences. Then, identify the use of the subordinate clause by writing above it *N* for *noun*, *ADJ* for *adjective*, or *ADV* for *adverb*.

Example **1.** Broccoli, <u>which is my favorite vegetable,</u> is rich in vitamin A.
                                         ADJ

11. Until plastic wrap was invented, most people used paper.

12. One mountain that is almost as tall as Mount Everest is K2.

13. Every day, the senator rides the train that runs from Delaware to Washington, D.C.

14. Bronze is what is created by mixing copper and tin.

15. Diamonds are rare although they are made of the widely distributed element carbon.

16. That decade was a time when great strides in civil rights were made.

17. Liang felt as if she had not slept in several days.

18. Mr. Martinez set his daughter on his shoulders so that she could watch the parade.

19. Maryland is one state where a person can find plenty of fresh seafood.

20. Ms. Desai reviewed with her students what they should study for the test.

Review C: **The Clause**

EXERCISE A In each of the following sentences, identify the underlined clause by writing on the line provided *IND* for *independent clause* or *SUB* for *subordinate clause*. Then, identify the use of each subordinate clause by also writing on the line *N* for *noun,* *ADJ* for *adjective,* or *ADV* for *adverb.*

Example 1. _____SUB–ADJ_____ The new exhibit includes poems that were written by children in

other countries.

1. _____ Burton showed his poems to whoever was willing to read them.

2. _____ Before we begin the video, let's make sure that everybody is comfortable.

3. _____ The house was now for sale, even though it needed extensive repairs.

4. _____ The clothes that got wet in the rain were soon dried.

5. _____ Dean picked up some of the broken glass before he swept.

6. _____ Martin looked as though he had lost his last friend.

7. _____ The truck driver decided not to try the freeway, which was covered with a

layer of ice.

8. _____ She agreed as soon as the situation had been explained to her.

9. _____ Finally, I remembered where I had left the keys.

10. _____ After the cat jumped down from the sofa, Maria sat.

EXERCISE B Underline the subordinate clause in each of the following sentences. Then, identify the use of the subordinate clause by writing above it *N* for *noun,* *ADJ* for *adjective,* or *ADV* for *adverb.*

                                         ADJ
Example 1. Vassily, who comes from Moscow, can sing several Beatles songs in Russian.

11. Since she was going downtown anyway, Clare offered to pick up the milk.

12. We decided to watch whatever Diego brought back from the video store.

13. Before he drove into the carwash, he rolled up all the windows.

14. The painting that had hung in the waiting room was now hanging in the doctor's office.

15. Ms. Johannsen stops at her uncle's house whenever she is in Portland.

16. What the butler saw was a matter of debate for weeks.

17. The CD, which had rolled across the carpet, came to rest against the cat.

18. Is she the singer for whom the song was written?

19. Although I had read *Moby-Dick* recently, I could not remember the narrator's name.

20. Our dog will eat whatever we put in front of her.

for **CHAPTER 6: THE CLAUSE** | *page 124*

Literary Model: Poetry

from "They Have Yarns"
by Carl Sandburg

(1) Of the man who drove a swarm of bees across the Rocky Mountains and the Desert "and didn't lose a bee,"

(2) Of a mountain railroad curve where the engineer in his cab can touch the caboose and spit in the conductor's eye, . . .

(3) Of the sheep counter who was fast and accurate: "I just count their feet and divide by four," . . .

(4) Of a cyclone that sucked cookstoves out of the kitchen, up the chimney flue, and on to the next town, . . .

(5) Of the man who killed a snake by putting its tail in its mouth so it swallowed itself, . . .

EXERCISE A Yarns are tall tales. In the poem "They Have Yarns," Carl Sandburg describes yarns from around the United States. Underline each adjective clause that appears in the lines above.

EXERCISE B

1. Use the model below to convert the information from the specified item number into two simple sentences that do not contain an adjective clause. The first sentence of the pair should begin with "They have yarns . . ."

(1) *They have yarns of a man. He drove a swarm of bees across the Rocky Mountains and the Desert and he "didn't lose a bee."*

(2) _____

(3) _____

(4) _____

(5) _____

Literary Model (continued)

2. Compare the simple sentences you wrote with the original phrases and clauses from the poem. If Sandburg had used only simple sentences in his poem, would (a) the connection between ideas be as tight or clear? (b) the flow or rhythm of the poem be affected? (c) the poem lose any of its humorous quality? Explain your answers.

_____

_____

_____

_____

_____

_____

EXERCISE C Based on Sandburg's model, write a poem in which you describe yarns, or tall tales, of your own creation. Be sure to use adjective clauses to combine ideas and to create a poetic rhythm. Underline each adjective clause.

_____

_____

_____

_____

_____

_____

_____

_____

_____

_____

_____

_____

EXERCISE D How would your poem be different if you could not use adjective clauses?

_____

_____

Writing Application: Letter

Writers can use adverb clauses to describe the conditions under which action takes place. The subordinating conjunctions that begin adverb clauses do more than simply introduce the clause. Subordinating conjunctions also show how sentence elements are logically related, so writers must choose these conjunctions carefully.

ILLOGICAL	Whether it stormed that day, we had to cancel our long-awaited trip to the beach.
	So that it stormed that day, we had to cancel our long-awaited trip to the beach.
LOGICAL	**Because** it stormed that day, we had to cancel our long-awaited trip to the beach.
	Since it stormed that day, we had to cancel our long-awaited trip to the beach.

As you can see, a writer must choose the subordinating conjunction that best describes the relationship between the idea expressed by the adverb clause and the idea expressed by the independent clause.

WRITING ACTIVITY

Eighth-grade students usually look forward to the day when they will first set foot on a high school campus. For most students, with the anticipation comes a little worry, too. Compose an e-mail or letter to a trusted older friend who is already wise in the ways of high school. Ask your friend for advice on three concerns, small or large, about high school. Use adverb clauses to describe how you think high school might be different from the school you now attend.

PREWRITING   You may feel confident about high school, or you may have dozens of questions about it. Either way, brainstorm to produce a list of possible concerns. Then, choose the three questions you would most like answered, keeping your audience in mind. Remember, your audience is a trusted friend who is in or has already been to high school.

WRITING   Letters to friends are informal, but that does not mean that they are unorganized or unclear. Treat each question in a separate, brief paragraph; and decide on the most effective order for the questions. Writers often begin with the least-pressing question and work toward the most-pressing question. Also, be specific about your concerns. "I'm worried that people will make fun of the way I dress" is less likely to get a helpful reply than "Because I have a quirky sense of style that others may not appreciate, I'm worried that people will make fun of the way I dress." Adverb clauses, as well as other types of clauses, can help you to add such details.

REVISING   Check your letter for errors in grammar, punctuation, and spelling. Letters to friends are informal, but that does not mean you can ignore all that you have learned about clear writing. The occasional fragment in informal writing is not a problem, but complete sentences tend to contain more complete meaning.

PUBLISHING   After checking your letter for errors, send it to your friend.

DEVELOPING YOUR WRITING

If you enjoyed this exercise, you could develop it into a longer writing project. Working with several friends, develop a pamphlet titled "How to Survive Your First Week in High School" to distribute to students going to high school. Ask a friend with artistic abilities to illustrate the pamphlet. Before distributing your pamphlet, be sure to get approval from your principal.

for **CHAPTER 7: SENTENCE STRUCTURE** `pages 139–47`

Choices: Exploring Sentence Structure

Here's your chance to step out of the grammar book and into the real world. You may not notice sentence structures, but you and the people around you use them every day. The following activities challenge you to find a connection between sentence structure and the world around you. Do the activity below that suits your personality best, and then share your discoveries with your class. Have fun!

WRITING ACQUISITION

Down Memory Lane

Do you have a few examples of writing that you did when you were younger? Well, find them and arrange them in order from those written earliest to the most current. Then, read each paper carefully. What do you notice about your sentence structure? How did your writing change from grade to grade? When did you start using compound and complex sentences? Write a brief report of what you have discovered about the development of your writing. You may be amazed at your progress!

REPRESENTING

Dashboard Delight

When a driver speeds down the highway, he or she has a dashboard that gives important information. Wouldn't it be nice if writers had a dashboard that they could check once in a while? You have learned most of the major building blocks of sentences—the parts of speech, phrases, and clauses. You also have learned the purposes of sentences, and you are learning about various kinds of sentence structures. Design a dashboard that will tell writers how they are doing. Include readings for each type of sentence structure. As for the rest, use your imagination.

WRITING

Shake, Rattle, and Roll

There are many verbs that are often used in pairs. *Read* and *write* are one pair; *sing* and *dance* are another. Brainstorm a list of up to ten of these pairs. Then, write two sentences for each pair. The first sentence should be a simple sentence that uses the pair as a compound verb. The second sentence should be a compound sentence that uses one half of each pair as the verb of each independent clause. If you think of trios of verbs, use them, too.

HISTORY

Dynamic Duos

Romeo and Juliet, Lewis and Clark, the turtle and the . . . well, you get the picture. Get together with a pal or two, and make a list of famous duos, or pairs. Write two sentences for each pair. One sentence will use the pair as a compound subject. The other sentence will be a compound sentence that uses one half of the duo as the subject of the first independent clause and the other half as the subject of the second independent clause. (It's a lot easier than it sounds.) Prepare a poster with two columns, one column displaying the simple sentences with compound subjects and the other column displaying the compound sentences. Be sure to highlight the subjects of each sentence.

COMPUTER SCIENCE

In the Pudding

Do grammar checkers really work? Find out! Create a test page. Include simple, compound, complex, and compound-complex sentences (the longer, the better). Also, include a few sentence fragments and anything else that you think might fool a program. In fact, get together with some friends and write some real doozies. Your sentences don't have to go together; they just have to attempt to fool the program. Then, run the grammar check. Make a note of each of the error messages that the program displays. Highlight each error. Tell the program to suggest corrections for each error. When the corrections are made, print out the new version. Now, analyze the changes that the program suggested. How many of the changes are appropriate? When your work is complete, share your results with the class.

Simple Sentences

7a. A *simple sentence* contains one independent clause and no subordinate clauses.

                                                    S   V

    EXAMPLE   Along the edge of the porch, **we planted** some colorful flowers.

A simple sentence may have a compound subject, a compound verb, or both.

                       S   S V

    EXAMPLE   **Katya** and **I dug** four inches into the rich soil and **sowed** twelve grape hyacinth bulbs.

EXERCISE A   In each of the following sentences, draw one line under each subject and two lines under each verb.

   Example **1.** The monkeys and apes will stay here or move on.

  1. Sally and Anne both take music lessons weekly.

  2. I climbed that oak tree and swam in the creek.

  3. Steve helped Roseanne with the puzzle and then washed the dishes.

  4. The parrot said "Cat for sale" and flapped its wings.

  5. All of a sudden, Dale and Amy burst into the room and grabbed the water jug.

  6. In April the company will increase its profits.

  7. Kim and Ted will go to Africa with Jade and photograph wildlife.

  8. Both the painting and the sketch show the meadow in the morning.

  9. This one and that one will be sold at the auction tomorrow.

10. After all of the hurry and bustle, a week or two at the beach sounded wonderful.

EXERCISE B   On each of the lines below, write your own simple sentence. Then, circle each subject and each verb.

   Example **1.** The (sun) (rose) and (warmed) the hillside. _____

11. _____

12. _____

13. _____

14. _____

15. _____

Compound Sentences

7b.   A *compound sentence* contains two or more independent clauses and no subordinate clauses.

The clauses of a compound sentence may be joined by
- a comma and a coordinating conjunction (*and, but, for, nor, or, so,* or *yet*)
- a semicolon
- a semicolon, a conjunctive adverb, and a comma

EXAMPLES   **Luisa Ortega is in my English class, and we have become good friends this year.**

Recently, the Ortegas invited me to a campground for the weekend; I eagerly accepted the invitation.

The family brought along a large tent; however, they did not use it for sleeping.

EXERCISE   Underline the independent clauses in each of the following sentences. Then, write *S* above each subject and *V* above each verb.

Example 1. The Ortegas put their sleeping bags out under the stars, but I preferred the tent.

1. I fear all kinds of wild creatures, but the family very kindly did not tease me about my apprehensions.

2. The family's black Labrador retriever evidently shared my fears, for he joined me in the tent.

3. In the middle of the night, I awoke to a strange sound; I immediately became frightened.

4. I was alone in the tent, for the dog had left.

5. Suddenly, the dog bounded into the tent, and within seconds the tent collapsed on top of us both!

6. The noise awoke the others, and I felt embarrassed!

7. Luisa crawled out of her sleeping bag, and together we pitched the tent again.

8. Then, Luisa returned to her sleeping bag, and I lay down on my cot in the tent.

9. Later that night, it rained, so the Ortegas ran to the tent.

10. I, along with the dog, remained dry; however, the Ortegas, in their scramble to the tent, were drenched!

for **CHAPTER 7: SENTENCE STRUCTURE** `pages 140–42`

Simple Sentence or Compound Sentence?

7a. A *simple sentence* contains one independent clause and no subordinate clauses.

7b. A *compound sentence* contains two or more independent clauses and no subordinate clauses.

Do not confuse a compound sentence with a simple sentence that contains a compound subject, a compound verb, or both.

SIMPLE SENTENCE   Coach Mendes and her team lost the first game of the double-header but won the second. [one independent clause with a compound subject and a compound verb]

COMPOUND SENTENCE   Sammi can play several instruments, but the banjo is her favorite. [two independent clauses]

EXERCISE In each of the following sentences, draw one line under each subject and two lines under each verb. Then, on the line provided, identify the sentence by writing *S* for *simple* or *Cd* for *compound*.

Example ___S___ **1.** David Attenborough has studied many unusual creatures and has written about their unique habitats and behaviors.

_____ **1.** I hurried over to Michael's house and met Rafiq on the way.

_____ **2.** The lightning struck the radio towers on the hill several times but did not damage them.

_____ **3.** The blinking light grew dim, and then it flashed several times.

_____ **4.** The gulls circle the fishing boat; they are hoping for a quick meal.

_____ **5.** The purple lantana and the red salvia look pretty and attract both bees and butterflies.

_____ **6.** After school I feed the rabbits, and Kris looks after the guinea pigs.

_____ **7.** In the evening the Korean restaurant opens and welcomes crowds of hungry diners.

_____ **8.** Patty and Carla are throwing Hilton a surprise party in their big backyard sometime next weekend.

_____ **9.** The crab scuttled quickly into the water, for it saw a heron nearby.

_____ **10.** I left, but Marcy stayed.

Complex Sentences

7c. A *complex sentence* contains one independent clause and at least one subordinate clause.

                                   S V   S   V

        EXAMPLE   Even though **it was** a gray, rainy day, **Pilar looked** forward to her walk in the park.

    INDEPENDENT CLAUSE Pilar looked forward to her walk in the park

   SUBORDINATE CLAUSE Even though it was a gray, rainy day

EXERCISE In each of the following sentences, draw one line under the independent clause and two lines under each subordinate clause. Then, write *S* above each subject and *V* above each verb.

Example 1. At the park, Pilar fed the ducks and swans, which quickly swam toward her.

1. Pilar looked for tiny fish and snails where the pond was shallow.

2. As she watched the fish and snails, she thought about a career in marine biology.

3. Her career plans had been all that she could think about since the Science Club took a field trip to a well-known oceanographic center.

4. Because the center was on a quiet shoreline, the scientists could study hundreds of forms of marine life.

5. Some students who had gone to the center last year had snorkeled around the tide pools.

6. Pilar became interested in Scripps Institution of Oceanography, which is a well-known oceano-graphic institute in San Diego, California.

7. Because her school computer had Internet access, Pilar could learn more about Scripps and marine biology.

8. First, she learned about research ships and their equipment when she looked at the Scripps Web site.

9. After she read an interview with a marine biologist, Pilar felt confident that marine biology was the career for her.

10. From the interview she learned that a marine biologist should have a good education, care about the environment, and enjoy travel.

Compound Sentence or Complex Sentence?

7b.   A *compound sentence* contains two or more independent clauses and no subordinate clauses.

              S V   S V

EXAMPLE Today, no **humans live** on the island, but **it is** still home to a wide variety of birds.

INDEPENDENT CLAUSES Today, no humans live on the island

             it is still home to a wide variety of birds

7c.   A *complex sentence* contains one independent clause and at least one subordinate clause.

              S V   S V

EXAMPLE Although no **humans live** on the island today, **it is** still home to a wide variety of birds.

INDEPENDENT CLAUSE it is still home to a wide variety of birds

SUBORDINATE CLAUSE Although no humans live on the island today

EXERCISE In each of the following sentences, draw one line under each subject and two lines under each verb. Then, on the line provided, identify the sentence by writing *Cd* for *compound* or *Cx* for *complex*.

Example _____Cx_____ **1.** Louisiana and Mississippi, which are two Southern states, border the Gulf of Mexico.

_____ **1.** Iowa is not near any oceans, but the Mississippi River makes up its eastern border.

_____ **2.** On the west coast, California borders Mexico, and Washington borders Canada.

_____ **3.** Hawaii is the only state that does not lie on the North American mainland.

_____ **4.** I learned that the northernmost state is Alaska.

_____ **5.** Texas is quite big, but Alaska is bigger.

_____ **6.** If you visit Death Valley in California, you will be 282 feet below sea level.

_____ **7.** The longest river in the United States is the Missouri River; the largest lake in the United States is Lake Michigan.

_____ **8.** Michigan, which resembles a mitten, sits between Lake Michigan and Lake Huron.

_____ **9.** I looked at a map, and then I showed Dana my home state.

_____ **10.** Dana lived in Canada before her family moved to New York, where her mother taught English.

GRAMMAR

Compound-Complex Sentences

7d. A *compound-complex sentence* contains two or more independent clauses and at least one subordinate clause.

<table>
<tr><td>EXAMPLE</td><td>$\overset{S}{Matt}$ $\overset{V}{would\ have\ broken}$ the school record, but $\overset{S}{he}$ $\overset{V}{stumbled}$ when his
right $\overset{S}{foot}$ $\overset{V}{hit}$ the last hurdle in the race.</td></tr>
<tr><td>INDEPENDENT CLAUSES</td><td>Matt would have broken the school record
he stumbled</td></tr>
<tr><td>SUBORDINATE CLAUSE</td><td>when his right foot hit the last hurdle in the race</td></tr>
</table>

EXERCISE In each of the following sentences, draw one line under every independent clause and two lines under every subordinate clause. Then, write *S* above each subject and *V* above each verb.

Example 1. When $\overset{S}{Thora\ Andersen}$ $\overset{V}{came}$ to this country, $\overset{S}{she}$ $\overset{V}{enjoyed}$ her new freedom, but
$\overset{S}{she}$ also $\overset{V}{worked}$ very hard.

1. Cece went to Chile during the winter vacation, but her older brother stayed home because he had made plans with some friends.

2. When Mr. Tolstoi entered the United States, he knew only a few words of English, but his wife was fluent in the language.

3. The two young men had avoided injuries because they had worn their seat belts, but the driver of the other car was not as fortunate.

4. Vegetarians, who do not eat meat, should watch their diets; they should eat nutritionally balanced meals.

5. Although both were tired, Ahnawake went to her soccer practice, and Carl went to his piano lesson.

6. The two dogs barked at each other constantly until the sun rose; consequently, none of us got much sleep last night.

7. You should shut the gate whenever you leave the backyard; otherwise, the dogs may get out.

8. When we went to the science museum, we attended a lecture on electricity; after the lecture, we visited some of the exhibits.

9. As we left the library, the rain pelted down, so we rushed back inside.

10. Aunt Eudora was born in Nashville, but when she was five years old, she and her family moved to Memphis, where she lived for the rest of her life.

Complex or Compound-Complex?

7c. A *complex sentence* contains one independent clause and at least one subordinate clause.

EXAMPLE Although **Emma is** a talented singer, **she did** not **audition** for the eighth grade's musical play.

INDEPENDENT CLAUSE she did not audition for the eighth grade's musical play

SUBORDINATE CLAUSE Although Emma is a talented singer

7d. A *compound-complex sentence* contains two or more independent clauses and at least one subordinate clause.

EXAMPLE **Emma is** a talented singer, but **she did** not **audition** for the eighth grade's musical play because **she needed** more time for her studies.

INDEPENDENT CLAUSES Emma is a talented singer

she did not audition for the eighth grade's musical play

SUBORDINATE CLAUSE because she needed more time for her studies

EXERCISE In each of the following sentences, draw one line under each subject and two lines under each verb. Then, on the line provided, identify the sentence by writing *Cx* for *complex* or *Cd-Cx* for *compound-complex*.

Example *Cd-Cx* **1.** I believe that my birthstone is the sapphire; Roseanne's is the opal.

_____ **1.** A gem is a mineral or other material that is used in jewelry and other ornaments.

_____ **2.** Some of the gems that you see are natural; others are artificial.

_____ **3.** Laney said that scientists can make sapphires, rubies, and emeralds in laboratories.

_____ **4.** Some gems occur in igneous rock, which forms when hot, molten material cools.

_____ **5.** Other gems occur in metamorphic rock, which forms under great heat and pressure; still others occur in sedimentary rock, which typically forms when water, wind, or ice deposits sand, gravel, and other materials.

_____ **6.** I asked Mr. Catalano whether pearls are made by oysters, and he said yes.

_____ **7.** When light travels through a well-cut diamond, the diamond glitters with different colors.

_____ **8.** The type of gem cut that is called the brilliant cut has fifty-eight facets.

_____ **9.** Diamonds are very valuable because they are very durable and brilliant, but some emeralds are even more valuable.

_____ **10.** Perhaps the most beautiful of all pearls is La Pellegrina, which is from India.

Review A: Classifying Sentences According to Structure

EXERCISE A In each of the following sentences, draw one line under every independent clause and two lines under every subordinate clause. Then, on the line provided, classify the sentence by writing *S* for *simple, Cd* for *compound, Cx* for *complex,* or *Cd-Cx* for *compound-complex.*

Example ___*Cx*___ **1.** Many of the novels that Agatha Christie wrote have been made into films.

_____ **1.** Suspense novels are extremely popular, and many readers especially enjoy those by Agatha Christie.

_____ **2.** Christie's first detective novel was *The Mysterious Affair at Styles.*

_____ **3.** Hercule Poirot, who is perhaps her most famous character, is the Belgian detective who solves the murder cases in many of her books.

_____ **4.** In *Murder on the Orient Express,* Poirot expertly interrogates many of the passengers on the train before he solves the case.

_____ **5.** Miss Marple, another detective of Christie's, is my favorite character.

_____ **6.** My introduction to Miss Marple came when I read *The Body in the Library.*

_____ **7.** In this mystery several people are suspects, for each has a possible motive, but Miss Marple sets an ingenious trap for the murderer.

_____ **8.** When I visited England last summer, I saw *The Mousetrap,* a suspense play by Christie, and I also toured her home in Devon.

_____ **9.** Because the clues in *The Mousetrap* were hidden so well, the ending surprised nearly everyone in the audience.

_____ **10.** Currently, I am reading *Death on the Nile;* I have not seen the movie yet.

EXERCISE B Classify each of the following sentences by writing on the line provided *S* for *simple, Cd* for *compound, Cx* for *complex,* or *Cd-Cx* for *compound-complex.*

Example ___*Cx*___ **1.** Do you know what the principal cause of most forest fires is?

_____ **11.** I will make the salad if you will make the lemonade.

_____ **12.** Amy, who is a three-year-old with an odd sense of humor, sometimes hides in strange places; yesterday I found her in the broom closet.

_____ **13.** What kinds of tricks does your dog do, Darren?

_____ **14.** The person in the middle is my cousin Josie, and the one to her left is Uncle Timothy.

_____ **15.** When I have finished all of my chores, I will sit outside for a while and read.

Review B: **Classifying Sentences According to Structure**

EXERCISE A   In each of the following sentences, draw one line under every independent clause and two lines under every subordinate clause. Then, on the line provided, classify the sentence by writing *S* for *simple*, *Cd* for *compound*, *Cx* for *complex*, or *Cd-Cx* for *compound-complex*.

Example   _____*Cx*_____ **1.** Did you know that some bored surfers created the sport of skateboarding?

_____ **1.** If you are a surfer, you may enjoy skateboarding, for the sport is similar to surfing.

_____ **2.** Some skateboards are made from wood; others are made from plastic or fiberglass.

_____ **3.** At first, skateboards had roller-skate wheels, but today's boards have special wheels that are much easier to control.

_____ **4.** I bought an inexpensive skateboard and customized it.

_____ **5.** When the skater shifts his or her weight, the board turns.

_____ **6.** My brother taught me how to skate.

_____ **7.** Some skaters practice every day, but I practice only on weekends.

_____ **8.** When you skate, you should wear kneepads, elbow pads, and a helmet.

_____ **9.** Schools in my area often sponsor contests for skateboarders; in fact, Lakeside Middle School is holding a contest this Saturday.

_____ **10.** I will not compete in the contest, but I will watch my brother as he competes.

EXERCISE B   Classify each of the following sentences by writing on the line provided *S* for *simple*, *Cd* for *compound*, *Cx* for *complex*, or *Cd-Cx* for *compound-complex*.

Example   _____*S*_____ **1.** Tyrone and I saw a horror movie together.

_____ **11.** Some scenes in the movie became too scary for me; consequently, I excused myself and went to the lobby.

_____ **12.** I think that many people in the audience left during the scariest scenes.

_____ **13.** At one point Tyrone got the hiccups and rushed out for some water.

_____ **14.** At times while Tyrone was gone, I turned my head away from the screen and closed my eyes, but I still saw the ugly monster with the glaring yellow eyes.

_____ **15.** As we rushed out of the theater to meet our parents, both Tyrone and I said that we could hardly wait to see the sequel.

Review C: **Classifying Sentences According to Structure**

EXERCISE On the lines provided, write your own sentences, using a variety of sentence structures. Circle each subject and each verb. Then, classify each sentence as *simple, compound, complex,* or *compound-complex.*

Example 1. (Lynette) and (I) (will study) math as soon as (we) (get) back from soccer practice.—Complex

1. _____
   _____

2. _____
   _____

3. _____
   _____

4. _____
   _____

5. _____
   _____

6. _____
   _____

7. _____
   _____

8. _____
   _____

9. _____
   _____

10. _____
    _____

for **CHAPTER 7: SENTENCE STRUCTURE**   pages 139–47

Literary Model: Sentence Structures in Tall Tales

Pecos Bill wanted a horse. To be exact, he wanted the Famous Pacing Mustang of the Prairies.

No one had ever been able to catch the mustang and ride him. They said even bullets could not stop him. Few men had ever even seen him. . . .

He gasped when he saw the horse. He was a palomino. His shining coat was the color of a new-minted gold coin. His mane and tail were snowy white. He had four white stockings and a white blaze between the eyes, and Bill made up his mind to capture him that very day.

—from "Pecos Bill and the Mustang" by Harold W. Felton

Wherever you go in this big country, you're likely to find somebody who'll tell you that Paul Bunyan's been there. . . .

You'll hear that Kansas used to be full of mountains before Paul Bunyan came. He turned it upside-down. Now it's flat as a pancake because all its mountain peaks are inside the ground, pointing to the center of the earth.

You'll hear that Paul got so sad at what he saw going on in New York City that he fell to crying, and his tears started the Hudson River.

Western deserts or Southern swamps, Eastern shores or Northern forests, Paul is said to have been there and done things. And if by chance you can't find any stories about his having been in your neck of the woods, fix some up. Everybody else has.

Right now, let's stick to the Northern forests, because we know for sure that Paul was there. . . .

—from "Paul Bunyan's Been There," retold by Maurice Dolbier

EXERCISE A Read the passages to yourself, and compare the styles of the two passages. Which passage contains mostly simple sentences? How does it sound different from the passage that contains compound, complex, and compound-complex sentences? Explain your answer.

_____

_____

_____

_____

Literary Model (continued)

EXERCISE B

1. Invent a character who might have lived in the Wild West of the nineteenth century. Write a

   brief passage about this character. Try to use mostly simple sentences. _____

   _____

   _____

   _____

   _____

   _____

   _____

   _____

   _____

2. Rewrite your passage so that almost all the sentences are either compound, complex, or

   compound-complex. _____

   _____

   _____

   _____

   _____

   _____

   _____

   _____

   _____

   _____

EXERCISE C   Which version of your paragraph do you think would appeal more to readers? Explain your

answer. _____

_____

_____

_____

GRAMMAR | Language in Context: Literary Model

for **CHAPTER 7: SENTENCE STRUCTURE**   *pages 139–47*

Writing Application: Description

Careful writers almost always use a variety of sentence structures. They know that using only simple sentences can produce choppy, repetitious text.

CHOPPY   Our house is somewhat small. It is clean, though. It is near the park. I like it.

SMOOTH   Our house is somewhat small, but because it is clean and near the park, I like it.

WRITING ACTIVITY

In your geometry class, you are using blueprints of houses to apply what you have learned about geometrical shapes. Your teacher has asked you to create a blueprint for your dream house. Before you sketch it out, describe it in a few paragraphs that you will turn in with your blueprint. Avoid producing a list of your dream house's traits. Instead, use complex, compound, and compound-complex sentences as well as simple sentences as you write your descriptive paragraphs.

PREWRITING   First, imagine the house you dream of building. You can plan realistically, or you can dream big and plan a mansion on rolling acreage. Just remember that you will have to produce the blueprint, with all its measurements, for the house's design. List the "must haves" and "would like to haves"; then, decide how to organize your paragraphs. Will you discuss the floor plan, then the interior, then landscaping? Will you imaginatively open the front door and walk through the house, room by room?

WRITING   With your lists and plan of organization in front of you, write the first draft of your description. Then, read your draft and try to sketch the floor plan and yard of the house. If you can't tell where a wall goes or how large to draw the kitchen, your draft needs more detail. Move from draft to drawing and back until the basics of the house are clear in both.

REVISING   Your audience for these paragraphs is your classmates, your teacher—and you. Adjust the formality of your writing so that it will interest students and also meet the more formal requirements of writing submitted to teachers. Check to be sure that you have used a variety of sentence patterns, including several complex and compound-complex sentences.

PUBLISHING   Check your paragraphs for errors in spelling and punctuation. Check your math, too. Then, print your description and your blueprint neatly and submit them together to your teacher. Later, with your teacher's permission, you and your classmates may wish to display your dream house plans on a bulletin board.

EXTENDING YOUR WRITING

If you enjoyed this exercise, you could develop it into a longer writing project. For a home economics class, you could compare and contrast living in a house with living in an apartment. For a history class, you could research a type of house built in the past—a sod house on the prairie, perhaps, or a log cabin in the woods of the northeastern states. What was life like in such a house?

Choices: Examining Agreement

The following activities challenge you to find a connection between agreement and the world around you. Do the activity below that suits your personality best, and then share your discoveries with your class. Have fun!

Don't You Dare?

Here is a game for a group of seven or eight. Get that old beanbag out. If you don't have a beanbag, use a ruler or an eraser. Have the group stand in a circle. You begin the game by saying either *Don't* or *Doesn't* as you pass the beanbag to the person next to you. Let's call her Carla. Carla hands the beanbag to the next person, who quickly hands it to the next, and so on. As the beanbag goes around the circle, Carla must add a subject to *Don't* or *Doesn't* and complete the question. For instance, she might say, "Don't they go to our school?" The trick is that Carla must complete the question before the beanbag comes back round to her. If she does, she wins a point, calls either *Don't* or *Doesn't*, and hands the beanbag to the next person.

Better Business Bureau

Get a telephone book and make a list of businesses and organizations that use plural nouns in their names. Choose organizations that you know well, such as the theaters you frequent, the stores you like, and clubs you enjoy. For each business, write a sentence. If you're musical, you could turn your sentences into a hometown rap. Just make sure that you position these business and organization names as subjects that agree with present tense verbs. Use some names as antecedents to pronouns, too. Read or perform your sentences for the class.

All for Nothing

What's the use of identifying usage errors if you don't learn from them? It's all for nothing! Create a form that you and your classmates can use to keep track of usage errors. Include columns for the error, the correction, and classification of the error. Pass out copies to all your classmates.

Jingle Jangle

Ask your classmates or your teacher which agreement error seems to be the most frequent. Then, write a mnemonic device to help everyone remember the rule easily. You could write a rhyme, a rap, or some other memory aid. Write a memo that includes your study aid, and pass out copies to the class.

One, Not Two

Compound subjects joined by *nor* can be confusing. After all, compound subjects name two or more nouns or pronouns. These subjects seem plural, but they aren't always plural. Help your classmates see why singular subjects joined by *or* or *nor* require a singular verb. Create six to eight examples of this type of sentence, and ask permission to act them out for the class. You'll need at least three people: a reader and two performers.

The Philippines

Lots of countries, cities, and towns have names that sound plural. The Philippines is one example. Does it seem strange to read *The Philippines is* instead of *The Philippines are*? Help your classmates get used to hearing and seeing such names as singular nouns that take singular verbs and pronouns. Get a world or national map. Mark the map with a dozen plural place names. Then, write a sentence for each place name. In your sentence, use a singular pronoun to refer to the place name. For instance, you could write *The Philippines relies on fishing for its food supply.* Ask to present your map to the class, reading each of your sentences as you point to the appropriate place.

Subject-Verb Agreement A

Number is the form a word takes to indicate whether the word is singular or plural.

8a. | When a word refers to one person, place, thing, or idea, it is ***singular*** in number. When a word refers to more than one person, place, thing, or idea, it is ***plural*** in number.

SINGULAR   lesson, box, child, him, each
PLURAL   lessons, boxes, children, them, many

EXERCISE A Above each of the following words, write *S* for *singular* or *P* for *plural*.

Examples 1. woman *S*

          2. women *P*

1. cases
2. us
3. clock
4. book
5. pencil
6. stereos
7. them
8. wish
9. mice
10. knuckle

11. feet
12. she
13. few
14. spoons
15. pin
16. lemon
17. plate
18. tribes
19. shelves
20. yam

EXERCISE B On the lines provided, write the plural form of each of the following words.

Example 1. chicken _____*chickens*_____

21. person _____
22. dentist _____
23. cup _____
24. audience _____
25. reporter _____

26. hawk _____
27. actor _____
28. cow _____
29. scientist _____
30. potato _____

USAGE

Subject-Verb Agreement B

8b. A verb should agree in number with its subject.

(1) Singular subjects take singular verbs.
(2) Plural subjects take plural verbs.

When a sentence contains a verb phrase, the first helping verb in the verb phrase agrees with the subject.

> **EXAMPLES** Our favorite **sport is** soccer. [The singular verb *is* agrees with the singular subject *sport*.]
>
> **We have been playing** soccer in the park. [The plural helping verb *have* agrees with the plural subject *We*.]

EXERCISE A In each of the following sentences, underline the verb in parentheses that agrees with its subject.

Example 1. Soccer *(is, are)* the world's most popular team sport.

1. Our cat *(like, likes)* to watch television with us, especially the nature shows.

2. All the students *(enjoy, enjoys)* the reading assignment every week.

3. Before he became a lawyer, my uncle Nacio *(was, were)* a high-wire performer in the circus.

4. This music *(has, have)* elements of harmony that are very complex.

5. *(Is, Are)* Rafael usually first in line for every new movie in town?

6. As the final plot twist is revealed, the reader *(start, starts)* to understand why the butler left the French doors open.

7. My mother *(prefer, prefers)* a good book to a good movie.

8. Many passersby *(are, is)* curious about the mysterious building being constructed downtown.

9. Before they leave for vacation, the women *(ask, asks)* their neighbors to look after their house.

10. The grass *(is, are)* always greener after a good rain.

EXERCISE B In each of the following sentences, underline the helping verb in parentheses that agrees with its subject.

Example 1. Jacob *(has, have)* been exploring a salt marsh.

11. Over the past year, Jonelle *(has, have)* been collecting articles about Olympic gymnasts.

12. I read that the English actor Ralph Fiennes *(is, are)* appearing in *Hamlet* this season in London.

13. *(Do, Does)* she know yet about the letter from her brother?

14. They *(has, have)* been thinking about adopting a dog for some time now.

15. Certainly Mr. Iwaye *(do, does)* understand the importance of meeting the deadline.

Subject-Verb Agreement C

8c.   The number of a subject is not changed by a phrase or clause following the subject.

> **EXAMPLES**   This **collection** of myths and legends **is** fascinating.
>
> The **flowers** that I planted in the front yard **are** in need of water.

USAGE

EXERCISE A   In each of the following sentences, underline the verb in parentheses that agrees with its subject.

Example 1. The book in which I found these facts and figures (*belongs*, *belong*) to Ms. Najera.

1. The last people off the ship (*carry*, *carries*) their own luggage.

2. This anthology of short stories (*include*, *includes*) at least one story by Charles Baxter.

3. Songs about love often (*make*, *makes*) me cry.

4. Jim's brother, who is an art director for television sitcoms in Hollywood, (*is*, *are*) a graduate of Carnegie Mellon University in Pittsburgh, Pennsylvania.

5. The demolition of a skyscraper always (*draw*, *draws*) a crowd.

6. At the end of the story, the king of the birds (*declare*, *declares*), "I grant the eagle's request!"

7. The solution to all of our problems (*is*, *are*) to start the project over again from scratch.

8. The potatoes from the garden (*was*, *were*) peeled before they were put into the pot.

9. Two types of salad (*was*, *were*) served first.

10. The sound of the passing ships (*echo*, *echoes*) through the fog.

EXERCISE B   In each of the following sentences, circle the subject of the verb in parentheses. Then, underline the verb in parentheses that agrees with the subject.

Example 1. My favorite (book) of short stories (*is*, *are*) *Tales of Mystery and Imagination* by Edgar Allan Poe.

11. The students in my karate class (*watch*, *watches*) carefully whenever the instructor demonstrates a move.

12. The jar of lima beans (*was*, *were*) stored in the coolest section of the cellar.

13. The birthday cards that I received this year (*is*, *are*) mostly from out of town.

14. The two men, who both work the third shift at the police department, (*sleep*, *sleeps*) during the day.

15. The judges on the panel (*decide*, *decides*) which skaters will continue to the semifinals.

Language and Sentence Skills Practice

Subject-Verb Agreement D

8d. The following indefinite pronouns are singular: *anybody, anyone, anything, each, either, everybody, everyone, everything, neither, nobody, nothing, no one, one, somebody, someone,* and *something.*

EXAMPLE   **Everyone is** responsible for bringing his or her own lunch.

8e. The following indefinite pronouns are plural: *both, few, many,* and *several.*

EXAMPLE   **Both** of the girls **excel** at basketball.

8f. The indefinite pronouns *all, any, more, most, none,* and *some* may be singular or plural, depending on their meaning in a sentence.

Often, the object in a prepositional phrase that follows the pronoun indicates whether the pronoun is singular or plural. Usually, if the object of the preposition is singular, the pronoun is singular. If the object is plural, the pronoun is plural.

EXAMPLES   **Some** of the carrots **have** been sliced. [*Some* refers to the plural object *carrots.*]
　　　　　　 Some of the salad **is** in the refrigerator. [*Some* refers to the singular object *salad.*]

EXERCISE   Circle the indefinite pronoun in each of the following sentences. Then, underline the correct form of the verb in parentheses.

Example 1. (Most) of the cups *(was, were)* unbroken after the earthquake.

1. Something about the candidate's answers *(has, have)* been bothering me ever since the debate.

2. Both of the dogs *(has, have)* already been treated for heartworm.

3. All of the stuff in the attic *(need, needs)* to be dusted before the yard sale.

4. Neither of the movies *(is, are)* very good.

5. *(Have, Has)* not several of these dogs already won awards?

6. Everybody who is registered for the class *(read, reads)* the same books.

7. No one in the play *(was, were)* prepared for the overwhelming response of the audience on opening night.

8. *(Is, Are)* any of the dough ready to be baked?

9. The director is pleased that more of the singers *(have, has)* memorized the score for this rehearsal than for the last rehearsal.

10. Somebody among the reporters covering the trial *(is, are)* getting inside information from the district attorney.

Subject-Verb Agreement E

| **8d.** | The following indefinite pronouns are singular: *anybody, anyone, anything, each, either, everybody, everyone, everything, neither, nobody, nothing, no one, one, somebody, someone,* and *something.* |

   EXAMPLE   **Each** of these lakes **has** good fishing and boating.

| **8e.** | The following indefinite pronouns are plural: *both, few, many,* and *several.* |

   EXAMPLE   **Few** of the trails **are** rocky.

| **8f.** | The indefinite pronouns *all, any, more, most, none,* and *some* may be singular or plural, depending on their meaning in a sentence. |

Often, the object in a prepositional phrase that follows the pronoun indicates whether the pronoun is singular or plural. Usually, if the object of the preposition is singular, the pronoun is singular. If the object is plural, the pronoun is plural.

   EXAMPLES   **Most** of the campground **is occupied.** [*Most* refers to the singular object *campground.*]

   Most of the campsites **are occupied.** [*Most* refers to the plural object *campsites.*]

EXERCISE   Circle the indefinite pronoun in each of the following sentences. Then, underline the correct form of the verb in parentheses.

Example   1. (Many) of the ocean's creatures (*looks,* <u>look</u>) strange to us.

1. Few of the world's sharks (*grows, grow*) to be sixty feet long.

2. One of the most interesting sharks (*is, are*) the whale shark.

3. Each of a whale shark's eggs (*is, are*) quite large.

4. "(*Has, Have*) anyone here ever seen a whale shark's egg?" asked the tour guide.

5. None of the sharks (*swims, swim*) toward the visitors.

6. Some of the other sea creatures (*is, are*) frightening, too.

7. Many of the visitors (*screams, scream*).

8. Few of us (*has, have*) seen a giant jellyfish before.

9. Several of the park's divers (*follows, follow*) a manta ray.

10. Everyone in our class (*seems, seem*) to be having a good time at the ocean park.

USAGE

Subject-Verb Agreement F

| **8g.** | Subjects joined by *and* usually take a plural verb. |

A compound subject that names only one person or thing takes a singular verb.

EXAMPLES   **Franco** and **I look** for a book about the life of George Washington Carver.

One respected **professor** and **researcher** at Tuskegee Institute **was** George Washington Carver.

| **8h.** | Singular subjects joined by *or* or *nor* take a singular verb. Plural subjects joined by *or* or *nor* take a plural verb. |

EXAMPLES   Neither **poverty** nor any other **hardship was** too great an obstacle for Carver.

Neither difficult **times** nor **disappointments were** too great an obstacle for Carver.

| **8i.** | When a singular subject and a plural subject are joined by *or* or *nor*, the verb agrees with the subject nearer the verb. |

EXAMPLE   At first, neither the local **farmers** nor Carver's closest **friend was interested** in his ideas.

EXERCISE   Circle the subjects of the verb in parentheses in each of the following sentences. Then, underline the correct form of the verb in parentheses.

Example   1. (Plants) (flowers) and (soil) *(was, were)* interesting to Carver.

1. Plants and flowers *(is, are)* featured on the cover of this book about Carver's life.

2. The author and illustrator of the book *(is, are)* the same person.

3. According to the book, grief and sorrow *(was, were)* part of Carver's early life.

4. Neither his mother nor his father *(was, were)* alive to raise Carver.

5. At the time, slaveholding and slave trading *(was, were)* widespread.

6. Neither Carver nor many other African Americans *(was, were)* able to find a college that would enroll them.

7. Neither the large universities nor the local college *(was, were)* accepting applications from African Americans.

8. Just laws and the strict enforcement of them *(was, were)* needed.

9. Also described in the book *(is, are)* Carver's experiments and discoveries.

10. An innovative educator and scientist *(was, were)* George Washington Carver.

Subject-Verb Agreement G

8j. When the subject follows the verb, find the subject and make sure the verb agrees with it.

EXAMPLES   Here **is** the **list** of topics from which you may choose.
When **are** these **books** due back to the library?

EXERCISE A   For each of the following sentences, underline the word or word group in parentheses that correctly completes the sentence.

Example 1. When (do, *does*) the teacher want us to finish the assignment?

1. Why (is, are) your parents going to Beijing?

2. Here (is, are) the magazines you were looking for.

3. (Has, Have) the students returned from their field trip yet?

4. (There is, There are) a snail crawling across the aquarium.

5. Where (is, are) the cat?

6. (Do, Does) all of your brothers and sisters speak Vietnamese?

7. When (was, were) the latest episodes of the program scheduled to begin?

8. There (is, are) many reasons you should read that book.

9. How (do, does) those new shoes feel?

10. Brittany, here (is, are) the books on astronomy you ordered.

EXERCISE B   Circle the subject or subjects of the verb in parentheses in each of the following sentences. Then, underline the word or word group in parentheses that correctly completes the sentence.

Example 1. (Has, *Have*) anyone in your family ever learned to water-ski?

11. (Are, Is) your little brother a finalist in the state gymnastics tournament?

12. (There's, There are) over forty species of birds that pass through my backyard.

13. How (do, does) bees make honey?

14. Here (lie, lies) the ruins of the colony.

15. When (is, are) your cousins from Guatemala coming to visit?

16. (Do, Does) anyone here have change for a twenty-dollar bill?

17. There (was, were) no excuses for what Dudley had done.

18. What (do, does) the Andersons want to know about the school system?

19. (Has, Have) someone told you the rules of our game?

20. Here (is, are) Amy and her sisters!

USAGE

Subject-Verb Agreement H

8k. The contractions *don't* and *doesn't* should agree with their subjects.

> **EXAMPLES**   These **shoes don't** fit me very well.
> **Doesn't she** go to your school?

EXERCISE A   In each of the following sentences, underline the word in parentheses that correctly completes the sentence.

Example 1. This old recording (*don't,* <u>*doesn't*</u>) sound like me.

1. Minneapolis and Toronto (*don't, doesn't*) have the climate for palm trees.

2. They (*don't, doesn't*) plan to attend the concert tonight.

3. (*Don't, Doesn't*) her brothers have a copy of the book?

4. They (*don't, doesn't*) plan to go to the reunion.

5. Macaroni and cheese (*don't, doesn't*) sound very good to me when I'm sick.

6. Only a few of the choir (*don't, doesn't*) know the words to the song.

7. (*Don't, Doesn't*) she attend ballet class with your brother?

8. It (*don't, doesn't*) matter how you fix the bicycle as long as you do it by Friday.

9. Anyone who thinks cricket is easy (*don't, doesn't*) understand the game.

10. (*Don't, Doesn't*) everyone wonder about where the stars come from?

EXERCISE B   Complete each of the following sentences by inserting the correct contraction, *doesn't* or *don't,* on the line provided.

Example 1. She _____*doesn't*_____ think she can finish the project on time.

11. Mr. Maduzia _____ know anyone else on the softball team.

12. _____ someone have the answer to my question?

13. Dr. Anna Kim _____ work at this clinic any longer.

14. Paolo _____ believe in UFOs, but he does believe in ghosts.

15. These ficus plants _____ look very healthy to me.

16. _____ you think we should begin the test now?

17. The video box _____ say who directed the film.

18. He _____ think you should go, does he?

19. The opera _____ seem as long in performance as it did in rehearsal.

20. Anyone who _____ own a dog or a cat wouldn't understand how I feel.

Subject-Verb Agreement I

USAGE

8l. A collective noun may be either singular or plural, depending on its meaning in a sentence.

The singular form of a **collective noun** names a group of persons, animals, or things. It takes a singular verb when it refers to the group as a unit. It takes a plural verb when it refers to the individual parts or members of the group.

EXAMPLES   The **team has been practicing** since March. [The team practices as a unit.]

The **team have been discussing** their strategies with one another. [Individual members discuss with one another.]

EXERCISE A   In each of the following sentences, underline the correct form of the verb in parentheses.

Example 1. The orchestra (*is, are*) rehearsing this afternoon at three o'clock.

1. Before each game, the team (*practice, practices*) their kicks.

2. As Napoleon once said, an army (*travel, travels*) on its stomach.

3. The committee generally (*decide, decides*) on its course of action pretty quickly.

4. After the rain, the entire herd (*graze, grazes*) peacefully along the hillside.

5. The Activist Alliance (*hold, holds*) its annual meeting this week in Fargo.

6. As the comedian leaves the stage, the audience (*applaud, applauds*) wildly.

7. The flock (*lift, lifts*) into the air a few birds at a time.

8. The evening before the big battle, the army (*clean, cleans*) their weapons.

9. Our family (*has, have*) never been able to agree on our destination for summer vacation.

10. The team (*are, is*) receiving awards for their individual achievements.

EXERCISE B   On the line provided in each of the following sentences, write the correct present tense form of the verb in parentheses.

Example 1. The crowd _____surges_____ toward the stage. (*surge*)

11. The team _____ among themselves over who gets to go first. (*bicker*)

12. The committee _____ gone their separate ways for lunch. (*have*)

13. Every Saturday, the troop _____ individual projects to their parents. (*present*)

14. The public _____ each new CD from Bryn Terfel with even greater acclaim than the one before. (*greet*)

15. The posse _____ which among them would bring the prisoner back to town. (*discuss*)

Subject-Verb Agreement J

USAGE

8m. An expression of an amount (a measurement, a percentage, or a fraction, for example) may be singular or plural, depending on how it is used.

> **EXAMPLES** **Ten dollars was** my weekly allowance when I was twelve years old.
>
> **Ten dollars** with consecutive serial numbers **were lying** on the counter.

8n. Some nouns that are plural in form take singular verbs.

> **EXAMPLE** **Is mumps** a contagious disease?

Some nouns that are plural in form and that name singular objects take plural verbs.

> **EXAMPLE** Where **are** the **scissors**?

EXERCISE A In the following sentences, underline the verb form in parentheses that agrees with the subject.

Example 1. Twenty percent of the class (*is, are*) absent today.

1. Fifteen dollars (*was, were*) a fair price for that teapot.

2. Sixty yards of fabric (*is, are*) necessary to make the banners for the homecoming parade.

3. Eight percent of the microchips (*was, were*) defective.

4. Twelve miles (*seem, seems*) like a long distance if you're walking.

5. About half of the members of the club (*was, were*) aware of the emergency.

6. The three weeks before Christmas (*feel, feels*) like forever.

7. One quarter of the flour (*is, are*) reserved for breading the cutlets.

8. Three casseroles (*was, were*) sitting in a row on the table.

9. Three fourths of the book club's members (*has, have*) not read the book yet.

10. Four gallons of gasoline (*is, are*) enough to get us to Grand Rapids and back.

EXERCISE B In the following sentences, underline the verb form in parentheses that agrees with the subject.

Example 1. The news today from Kosovo (*is, are*) surprisingly good.

11. The Olympics (*was, were*) in Munich, Germany, that year.

12. Physics (*is, are*) my first class of the day.

13. (*Is, Are*) civics the study of the duties and rights of citizenship?

14. As she tips her head forward, Charlene's eyeglasses (*slip, slips*) down her nose.

15. A summons (*was, were*) issued for the witness to appear in court the next day.

Subject-Verb Agreement K

| **8o.** | Even when plural in form, the title of a creative work (such as a book, song, movie, or painting) or the name of a country, city, or organization generally takes a singular verb. |

EXAMPLES   **"The Fox and the Grapes" is** a fable by Aesop.

   The Cayman Islands is a beautiful vacation spot.

| **8p.** | A verb agrees with its subject but not necessarily with a predicate nominative. |

EXAMPLES   **Oranges are** a good **source** of vitamin C. [The verb *are* agrees with the plural subject *Oranges*, not with the singular predicate nominative *source*.]

   A good **source** of vitamin C **is oranges.** [The verb *is* agrees with the singular subject *source*, not with the plural predicate nominative *oranges*.]

EXERCISE A   In each of the following sentences, underline the verb form in parentheses that agrees with the subject.

Example 1. *The Confessions of St. Augustine* still (<u>has</u>, have) relevance for a modern reader.

1. *The Birds (is, are)* one of the scariest novellas I've ever read.

2. He is from the Seychelles, which *(is, are)* a small island nation in the Indian Ocean.

3. *Quaker Ladies*, by Andrew Wyeth, *(is, are)* a painting that appears in my literature textbook.

4. *(Is, Are) The Railway Children* your favorite book?

5. Big Rapids *(seem, seems)* to be a nice place to grow up.

6. What an unsettling story *(is, are)* "The Willows," by Algernon Blackwood!

7. *The Lusiads (is, are)* an epic poem about the Portuguese explorer Vasco da Gama.

8. This year, the Friends of American Writers *(award, awards)* its literature prize to *The Wild Colonial Boy.*

9. *The Bells of St. Mary's (star, stars)* Bing Crosby and Ingrid Bergman.

10. "The Bells," by Anne Sexton, *(feel, feels)* like a cry from the heart.

EXERCISE B   In each of the following sentences, underline the verb form in parentheses that agrees with the subject.

Example 1. The secret ingredient in my mother's spaghetti sauce (<u>is</u>, are) four cloves of garlic.

11. Potatoes *(is, are)* the chief crop of my grandfather's farm in Idaho.

12. Weekday afternoons *(is, are)* the best time to reach Julia at work.

13. A good present for Tara *(is, are)* stereo headphones.

14. The most famous product of Detroit, Michigan, *(is, are)* automobiles.

15. *(Is, Are)* books an appropriate gift for a six-month-old child?

Pronoun-Antecedent Agreement A

A pronoun usually refers to a noun or another pronoun called its *antecedent*.

8q. A pronoun should agree in number and gender with its antecedent.

EXAMPLES   **Alicia** left **her** book bag on the school bus.

Many people like the **movie** because of **its** special effects.

The **musicians** are practicing for **their** spring concert.

Not every **student** has returned **his or her** permission slip for the field trip.

EXERCISE   On the line provided in each of the following sentences, write a pronoun that agrees with the antecedent. Then, circle each antecedent.

Example   1. (Paul) loaned Nell _____*his*_____ jacket.

1. Mary Ellen took _____ dog for a walk after dinner.

2. One of the men bent to pick up _____ tools.

3. Somebody left _____ books on the lawn last night.

4. Sean said that _____ was too tired to come with us to the movies.

5. Out of sheer boredom, the cat chased _____ own tail.

6. Stanley went up to _____ room to do the homework assignment.

7. Miranda hung the diploma on the wall of _____ bedroom.

8. Each of the girls on the soccer team received _____ own jersey yesterday.

9. As the sun set, the mountain cast _____ shadow across the desert.

10. Pick up the frying pan and bring _____ to me, please.

11. We stayed awake to watch the film until _____ was over.

12. If your sister gets here after I leave, tell _____ I left a casserole in the fridge.

13. Neither of the boys remembered where _____ baseball glove was.

14. That afternoon Uncle Oliver told us stories about _____ experiences in Vietnam.

15. Either of the men is willing to tell you what _____ saw at the accident scene.

16. Emily Dickinson often gave _____ poems away as gifts to neighbors.

17. Everybody at the office put flowers in _____ cubicle.

18. The author of *The Adventures of Huckleberry Finn* changed _____ name from Samuel Clemens to Mark Twain.

19. Each of the nuns lifted _____ hand to make the sign of the cross.

20. Someone hung _____ wet towel over the shower curtain.

USAGE

Pronoun-Antecedent Agreement B

| **8r.** | Use a singular pronoun to refer to two or more singular antecedents joined by *or* or *nor*. |

  EXAMPLE   Neither **Ramona nor Gloria** could find **her** library card.

| **8s.** | Use a plural pronoun to refer to two or more antecedents joined by *and*. |

  EXAMPLE   **Vincent and Jules** have learned all of **their** lines in the play.

EXERCISE A   On the line provided in each of the following sentences, write a pronoun that agrees with the antecedent or antecedents. Then, circle each antecedent.

Example 1. Every Sunday (Maggie) and (Roger) watched _____*their*_____ favorite television show.

1. When we're playing tennis, my brother and I never let the other players intimidate

  _____.

2. Either Jason or Raul will bring _____ tool kit to the bicycle race.

3. Brenda and Caitlin told us that _____ didn't plan to come to the party.

4. If either Brittany or Celine wants to be a successful writer, _____ will need to

  work hard.

5. Leora and Annette pooled _____ resources to buy a birthday present for Jim.

6. Please ask Glendon and Maria if _____ science fair project is ready yet.

7. Did Lauryn or Marian say if _____ was going to the mock trial?

8. Karen and I discussed _____ difference of opinion quite calmly.

9. Frank and Tina would like the class to help _____ set up their display.

10. Let Kathryn and Michael know in advance if _____ should bring a dish to the party.

EXERCISE B   Each of the following sentences contains an error in pronoun-antecedent agreement. Cross out the error, and write the correct pronoun above it. Then, circle each antecedent.

Example 1. Either (Denzel) or (Malcolm) will bring ~~their~~ *his* soccer ball to the game.

11. Julio and Spike have brought all of his CDs to the dance.

12. Neither Faith nor Deanna knew where their bicycle was.

13. Is Melissa or Martina sure they won't join us?

14. Let's ask Antonia and Belle if she read the article about comets.

15. Does Dutch or Pike have their notebook with him?

USAGE

Pronoun-Antecedent Agreement C

8t. Some indefinite pronouns are plural, some are singular, and some may be either.

(1) Use a singular pronoun to refer to *anybody, anyone, anything, each, either, everybody, everyone, everything, neither, nobody, nothing, no one, one, somebody, someone,* and *something*.

> **EXAMPLES**   **Each** of the boys likes **his** new uniform.
>
> Has **everybody** in the club paid **his or her** dues?

(2) The following indefinite pronouns are plural: *both, few, many,* and *several.*

> **EXAMPLE**   **Few** of the explorers became lost on **their** way out of the cave.

(3) The indefinite pronouns *all, any, more, most, none,* and *some* may be singular or plural, depending on their meaning in a sentence.

> **EXAMPLES**   **Most** of the forest has already been cut down, hasn't **it**? [*Most* refers to the singular noun *forest*.]
>
> **Most** of the trees have already been cut down, haven't **they**? [*Most* refers to the plural noun *trees*.]

EXERCISE   Each of the following sentences contains an error in pronoun-antecedent agreement. Draw a line through each incorrect pronoun, and write the correct form above it. Then, circle the antecedent.

Example   1. (Each) of the cats has ~~their~~ *its* own special hiding place.

1. Some of the CDs have lost its jewel cases.

2. Few of the women's soccer team enjoyed her stay in Helsinki.

3. Either of the brothers is willing to bring their baseball glove to the game.

4. Hasn't anybody announced their intentions yet?

5. Many of the reporters do his or her own research.

6. All of the rosebushes in the garden have thorns on it.

7. Everyone in the class is aware of their responsibility to bring a note from home.

8. Someone on the swimming team left their goggles by the side of the pool.

9. Several of the boys joined the military after he graduated from high school.

10. Some of the people in the audience got the joke, and it laughed heartily.

Pronoun-Antecedent Agreement D

8t.   Some indefinite pronouns are plural, some are singular, and some may be either.

(1) Use a singular pronoun to refer to *anybody, anyone, anything, each, either, everybody, everyone, everything, neither, nobody, nothing, no one, one, somebody, someone,* and *something.*

> **EXAMPLES**   Has **anyone** lost **his or her** keys?
>
> **Each** of the recipes calls for wheat as **its** main ingredient.

(2) The following indefinite pronouns are plural: *both, few, many,* and *several.*

> **EXAMPLE**   **Several** of the teachers ordered **their** textbooks early.

(3) The indefinite pronouns *all, any, more, most, none,* and *some* may be singular or plural, depending on their meaning in a sentence.

> **EXAMPLES**   **All** of the money retained **its** value. [*All* refers to the singular noun *money.*]
>
> **All** of the vases retained **their** value. [*All* refers to the plural noun *vases.*]

EXERCISE   On the line provided in each of the following sentences, write a pronoun that agrees with its antecedent. Then, circle the antecedent.

Example 1. (Several) of the houses lost _____*their*_____ roofs during the storm.

1. Each of my sisters has _____ own pogo stick.

2. None of the employees should reveal _____ password to anyone.

3. Everything the teacher said made sense the moment he said _____.

4. Both of the astronomical calendars have the same nebula on _____ covers.

5. Several of the police officers spent _____ holidays volunteering at the new community center.

6. If you have anything to say during the debate, please say _____ as succinctly as possible.

7. Neither of my grandmothers has ever revealed _____ secret for making jambalaya.

8. More of the palm trees have been planted this year because _____ look so striking along the beach.

9. One of the male interns put _____ clipboard down to pick up the baby.

10. Most of the radio program was written by Marta, but a few minutes of _____ were written by Tish.

USAGE

Pronoun-Antecedent Agreement E

8u. Either a singular or a plural pronoun may be used to refer to a collective noun, depending on the meaning of the sentence.

A collective noun is singular when it refers to the group as a unit and plural when it refers to the individual parts or members of the group.

SINGULAR   The **band** made **its** debut in November 1999.

PLURAL   The **band** happily signed autographs for **their** fans.

EXERCISE A   In each of the following sentences, circle the antecedent for the pronouns in parentheses. Then, underline the pronoun that agrees with the antecedent.

Example   1. After hearing all the evidence, the (jury) made (*its*, *their*) decision quickly.

1. The thundering herd left a wide swath of flattened grass in (*its, their*) wake.

2. As the team entered the lobby, the fans began to ask for (*its, their*) autographs.

3. After debating all of (*its, their*) options, the commission issued its report.

4. The readership of the newspaper were not shy about making (*its, their*) opinions known.

5. The jury could not agree among (*itself, themselves*) what to order for lunch.

6. During the intermission, the ensemble tuned (*its, their*) instruments.

7. The majority of the class took (*its, their*) work home last night.

8. The Fantasy Society voted *The Lord of the Rings* (*its, their*) choice for Book of the Century.

9. The cast of the play took (*its, their*) curtain calls one at a time.

10. The crowd voted with (*its, their*) feet and left the debate early.

EXERCISE B   On the line provided in each of the following sentences, write a pronoun that agrees with its antecedent. Then, circle the antecedent.

Example   1. The (class) agreed to hold _____*its*_____ annual party next month.

11. The troupe of actors looked good in _____ costumes.

12. The entire staff lined up in the parking lot to have _____ picture taken.

13. The committee cannot even agree among _____.

14. After a fierce battle, the platoon took _____ position at the top of the ridge.

15. After winning, the team posed for photographs with _____ ecstatic fans.

Pronoun-Antecedent Agreement F

USAGE

8v. An expression of an amount may take a singular or plural pronoun, depending on how the expression is used.

    SINGULAR I paid **twenty dollars** for these skates. I thought **it** was a reasonable price.
      PLURAL I have **twenty dollars,** but one of **them** has been torn in half.

8w. Some nouns that are plural in form take singular pronouns.

    SINGULAR I have good **news.** Would you like to hear **it**?
      PLURAL Where are the **scissors**? Oh, here **they** are.

EXERCISE A In each of the following sentences, circle the antecedent for the pronouns in parentheses. Then, underline the pronoun in parentheses that agrees with the antecedent.

Example 1. Jerrold enjoyed studying (genetics) because (*it*, *they*) combined biology and chemistry.

1. If I make fifty dollars from the carwash this weekend, I can use (*it*, *them*) to put a down payment on a bicycle.

2. After Luther oiled the shears, (*it*, *they*) were ready to use again.

3. Michiko poured the molasses and watched (*it*, *them*) cover the bottom of the pan.

4. Now that you've heard the news, do you think (*it*, *they*) will affect how you vote?

5. If you want to go to the Olympics, you have to train for (*it*, *them*).

6. Sue had three dollars in her wallet, but now one of (*it*, *them*) is missing.

7. Vera dropped the pliers in the grass and then spent an hour looking for (*it*, *them*).

8. Mathematics was more than an interest for Leora; (*it*, *they*) became a passion.

9. Roxanne decided not to wear her shorts because (*it*, *they*) had become threadbare.

10. He had only seventy-five cents; would (*it*, *they*) be enough to pay for the juice?

EXERCISE B Each of the following sentences contains an error in pronoun-antecedent agreement. Cross out each incorrectly used pronoun, and write the correct pronoun above it. Then, circle the antecedent.

Example 1. Please put the (scissors) back when you are finished with ~~it.~~ *them*

11. Francesca decided to take civics because she could fit them into her schedule.

12. Malik has lost his eyeglasses; he needs it for basketball.

13. Take the binoculars out of its case, please.

14. Did you hear the news? Could they be any worse?

15. Of all the pants you could have worn, that could be the worst.

USAGE

Pronoun-Antecedent Agreement G

| **8x.** | Use a singular pronoun to refer to the title of a creative work (such as a book, song, movie, or painting). |

EXAMPLE   Have you read **"The Bells"** by E. A. Poe? **It** is one of my favorite poems to read aloud.

| **8y.** | Use a singular pronoun to refer to the name of a country, city, or organization. |

EXAMPLE   **Calloway Motors** will have **its** grand opening on Saturday.

EXERCISE   Most of the following sentences contain an error in pronoun-antecedent agreement. Draw a line through each incorrectly used pronoun, and write the correct pronoun above it. If a sentence is already correct, write *C* next to the sentence number.

Example   1. Hartwig Interiors is redesigning ~~their~~ *its* own showroom.

1. Discount Appliances used to be located on Burnet Avenue; they stood where a beautiful orchard used to grow.

2. *The Cowboys* is one of my dad's favorite movies, and he has seen it several times.

3. After Tranh was assigned to read *Great Expectations*, the Charles Dickens masterpiece, he managed to finish them over the weekend.

4. The Netherlands is also known as Holland, and its citizens are known as the Dutch.

5. The Sons of the Desert, devoted to the comic films of Laurel and Hardy, was founded in 1964, and my grandfather has been a member of them since 1967.

6. After I read "Flowers for Algernon," I found out that Hollywood has adapted them for the movies twice.

7. As you read T. S. Eliot's "The Hollow Men," consider the effect of them on your imagination.

8. Jacques Offenbach never completed his opera *The Tales of Hoffmann;* Ernest Guiraud finished them after Offenbach's death.

9. When you come to the Narrows, where so many ships have gone down, go around them.

10. Several of my uncles are members of the Knights of Columbus; my father has also been a member of it.

USAGE

Review A: **Subject-Verb Agreement**

EXERCISE A Circle the subject in each of the following sentences. If the underlined verb does not agree with the subject, cross out the verb and write the correct verb above it. If the sentence is already correct, write *C* before the sentence number.

Example 1. The (sailors) on the ship has *[have]* all been granted shore leave.

1. My shoes and my shirt lies at the end of the bed.

2. Either Dr. Chen or Dr. Montoya plan to perform the operation.

3. Don't someone who has read the books have something to say?

4. One by one, the flock of birds have descended into the trees.

5. Afternoons are the best time for a nap.

6. The officers of the Forest Service doesn't approve of campfires during a drought.

7. Gymnastics or electronics is the only class with spaces available.

8. There are many students who use study hall to finish their homework.

9. Most of the horses grazes in the upper pasture during the summertime.

10. Both of the flute players hopes to audition for the first chair in the orchestra.

EXERCISE B Circle the subject in each of the following sentences. Then, underline the form of the verb or contraction in parentheses that agrees with the subject.

Example 1. (Everyone) in the senior class *(is, are)* looking forward to the field trip.

11. Neither Jay nor Sonya *(is, are)* going to the folk festival this year.

12. Each of the children *(has, have)* gone to bed by now.

13. Anyone who listens to the singer's music *(has, have)* to get up and dance.

14. Our cat Conrad and our dog Padgett *(like, likes)* to sleep on the bed.

15. Katherine told me that the League of Women Voters *(is, are)* sponsoring a debate between the two candidates this Wednesday.

16. All of my aunts and uncles *(remember, remembers)* when my grandmother's birthday is.

17. *(Doesn't, Don't)* most people in our town recycle their bottles and cans?

18. Either of the girls *(is, are)* happy to help you rake your lawn.

19. When *(is, are)* the football team scheduled to play Reed City?

20. Enrique told me that he *(don't, doesn't)* care for okra.

Review B: **Pronoun-Antecedent Agreement**

USAGE

EXERCISE A Circle the antecedent for the underlined pronoun in each of the following sentences. If the underlined pronoun does not agree with the antecedent, cross out the pronoun and write the correct pronoun over it.

Example 1. (All) of the young men have left ~~his~~ *their* childhoods behind.

1. Many of the science fair contestants have brought <u>his or her</u> own equipment.

2. One of the girls has gotten mud all over <u>their</u> shoes.

3. Every member of the class brought <u>their</u> own pencil to the test on Friday.

4. Either Sergio or Michael will need to bring <u>their</u> boombox to the party.

5. No one in the family remembered to bring <u>their</u> key to the cabin by the lake.

6. Aren't all of your uncles taking a fishing pole with <u>him</u> on vacation?

7. A few of the students told <u>his or her</u> parents about the pop quiz on Friday.

8. Each of the kittens cried for <u>their</u> mother.

9. One of the young women was certain that the award for Best Class Song was going to <u>them</u>.

10. Some of the books showed Princess Diana on <u>its</u> covers.

EXERCISE B In each of the following sentences, circle the antecedent for the pronouns in parentheses. Then, underline the pronoun in parentheses that agrees with the antecedent.

Example 1. (Each) of the children handed the teacher (*his or her*, *their*) answer sheet.

11. *The Barretts of Wimpole Street* is my mother's favorite film; she has seen (*it*, *them*) several times.

12. The cast of the play decided to have a party after (*its*, *their*) last performance.

13. One of the ships was able to unload most of (*its*, *their*) cargo before the hurricane struck.

14. The Center for South and Southeast Asian Studies will publish Professor Becker's book as part of (*its*, *their*) publication series.

15. Having mastered electronics, Judith is very good at explaining (*it*, *them*) to the class.

16. Have you ever wondered why birds resting on a branch or a telephone wire tuck (*its*, *their*) heads under their wings during a storm?

17. The council didn't get to (*its*, *their*) final vote until nine o'clock that night.

18. Someone from the boys' basketball team left (*his*, *their*) shoes on the bench.

19. Those young women will carry (*her*, *their*) own luggage onto the plane.

20. Neither of the girls can tell me where (*her*, *their*) sleeping bag is.

Review C: Agreement

EXERCISE A Most of the following sentences contain an error in subject-verb agreement. Cross out the incorrect form of the verb, and write the correct verb form above it. If a sentence is already correct, write *C* next to the sentence number.

Example 1. Grand Rapids, Michigan, ~~are~~ *is* a center of furniture manufacturing.

1. The sound of all these birds echo all around the courtyard.

2. Economics seem like a difficult subject to some people.

3. Fifteen feet of rope were necessary to secure the boat to the dock.

4. Moving with one mind, the crowd surge toward the stage.

5. Don't he know which way he's going?

6. Where is the books that I left on the kitchen counter?

7. Either Kadonna or her brother is responsible for sending out the invitations for the reunion.

8. Everybody who contributed to the charities are welcome at the annual dinner.

9. About ten percent of the furniture are sitting in a warehouse.

10. Monday afternoons are the best time to make an appointment with Dr. Secada.

EXERCISE B Most of the following sentences contain an error in pronoun-antecedent agreement. Cross out the incorrect pronoun, and write the correct pronoun form above it. If a sentence is already correct, write *C* next to the sentence number.

Example 1. The Netherlands is in Europe; adjacent to ~~them~~ *it* are Belgium and Germany.

11. Mikki has saved fifty dollars; she plans to use them to buy a present.

12. As soon as we heard the news from France, we passed them along to our friends at home.

13. After seeing the film *Darby O'Gill and the Little People,* Declan recommended them to his brother.

14. Candace or Melanie will bring their soccer ball to the championship match.

15. The gymnastics team discussed their fears about going to the meet.

16. No one who has ever seen Angkor Wat will ever forget their first impression of it.

17. We heard that some of the boys' ski team are bringing his own skis.

18. Carl or David will bring his football to the game.

19. After you're done with the binoculars, please put it back in the case.

20. The jury debated the verdict among itself.

USAGE

Review D: Agreement

EXERCISE Each of the following sentences contains an error in pronoun-antecedent agreement or subject-verb agreement. Draw a line through each incorrect verb or pronoun, and write the correct verb form or pronoun form above it.

Examples 1. Neither Los Angeles nor San Francisco ~~are~~ *is* the capital of California.

2. Either Dad or Uncle Tom will pick us up in ~~their~~ *his* car.

1. Nicoletta or Jacqueline will present their book report to the class tomorrow.

2. Everybody in our classes were informed in advance about the change in schedule.

3. Some of the best paintings are next-door; let's look at it first.

4. Here is the books you ordered online, Ms. Shimeda.

5. Each of the teachers spoke to their own class.

6. Some of the groceries has already been placed in the pantry.

7. Either the players or the coach call timeout.

8. A theater and a rehearsal room was added to the high school last year.

9. Everyone who completed their project on time was rewarded with a bright, shiny apple.

10. Nobody in the caravan were paying attention when the camel went astray.

11. The Cho family will take their vacation this year in Thailand.

12. When the shears were broken, Eric found time to repair it.

13. Doesn't the dog and cat get along?

14. Macaroni and cheese are my favorite dish.

15. If you spill all of the cereal, make sure to clean them up.

16. Neither Uncle Lyle nor Uncle Tector remembered where their boots were.

17. The presence of thousands of peacekeeping troops assure the villagers of their safety.

18. When presented with a legal summons, a citizen has an obligation to respond to them.

19. We will listen to half of *Nights in the Garden of Spain* this morning, and we will hear the rest of them this afternoon.

20. Neither the students nor the players is likely to forget the homecoming game.

for **CHAPTER 8: AGREEMENT**   *pages 155–79*

Proofreading Application: Speech

Good writers are generally good proofreaders. Readers tend to admire and trust writing that is error-free. Make sure that you correct all errors in grammar, usage, spelling, and punctuation in your writing. Your readers will have more confidence in your words if you have done your best to proofread carefully.

Even though a speech is meant to be heard, not seen, a speaker who violates the rules of agreement covered in this chapter still runs the risk of confusing listeners. Agreement errors can potentially cloud the meaning of your ideas and diminish your credibility as a speaker. Therefore, before you give a speech or an oral report, you should make sure that the words you will deliver are free of agreement errors. After all, as a speaker, you want listeners to focus on your words, not on your mistakes.

PROOFREADING ACTIVITY

Find and correct the agreement errors in the following speech. Use proofreading symbols to make your corrections.

Example *Over the past month, the whole orchestra* ~~have~~ *has been practicing for its annual concert.*

Mr. Frost, our conductor, and the orchestra welcomes you to our first annual concert and chorus. Each of the members of our orchestra has spent many hours of their own free time practicing for this event. Most of the selections tonight was written or arranged by American composers. We are proud to say that several of our own students have contributed his or her own compositions to the evening's entertainment. A few of our selections includes choral accompaniment. Our chorus are directed by Mrs. Theresa Fernandez. Either Mrs. Fernandez or Mr. Frost will be introducing their selections as the evening continues. "The Stars and Stripes Forever" are our first piece.

Anyone wishing to make a donation to the music department may give their contribution to the students at the table in the front hall. All of us at King Middle School invites you to sit back and enjoy the show.

Literary Model: Short Story

> "Sam," says Bill, "I suppose you'll think I'm a renegade, but I couldn't help it. . . . The boy is gone. I sent him home. All is off. There was martyrs in old times," goes on Bill, "that suffered death rather than give up the particular graft they enjoyed. None of 'em ever was subjugated to such supernatural tortures as I have been. . . ."
>
> "What's the trouble, Bill?" I asks him.
>
> "I was rode," says Bill, "the ninety miles to the stockade, not barring an inch. Then, when the settlers was rescued, I was given oats. . . . I tell you, Sam, a human can only stand so much. I takes him by the neck of his clothes and drags him down the mountain. On the way he kicks my legs black and blue from the knees down. . . ."
>
> —from "The Ransom of Red Chief" by O. Henry

EXERCISE A   In the excerpt above, underline each sentence that contains an error in subject-verb agreement. Then, on the lines provided, write these sentences, circling each subject and each verb that do not agree in number.

_____

_____

_____

_____

_____

_____

EXERCISE B   Describe the characters in this excerpt. Why do you think O. Henry has his characters speak in such a manner?

_____

_____

_____

_____

_____

_____

_____

Literary Model (continued)

EXERCISE C   Write a dialogue between two characters: the first, a person who uses standard English grammar; the second, a person who does not. Have the second character use verbs that do not agree with their subjects. Underline each verb that does not agree with its subject.

_____

_____

_____

_____

_____

_____

_____

_____

_____

_____

_____

_____

_____

_____

EXERCISE D

1. How does the second character's use of verbs that do not agree with their subjects help to characterize him or her?

_____

_____

_____

2. In what ways was writing your dialogue challenging?

_____

_____

_____

_____

for **CHAPTER 8: AGREEMENT**   pages 158–59

Writing Application: Directions

Sometimes, phrases and clauses that come between a subject and its verb can trick writers into agreement problems. One quick way to check for correct agreement is to block out the intervening phrase or clause with your thumb and read the sentence aloud. Another way is to bracket the intervening phrase or clause and read the subject and its verb together. In most cases, by focusing on the subject and its verb in a sentence, you will be able to decide whether the sentence contains an agreement error.

AGREEMENT PROBLEM   The labels on the suitcase has fallen off.

CORRECT AGREEMENT   The labels [on the suitcase] ~~has~~ *have* fallen off.

WRITING ACTIVITY

The elementary school you attended needs help with a nature scavenger hunt. You will write directions for kids to use as they collect various natural items to bring back to their science classes. Write clues that will help kids find six items, using prepositional phrases to tell kids where to look. For instance, you might say, "These things on the oak tree turn into leaves." Be sure that the subject of the sentence agrees with its verb.

PREWRITING   First, choose six items that kids can find easily and that will prove interesting in the science classroom. Obviously, you will not ask the kids to find anything that might hurt them—no stinging insects or thorny briars! Think of things that kids can locate while walking around school grounds with their teachers.

WRITING   Next, for each item, devise clues that require kids to puzzle out what and where the items are. Your first goal is clarity: Will the clues guide kids to the items, challenging them to think hard but not frustrating them? Use prepositional phrases to point out the items' locations. Second, consider diction, or word choice. Use simple words and sentences that school children will understand.

REVISING   Directions, whether straightforward or purposefully puzzling, should be tested for accuracy. Follow your own directions to be sure that they work. Finally, consider your tone. The scavenger hunt should be a fun outdoor activity, and the kids will be excited to be out of their classrooms for a while. Match their excitement with your word choice and energetic tone.

PUBLISHING   Check your directions for errors in grammar, usage, spelling, and punctuation. Also, be sure to look for errors in subject-verb agreement. Do not let mistakes throw the kids off track as they hunt! Then, meet with the kids' teachers and make any final adjustments needed.

EXTENDING YOUR WRITING

If you enjoyed this exercise, you could develop it into a longer writing project. You may have heard the idea that people truly know a subject when they can teach it. You might develop a guided discussion and work sheets for the kids to use when they return to the classroom with their items. Then, lead them through a period of study, using your written materials.

Choices: Investigating Verbs

Here's your chance to step out of the grammar book and into the real world. You may not realize it, but examples of usage appear in your life every day. The following activities challenge you to find a connection between verbs and the world around you. Do the activity below that suits your personality best, and then share your discoveries with your class. Have fun!

GAME

Every Word Counts

What is the longest verb phrase (no compound verbs!) that you can think of? Use as many modals as you can. Challenge your classmates to a duel. To the victor goes the snack!

CONTEST

Come to Order

Hold a contest. Begin by making a list of all the tenses. Then, write a sentence for each tense. Divide the class into groups of three or four. Make one copy of your sentences for each group. Pass out the sentences, and tell everybody to cut the sentences out so that they'll be on strips of paper. On your signal, each group should place the sentences in order from past to future. The first group to do so correctly wins.

TECHNOLOGY

Magnifying Glass

Choose twenty of the peskiest verbs in the chapter. Type them into a word processor. Then, enlarge the size of the letters that change for each form. For instance, for the past participle of the word *swim*, you would see the letters *s*, *w*, and *m* in small letters and the letter *u* in a large letter. You may wish also to boldface the "magnified" letters. Pass out copies of your list to your classmates.

COMPUTER ART

Sit Down, You're Rockin' the Boat!

Use a public domain illustration library to create small posters illustrating the proper use of *sit/set*. If you want to go really wild, you could design a deck of playing cards, with each card illustrating a situation in which one form of these verbs is used correctly. Naturally, you'll need to include the sentence that each picture illustrates.

WRITING

One by One

Whether you know it or not, verb tenses are part of your life. Make a list of all the tenses, including emphatic tense. For each tense, write one sentence about you and your life. Underline each verb or verb phrase.

WRITING

Tense Situations

Why do you think it is so important to maintain consistency of verb tenses when writing about past events? Try this activity. Write a description of an event that happened to you or to someone you know, but don't pay close attention to the verb tenses. In fact, mix them up a bit. Next, rewrite your description, this time focusing on consistent verb tenses throughout. Now, read your first version aloud to a classmate. Have him or her write down the sequence of events as he or she believes they happened. Finally, read your second version to your classmate and have him or her do the same thing. Is there a difference in your classmate's perception of which event happened before or after another?

ANALYZING

The "Voice" of Reason

Your textbook offers a reliable explanation of how sentences containing active-voice verbs are transformed into sentences containing passive-voice verbs, but there may be more to it than that. Is it always the case that only the object of an active-voice verb can become the subject of a passive-voice verb, or can something else, such as the object of a preposition, become the subject? For example, can't you say "The house was broken into"? Think about these questions, and come up with at least fifteen sentences that illustrate different kinds of passive constructions.

USAGE

The Principal Parts of Verbs

9a.   The four principal parts of a verb are the ***base form,*** the ***present participle,*** the ***past,*** and the ***past participle.***

BASE FORM	PRESENT PARTICIPLE	PAST	PAST PARTICIPLE
arrive	[is] arriving	arrived	[have] arrived
talk	[is] talking	talked	[have] talked
swim	[is] swimming	swam	[have] swum

EXERCISE In each of the following sentences, identify the form of the underlined verb by writing above it *B* for *base form*, *PresP* for *present participle*, *P* for *past*, or *PastP* for *past participle*.

                                  PresP
Example 1. The dogs are <u>rolling</u> in the grass.

1. Let's <u>sing</u> another song.

2. He has <u>heard</u> about the failed experiment.

3. Indira <u>left</u> for Africa late Sunday afternoon.

4. The ducks have been <u>paddling</u> around on the surface of the lake.

5. I <u>understood</u> the speech, but I didn't agree with it.

6. Jonathan had <u>been</u> to England once before.

7. In the morning, the eagle's eggs <u>hatched</u>.

8. Will you help Gina <u>clean</u> the kitchen, please?

9. The helicopters have <u>landed</u> next to the soccer field.

10. To save money, I am <u>trying</u> to bring my lunch to school more often.

11. Is it true that she made them <u>leave</u> early?

12. The sun has <u>set</u> already, hasn't it?

13. Suddenly, the snake <u>slithered</u> quietly away.

14. The Ferris wheel is slowly <u>coming</u> to a halt.

15. Astonished by the crowds, we <u>stood</u> in a doorway and waited.

16. Cynthia, have you ever <u>seen</u> a morning glory open?

17. The goalie leaped into the air and <u>grabbed</u> the ball.

18. I hope the guards let us <u>get</u> close enough to see the queen.

19. After they had <u>swept</u>, they carried out the recycling.

20. I thought you were <u>singing</u> in tonight's performance, Mikki.

Regular Verbs

9b. A *regular verb* forms its past and past participle by adding –d or –ed to the base form.

  EXAMPLE   We recently **adopted** a Chihuahua puppy.

EXERCISE On the blank in each of the following sentences, write the correct past or past participle form of the verb given in parentheses.

Example 1. (collect) How many baseball cards have you _____ *collected* _____?

1. (talk) When he first _____ to me, I thought he was from Georgia.

2. (suppose) They were _____ to help put up the decorations.

3. (land) The spaceship _____ on the cold surface of the planet.

4. (name) Kelly has a dog that she _____ Soda.

5. (enjoy) Carla has _____ the classes she is taking.

6. (consider) I _____ him my best friend.

7. (close) Have you _____ the front door?

8. (open) The archaeologists carefully _____ the door to the tomb.

9. (please) The jester _____ the court with his antics.

10. (stay) Have you _____ with her before, Susan?

11. (predict) On the news last night, the forecaster _____ snow.

12. (watch) The mother cat has _____ over her kittens carefully.

13. (roar) The lion _____ , and the tiger growled.

14. (cheer) Your funny story _____ her up.

15. (wait) The patients have all _____ here for a while now.

16. (gain) What, after all, have they _____ by being spiteful?

17. (promise) If she has _____ , I know she will keep her word.

18. (walk) The last people to finish the 10K race waved to me as they _____ across the finish line.

19. (return) I _____ to my seat and buckled my seat belt.

20. (expect) The dogs had _____ to go for a walk.

USAGE

Irregular Verbs A

9c. | An *irregular verb* forms its past and past participle in some other way than by adding *–d* or *–ed* to the base form.

An irregular verb forms its past and past participle in one of these ways: changing consonants, changing vowels, changing consonants and vowels, or making no change at all.

EXAMPLES   The ship **sank** in 1912.

Have you **read** *The Pearl* by John Steinbeck?

EXERCISE   In each of the following sentences, underline the correct verb form in parentheses.

Example 1. Have you (*saw, seen*) any of the movies showing now?

1. The strong wind has (*blew, blown*) the papers about the room.

2. In the morning, the delivery van (*come, came*) with our new washing machine.

3. The mosquito (*bited, bit*) my leg twice.

4. Something the puppy had (*ate, eaten*) made it feel unwell.

5. I have (*become, became*) sleepy.

6. Have you ever (*broken, broke*) any bones?

7. We (*brought, bringed*) some pecans from our yard, Grandma.

8. When was that project (*began, begun*)?

9. I think the inner tube in my front tire (*bursted, burst*) when I went over the curb.

10. What have you (*buyed, bought*), Tony?

11. Have you (*cut, cutted*) any daisies to put on the dinner table?

12. The boy (*chose, choosed*) the straighter path.

13. What kind of table have you two (*built, build*)?

14. I think that lunch (*costed, cost*) more than Laura thought it would.

15. Daniel or Frank (*caught, catched*) a baseball that was batted into the bleachers.

16. Julie, has something (*fallen, fell*) over in there?

17. Roseanne had (*drawn, drew*) a picture of a mockingbird.

18. We just (*drove, drived*) to Cassville, Missouri.

19. Have you (*drank, drunk*) all the milk?

20. Janette (*did, done*) more than anyone else to make sure they succeeded.

Irregular Verbs B

9c. | An *irregular verb* forms its past and past participle in some other way than by adding *–d* or *–ed* to the base form.

An irregular verb forms its past and past participle in one of these ways: changing consonants, changing vowels, changing consonants and vowels, or making no change at all.

EXAMPLES   For a snack I **ate** some grapes.

Has he **fed** the horses?

EXERCISE In each of the following sentences, underline the correct verb form in parentheses.

Example 1. Have you two (_lent_, lended) Tom your notes?

1. Have the sisters (*forgave, forgiven*) each other?

2. The two sides had (*fought, foughten*) about the terms of the treaty.

3. How many home runs have you (*hitted, hit*) this season?

4. How many times has that jet (*flew, flown*) across the Atlantic?

5. I think that Jorge (*feeled, felt*) bad about the argument.

6. The water in the ice trays has not (*frozen, froze*) yet.

7. Peter had (*went, gone*) to church before I arrived.

8. Grandma had (*gave, given*) Aunt Jean a new vase.

9. After we had dismounted, we (*lead, led*) the horses to the stream.

10. What kinds of native plants (*grown, grew*) there?

11. Have you (*hurted, hurt*) yourself, Amelia?

12. We both (*heared, heard*) the same rumor.

13. The cat (*hid, hidden*) under Michelle's bed and would not come out.

14. The anthropologist (*found, finded*) several cave dwellings in that area.

15. The mailbox (*held, holded*) seven catalogs and three bills.

16. I think that the two of them (*had, haved*) a better time than they thought they would.

17. I have always (*keeped, kept*) secrets well.

18. William had long (*knowed, known*) Rabbi Goldstein.

19. They (*laid, lay*) the quilts on the bed.

20. The two soldiers (*got, gotten*) ready for the advance.

USAGE

Irregular Verbs C

9c. An *irregular verb* forms its past and past participle in some other way than by adding –d or –ed to the base form.

An irregular verb forms its past and past participle in one of these ways: changing consonants, changing vowels, changing consonants and vowels, or making no change at all.

EXAMPLES When **was** the Great Wall of China **built**?

Each student **has written** an essay about an endangered species.

EXERCISE On the blank in each of the following sentences, write the correct past or past participle form of the verb given in parentheses.

Example 1. (*let*) Yesterday, the O'Daniels _____ *let* _____ their cats go outside.

1. (*shake*) We had _____ the rugs out.

2. (*light*) The hostess _____ the candles.

3. (*lose*) The boys have _____ no time getting comfortable.

4. (*ride*) The jockey _____ the thoroughbred across the finish line.

5. (*meet*) The plan has _____ with strong opposition.

6. (*pay*) I _____ a little more to get tools of better quality.

7. (*put*) Yesterday, Aunt Elma _____ a blooming rose in a vase on the table.

8. (*make*) Has he ever _____ grits before?

9. (*read*) After you have _____ the chapter, answer the review questions.

10. (*ring*) Have you _____ the bell?

11. (*rise*) They _____ at dawn to begin harvesting the fruit.

12. (*sell*) Has he _____ any of the raffle tickets?

13. (*say*) Uncle Juan _____ that Charley would be late.

14. (*run*) Have you ever _____ for a position on the student council?

15. (*seek*) The hawk _____ its prey.

16. (*see*) You both _____ what happened, didn't you?

17. (*send*) She has _____ the package to Baton Rouge.

18. (*set*) Aunt Shirley _____ the grandfather clock.

19. (*lie*) I had just _____ down to rest when the doorbell rang.

20. (*sing*) All of the eighth graders _____ the national anthem.

USAGE

Irregular Verbs D

9c. | An *irregular verb* forms its past and past participle in some other way than by adding *–d* or *–ed* to the base form.

An irregular verb forms its past and past participle in one of these ways: changing consonants, changing vowels, changing consonants and vowels, or making no change at all.

EXAMPLES   Who **drew** this sketch of the White House?

Marcia **had hurt** her right arm during softball practice.

EXERCISE   On the blank in each of the following sentences, write the correct past or past participle form of the verb given in parentheses.

Example 1. (swing)   The engine _____*swung*_____ from a block and tackle.

1. (sink)   In a few short hours, the boat had _____.

2. (sit)   Had they already _____ down?

3. (speak)   I believe the guests have _____ to the staff about the mishap.

4. (spend)   Has he ever _____ a week there before?

5. (spin)   We _____ the wheels in the loose sand.

6. (spread) Our cousins _____ the picnic supplies out on the blanket.

7. (stand)   Denny _____ on his head and sang a silly song.

8. (steal)   The thief had _____ very little of value.

9. (swim)   Have you _____ laps here before?

10. (swing)   We had _____ across the gully on a sturdy rope.

11. (take)   You two have _____ the best seats.

12. (teach)   Ms. Lawson _____ Latin for seventeen years.

13. (tear)   The paper _____ easily.

14. (tell)   The clock _____ time inaccurately.

15. (think)   I _____ I would go early.

16. (throw)   Has he _____ the first pitch?

17. (wear)   It _____ out in less than a year.

18. (win)   My mother _____ the door prize.

19. (sink)   The lead weights _____ to the bottom.

20. (sit)   Seventeen tigers _____ and licked their chops.

Language and Sentence Skills Practice

185

Irregular Verbs E

USAGE

| **9c.** | An ***irregular verb*** forms its past and past participle in some other way than by adding –*d* or –*ed* to the base form. |

An irregular verb forms its past and past participle in one of these ways: changing consonants, changing vowels, changing consonants and vowels, or making no change at all.

    EXAMPLES   We **sent** the package to you yesterday.

                 Bradley **had bought** the bicycle at a rummage sale.

EXERCISE On the blank in each of the following sentences, write the correct past or past participle form of the verb given in parentheses.

Example 1. (*become*)   What had _____*become*_____ of the treasure map?

1. (*begin*)   Sara had _____ saving for college when she was very young.

2. (*burst*)   The balloon _____ when it hit the ceiling.

3. (*choose*)   I _____ a simple black sweater.

4. (*cost*)   How much time has that mistake _____ us?

5. (*drink*)   We had _____ a lot of water , but we were still thirsty.

6. (*eat*)   The frogs _____ the flies that were buzzing around the pond.

7. (*give*)   Has Uncle Sal _____ you a copy of the family tree?

8. (*go*)   She has _____ to the launchpad.

9. (*know*)   What had you _____ about jellyfish before you took biology?

10. (*lie*)   The German shepherds _____ down to nap in the sun.

11. (*lead*)   Have you _____ them across the desert?

12. (*lay*)   The squirrel_____ a leaf where it had buried the pecan.

13. (*lend*)   I have _____ him money for the pay phone.

14. (*ring*)   The cathedral bells _____ out in the morning.

15. (*run*)   They had _____ a great distance.

16. (*see*)   Two of the deer _____ a wolf at the edge of the clearing.

17. (*swing*)   The monkeys _____ from limb to limb.

18. (*wear*)   The Mullaney children always _____ their seat belts.

19. (*be*)   Last week, Donna and Tressa _____ sure they would be able to run in the 10K race.

20. (*rise*)   The temperature had _____ since morning.

USAGE

Tense

9d. The *tense* of a verb indicates the time of the action or state of being expressed by the verb.

PRESENT TENSE	I give	**PRESENT PERFECT TENSE**	I have given
PAST TENSE	I gave	**PAST PERFECT TENSE**	I had given
FUTURE TENSE	I will (shall) give	**FUTURE PERFECT TENSE**	I will (shall) have given

The *progressive form* of each tense expresses continuing action or state of being. It consists of a form of the verb *be* plus the present participle of a verb.

EXAMPLE   The candidates **will be giving** their speeches Friday. [future progressive]

EXERCISE   Underline the verb in each of the following sentences. Then, above the verb, identify its tense. Also, indicate if the verb is in the progressive form.

Example 1. I <u>am going</u> to the market. *present progressive*

1. The Reigers have moved to San Antonio, Texas.

2. I run three miles every day after school.

3. Today, we will be meeting the President of the United States.

4. We climbed Mount Monadnock.

5. As of next Thursday, you will have been a United States citizen for one year.

6. I have written to my congresswoman about the homeless people in our town.

7. Beatrice had spent the summer with her favorite cousin.

8. Sara Luisa is now living in Lima, Peru.

9. By next Friday, we shall have finished the construction of the set for the new play.

10. By then, the orchestra had already learned the new piece of music.

11. Has the waiter brought your water yet?

12. Nicci will be attending music camp this summer.

13. The author had published her first book at the age of twenty-four.

14. Next year, the wax museum will have been open for two hundred years.

15. I enjoy fresh orange juice every morning.

16. Will the composer be present for the concert?

17. The pilot flew to fifteen cities in three days.

18. We had sent the package by airmail.

19. I have never heard of that film.

20. By the end of the month, I will have been here six months.

Consistency of Tense

9e. Do not change needlessly from one tense to another.

When describing events that occur at the same time, use verbs in the same tense. When describing events that occur at different times, use different tenses to show clearly the order of events.

EXAMPLES   Everyone in the audience **stood** and **applauded.** [Both verbs are past tense because both actions occurred at the same time in the past.]

The spelunkers **thought** that they **had found** a valuable treasure. [Because the action of finding was completed in the past before the action of thinking was completed, *had found* is past perfect tense, and *thought* is past tense.]

EXERCISE   Read the following passage. Decide whether it should be written in the present or the past tense. Above each underlined verb, either rewrite the verb to correct any unnecessary changes in tense or write *C* if the verb tense is already correct.

Examples I **[1]** went to New Orleans and **[2]** see the French Quarter. *or*

I **[1]** went to New Orleans and **[2]** see the French Quarter.

  I **[1]** traveled all the way from Indiana to visit my cousins in New Orleans. I **[2]** went by airplane. The trip **[3]** is long and a little tiring. My cousins, Larry and Dana, **[4]** were very happy to see me and **[5]** hug me when I **[6]** see them at the airport gate. Then we all **[7]** went back to their house on Algiers Point. After resting, we **[8]** took the Algiers ferry to the east bank of the Mississippi River. From there, we **[9]** walk a short distance to the French Quarter. We **[10]** visited Jackson Square, which is in front of St. Louis Cathedral. Then we **[11]** ate gumbo and po' boy sandwiches while we **[12]** sit on a bench on the Moon Walk, a boardwalk overlooking the Mississippi River. The next day, we **[13]** visited the Aquarium of the Americas, **[14]** take a streetcar uptown, and **[15]** went to the zoo in Audubon Park. There, we **[16]** saw white alligators, nutria, and other animals that live in the swamps of southern Louisiana. We **[17]** spend the last day of my visit visiting with other members of my family. My aunt Nell **[18]** made red beans and rice for everybody, and we **[19]** sat around telling stories until we **[20]** are sleepy.

NAME _____ CLASS _____ DATE _____

for **CHAPTER 9: USING VERBS CORRECTLY**   pages 200–201

Active and Passive Voice

9f. A verb in the ***active voice*** expresses an action done by its subject. A verb in the ***passive voice*** expresses action done to its subject.

EXAMPLES   I. M. Pei **designed** this building. [The subject, *I. M. Pei*, performs the action.]
This building **was designed** by I. M. Pei. [The subject, *building*, receives the action.]

EXERCISE On the line provided, write *AV* if the underlined verb in the sentence is in the active voice. Write *PV* if it is in the passive voice.

Example __PV__ **1.** Our cats, Spooky and Shine, <u>were fed</u> by our neighbor John.

_____ **1.** We <u>adopted</u> Spooky last year.

_____ **2.** As kittens, Spooky and several other cats <u>were dumped</u> nearby.

_____ **3.** Their owner <u>did</u> not <u>want</u> them.

_____ **4.** The owner <u>should</u> not <u>have left</u> them to fend for themselves.

_____ **5.** They mostly stayed hungry until we <u>found</u> them.

_____ **6.** They were sick and skinny, and they <u>were frightened</u> by just about anything.

_____ **7.** My mother and I <u>spent</u> many days making friends with them.

_____ **8.** We <u>brought</u> them food and talked to them quietly while they ate.

_____ **9.** We <u>had been warned</u> that they might be too skittish to come near us.

_____ **10.** However, they acted as if they <u>knew</u> we were there to help.

_____ **11.** Quite a lot of food <u>was eaten</u> by them.

_____ **12.** Two of the kittens, calico cats, <u>had</u> black, tan, and white patches.

_____ **13.** The other two <u>were covered</u> by thick black coats.

_____ **14.** We <u>named</u> one of the black ones Spooky because she ran away at the slightest movement or noise.

_____ **15.** It was a long time before we <u>were allowed</u> to pet her.

_____ **16.** They were all <u>taken</u> to a veterinarian, who gave them shots.

_____ **17.** Spooky <u>was spayed</u> as soon as she was old enough.

_____ **18.** Our friend Eileen <u>helped</u> us find homes for the other three.

_____ **19.** They were all <u>neutered</u> before they were a year old.

_____ **20.** By spaying and neutering the cats, we <u>are helping</u> to reduce the problem of unwanted pets.

Language and Sentence Skills Practice   **189**

USAGE

Sit and Set

The verb *sit* means "to rest in an upright, seated position" or "to be in a place." *Sit* seldom takes an object. The verb *set* means "to put (something) in a place." *Set* usually takes an object.

EXAMPLES   Angelo **sat** between Dominic and me. [past tense of *sit*]

Karen **set** a vase of flowers on the piano. [past tense of *set*]

EXERCISE   Write the correct form of *sit* or *set* on the line provided.

Example 1. We had ___*sat*___ down to rest just before we heard the siren go off.

1. _____ that bowl of noodles over there, please.

2. Will you three _____ down for a minute or two?

3. Yesterday morning, I _____ the papers on that ledge.

4. Off and on last week, the cardinal _____ on the bird feeder and sang.

5. Are you _____ the tomatoes on the windowsill to ripen?

6. Is Joe _____ next to the radiator, Wanda?

7. The two old benches had _____ on the front porch for about twenty years.

8. Have you _____ the Easter eggs in the dye bath?

9. We usually _____ here to wait for the election results.

10. _____ your piggy bank in a place where you'll remember to drop coins into it.

11. The newspaper _____ on the table all afternoon last Sunday.

12. Has the student _____ down her pencil yet?

13. Is the pencil _____ on the desk?

14. How long has the dog been _____ there?

15. They both _____ down on the stage and took off their shoes.

16. I grabbed the book and _____ it next to my backpack.

17. The bicycle pump had _____ in the garage for years without anyone using it.

18. He has _____ the signal flare where we can see it.

19. Nigel was _____ the dishes in the cabinet when you startled him.

20. Have Sarah and Laney _____ on the new sofa?

Lie and *Lay*

The verb *lie* means "to rest," "to recline," or "to be in a place." *Lie* does not take an object. The verb *lay* means "to put (something) in a place." *Lay* usually takes an object.

EXAMPLES   Dad **lay** down on the sofa and took a short nap. [past tense of *lie*]

He **laid** his eyeglasses beside his book. [past tense of *lay*]

EXERCISE   Write the correct form of *lie* or *lay* on the line provided.

Example 1. They had ___*lain*___ down to sleep an hour earlier.

1. _____ that quilt in the cedar chest.

2. Is it _____ there now?

3. She _____ the ring on top of the dresser.

4. The emerald ring _____ at the back of the drawer where nobody could find it.

5. Have your slippers been _____ next to the fireplace?

6. Has our dog Banjo _____ your slippers next to the fireplace?

7. Yesterday I _____ the report on your desk.

8. It has _____ on your desk since then.

9. Use sunscreen when you are _____ in the sun.

10. We had _____ in the sun too long.

11. Will you _____ there all morning?

12. Will you _____ your work down?

13. San Antonio _____ southwest of Austin.

14. The map shows where the ghost town once _____.

15. After lunch today I was sleepy, so I _____ down for a nap.

16. I _____ down my books and went for a walk.

17. The clothes had _____ out where the cat could lie on them.

18. Are you _____ your clothes out for tomorrow?

19. _____ on the ground, Mike, and look up at the stars.

20. Mike had _____ a blanket on the cold ground.

USAGE

Rise and *Raise*

The verb *rise* means "to go up" or "to get up." *Rise* does not take an object. The verb *raise* means "to lift up" or "to cause (something) to rise." *Raise* usually takes an object.

EXAMPLES Gasoline prices **have risen** recently. [present perfect tense of *rise*]

Oil producers **have raised** gasoline prices. [present perfect tense of *raise*]

EXERCISE Write the correct form of *rise* or *raise* on the line provided.

Example 1. ____*Rise*____ up and make your voices heard!

1. _____ your voice a little please.

2. Has the price _____ recently?

3. Esther _____ a good point at yesterday's meeting.

4. One issue _____ in importance above all others.

5. Are those balloons _____ very high?

6. We will _____ early in the morning when we go camping.

7. I had _____ the blinds so I could see who was making the noise.

8. It has been _____ steadily since Tuesday.

9. I am slowly _____ my eyes to look at the screen.

10. We _____ as a group and went outside.

11. Last week Sergio _____ the flag each morning.

12. Have you _____ your hand?

13. After the Vice President had spoken, the Congressional representative _____ quickly to make her point.

14. Has the sun _____ before 6:30 this month?

15. I often _____ my binoculars to watch the elk grazing.

16. The price of fuel generally _____ as demand increases.

17. When you _____ that point, what did Bob say?

18. His temperature has _____ since this afternoon.

19. I am _____ my expectations.

20. My expectations _____ as I see my goals more clearly.

USAGE

Six Troublesome Verbs

The verb *sit* means "to rest in an upright, seated position" or "to be in a place." *Sit* seldom takes an object. The verb *set* means "to put (something) in a place." *Set* usually takes an object.

The verb *lie* means "to rest," "to recline," or "to be in a place." *Lie* does not take an object. The verb *lay* means "to put (something) in a place." *Lay* usually takes an object.

The verb *rise* means "to go up" or "to get up." *Rise* does not take an object. The verb *raise* means "to lift up" or "to cause (something) to rise." *Raise* usually takes an object.

EXERCISE A In each of the following sentences, underline the correct verb form in parentheses.

Example 1. Carmen (*lay*, *laid*) on the beach and watched the sailboat regatta.

1. I had (*set*, *sat*) the scissors down in the kitchen.

2. The cattle had (*lain*, *laid*) under the oak trees for quite a while.

3. Has the price of wheat (*risen*, *raised*) again?

4. Has the puppy (*lain*, *laid*) the chew toy down yet?

5. After that, we both (*sat*, *set*) quietly and thought about the future.

6. Please do not (*rise*, *raise*) the umbrella in the house.

7. Were you (*laying*, *lying*) in the hammock?

8. Myron is (*sitting*, *setting*) colorful napkins next to the plates.

9. She (*raised*, *rose*) up and started to protest.

10. I (*lay*, *laid*) there for a while.

EXERCISE B Decide whether the underlined verb in each of the following sentences is correct. If the verb is incorrect, write the correct form above it. If the verb is correct, write *C* above it.

Example 1. Who is <u>setting</u> next to Mr. Mitchell? *(sitting)*

11. <u>Sit</u> the new trophy on the mantel with the others.

12. Our hopes for the soccer championship have <u>raised</u>.

13. I <u>sat</u> on the dock for three hours waiting for the ferry to return.

14. Philip's bicycle is <u>laying</u> in the middle of the driveway.

15. The stage manager had <u>lain</u> the props in the wrong places.

Review A: **Principal Parts of Verbs**

EXERCISE On the line provided in each of the following sentences, write the correct form (past or past participle) of the verb given in parentheses.

Example 1. *(fall)* The last Russian czar had ____*fallen*____ from power in 1917.

1. *(carve)* The Navajo artist has _____ a special design on his front door.

2. *(claim)* The defendant _____ that she was out of the country at the time of the crime.

3. *(be)* Cecile and I have _____ friends since the third grade.

4. *(dance)* Ginger Rogers _____ with Fred Astaire in the days of ball gowns and top hats.

5. *(make)* I have _____ the basketball team two years in a row.

6. *(start)* The Coast Guard officer _____ the boat's engine and headed toward the wreck.

7. *(write)* The mystery writer has _____ twelve books to date.

8. *(begin)* The mayor has already _____ her reelection campaign.

9. *(fight)* The boxing champion announced that he had _____ his last bout.

10. *(swim)* Have you ever _____ in the ocean?

11. *(draw)* Maraya _____ a stunning picture of the Egyptian pyramids.

12. *(come)* Have the O'Briens _____ back from their vacation in Ireland?

13. *(give)* The judge _____ the jurors their instructions.

14. *(work)* During the summer Molly _____ at the animal clinic.

15. *(teach)* Who _____ you to water-ski?

16. *(send)* Aunt Bernice _____ me a book of poems by Langston Hughes.

17. *(go)* Steven has _____ to the store to buy some dog food.

18. *(win)* Ben and I _____ first prize in the three-legged footrace.

19. *(break)* Is your new wristwatch _____?

20. *(know)* I have _____ Dr. Stamos all my life.

Review B: **Verb Tense and Voice**

EXERCISE A On the line provided, identify the tense of the verb in each of the following sentences. Then, circle the verb if it is in the progressive form.

Example _present_ **1.** The train is leaving in ten minutes.

_____ **1.** Toadstools had grown in a ring on the lawn.

_____ **2.** We are going to school now.

_____ **3.** I crossed my arms.

_____ **4.** Will you have finished by then?

_____ **5.** I shall succeed, Melinda.

_____ **6.** The goldfish was swimming around the new water plant.

_____ **7.** He has turned on the flashlight.

_____ **8.** Jean and Nick have been taking piano lessons.

_____ **9.** The volcano had erupted very suddenly.

_____ **10.** Will you be there?

EXERCISE B On the line provided, identify the voice of the verb in each of the following sentences. Use *AV* for *active voice* and *PV* for *passive voice*.

Example _PV_ **1.** We were left with little to do.

_____ **11.** The cold wind chilled the weary passengers.

_____ **12.** I was given a silver dollar by my great-uncle.

_____ **13.** The newsletters were all delivered in the Dawson neighborhood.

_____ **14.** Russell wrote an article about the creeks in the area.

_____ **15.** The turtle is crossing the pond.

Review C: Six Troublesome Verbs

USAGE

EXERCISE Proofread the following sentences for errors in the use of *sit, set, lie, lay, rise,* and *raise.* Cross out each incorrect verb form, and write the correct form above it. If the verb form is already correct, write *C* above it.

Example 1. The panther had ~~laid~~ *lain* in the sun all morning.

1. I quickly sat the colander down and went to see what was the matter.

2. We lay the embroidery on the table to show Grandma.

3. How high has the balloon raised?

4. The warriors laid their weapons on the sand.

5. The old cart has set there for at least a year.

6. Had you sat there long before Steve arrived?

7. Tania is laying down to rest after work.

8. The president of the club raised and went to the podium.

9. Please sit that where your cousin will see it.

10. Have the lions laid in the shade all day long?

11. Is the toad still setting near the drain?

12. I have just laid down to do some stretching.

13. The corner market has just risen its prices again.

14. Yesterday I sat the flowerpot on the deck.

15. Please lie the seed packets down and come look at this tomato.

16. Are the temperatures raising?

17. All morning long last Sunday, the dog set there and looked hopefully at the back door.

18. The tools lay on the garage floor until I picked them up.

19. The football set forgotten on the floor of Tony's closet all through last summer.

20. We rose several objections to the plan.

Review D: **Correct Use of Verbs**

EXERCISE A Underline the verb in each of the following sentences. Then, above the verb, identify its tense. Also indicate whether the tense is in the progressive form and whether it is in the active voice or passive voice.

present, progressive, active voice
Examples 1. He is <u>making</u> bread for the bake sale.

past perfect, passive voice
      2. We had been <u>given</u> daisies.

1. The team is finishing its work now.

2. I have read *The Lion, the Witch, and the Wardrobe.*

3. I am called Kate by my relatives.

4. The avalanche will have destroyed the village.

5. The dye has been staining the counter.

6. I shall interview several people for the position.

7. The story was told to everyone nearby.

8. Desirée had thanked Aunt Kendra for the birthday present.

9. We have looked everywhere for the fake mustaches.

10. Danielle and Sara are leaving Muskogee.

EXERCISE B Proofread the following sentences for errors in the use of verbs. Cross out each incorrect verb form, and write the correct form above it.

brought
Example 1. I have ~~brung~~ my stamp collection to show you.

11. I went up to Larry and tells him my name.

12. They been asked not to make so much noise.

13. Marcel and Reginald have lead the hikers across the snowy ridge.

14. Mr. Benedict builded several houses with energy-efficient appliances.

15. The blue jay seen the cat before it pounced.

16. The king had soon forgave the duke for his angry words.

17. Have you two set outside very long?

18. The cheetah had ran across the grassy plain.

19. I use to live in Baltimore.

20. She was laying down when the news came.

Proofreading Application: Process

Good writers are generally good proofreaders. Readers tend to admire and trust writing that is error-free. Make sure that you correct all errors in grammar, usage, spelling, and punctuation in your writing. Your readers will have more confidence in your words if you have done your best to proofread carefully.

Education today focuses on the process of learning. It's not enough to answer a question or solve a problem correctly; you need to be able to explain your answer. You need to be able to tell how you arrived at your answers. Many times, you will be required to write paragraphs that explain your thought processes.

Whenever you explain a process, you will be using verbs. These verbs must be correct in form and tense, and consistent with each other. If they are not, your explanation will not make sense. Your reader will not be sure about what happened, when it happened, or how it happened. Whenever you explain a process, be sure to proofread your verbs carefully.

PROOFREADING APPLICATIONS

Find and correct the errors in verb usage. Use proofreading symbols to make your corrections.

Example If two consecutive page numbers add up to 635, what ~~were~~ the
            are

         page numbers?

Yikes! How was I suppose to figure this one out? At first, I
just set there, trying to figure out what to do. Then, I decided
to start with what I knowed.

I seen that the numbers would be close to each other.
Consequently, I divided the numbers by two and comed up with 317
and a half. Of course, a page don't come in halves. So, I taked
that number as a starting point.

I letted one page be 317. Then, I rose the other page number to
318. As soon as I had wrote down the numbers, I realized that I
had the answer.

for **CHAPTER 9: USING VERBS CORRECTLY**   *pages 186–205*

Literary Model: Narrative

> The morning after the funeral Tom took Huck to a private place to have an important talk. . . . Huck's face saddened. He said:
> "I know what it is. You got into [Room] No. 2 and never found anything. . . . Nobody told me it was you; but I just knowed it must a ben you, . . . and I knowed you hadn't got the money becuz you'd a got at me some way or other and told me even if you was mum to everybody else. Tom, something's always told me we'd never get holt of that swag.". . .
> "Huck, that money wasn't ever in No. 2! . . . The money's in the cave!"
>
> —from *The Adventures of Tom Sawyer* by Mark Twain

EXERCISE A   Rewrite Huck's lines in standard English.

_____

_____

_____

_____

_____

_____

EXERCISE B

1. What verbs did you change, and why did you change them? _____

_____

_____

_____

2. Why do you think Mark Twain had Huckleberry Finn speak in nonstandard English? _____

_____

_____

_____

_____

Language and Sentence Skills Practice

Literary Model (continued)

USAGE | Language in Context: Literary Model

EXERCISE C   Write a brief dialogue using verb forms (either standard or nonstandard) to create realistic characters.

_____

_____

_____

_____

_____

_____

_____

_____

_____

_____

_____

_____

_____

_____

_____

_____

_____

_____

EXERCISE D   Read through your dialogue, or perform it with a friend. Then, ask yourself why you used the forms you did. What impression were you trying to make on the reader? What do the verb forms you used say about the characters in your dialogue?

_____

_____

_____

_____

_____

_____

_____

_____

_____

Writing Application: Personal Goals

Future perfect is probably the least used of the six verb tenses, but it performs an important function when we do use it. With it, we speak or write of what will have been accomplished by some point in the future. Future perfect allows us to make predictions about what will have happened and what we will have done at a stated time in the future.

> **FUTURE**   The district will replace the old, torn texts if the bond election goes well.
>
> **FUTURE PERFECT**   The district will have replaced the old, torn texts by next fall.

WRITING ACTIVITY

Future perfect is a good tense to use when setting goals. "I will improve my serve" is a good goal for a volleyball player, but "I will have improved my serve by the time spring tryouts come around" is better. It *assumes* success—"I *will have done* it!"—and gives the player a due date for achieving the goal. Most students have subjects and activities that come easily to them as well as subjects and activities that challenge and even frustrate them. Choose your hardest subject and write a paragraph in which you use future perfect tense to set three specific goals that will guide you to improve your skills and build your confidence.

PREWRITING   Select a school subject in which you would like to perform better. Then, take a few minutes to produce two lists, one of your strengths in the subject and one of skills that need development. Be honest and encouraging—even the strongest student can better his or her skills. Phrase your self-critique in positive terms. Then, choose the three skills you would most like to improve.

WRITING   For each skill, draft a paragraph that states your current level of ability, the level of ability you want to achieve, and steps you can take to achieve it. Build into the paragraph a time in the future by which you will have achieved the goal. Goals that nudge you toward improvement are realistic, so challenge yourself gently to avoid frustration and a sense of failure.

REVISING   Let a trusted adult or older friend read your paragraphs. Perhaps he or she will suggest a method for reaching your goals that had not yet occurred to you. Enlist this person to check on your progress and encourage you occasionally as you work toward the goals.

PUBLISHING   Check your paragraphs for errors in grammar, usage, spelling, and punctuation. Then, write neatly or print out two copies. Post one where you do your homework each day, and tape the other inside the folder where you keep the challenging subject's work. Each time you tackle work in the subject, read your goals and focus on the steps toward achieving them that you have outlined.

EXTENDING YOUR WRITING

If you enjoyed this exercise, you could develop it into a longer writing project. You have probably heard the saying, "Nothing breeds success like success." For an English class, write a personal narrative about a challenge that you thought you could not overcome. Explain how you eventually met that challenge and what you learned from the experience.

for **CHAPTER 10: USING PRONOUNS CORRECTLY**   *pages 216–31*

Choices: Investigating Pronoun Usage

Here's your chance to step out of the grammar book and into the real world. You may not realize it, but examples of pronoun usage appear in your life every day. The following activities challenge you to find a connection between pronoun usage and the world around you. Do the activity below that suits your personality best, and then share your discoveries with your class. Have fun!

DISCUSSION

Get Real

In common usage, *whom* is heard less often than *who*, regardless of the case required by the sentence. Why? What's the big deal? Is thinking about case too much trouble? Why was *who* chosen and not *whom*? Lead a discussion of these questions.

LINGUISTIC HISTORY

Ye Merry Gentlemen

Luckily, *you* is one pronoun that we don't need to divide into nominative and objective cases, but such was not always the case. Do a little research. (The *Oxford English Dictionary* would be an excellent source.) What is the history of the second-person pronoun? When did *you* first come into general use? How does *ye* fit into the picture? Then, fill your classmates in on a little bit of the history of the English language.

GRAPHICS

Fill in the Blank

Create a diagram that illustrates the use of personal pronouns in sentence structure. Your diagram will include two versions of the same sentence. To begin, write a sentence with four nouns—a subject, an indirect object, a direct object, and an object of a preposition. Then, write the sentence again, this time replacing each noun with a blank line to be filled in with a personal pronoun. Draw a vertical line that extends down from each blank, and then surround each vertical line with a list of personal pronouns that make sense in that position. These pronouns don't have to refer to the nouns in your original sentence; this is your chance to create new possibilities. Transfer your diagram to poster board, and with your teacher's permission, hang it in the classroom.

LINGUISTICS

Y'all Come Back

Standard English has no special pronoun for second-person plural. However, regional dialects of English do. In fact, there are several different expressions. What are these expressions? In what regions are they used? Let your classmates know the answers to these questions.

DISCUSSION

She's a Grand Old Flag

The form of a personal pronoun can indicate the pronoun's case, but it can also indicate the pronoun's gender. Why do we use feminine pronouns to refer to some objects? Think about this question. Begin by making a list of things, such as cannons, that are often called *she*. Why do you suppose these things were chosen and not others? Do other languages also use feminine-case pronouns similarly? If so, what objects do these languages label as feminine? Lead a discussion of these questions.

STUDY AID

"Unruly" Conduct

Create a list of all the rules in this chapter and provide at least one example sentence for each. Highlight in color important rules such as pronouns that are predicate nominatives and *who* versus *whom*. Make copies for your classmates and hand them out.

WRITING

Good Times, Good Friends

Write a page that tells the good things about three friends of yours. What's so hard about that? Use at least ten pronouns, but don't use any nominative-case pronouns.

Case Forms

Case is the form that a noun or a pronoun takes to show its relationship to other words in a sentence. In English, there are three cases: *nominative*, *objective*, and *possessive*.

NOMINATIVE CASE	That **author** is my favorite. **He** is my favorite. [subjects]
OBJECTIVE CASE	I gave **him** a **book** with **pictures**. [objects]
POSSESSIVE CASE	**My** sister likes that **author's** books. [possessive pronoun and possessive noun]

EXERCISE   Above each underlined word in the following sentences, write *N* for *nominative case*, *O* for *objective case*, or *P* for *possessive case*.

Example 1. I read an article about a famous explorer.

1. She went to the bottom of the ocean.

2. Another diver followed her as a safety precaution.

3. The divers used hand signals to communicate underwater.

4. Near the shore, they saw a shelf of land.

5. This shelf's name is the continental shelf.

6. A shelf can slope many fathoms under water.

7. These shelves attract explorers from around the world.

8. Scuba divers wear special equipment for exploring.

9. A diver's mask is a window to an exciting, new world.

10. Its fit helps to ensure a safe and comfortable dive.

11. Hers is equipped with a purge valve that helps to remove water.

12. Fins increase a diver's swimming power.

13. A snorkel is attached to the mask strap on the left side.

14. It helps a diver on the surface to conserve air.

15. When they wear scuba tanks, divers take their air supply with them.

16. We want to learn to scuba dive.

17. Mr. Jesse will teach us.

18. He teaches his classes at the city pool.

19. Our final dive, or checkout dive, would be at Lake Travis.

20. Will Tana's soccer schedule interfere with scuba classes?

Language and Sentence Skills Practice

The Nominative Case

10a.   The *subject* of a verb should be in the nominative case.

    EXAMPLE   Did **he** and **she** design the Web site? [*He* and *she* are the subjects of *Did design*.]

10b.   A *predicate nominative* should be in the nominative case.

    EXAMPLE   The judges will be **they.** [*They* follows the linking verb *will be* and identifies the subject *judges*.]

EXERCISE A   For each of the sentences below, underline the correct pronoun form in parentheses.

   Example 1. Al and (<u>they</u>, *them*) volunteered at the homeless shelter.

1. *(We, Us)* play chess every afternoon.

2. Everyone could see it was *(he, him)*.

3. Did the Jenkins family or *(they, them)* host the picnic?

4. The French government and *(we, us)* have a good relationship.

5. On our team the high scorers were *(he, him)* and I.

6. The only people to understand the poem were *(they, them)*.

7. The police officer and *(we, us)* were the ones who saw the UFO.

8. Stephanie and *(he, him)* thought the joke was hilarious.

9. Either Toni or *(she, her)* will pick you up after the show.

10. Wasn't it *(he, him)* who reported the missing bicycle?

EXERCISE B   Each of the following sentences contains an underlined pronoun. Write *C* above the under-lined pronoun if its form is correct. If the pronoun form is incorrect, cross it out and write the correct form above it.

   Example 1. The tutors will be <s>her</s> *she* and I.

11. Grandma and <u>me</u> went to a class to learn about computers.

12. After the replay, the referee said the winners were <u>us</u>.

13. The photographers should have been <u>them</u>.

14. The first to perform are <u>we</u>.

15. The most valuable player might have been <u>her</u>.

USAGE

The Objective Case

10c. A **direct object** should be in the objective case.

   EXAMPLE   Lisa asked **me** to go to the library. [*Me* tells *whom* Lisa asked.]

10d. An **indirect object** should be in the objective case.

   EXAMPLE   The teacher gave **us** a test. [*Us* tells *to whom* the teacher gave a test.]

10e. An **object of a preposition** should be in the objective case.

   EXAMPLE   No one except **Oscar** and **him** speaks Spanish. [*Oscar* and *him* are the objects of the
   preposition *except*.]

EXERCISE A   For each of the sentences below, underline the correct pronoun form in parentheses.

Example 1. Did you go with Conchita and *(he, him)* to the party?

1. The clown chose Mike and *(she, her)* from the audience.

2. He offered *(we, us)* some kimchi, a Korean salad.

3. Everyone applauded the performers and *(he, him)*.

4. Between you and *(I, me)*, the Hornets are my favorite team.

5. The crossing guard gave Racquel and *(I, me)* some good advice.

EXERCISE B   Each of the following sentences contains at least one underlined pronoun. Write *C* above
the underlined pronoun if its form is correct. If the pronoun form is incorrect, cross it out and write the
correct form above it.

Example 1. Will you show him and ̶I̶ your science project?
                        C   me

6. There are several seats between her and we.

7. Mr. Yakanura made us tempura for dinner.

8. Mr. Hinds gave Peggy and she directions.

9. She gave the CD-ROM to we.

10. When we visited China, Grandma took me to a festival.

11. Will you give her and I your e-mail address?

12. We played against the Raiders and they at the end of the season.

13. Will our class send him a get-well card?

14. The soothing piano music calmed she and I.

15. For he and I, Ms. Tompkins drew a huge cat.

USAGE

Nominative and Objective Case A

The *subject* of a verb and a *predicate nominative* should be in the nominative case.

> **EXAMPLES**   May **we** go to the art exhibit? [subject]
>
> My favorite artists are **Frida Kahlo** and **she**. [predicate nominatives]

A *direct object*, an *indirect object*, and an *object of a preposition* should be in the objective case.

> **EXAMPLES**   Mother took **her** and **me** to the gallery opening. [direct objects]
>
> Show **us** your latest charcoal drawing. [indirect object]
>
> For **Sue** and **them**, the guide gave a special tour. [objects of a preposition]

EXERCISE   For each of the following sentences, underline the correct pronoun form in parentheses.

Example 1. They and (*I, me*) visited the Metropolitan Museum of Art.

1. The guide showed (*we, us*) the Yoruba sculpture exhibit.

2. Tell (*I, me*) more about this African art form.

3. (*We, Us*) think this terra-cotta sculpture is fascinating!

4. The last to leave the exhibit was (*she, her*).

5. Greta and (*he, him*) were eager to see "Mirror of the Medieval World."

6. They waited for (*we, us*) at the door.

7. Art of the Middle Ages interests (*they, them*).

8. (*We, Us*) saw works of art created between the fourth and sixteenth centuries.

9. The group members most interested in medieval art are (*we, us*).

10. The guide directed (*I, me*) to an American Indian art exhibit.

11. Everyone except (*they, them*) followed me.

12. Hal and (*he, him*) were amazed by the quilled and beaded work.

13. Drawings on painted buffalo skins told (*we, us*) stories.

14. Kim showed (*I, me*) a basket woven by Datsolalee.

15. One of the best-known of all American Indian basket weavers is (*she, her*).

16. Between you and (*I, me*), the wooden masks seemed scary.

17. The guide gave (*we, us*) pamphlets about the exhibit.

18. It was (*I, me*) who begged to stay.

19. My sister should have come with (*we, us*).

20. I bought (*she, her*) a book from the museum's bookshop.

Nominative and Objective Case B

The *subject* of a verb and a *predicate nominative* should be in the nominative case.

A *direct object*, an *indirect object*, and an *object of a preposition* should be in the objective case.

EXERCISE Each of the following sentences contains at least one underlined pronoun. Write *C* above the underlined pronoun if its form is correct. If the pronoun form is incorrect, cross it out and write the correct form above it.

Example 1. Our visitors might have been <u>she</u> (*C*) and <u>him</u> (*he*).

1. Did you see the photographs by Dorothea Lange and <u>she</u>?

2. The winner in the Fun Run's wheelchair division was <u>he</u>.

3. Dr. Chen showed <u>her</u> and <u>I</u> his acupuncture clinic.

4. The volunteer coordinator should be <u>her</u>.

5. Will you play a game with <u>he</u> and <u>I</u>?

6. <u>Him</u> and <u>me</u> are building a model of the White House.

7. Did you see <u>him</u> and <u>her</u> at the grocery store?

8. Grandpa taught <u>he</u> and <u>I</u> some yoga postures.

9. Your biggest fans are <u>her</u> and <u>me</u>.

10. Will you go with Claire and <u>I</u> to hear the violinist Itzhak Perlman?

11. I made <u>her</u> and <u>him</u> a nutritious snack.

12. <u>We</u> and <u>they</u> meet on Thursdays for chess games.

13. Mother and <u>me</u> designed a new birdhouse.

14. Daisuke told <u>she</u> and <u>I</u> about his trip to Tokyo.

15. Did you choose <u>him</u> or <u>I</u>?

16. Juanita, Malcolm, and <u>me</u> collaborated on a science project.

17. Is the author of the skit <u>her</u> or <u>him</u>?

18. Uncle Stuart gave <u>him</u> and <u>I</u> bicycles for our shared birthday.

19. The awards presented to <u>she</u> and <u>I</u> were hung over the mantelpiece.

20. We may have to go to the mall without <u>her</u>.

USAGE

The Possessive Case

10f. The personal pronouns in the possessive case—*my, mine, your, yours, his, her, hers, its, our, ours, their, theirs*—are used to show ownership or possession.

EXAMPLES Have you seen **my** sweater?
I believe these books are **theirs.**

EXERCISE A In each of the following sentences, underline the personal pronoun in the possessive case.

Example 1. <u>Mine</u> has white stripes.

1. Did Jenny try on her kimono?

2. With yours, the class has now collected over one hundred cans.

3. My report is about the history of skateboarding.

4. Mine is hanging in the closet.

5. Has theirs ever been tested for safety?

6. Our piñata is filled with fruit, nuts, and small toys.

7. A vegetarian restaurant is their choice.

8. Hers is the only project about volcanoes.

9. Where are your new glasses?

10. Its nest is made of twigs, leaves, and bits of yarn.

EXERCISE B Choose appropriate possessive-case pronouns for the blanks in the following sentences. Use a variety of pronouns.

Example 1. Is this video game _____*yours*_____?

11. Will _____ poem appear in our school's literary magazine?

12. _____ stamp collection is not for sale.

13. Place your trophy next to _____.

14. I want to leave my suitcase here with _____.

15. _____ Web page design looks professional.

16. Has _____ piano been tuned lately?

17. _____ opinions differ on that issue.

18. _____ was chosen first.

19. Did _____ basketball coach offer any helpful suggestions?

20. Most of _____ clothes are made of cotton.

Who and Whom

USAGE

10g. The use of *who* or *whom* in a subordinate clause depends on how the pronoun functions in the clause. The nominative form is *who*. The objective form is *whom*.

EXAMPLES Do you know **who** he is? [predicate nominative of the subordinate clause *who he is*]

Leslie Marmon Silko is an author **whom** our class enjoys. [direct object of the subordinate clause *whom our class enjoys*]

EXERCISE A For each of the sentences below, underline the correct pronoun form in parentheses.

Example 1. The person *(who, whom)* she invited is a secret.

1. The woman *(who, whom)* fixed our stereo just called.

2. Taro is the one *(who, whom)* gave me the letter.

3. Justice O'Connor, *(who, whom)* I admire, was on the Supreme Court.

4. Do you know *(who, whom)* is on the committee?

5. I don't know to *(who, whom)* this address book belongs.

6. The dedication page tells for *(who, whom)* the book was written.

7. Aborigines are the only people *(who, whom)* live in some parts of Australia.

8. We need a business leader *(who, whom)* can speak Japanese.

9. The girl to *(who, whom)* I was speaking is my cousin.

10. Coretta Scott King is a woman *(who, whom)* I respect.

EXERCISE B In each of the following sentences, write *C* above the underlined pronoun if its form is correct. If the pronoun form is incorrect, cross it out and write the correct form above it.

Example 1. I listed only those ~~whom~~ who raised their hands.

11. Ask her to <u>whom</u> we should mail the package.

12. We need an assistant coach <u>whom</u> is enthusiastic.

13. I send e-mail to a pen pal <u>who</u> lives in Italy.

14. Is this your new friend <u>who</u> you met yesterday?

15. Can you tell me <u>whom</u> invented the light bulb?

16. My uncle, <u>whom</u> is from Zambia, has an African mask collection.

17. Are you the team to <u>whom</u> these uniforms belong?

18. Mrs. Jones, <u>who</u> I visit daily, appreciates my help.

19. I like the band <u>who</u> sings this song.

20. Mohandas Gandhi, <u>who</u> we honor, used nonviolence to help bring freedom to India.

Appositives and Reflexive Pronouns

10h. A pronoun used as an appositive is in the same case as the word to which it refers.

> **EXAMPLE** **We** bowlers play every Saturday. [The pronoun *We* is in the nominative case because it is used as an appositive of the subject, *bowlers*.]

Reflexive pronouns such as *himself* and *themselves* can be used as objects. Do not use the non-standard forms *hisself* and *theirselfs* or *theirselves* in place of *himself* and *themselves*.

> **NONSTANDARD** He reminded hisself to turn off the computer.
> **STANDARD** He reminded **himself** to turn off the computer.

EXERCISE A In each of the sentences below, underline the correct prounoun form in parentheses. Then, circle the noun to which the underlined pronoun refers.

Example 1. Shelby sent *(we, us)* children boots for the winter.

1. Mrs. Woo thanked *(we, us)* traffic-safety helpers.

2. *(We, Us)* girls were first-string on the basketball team.

3. The league leaders were *(we, us)* Sentinels.

4. Mark wrote a postcard to *(we, us)* scouts.

5. Did you invite *(we, us)* group leaders?

6. The first people on the program were *(we, us)* twirlers.

7. *(We, Us)* brothers were known as the Great Beninos.

8. The teacher called *(we, us)* students up to the stage.

9. Nurse Anthony gave a plaque to *(we, us)* volunteers.

10. *(We, Us)* boys plan to help with the park cleanup.

EXERCISE B For each of the sentences below, underline the correct pronoun form in parentheses.

Example 1. Omar treated *(himself, hisself)* to a new basketball.

11. Did they make *(theirselves, themselves)* enough food?

12. Jake will finish the project by *(himself, hisself)*.

13. The girls announced *(themselves, theirselves)* the winners.

14. The guests helped *(theirselfs, themselves)* to the appetizers.

15. Is he going to the movies by *(hisself, himself)*?

Clear Pronoun Reference A

USAGE

10i. Avoid an *ambiguous reference,* which occurs when any one of two or more words could be a pronoun's antecedent.

AMBIGUOUS   Rick said goodbye to John before he boarded the airplane.

CLEAR   Before Rick boarded the airplane, he said goodbye to John.

EXERCISE Revise each of the following sentences by correcting each unclear pronoun reference. Write your revisions on the lines provided.

Example 1. Liz was surprised to see Pam when she walked into the room.

When Liz walked into the room, she was surprised to see Pam.

1. After our dog met our new cat, it was very scared for a few days.

_____

2. Jenny and Sandy are going to their first concert, and she is very excited.

_____

3. Joan and Nina submitted projects for the science fair, and she won first prize in her category.

_____

4. Gary asked Bill to pass his notebook.

_____

5. Jenna called Ms. Adams because she was writing an article for the newspaper.

_____

6. After talking to Donna, Sarah felt better about her questions.

_____

7. Cynthia called Mary while she was visiting San Francisco.

_____

8. Did Ed and Antonio congratulate the men's soccer team after they finished eating dinner?

_____

9. Mom asked Claire where her hairbrush was.

_____

10. When Mr. Mercado and his son return from Mrs. Bray's office, please give this letter to him.

_____

Clear Pronoun Reference B

USAGE

10j. Avoid a *weak reference,* which occurs when a pronoun refers to an antecedent that has been suggested but not expressed.

WEAK   Belinda enjoyed visiting her mother, a nurse, at work; she plans to study it in college.

CLEAR   Belinda enjoyed visiting her mother, a nurse, at work; she plans to study nursing in college.

EXERCISE   Revise each of the following sentences by correcting each unclear pronoun reference. Write your revisions on the lines provided.

Example 1. It has not rained here in two months; we really need some.

It has not rained here in two months; and we really need some rain.

1. Betsy and Robbie enjoy bird-watching, but last week they didn't see many.

_____

2. When the bus's door opened, we all climbed in it.

_____

3. This morning on the radio, they announced the newly elected senators.

_____

4. Ken has been playing basketball for several years and hopes to become a professional one.

_____

5. Once the tree is bare, please rake them into a pile.

_____

6. To help the community, they are holding a food drive at our school.

_____

7. The four-year-olds have storytelling every day at 10 A.M.; they really like them.

_____

8. Harry played the leading role, and it was wonderful.

_____

9. Jennifer's father works in computer programming, and Jennifer thinks she may want to be one herself.

_____

10. I can't play racquetball today because I broke mine last week.

_____

USAGE

Special Pronoun Problems

10g. The use of *who* or *whom* in a subordinate clause depends on how the pronoun functions in the clause.

> **EXAMPLE**   Do you know **who** won the wheelchair division of the race? [subject]

10h. A pronoun used as an appositive is in the same case as the word to which it refers.

> **EXAMPLE**   **We** spectators waited anxiously. [The pronoun *We* is in the nominative case because it is used as an appositive of the subject, *spectators*.]

Reflexive pronouns such as *himself* and *themselves* can be used as objects. Do not use the nonstandard forms *hisself* and *theirselfs* or *theirselves* in place of *himself* and *themselves*.

NONSTANDARD   Did Jim build the racing chair by hisself?

STANDARD   Did Jim build the racing chair by **himself**?

EXERCISE   Each of the following sentences contains at least one underlined pronoun. Write *C* above the underlined pronoun if its form is correct. If the pronoun form is incorrect, cross it out and write the correct form above it.

Example 1. Ask them to whom <u>us</u> racers should report. *[C over "whom", we over "us"]*

1. In 1977, <u>we</u> wheelchair racers competed in the Boston Marathon for the first time.

2. The seven racers readied <u>theirselves</u> for the race.

3. Do you know <u>who</u> won the race in 1978?

4. All athletes <u>who</u> complete such a long, difficult race should declare <u>themselves</u> winners.

5. A foundation, to <u>whom</u> we are grateful, gave traveling assistance to <u>we</u> racers.

6. In 1980 Sharon Limpert, <u>whom</u> won the women's title, became the first woman to break three hours.

7. The 1998 Boston Marathon offered finish-line excitement for <u>we</u> fans.

8. It looks like a tie! To <u>whom</u> do you think they will give the medal?

9. The race officials, <u>who</u> we respect, asked <u>we</u> spectators to step back.

10. The racers usually ask <u>theirselfs</u> what they can do to improve their speed.

Review A: **Case**

EXERCISE A   Each of the following sentences contains an underlined pronoun. Write *C* above the under-lined pronoun if its form is correct. If the pronoun form is incorrect, cross it out and write the correct form above it.

Example 1. I will meet Lili and ~~she~~ *her* at the bus.

1. Our band and <u>them</u> are performing at the Fall Marching Festival.

2. Judges rank <u>us</u> according to musical skill and technique.

3. Did you save a seat for Lili and <u>I</u>?

4. The instruments were loaded carefully by <u>they</u>.

5. On the bus Kirby and <u>he</u> made up a pep song.

6. They taught Mary and <u>she</u> the song.

7. The boys and <u>we</u> took turns suggesting games to play.

8. The first to arrive at the field were <u>us</u>.

9. Our band director gave Bob and <u>I</u> some sunscreen.

10. Where should Carol and <u>he</u> put their trombone cases?

EXERCISE B   Choose appropriate pronouns for the blanks in the following sentences.

Example 1. Tamika and _____*she*_____ went skating last Friday.

11. Do Ray and _____ have time to practice?

12. Some of _____ talked to friends in other bands.

13. Is the drum major _____?

14. Sue reminded Lili and _____ to straighten our hats.

15. For the other bands and _____, weeks of practice are about to pay off!

EXERCISE C   Choose appropriate possessive-case pronouns for the blanks in the following sentences. Use a variety of pronouns.

Example 1. _____*Mine*_____ are too muddy to wear inside.

16. With only seconds left, _____ midcourt shot won the game!

17. Was _____ published in the school newspaper?

18. At the dog show, _____ collie won several blue ribbons.

19. _____ neighborhood's crime-prevention program won national recognition.

20. Does _____ family celebrate Hanukkah?

Review B: **Case and Special Pronoun Problems**

EXERCISE A Each of the following sentences contains an underlined pronoun. Write *C* above the underlined pronoun if its form is correct. If the pronoun form is incorrect, cross it out and write the correct form above it.

Example 1. They made a papier-mâché globe for ~~theirselfs.~~ *themselves*

1. Desmond and me looked at the map of the world.

2. Mr. Rudolph pointed out the Indian subcontinent to us.

3. The students helped theirselves to pushpins for marking countries of special interest.

4. My favorite country is Italy because of its interesting shape.

5. Did you know that my favorite country is also theirs?

6. Della was the student who gave a report about Asia.

7. The amount of water seemed enormous to we students.

8. Whom can say how much of the earth is water?

9. Neither Mr. Singh nor him has visited relatives in India.

10. Juan surprised hisself by naming all of Africa's countries without looking at the map.

EXERCISE B Each of the following sentences contains an underlined pronoun. Write *C* above the underlined pronoun if its form is correct. If the pronoun form is incorrect, cross it out and write the correct form above it.

Example 1. Kamika told us who the leader of Pakistan is. *C*

11. The expert on geography was him.

12. We can ask Juan or he for help if we need it.

13. My mother gave my sister and I a Mercator projection map.

14. It was my sister who really wanted it.

15. The proud new owners of the map were us.

16. Us children hung it on the wall of the basement.

17. My uncle and he checked to see whether the country, Burkina Faso, was on it.

18. Between my sister and I, we found 107 countries.

19. Both of we enjoyed studying the map.

20. Someday, two experts on the globe will be Erica and she.

USAGE

Review C: **Clear Reference**

EXERCISE Rewrite each of the following sentences to correct any ambiguous or weak pronoun references. Write your new sentences on the lines provided.

Example 1. My mother called her sister after she got home

After she got home, my mother called her sister.

1. Mr. Jennings asked Mr. Ruiz when he would be presenting the award. _____

_____

2. When Kevin passed the basketball to Carlton, he stepped out of bounds. _____

_____

3. Gail told Aunt Judy that she had a spaghetti stain on her shirt. _____

_____

4. The Olympic gymnasts hoped to win a gold or silver medal, and they celebrated when they

won it. _____

_____

5. Yvonne asked Jill if she could join the softball team. _____

_____

6. Jerry teaches guitar lessons, and he wants to make it a full-time job. _____

_____

7. The lead actor is talented. One of these is singing. _____

_____

8. The art teacher encourages creative students, and she says that is easy to find. _____

_____

9. Luisa wants to learn that computer language. She will take it as a class. _____

_____

10. When we take Spot and Rover on a walk, it usually barks at the neighbor's dog. _____

_____

216

Literary Model: Poetry

I take him outside
under the trees,
have him stand on the ground.
We listen to the crickets,
cicadas, million years old sound.
Ants come by us.
I tell them,
"This is he, my son.
This boy is looking at you.
I am speaking for him."

The crickets, cicadas,
the ants, the millions of years
are watching us,
hearing us.
My son murmurs infant words,
speaking, small laughter
bubbles from him.
Tree leaves tremble.
They listen to this boy
speaking for me.

—"Speaking"
by Simon J. Ortiz

EXERCISE A Write the ten different personal pronouns that appear in the poem. After each pronoun, indicate its case (nominative, objective, or possessive)—that is, the form of the pronoun that shows its use in the sentence or clause.

_____

_____

_____

_____

_____

EXERCISE B The author uses the pronouns *he* and *him* a few times before he identifies the person (called the antecedent) to whom those pronouns are referring. What do you think the author's purpose was in using this technique? Support your response with information from the poem.

_____

_____

_____

_____

_____

USAGE | Language in Context: Literary Model

Literary Model (continued)

EXERCISE C Two relationships are discussed in this poem: the relationship between people and nature and the relationship between two people. Write a short poem or piece of prose whose theme is one of these types of relationship, or both. As Ortiz did, include many personal pronouns, and do not immediately establish the antecedent of at least one of them.

_____

_____

_____

_____

_____

_____

_____

_____

_____

_____

EXERCISE D

1. Explain your use of personal pronouns in your poem. What effect were you trying to achieve?

_____

_____

_____

_____

_____

_____

2. Do you think it would be effective to use so many personal pronouns in other forms of writing—for example, in book reports, essays, or business letters? Explain your answer.

_____

_____

_____

_____

_____

_____

_____

Proofreading Application: Personal Essay

Good writers generally are good proofreaders. Learn to become a careful proofreader so that you can correct errors in grammar, usage, spelling, and punctuation. Readers will have more trust in what you are communicating if you do your best to make sure that your writing is free of errors.

The grammar you use when you communicate informally with family and friends may differ from the grammar you use in a formal writing assignment. Remember, to communicate most effectively with the widest variety of people and to persuade your readers that you are a careful and thoughtful writer, you should follow the rules of standard English.

PROOFREADING ACTIVITY

The following excerpt from a personal essay contains errors in pronoun usage. Find the errors and correct them, using proofreading symbols to replace incorrect words.

Example   Improving our strength and flexibility was a priority for my
friend and ~~I~~ *me*.

Coach Fernandez told us that stretching would improve our speed, so Joe and me decided to sign up for yoga. Him and me thought it would be so easy, but we were wrong! Us big, strong football players, whom work out at least three hours a day, were groaning in the first posture.

Everyone except us seemed so calm and relaxed. The teacher, who we respect, offered Joe and I some helpful suggestions about our breathing. Another student and her demonstrated a deep-breathing exercise to increase lung capacity. I had felt tired when we started, so I was amazed at how much energy I had after breathing deeply.

Once we had been calmed and energized by deep-breathing, the teacher warned we boys that the real work would begin! Our first attempt to shape our bodies like half-moons left us weak and shak-

Writing Application: Newspaper Article

Your purpose for writing and speaking determines the kind of language you will use. For example, you might use nonstandard English to communicate informally with a friend—in conversation, in a note, or by e-mail; however, formal speaking and writing occasions require standard English.

NONSTANDARD Are you sure it was her?

STANDARD Are you sure it was **she**?

Think of other examples of nonstandard pronoun usage that you have used or heard in informal situations.

WRITING ACTIVITY

Imagine you are a reporter for your school newspaper. You have been asked to cover an important school event. Write the newspaper article, using personal pronouns in your account of who did what. Be sure to use standard English.

PREWRITING Attend a school event or imagine one. It could be a fine arts, academic, or sporting event. To gather details about the event, use the *5W-How?* questions: *Who? What? Where? When? Why?* and *How?* Interview both participants and spectators at the event.

WRITING Try to organize your information so the most important details come first. Readers of newspaper articles often scan quickly, so give them the essentials as early in the article as possible. Then, elaborate with supporting details. Also, create a headline that attracts attention and announces your subject.

REVISING Ask peer editors to read your article. Ask them to determine whether all the necessary information is included. Ask the readers to find answers to all of the *5W-How?* questions.

PUBLISHING Check your article for errors in punctuation and spelling. Make sure that the pronouns you use are correct according to the rules of standard English. With your teacher's permission, post your article on the bulletin board.

EXTENDING YOUR WRITING

You may wish to develop this writing exercise further. You could adopt the point of view of one of the event's participants and write a letter about the event to a friend. Or you might want to take notes on other school functions and write a magazine article about the extra-curricular activities your school offers.

for **CHAPTER 11: USING MODIFIERS CORRECTLY**   `pages 238–56`

Choices: Exploring Modifiers

Here's your chance to step out of the grammar book and into the real world. You may not notice modifiers, but you and the people around you use them every day. The following activities challenge you to find a connection between modifiers and the world around you. Do the activity below that suits your personality best, and then share your discoveries with your class. Have fun!

ART

Metamorphoses

Artists create illusions. When an artist wants to show that one object is farther away than another object, how does he or she do so? The artist must transform degrees of distance into degrees of size, and, possibly, of color. Try your hand at this illusion. Draw three objects—one far, one farther, and one farthest. Be sure to title your illustration. Then with your teacher's permission, display your creation in your classroom.

WORD ASSOCIATION

The Best of the Best

Everybody has an opinion on superlatives, and here's your chance to prove it. Here are your categories: movies, books, CDs, and places to visit. Find out your classmates' thoughts on these topics by having everyone list good, better, and best for each of these categories. Get into groups of four or fewer, and have each group member share his or her own opinions.

DEMONSTRATION

Mix and Match

You're going to need at least five people for this project. Write three or four relatively short sentences that each include a misplaced modifier—a word, phrase, or clause. Then, in bold red marker, transfer each misplaced modifier onto its own large piece of paper or poster board. Write the other words from each sentence in black, one to a piece of poster board. In the order of each original sentence, have each group member stand in front of the class and hold up a word or two. Ask the class where the person holding the misplaced modifier should stand. In how many places can the modifier sensibly fit?

GAME SHOW

Lightning Round

Test your classmates' speed with your own version of a game show's final round. Write ten of your favorite adjectives and adverbs on a sheet of paper. Then, cut each word onto its own strip. Pull a modifier from a container holding your paper strips, announce the word to the contestants (your classmates), and have each person write a sentence that includes the modifier. The first contestant to insert the modifier correctly in a complete sentence wins a point. Continue the game until you have used all ten modifiers; the contestant with the most points at the end of round ten wins.

WRITING

Personal Best

There are the things you do well, the things you do better, and the things you do best. What are they? Write ten sentences about these things. In each sentence, use one of the forms of *well.* Don't be shy. Brag a little! Publish these sentences in a letter to your teacher, a relative, or a friend.

CREATIVE GROUP PROJECT

Adding On

Get into groups of four or fewer. Have each group member write a short, dull sentence such as "The girl woke up." Then, as a group, spice up each sentence. After passing all sentences to the person on the left, each group member gets to add one adjective, adverb, or prepositional phrase to the new sentence. Keep passing the sentences around until every group member makes an addition to each sentence. When all sentences are finished, go through them one by one and correct any modifiers that are confusing or incorrectly placed.

Language and Sentence Skills Practice

USAGE

What Is a Modifier?

A *modifier* is a word or word group that makes the meaning of another word or word group more specific. *Adjectives* modify nouns and pronouns. *Adverbs* modify verbs, adjectives, and other adverbs.

ADJECTIVES	My **green** dress is here. [*Green* modifies the noun *dress*.]
	This one is **fast**. [*Fast* modifies the pronoun *one*.]
ADVERBS	Eli spoke **softly**. [*Softly* modifies the verb *spoke*.]
	I feel **too** tired. [*Too* modifies the adjective *tired*.]
	You work **more** quickly than I. [*More* modifies the adverb *quickly*.]

EXERCISE   In each of the following sentences, circle the word that modifies the underlined word or word group. Do not include the articles *a, an,* and *the*.

Example   1. Will you try (harder)?

1. The bright <u>sun</u> hurts my eyes.

2. That dancer <u>moves</u> gracefully.

3. This popcorn seems much <u>saltier</u>.

4. Paris is an exciting <u>city</u>.

5. The downpour almost <u>completely</u> flooded our yard.

6. Leaves provide food for small <u>animals</u>.

7. Your report was extremely <u>interesting</u>.

8. She talks rather <u>softly</u>.

9. <u>Will</u> you <u>listen</u> carefully?

10. Send us another <u>one</u>.

11. Several <u>others</u> have voted.

12. I could almost <u>taste</u> it!

13. This room is slightly <u>cooler</u>.

14. The steaming <u>drink</u> warmed us.

15. You are very <u>late</u>!

16. We were too <u>late</u> for front-row seats.

17. He <u>answered</u> the question intelligently.

18. Your e-mail message was so <u>funny</u>!

19. I <u>will</u> gladly <u>help</u> you.

20. Samone is unusually <u>quiet</u> today.

USAGE

Adjective or Adverb?

To decide whether a word is an adjective or adverb, determine how the word is used in the sentence.

11a. If a word in the predicate modifies the subject of the verb, use the adjective form. If it modifies the verb, use the adverb form.

    ADJECTIVE Jenny's performance was **beautiful.** [*Beautiful* modifies the noun *performance*.]

    ADVERB Jenny performed **beautifully.** [*Beautifully* modifies the verb *performed*.]

EXERCISE Each of the following sentences contains an underlined modifier. If the underlined word is used as an adjective, write *ADJ* above the word. Write *ADV* if the word is used as an adverb.

    Example 1. Our long-distance runner is <u>sick</u>. [ADJ]

1. We arrived <u>late</u> for the track meet.

2. I <u>hurriedly</u> dressed in my uniform.

3. The locker room smelled <u>musty</u>.

4. Will the first event begin <u>soon</u>?

5. The <u>anxious</u> participants filled the bleachers.

6. Can you line up <u>quickly</u>?

7. The runner beside me looked so <u>serious</u>.

8. I can't believe I finished <u>first</u>!

9. The distance to the finish line seemed <u>endless</u>.

10. I have never run so <u>fast</u>.

11. The crowd cheered <u>enthusiastically</u> for all the runners.

12. Our team is so <u>excited</u> about the 400-meter relay.

13. We have the <u>best</u> record in our region.

14. Eli ran a surprisingly <u>fast</u> time in the trial.

15. He walked <u>confidently</u> to the starting blocks.

16. Is the high jump the <u>first</u> field event?

17. Pedro jumped <u>easily</u> and cleared the bar.

18. Our whole team performed <u>fantastically</u>.

19. Coach Williams <u>proudly</u> accepted our trophy.

20. We looked <u>exhausted</u>, but we felt great!

Language and Sentence Skills Practice

223

USAGE

Good and *Well*

Good is an adjective. It should be used to modify a noun or a pronoun. Use *well* to modify a verb.

> **EXAMPLES**   Ramón's paintings look **good**. [*Good* modifies the noun *paintings*.]
> Ramón paints **well**. [*Well* modifies the verb *paints*.]

Well may be used either as an adjective or as an adverb. As an adjective, *well* has two meanings: "in good health" or "satisfactory."

> **EXAMPLES**   Ramón feels **well** today. [Meaning "in good health," *well* modifies the noun *Ramón*.]
> All is **well** at his studio. [Meaning "satisfactory," *well* modifies the pronoun *All*.]

EXERCISE A   For each of the sentences below, underline the correct modifier in parentheses.

Example 1. Everything is (*good*, *well*) with my favorite band.

1. We didn't have (*good*, *well*) seats at the concert.

2. Inge and I couldn't hear the lead singer very (*good*, *well*).

3. The band performed as (*good*, *well*) as we had hoped.

4. The drummer looked (*good*, *well*) in that silver outfit.

5. It was so hot in the concert hall that I didn't feel (*good*, *well*).

6. Being a (*good*, *well*) friend, Janeatha bought me a cup of cold apple juice.

7. The apple juice tasted (*good*, *well*).

8. How (*good*, *well*) was the concert?

9. I was surprised that the bass guitarist sang so (*good*, *well*).

10. His voice is so (*good*, *well*) that I think he should become the lead singer.

EXERCISE B   The following paragraph contains errors in the use of *good* and *well*. Cross out the errors and write the correct modifier above each word that you have crossed out.

Example [1] All is ~~good~~ *well* with me today.

[11] How good, or healthy, I feel depends on how good I take care of myself. [12] A good breakfast gives me a well start on my day. [13] Foods low in sugar are well choices. [14] My family and I work good together to make healthy foods that taste well. [15] Exercise is important, too. [16] I can't run very good, but a long walk gives me energy. [17] I also play basketball very good, so I get plenty of exercise. [18] How good I sleep at night also affects the way I feel. [19] I need at least eight hours to perform good at school the next day. [20] Diet, exercise, and rest will help me live a well, long life.

Regular Comparison

11b. The three degrees of comparison are the *positive,* the *comparative,* and the *superlative.*

In regular comparison, modifiers form the comparative degree by adding *–er* or using *more/less.* They form the superlative degree by adding *–est* or using *most/least.*

POSITIVE	COMPARATIVE	SUPERLATIVE
new	newer	newest
quickly	more quickly	most quickly
careful	less careful	least careful

EXERCISE Complete the following chart by filling in the two missing forms for each modifier given.

	Positive	Comparative	Superlative
Example 1.	*juicy*	juicier	*juiciest*
1.	small	_____	_____
2.	_____	_____	most cheerfully
3.	_____	prettier	_____
4.	often	_____	_____
5.	_____	more improbable	_____
6.	_____	_____	most smoothly
7.	dirty	_____	_____
8.	_____	less desirable	_____
9.	_____	_____	crankiest
10.	boastful	_____	_____
11.	_____	sweeter	_____
12.	grateful	_____	_____
13.	_____	_____	chilliest
14.	hot	_____	_____
15.	_____	sillier	_____
16.	_____	_____	most wonderful
17.	blue	_____	_____
18.	famous	_____	_____
19.	_____	more fickle	_____
20.	_____	_____	least salty

Language and Sentence Skills Practice

225

USAGE

Irregular Comparison

11c. The comparative and superlative degrees of some modifiers are not formed by the usual methods.

POSITIVE	COMPARATIVE	SUPERLATIVE
good	better	best
bad	worse	worst
little	less	least

EXERCISE Complete each sentence below by writing the modifier specified in the parentheses on the line provided.

Example 1. (superlative of *little*)   Orange is my ___*least*___ favorite color.

1. (superlative of *much*)   The _____ common form of Nigerian jewelry is a long string of beads.

2. (comparative of *good*)   Both of the charcoal drawings were exceptional, but I thought Ian's was _____.

3. (comparative of *little*)   I have _____ time to practice the piano today than I had yesterday.

4. (superlative of *good*)   Tony has the _____ scoring record on our team this year.

5. (superlative of *bad*)   This is the _____ movie I have ever seen!

6. (comparative of *much*)   Joseph Bruchac's "Birdfoot's Grampa" is the _____ interesting of the two poems.

7. (superlative of *well*)   Of all the musicians who performed last night, I think Wynton Marsalis played the _____.

8. (comparative of *many*)   There were _____ people at this year's school carnival than at last year's.

9. (superlative of *far*)   Which of the following Tanzanian cities is _____ from Mtwara: Lindi, Songea, or Tabora?

10. (comparative of *well*)   I feel much _____ today than I did yesterday.

Regular and Irregular Comparison A

11b. The three degrees of comparison are the *positive,* the *comparative,* and the *superlative.*

POSITIVE	COMPARATIVE	SUPERLATIVE
happy	happier	happiest
skillfully	more skillfully	most skillfully
much	more	most

USAGE

EXERCISE Complete the following chart by filling in the two missing forms for each modifier given.

	Positive	Comparative	Superlative
Example 1.	*bossy*	*bossier*	bossiest
1.		more believable	
2.	angrily		
3.			dimmest
4.	good		
5.		drier	
6.			least bitter
7.			most observant
8.		worse	
9.	warm		
10.	many		
11.		farther	
12.			perkiest
13.	well		
14.	little money	_____money	_____money
15.		more ridiculous	
16.	much		
17.			saddest
18.		slyer	
19.	happily		
20.			grumpiest

Regular and Irregular Comparison B

11b. The three degrees of comparison are the **positive,** the **comparative,** and the **superlative.**

POSITIVE   An anglerfish is a **big** saltwater fish.
COMPARATIVE   A barracuda is **bigger** than an anglerfish.
SUPERLATIVE   The bluefin tuna is the **biggest** of the three fish.

EXERCISE Complete each sentence below by writing the modifier specified in the parentheses on the line provided.

Example 1. (superlative of *exciting*) The ____*most exciting*____ spot our family has ever visited is the Monterey Bay Aquarium.

1. (superlative of *large*) Most of the aquarium's permanent exhibits focus on Monterey Bay, the nation's _____ national marine sanctuary.

2. (comparative of *many*) The aquarium had _____ exhibits than our family could visit in one day.

3. (superlative of *well*) Because a diver hand-fed sharks in the Kelp Forest exhibit, Stephen liked that exhibit _____.

4. (superlative of *odd*) The _____ fish in the Outer Bay exhibit was the ocean sunfish, which looked like a big leather disk.

5. (comparative of *much*) In the Mystery of the Deep exhibit, visitors can learn _____ information about the deep sea.

6. (superlative of *deep*) Some of the animals we saw from the _____ waters—as deep as 3,300 feet—were Pacific hagfish, mushroom corals, and squat lobsters.

7. (superlative of *interested*) Of all the members of my family, I am the _____ in deep-sea life.

8. (comparative of *gracefully*) In the Splash Zone exhibit, my little sister Kate crawled _____ through the coral reef structures than I did.

9. (superlative of *cute*) She decided that the _____ animal she saw was the black-footed penguin.

10. (comparative of *far*) On that exciting day Kate, who usually complains, walked _____ than she ever had before!

Use of Comparative and Superlative Forms A

11d. Use the comparative degree when comparing two things. Use the superlative degree when comparing more than two.

COMPARATIVE	Of the two boys, he is **more bashful.**
	Rosa's dive was **better** than mine.
SUPERLATIVE	Is he the **most bashful** of all the boys?
	She performed her **best** dive ever.

EXERCISE In the following sentences, if an underlined modifier is incorrect, cross it out and write the correct form above it. If the underlined modifier is correct, write *C* above it.

                                    more destructive
Example 1. Which is ~~most destructive~~ to an archaeological site: wind or water?

1. The tomb of Qin Shihuangdi has been called "the <u>greater</u> archaeological find of our time."

2. Of the more than 7,000 life-size warriors, horses, and chariots, which looked <u>more realistic</u>?

3. It was the <u>more amazing</u> thing I had ever seen!

4. Since 1974, archaeologists in China have been putting forth their <u>better</u> efforts to rebuild the lifelike terra-cotta army.

5. Rebuilding the statues was probably <u>hardest</u> than unearthing them.

6. Some of the smallest pieces provide the <u>best</u> clues about sculpting techniques during the emperor's time.

7. Amy knows <u>more</u> information about China's first emperor than I do.

8. Were the chariots or the horses buried <u>deepest</u>?

9. Of all the farmers who found the first clay head, he was <u>more terrified</u>.

10. Do you have a <u>more current</u> account than this one?

Use of Comparative and Superlative Forms B

11e. Include the word *other* or *else* when comparing one member of a group with the rest of the group.

NONSTANDARD	The blue whale is larger than any animal.
STANDARD	The blue whale is larger than any **other** animal.
NONSTANDARD	I finished my report before anyone in my class did.
STANDARD	I finished my report before anyone **else** in my class did.

EXERCISE Some of the following sentences need *other* or *else* to complete their meaning. Insert a caret (∧) where the word *other* or *else* is needed, and write the omitted word on the line provided. If a sentence is already correct, write *C* on the line.

Example _____*else*_____ **1.** Julia is taller than anyone in her class.

_____ **1.** Can anyone else on the team run faster than he can?

_____ **2.** These scissors are sharper than any pair I could find.

_____ **3.** Berta has won more trophies for track and field than any athlete.

_____ **4.** She is more skillful than anyone in her art class.

_____ **5.** I write to my cousin more than I write to anyone in my family.

_____ **6.** Is jogging more effective for weight loss than any form of exercise?

_____ **7.** During free reading, short stories are more popular than any form of literature.

_____ **8.** Juan has done more volunteer work than anyone in his troop.

_____ **9.** This kitten is not as curious as all the kittens in its litter.

_____ **10.** Gina was more observant than anyone on the hike.

_____ **11.** This first song is better than any song on the CD.

_____ **12.** The cheetah can run faster than any land animal.

_____ **13.** The month of February has fewer days than any month.

_____ **14.** Houda speaks Arabic better than anyone in his family.

_____ **15.** This book has fewer pages than any book.

_____ **16.** Rachel scored more goals than anyone on her soccer team.

_____ **17.** Has Paul run more miles than anyone in his track club?

_____ **18.** A saltwater crocodile is larger than any other reptile.

_____ **19.** Our neighbor Mrs. Gold grows more flowers than anyone on our street.

_____ **20.** These pants are baggier than any other pants in my closet.

Double Comparisons and Double Negatives

11f. Avoid using double comparisons.

NONSTANDARD	This sweater is more warmer than my jacket.
STANDARD	This sweater is **warmer** than my jacket.

11g. Avoid using double negatives.

NONSTANDARD	I don't have no mail today.
STANDARD	I do**n't** have **any** mail today. *or* I have **no** mail today.

EXERCISE Most of the following sentences contain incorrect double comparisons or double negatives. Cross out any unnecessary words. Insert carets (∧) where words are needed, and write the needed words on the lines provided. If a sentence is already correct, write *C* on the line.

Example ___*any*___ **1.** I don't have ~~no~~ change.
∧

_____ **1.** I don't hardly know nothing about the country of Zambia.

_____ **2.** We have never had no problems with our car.

_____ **3.** These enchiladas are more tastier than the tacos.

_____ **4.** The most strangest noise is coming from behind that door.

_____ **5.** I haven't never watched the sun rise.

_____ **6.** Your explanation doesn't make no sense to me.

_____ **7.** If the water were more deeper, we could dive safely.

_____ **8.** I can't barely reach the top shelf.

_____ **9.** Is the most longest bridge in the world the Humber Bridge in England?

_____ **10.** Grandpa seems more wiser than anyone else I know.

_____ **11.** The black rock for these statues can't be found in no other place.

_____ **12.** That's the most funniest story I have ever heard!

_____ **13.** We didn't see no weeds in the garden.

_____ **14.** Could I try on this dress in a larger size?

_____ **15.** This discount store has the most cheapest prices on school supplies.

_____ **16.** I don't remember ever eating a plantain.

_____ **17.** The most oldest covered bridge in use is in New Hampshire.

_____ **18.** I never heard no one play the piano as well as Angela Cheng.

_____ **19.** Joe needs a more shorter board for the birdhouse floor.

_____ **20.** She never goes nowhere without her glasses.

USAGE

Misplaced Prepositional Phrases

| **11h.** | Place modifying words, phrases, and clauses as near as possible to the words they modify. |

| MISPLACED | We took our cat to the veterinarian with the sore paw. |
| CORRECT | We took our cat **with the sore paw** to the veterinarian. [The phrase modifies the noun *cat*.] |

EXERCISE A Underline the prepositional phrase in each of the following sentences. Then, circle the word that the phrase modifies.

Example 1. I (saw) in the newspaper a camera advertisement.

1. The ad said that the camera came with two extra lenses.

2. I called the phone number that was listed in the advertisement.

3. I wanted further information about the camera.

4. The camera dealer had satisfactory answers to my questions.

5. A camera of my own is a dream come true!

EXERCISE B Underline the misplaced prepositional phrase in each of the following sentences. Draw an arrow from the phrase to its correct location in the sentence.

Example 1. I saw a movie about spiders in my science class.

6. I took a nap and dreamed about a faraway castle on my blue couch.

7. Virgil found a book about prehistoric animals in the library.

8. The woman wrote a play about two elephants in the red dress.

9. Three men had to stop quickly while a goose crossed the road in a small car.

10. The water refreshed us from a fountain.

11. Did you see the medals that Aunt Elsa won in the attic?

12. This *daruma* doll is said to help wishes come true from Japan.

13. That boy will feed our dogs in the yellow shirt.

14. The rocks are from the playground in my shoes.

15. The book *Scorpions* describes two friends living in Harlem by Walter Dean Myers.

Misplaced and Dangling Participial Phrases

11h. Place modifying words, phrases, and clauses as near as possible to the words they modify.

MISPLACED	Buried in the yard, the dog dug up a bone.
CORRECT	The dog dug up a bone **buried in the yard.**
DANGLING	Planning a picnic, the rain was saddening.
CORRECT	**Planning a picnic,** we were saddened by the rain.
CORRECT	**Because we were planning a picnic,** the rain was saddening.

EXERCISE Rewrite the following sentences to correct the misplaced and dangling participial phrases.

Example 1. Addressing the crowd, Dr. Martin Luther King, Jr.'s speech was inspiring. *Addressing the crowd, Dr. Martin Luther King, Jr., gave an inspiring speech.*

1. Hoping to win the race, the fall was disappointing. _____

2. Grasped tightly in my hands, I urged the horse onward with the reins. _____

3. Vo, hidden in the closet, couldn't find his sleeping bag. _____

4. The log fit into the stove broken in half. _____

5. Running on empty, I needed to stop for gas. _____

6. Built into the cliffs, archaeologists have learned much from Anasazi dwellings. _____

7. Aunt Rosa offered grilled chicken to us wrapped in a flour tortilla. _____

8. Rested from a long nap, the afternoon hike seemed easy. _____

9. Traveling along the Congo River, exotic birds and brightly colored insects can be seen. _____

10. Leaping across the stage, the dancer's performance amazed us. _____

Misplaced Clauses

USAGE

11h. Place modifying words, phrases, and clauses as near as possible to the words they modify.

An *adjective clause* should be placed directly after the word it modifies.

MISPLACED CLAUSE He gave a turtle to his sister **that he found under the tree.**

CORRECT He gave a turtle **that he found under the tree** to his sister. [The clause modifies *turtle*, not *sister*.]

EXERCISE A In each of the sentences below, underline the adjective clause. Then, circle the noun or pronoun that the clause modifies.

Example 1. I have an (uncle) who lives in Hungary.

1. I really enjoyed the movie that we saw last night.

2. My sister, who lives in Oklahoma, is coming home for Thanksgiving.

3. I couldn't have finished without your help, which I really appreciate.

4. The man whose car had been dented filed an accident report.

5. The boy whom I invited to the dance will be unable to go.

EXERCISE B Rewrite the following sentences to correct the placement of adjective clauses.

Example 1. The bike is on sale this week that I want. *The bike that I want is on sale*
this week.

6. Jolene gave a bird to her brother that has white feathers. _____

_____

7. The pictures were of monkeys that we took. _____

_____

8. The trees held many birds' nests that lost their leaves in the hurricane. _____

_____

9. The burglar turned himself in to the police who had stolen my bracelet. _____

_____

10. The store is on Elm Avenue that offers secondhand clothing. _____

_____

Misplaced Phrases and Clauses

11h. Place modifying words, phrases, and clauses as near as possible to the words they modify.

| MISPLACED CLAUSE | The comic strip features Charlie Brown **that I like.** |
| CORRECT | The comic strip **that I like** features Charlie Brown. |

USAGE

EXERCISE Underline the misplaced phrase or clause in the following sentences. Then, draw an arrow from the phrase or clause to its correct location in the sentence.

Example 1. Charlie Brown and his gang teach readers valuable lessons, including a beagle and a bird.

1. Beth showed me a magazine article about Charles Schulz in the library.

2. Schulz created his comic strip for almost fifty years called *Peanuts*.

3. The comic strip was published in twenty-one different languages about a funny group of neighborhood children.

4. The comic strips are my favorites about sandlot baseball and the Great Pumpkin.

5. The one is about Charlie Brown that I like the most finally hitting a home run.

6. Charlie Brown worries about his batting ability, who loves baseball.

7. Charlie Brown's beagle has an adventurous personality whose name is Snoopy.

8. Snoopy flies an imaginary airplane in World War I called the *Sopwith Camel*.

9. The evil Red Baron often threatens Snoopy's safety, who also flies a World War I airplane.

10. The beagle is confident and comical, nicknamed "Joe Cool."

11. Snoopy writes novels sitting on his doghouse.

12. The bird Woodstock takes shorthand for Snoopy's great novels, who rarely speaks.

13. Linus sucks his thumb, carrying a security blanket.

14. He anxiously awaits Halloween hoping to see the Great Pumpkin.

15. Peppermint Patty and Marcie share a secret crush on Charlie Brown, who are pals.

16. Schulz's children talk of hope, faith, and love, whose problems are not always childhood ones.

17. *Peanuts* has given its millions of readers many laughs, originally called *L'il Folks*.

18. Did you see the box of *Peanuts* comic strips in the attic that Bill collected?

19. Bill was given the collection, whose father is a *Peanuts* fan, for his birthday.

20. Dating as far back as 1951, Bill has comic strips.

Review A: **Modifiers**

USAGE

EXERCISE A   In each of the following sentences, circle the word that modifies the underlined word or words. Do not include the articles *a, an,* and *the.*

Example 1. Can you whisper (quietly)?

1. The colorful headdress is from Jamaica.

2. Today I am unusually tired.

3. Few others have won the award.

4. The child waited anxiously.

5. He is moving rather slowly today.

EXERCISE B   For each of the sentences below, underline the correct modifier in parentheses.

Example 1. I waited (*patient, patiently*) for the bell to ring.

6. Do you speak Vietnamese as (*good, well*) as your brother does?

7. My baby sister cries (*loudly, loud*) at bedtime.

8. These Mongolian dumplings, called *buuz,* taste (*delicious, deliciously*).

9. Alice (*frantic, frantically*) rushed to catch the bus.

10. How (*well, good*) can Greg sing this Israeli song, "Hava-nagilah"?

11. My model of the Eiffel Tower turned out (*good, well*).

12. The park seems so (*peaceful, peacefully*) today.

13. Although she looks fine, Tina does not feel (*well, good*).

14. Fresh fruit and yogurt make a (*good, well*) dessert.

15. The sun shone (*bright, brightly*) on the morning of the swim meet.

16. I always speak (*respectfully, respectful*) to my parents and grandparents.

17. How (*well, good*) a hot, steamy bath will feel!

18. Everyone on the team played (*well, good*) tonight.

19. Jamal felt (*bad, badly*) after eating such a large meal.

20. How (*good, well*) did Rich play the part of Peter Van Daan in the play *The Diary of Anne Frank*?

         HOLT HANDBOOK | Second Course

Review B: **Comparisons and Double Negatives**

EXERCISE A   In the following sentences, if an underlined modifier is incorrect, cross it out and write the correct form above it. If the underlined modifier is already correct, write *C* above it.

Example   1. This book has fewer pictures than ~~any~~ *any other* book we have read.

1. During practice today, the trombone sounded louder than <u>any</u> instrument.

2. This is one of Henry Rowe Schoolcraft's <u>most finest</u> books about American Indian history and culture.

3. Both of the Assad brothers, who are classical guitarists, performed well, but I thought Odair's solos were <u>best</u>.

4. Carlos can run <u>farer</u> than anyone else in his class.

5. This little gray kitten is the <u>most cutest</u> of the litter.

6. Which of these two books by Lensey Namioka is <u>least expensive</u>?

7. Cold water tastes <u>gooder</u> than warm water.

8. Of everyone in our class, Sela collected the <u>most</u> cans.

9. Which of the following Tibetan cities is <u>larger</u>: Lhasa, Xungba, or Nagqu?

10. Olivia seems more daring than <u>anyone</u> on the playground.

EXERCISE B   The following sentences contain double negatives. Cross out any unnecessary words. Insert a caret (∧) where words are needed, and write the needed words on the lines provided.

Example ___*can*___ **1.** My baby sister ~~can't~~ ∧ barely climb the steps.

_____ **11.** Nobody in our neighborhood knows nothing about gardening.

_____ **12.** I won't never be able to play the guitar as well as B. B. King.

_____ **13.** The directions that José gave us don't make no sense.

_____ **14.** Although Carol has only one arm, she hasn't never lost the city tennis championship.

_____ **15.** Our family hardly never gets e-mail on Sunday.

Review C: Misplaced Modifiers

USAGE

EXERCISE A   Underline the misplaced phrase or clause in each of the following sentences. Then, draw an arrow from the phrase or clause to its correct location in the sentence.

Example 1. Felipe called <u>out of the yard</u> to tell us that our dog had jumped.

1. Chirping excitedly, I listened to the bird.

2. Lucas designed a costume for the play with red sequins.

3. Our family saw giraffes driving through the game preserve.

4. Jazz musician Stefon Harris plays the vibraphone, whose first album is called *A Cloud of Red Dust.*

5. I brought a scarf for Mother that is made of silk.

6. The giant land tortoise inhabits the Galápagos Islands which can live 200 years.

7. The man saw a movie about George Washington in the brown hat.

8. The bowl fell on the floor that was filled with fruit salad.

9. Ricardo discovered a book about rock climbing in the library.

10. I saw a petrified tree taking a shortcut through the woods.

EXERCISE B   Rewrite the following sentences to correct dangling participial phrases.

Example 1. Excited about tomorrow's race, sleep did not come easily. *Because I was excited about tomorrow's race, sleep did not come easily.*

11. Prepared for the test, it seemed easy. _____

_____

12. Excited about the party, the balloons were blown up. _____

_____

13. Sewing all day, my costume is finally finished. _____

_____

14. Soothed by the soft music, the baby's cries stopped. _____

_____

15. Traveling through the city of Ayuthaya in Thailand, the beautiful temple called Wat Tanot was seen. _____

_____

Review D: **Modifiers**

USAGE

EXERCISE A In most of the following sentences, a modifier is used incorrectly. Cross out any unnecessary or incorrect words. Insert a caret (∧), and write above it any words that need to be inserted. If a sentence is already correct, write *C* beside the sentence's number.

Example 1. Please speak ~~slow~~ *slowly* so everyone can hear you.

1. Karl hasn't never heard of the Paralympics.

2. Is the Sears Tower in Chicago the most tallest building in the United States?

3. Grandmother never hears no one who speaks softly.

4. Pluto is farther from the sun than any planet in our solar system.

5. Of the two jackets, this one will keep you warmest.

6. Many of the doors in Zanzibar are carved beautiful.

7. The comedian's jokes were more funnier than usual.

8. I enjoyed *Swan Lake* more than any other ballet I have seen.

9. Which of these three salsas is spicier?

10. Yo-Yo Ma plays the cello really good.

EXERCISE B Rewrite the following sentences to correct misplaced or dangling modifiers.

Example 1. Reading my mystery novel, the afternoon slipped away. *As I was reading my mystery novel, the afternoon slipped away.*

11. One player has a dog named Woofer on the team. _____

_____

12. Rushing to answer the telephone, the ringing stopped. _____

_____

13. Birds swooped to the bird feeder chirping loudly. _____

_____

14. Tumbling across the mat, the gymnast's strength and grace were amazing. _____

_____

15. The tired runner congratulated the winner, admitting defeat. _____

_____

for **CHAPTER 11: USING MODIFIERS CORRECTLY** | *pages 238–56*

Proofreading Application: Review

Good writers are generally good proofreaders. Readers tend to admire and trust writing that is error-free. Make sure that you correct all errors in grammar, spelling, usage, and punctuation. Your readers will have more confidence in your words if you have done your best to proofread carefully.

A modifier makes another word or word group more specific. For communication to be clear, however, writers must use modifiers correctly.

PROOFREADING ACTIVITY

Find and correct errors in the use of modifiers in the following excerpt from a movie review. Use proofreading symbols to make your corrections.

    The most best movie I have seen this year is *Genghis Blues*.
No documentary has never been so heartwarming. The film centers
on Paul Peña, a blind musician from San Francisco. Listening to
his radio one night, he hears some strangely music called
throatsinging. Because he hasn't never heard anything so unusual, he investigates. He discovers that the music is extreme popular in a region of Mongolia called Tuva. With practice, he
learns the art form good and sings for a group of visiting Tuvan
throatsingers. He sings so good that they ask him to travel to
Tuva to compete in a contest. No one had never been invited to
do that before. Because of his blindness and health problems,
Peña has a more harder time traveling than he imagined. In addition, Tuva is one of the more remote regions on earth.

Literary Model: Description

Alfonso sat on the porch trying to push his <u>crooked</u> teeth to where he thought they belonged. He hated the way he looked. Last week he did fifty sit-ups a day, thinking that he would burn those already apparent ripples on his stomach to even <u>deeper</u> ripples, dark ones, so when he went swimming at the canal next summer, girls in cut-offs would notice. . . .

Alfonso didn't want to be the <u>handsomest</u> kid at school, but he was determined to be <u>better</u> looking than average. . . . He asked his mother if he could have braces, like Frankie Molina, her godson, but he asked at the wrong time. . . . She glared at him. "Do you think money grows on trees?" . . . Their family ate a lot of frijoles, which was OK because nothing else tasted so <u>good</u>, though one time Alfonso had had Chinese pot stickers and thought they were the next <u>best</u> food in the world.

—from "Broken Chain" by Gary Soto

EXERCISE A Write each underlined modifier. Beside it, label it *positive, comparative,* or *superlative.*

_____

_____

_____

_____

EXERCISE B Write the words being modified by the underlined words in the excerpt.

_____

_____

_____

_____

_____

_____

Literary Model (continued)

EXERCISE C   Using the excerpt from Soto's story as a model, write a short description of a character's thoughts about himself or herself. Use several positive, comparative, and superlative forms of adjectives and adverbs in your description, and underline each one.

_____
_____
_____
_____
_____
_____
_____
_____
_____
_____
_____
_____
_____
_____
_____
_____
_____
_____
_____
_____
_____
_____

EXERCISE D   Why is it sometimes more effective to use comparative and superlative forms of modifiers instead of positive forms?

_____
_____
_____
_____

USAGE | Language in Context: Writing Application

Writing Application: Directions

Writers use modifiers to strengthen their writing and to make it more specific. If the modifiers are misplaced, however, the writing can be confusing and misleading. Notice how the meaning of the following sentence changes when the position of the phrase *with green onions* changes.

> **EXAMPLE**   To the pot add the rice **with green onions.**
>
>   To the pot **with green onions,** add the rice.

A reader following these instructions could become confused. Obviously, correct placement of modifiers is essential when explaining a process.

WRITING ACTIVITY

Imagine that you have been asked to teach your class how to do something. Write down your "how-to" directions so the other students will clearly understand the process. Be sure to place modifying phrases and clauses as near as possible to the words they modify.

PREWRITING   You can do many things that others might like to learn. Brainstorm things that you can do that would interest your classmates. To narrow down your list, ask yourself these two questions:

- What do I like doing?
- What can I do best?

After you have chosen the process you want to explain, write down the steps in chronological order. Be sure to list any materials that are needed.

WRITING   Introduce your paper by giving readers a reason for learning the process. Show that the process is entertaining, challenging, or useful. Then, list the materials needed, and give the steps of the process in chronological order. Use only details that will help your readers complete the process.

REVISING   Ask a friend to read your paper. Someone who is not already familiar with the process can quickly find information that is missing or misplaced. Add transitional words like *first, next,* and *after this*. To avoid confusion, pay special attention to placing modifiers as near as possible to the words they modify.

PUBLISHING   Because specific details are important in a process paper, you need to proofread carefully. Re-read your paper several times to catch errors in grammar, usage, punctuation, and spelling. Make sure that you have correctly used modifying phrases and clauses. Collect all the published "how-to" lists and make enough copies for each member of the class to have a complete set.

EXTENDING YOUR WRITING

You may wish to extend this exercise further. Review the guidelines for public speaking, and demonstrate your process to the class. You might also combine students' papers and create a class "How-to" booklet for your classroom or the library.

Choices: Practicing Correct Usage

Here's your chance to step out of the grammar book and into the real world. You may not notice them, but examples of usage appear in your life every day. The following activities challenge you to find a connection between using words correctly and the world around you. Do the activity below that suits your personality best, and then share your discoveries with your class. Have fun!

ART

Everyone Among Us

Lots of people misuse the prepositions *between* and *among*. Help these people out by illustrating the correct use of these prepositions. For example, you might draw two scenes: one of a person choosing between two things; the other of a person choosing among three or more things. As a caption for each of your pictures, write a sentence that correctly uses *between* or *among*. Then, post your illustrations in your classroom.

ETYMOLOGY

There You Go Again!

The words *their, there,* and *they're* may sound alike, but ask yourself this question: Did they all come from the same word originally? Look up the origins of these three words in a good dictionary. While you're at it, look up another set of words that sound alike, such as *affect* and *effect*. Then, write a paragraph or two describing your findings and share them with your class.

COMEDY

What I Meant to Say

Many comedians joke about usage errors. Go to the library and find a few anthologies of jokes. Do you see any jokes that involve usage errors or plays on words? Write several of these down, and share them with the class.

INTERNET SEARCH

Surfing Safari

Where can a writer go on the Internet to get help with using words correctly? Are there sites that include information on usage? If so, what are their addresses and what information do they have? Report your findings to the class. Give everyone in the class a list of Web sites, noting which sites are the most helpful.

LITERATURE

Outlaws of the English Language

As the old saying goes, "You've got to break eggs if you want to make an omelet." Most great writers have, at one time or another, broken an established usage rule, often for a good reason. Find some examples of this outlaw streak that runs through literature. Then, for each of your examples, write a few sentences that explain why you think the author broke usage rules.

GEOGRAPHY

Map It!

Many regions of the country have their own special ways of talking. Dictionaries may label these usages *dialect* or *regionalism*. Most of these usages are informal, but not necessarily incorrect. Research some regional usages (*reckon, y'all*), and place them on a map of the United States. On your map, include at least three words or expressions that are commonly used in each region you've specified. With your teacher's permission, post your map in the classroom.

WORD PROCESSING

If You Want Something Done Right

Some computer word processors automatically correct some mistakes for you. However, you may not wish to rely too heavily on this feature. Investigate a computer's automatic-correction feature. Identify the errors the feature will correct, and show the class how to select these corrections. Also, show your classmates how to turn this feature on and off. Then, lead a discussion about times when this feature is appropriate and times when it is best turned off.

Usage Glossary A

Review the glossary entries on pages 265–67 of *Holt Handbook* for information on the correct usage of the following terms:

a, an	*a lot*
accept, except	*anyways, anywheres, everywheres,*
affect, effect	*nowheres, somewheres*
ain't	*at*
all ready, already	*bad, badly*
all right	

USAGE

EXERCISE Two choices appear in parentheses in each of the following sentences. Circle the correct choice.

Example **1.** My sister cannot go (*anywhere*, *anywheres*) without our younger brother.

1. (*Anyways, Anyway*), as I was saying, the best part of the story happened after we got on the bus.

2. Did that woman tell her friends that their gift was too expensive for her to (*accept, except*)?

3. When my cousin returned from his week-long vacation, his refrigerator smelled (*bad, badly*).

4. Where did you say that Aunt Sally will (*live at, live*) when she moves across town in two weeks?

5. My father says that our grandfather was (*a, an*) honorable man.

6. Cherise was happy that there were (*a lot, alot*) of the same old choices on the new menu.

7. In 1972, every state (*accept, except*) Massachusetts favored Richard Nixon by a majority of electoral college votes.

8. Dad says that he would prefer to wait in the car until we are (*all ready, already*) to leave the house.

9. Darla's allergy to dogs does not (*effect, affect*) her sinuses as severely as her allergy to cats.

10. Is it (*allright, all right*) if we choose to eat lunch in the courtyard this afternoon?

11. Can you believe that those children (*all ready, already*) know how to speak three languages?

12. Though they were naturally athletic, the enthusiastic couple played tennis (*bad, badly*).

13. If we search every room, I am positive we'll find your address book (*somewhere, somewheres*).

14. This (*is not, ain't*) the most exciting book I have ever read.

15. If you have (*all ready, already*) made up your mind, I will not try to persuade you any more.

16. The marching band in the navy and gold uniforms received (*a, an*) high score in the competition.

17. The worried teenager could not remember where she had left her (*keys, keys at*).

18. The lawn looks (*bad, badly*) today; we have not mowed it for three weeks.

19. All of the jurors (*accept, except*) one believed that the defendant was guilty.

20. Do you think it would be (*allright, all right*) if we cooked spaghetti for dinner tomorrow night?

USAGE

Usage Glossary B

Review the glossary entries on pages 268–70 of *Holt Handbook* for information on the correct usage of the following terms:

between, among	fewer, less
bring, take	good, well
bust, busted	had ought, hadn't ought
could of	hardly, scarcely
doesn't, don't	

EXERCISE Two choices appear in parentheses in each of the following sentences. Circle the correct choice.

Example 1. Who would (*of,* (*have*)) guessed we'd be studying in Paris?

1. Even though she was nervous, Cleo played (*good, well*) at the piano recital last night.

2. There are far (*fewer, less*) bison today than there were one hundred fifty years ago.

3. If you ask me, that little boy (*doesn't, don't*) look too happy.

4. José shared the prize money (*between, among*) his many friends.

5. There are (*fewer, less*) jobs in manufacturing now than there once were.

6. Don't forget to (*bring, take*) your baseball mitt to my house tonight.

7. The extended school year was discussed (*among, between*) the three parents.

8. Derwood might (*have, of*) believed that story about Loch Ness, but I could not tell for sure.

9. Mi Ling won't be able to (*bring, take*) her dog along when she goes away to camp.

10. The child got (*busted, caught*) when he tried to stay up later than the baby sitter had instructed.

11. Many immigrants (*brought, took*) only what they could carry when they came here to the United States.

12. Dinah's opinion is that the novel (*ought not, hadn't ought*) to have ended so suddenly.

13. She put the flowers (*between, among*) two pages of a favorite childhood book.

14. Jimmy Carter (*is, is not*) hardly idle in his retirement from public office.

15. Let's put (*fewer, less*) walnuts in this batch of muffins than we put in the last.

16. We (*ought not, hadn't ought*) to wander off too far; the trails in this park can be confusing.

17. I could (*of, have*) predicted that the most popular song of the year would be that one.

18. Not only was the toddler's temperature too high, but we could tell that he did not feel (*good, well*).

19. When the temperature outside goes below freezing, we let the faucets drip to prevent the pipes from (*bursting, busting*).

20. The art teacher (*don't, doesn't*) mind if we talk while we work, as long as we talk quietly.

USAGE

Usage Glossary C

Review the glossary entries on pages 271–73 of *Holt Handbook* for information on correct usage of the following terms:

he, she, it, they   kind of, sort of
hisself   learn, teach
how come   leave, let
its, it's   like, as
kind, sort, type   like, as if, as though

EXERCISE   Two choices appear in parentheses in each of the following sentences. Circle the correct choice.

Example 1. Why don't you do your homework (*like,* (*as*)) I do, right after school?

1. Perry convinced (*himself, hisself*) that he was going to win the match.

2. The peacock spread (*its, it's*) feathers and strutted away from the turkey.

3. Abraham Lincoln was a quiet man, but his words can (*teach, learn*) us a lot.

4. The man looked (*like, as though*) he had a guilty conscience, but he was later proven innocent.

5. The poet was (*kind of, somewhat*) disappointed when the publisher misunderstood her latest poem.

6. Do you know (*how come, why*) we got chosen to wash dishes tonight?

7. Although (*its, it's*) not right to do so, some salespeople make exaggerated claims.

8. The pumpkin was (*kind of, rather*) small, but we made wonderful bread with it.

9. The old general looked (*like, as if*) he might cry when he talked about the war.

10. The small boy wanted to take the toy, but his cousin convinced him to (*leave, let*) it there.

11. Kurt Vonnegut (*is, he is*) one of Uncle Gene's favorite writers.

12. Will the lifeguard at camp this summer (*learn, teach*) us how to swim the butterfly stroke?

13. The professional photographer uses (*these type, this type*) of film more than any other.

14. I'd like to find out (*why, how come*) this batch of mashed potatoes turned out so lumpy.

15. Because I am good at math problems, I like to (*learn, teach*) other students how to do them.

16. The frantic baby sitter wished that the toddlers would (*let, leave*) her have peace for just one moment.

17. Model airplanes (*they are, are*) all over the desk in my nephew's room.

18. By the end of the boat ride, I was feeling (*kind of, slightly*) sick to my stomach.

19. (*These sorts, These sort*) of test questions are difficult until you get the chance to practice them.

20. The soccer forward decided to shoot right next to the post, just (*like, as*) Coach Weinberg had told the players to do.

Usage Glossary D

Review the glossary entries on pages 275–76 of *Holt Handbook* for information on the correct usage of the following terms:

of	*their, there, they're*
real	*theirself, theirselves*
reason . . . because	*them*
some, somewhat	*this here, that there*
than, then	*try and*

EXERCISE   Two choices appear in parentheses in each of the following sentences. Circle the correct choice.

Example 1. Would you get *(off,* off of) that roof?

1. The reason geese migrate is *(that, because)* they can't survive in frozen water.

2. The crowd revived *(somewhat, some)*, but Judy still thought the team deserved more support.

3. Cristina and Gil sent *(their, there)* regards from Niagara Falls.

4. From now on, I will *(try to, try and)* do my laundry more often so it won't pile up like this.

5. Although *(they're, their)* not large, shrews are quite strong.

6. When you finish your dinner, put your trash in one of *(them, those)* trash cans over there.

7. Robert Burns wrote the *(real, very)* lovely Scottish song "Auld Lang Syne."

8. The reason we can grow corn today is *(because, that)* the Maya cultivated the plant over two thousand years ago.

9. The opposing team scored one run more in the final game *(than, then)* our team did.

10. Although *(their, there)* coats are often white, Arabian horses have jet black hair underneath.

11. I was *(extremely, real)* sorry to hear that you lost your dog.

12. Argentina is farther south *(then, than)* Ecuador and has a cooler climate.

13. The reason the Appalachians are more rounded than the Rockies is *(that, because)* they are older than the Rockies.

14. Her family pays higher property taxes because they live *(outside of, outside)* the city limits.

15. In the past ten minutes, the sun has gone down *(somewhat, some)*.

16. Class, look *(inside, inside of)* this box and choose the book that you would like to read next.

17. I told Julia that I would *(try to, try and)* have lunch with her tomorrow.

18. *(This here, This)* rainbow trout is the largest fish that I have ever caught.

19. Irene, would you pass me *(them, those)* tasty-looking appetizers?

20. Can you even believe that those seventh-graders wrote this entire play by *(theirselves, themselves)*?

Usage Glossary E

Review the glossary entries on pages 277–78 of *Holt Handbook* for information on the correct usage of the following terms:

use to, used to,	*who, which, that*
suppose to, supposed to	*who's, whose*
way, ways	*without, unless*
when, where	*your, you're*
where	

EXERCISE   Two choices appear in parentheses in each of the following sentences. Circle the correct choice.

Example 1. It's only a short (*way,* *ways*); I think I'll walk.

1. Singing *a cappella* is (*when there's singing, singing*) without instrumental accompaniment.

2. This relay race is so confusing that I can't tell (*who's, whose*) turn it is to run.

3. Don't go swimming in the ocean (*without, unless*) you have someone with you.

4. Delia is the only child in her class (*who, which*) is from Peru.

5. Negotiation is (*where people discuss and compromise, discussing and compromising*) to reach an agreement.

6. (*Who's, Whose*) the congressperson for your district?

7. Old Dog Tray was the faithful dog (*that, who*) Stephen Foster owned.

8. Nobody should try out (*without, unless*) he or she is willing to rehearse daily.

9. A mosaic is (*when you have small pieces, small pieces*) of material, such as colored gravel, fitted together to create a design on a flat surface.

10. Did it feel unusual at all when you changed (*your, you're*) last name?

11. The ancient Egyptians had an underworld god (*who's, whose*) name was Osiris.

12. You can't travel to some countries (*without, unless*) you have a passport.

13. The bird (*that, who*) visited the speaker in Poe's famous poem was a raven.

14. The photographer used a special lens because her subject was a (*ways, way*) off.

15. The middle school science teachers are (*suppose, supposed*) to go to a conference next month.

16. In order to collect data from Mars, the satellite has to travel a long (*way, ways*).

17. Sheila read (*where, that*) the city of Austin is going to tear down that dance hall.

18. The flight attendant says that (*your, you're*) supposed to fasten your seat belt.

19. Nelson is not (*used to, use to*) animals, but he warmed up to the puppy right away.

20. The driving instructor pointed out a sign (*where, that shows*) the speed limit has changed.

Review A: **Usage Glossary**

USAGE

EXERCISE Two choices appear in parentheses in each of the following sentences. Circle the correct choice.

Example 1. Did you see that turtle before it slid (*off of*, *off*) the rock and into the water?

1. Jesse will hand me (*them*, *those*) paintbrushes when he is finished with them.

2. By the time we got around to raking the leaves in our front yard, winter had (*all ready*, *already*) come, and there were flurries of snow in the air.

3. Ms. Carbone (*she is*, *is*) my favorite counselor.

4. Red peppers have a powerful flavor, and so they (*affect*, *effect*) the taste of a dish more than most other vegetables do.

5. Can you believe that Martha (*doesn't*, *don't*) want to run for class president?

6. There (*was*, *was not*) scarcely any water in southern California until engineers built waterways from the mountains.

7. Although the chess champion had (*fewer*, *less*) pieces on the board than her opponent, she knew how she would win the game.

8. After World War II, several Allied nations divided Germany (*between*, *among*) themselves.

9. Did you really get (*caught*, *busted*) falling asleep in class?

10. Dad read in the paper (*where*, *that*) the city will let the voters decide whether to create a park here.

11. My Spanish is (*kind of*, *somewhat*) better than my French.

12. Miguel bought (*himself*, *hisself*) a good pen for his writing class.

13. I still do not understand (*why*, *how come*) getting in shape is so difficult while getting out of shape is so easy.

14. William Shakespeare's plays are more well known (*than*, *then*) those of his contemporaries.

15. The reason Lana got angry was (*because*, *that*) Kadeem criticized her unfairly.

16. President Kennedy told Americans to ask what they could do for (*their*, *there*) country.

17. Actually, I did not really want to go to the movies on Friday night (*anyway*, *anyways*).

18. Don't make a promise (*without*, *unless*) you can keep it.

19. Was it Great Britain (*whose*, *who's*) flag was first planted at the summit of Mount Everest?

20. The overanxious reporter did not (*leave*, *let*) the figure skaters have a moment to themselves before asking them how they felt.

Review B: **Usage Glossary**

EXERCISE Two choices appear in parentheses in each of the following sentences. Circle the correct choice.

Example 1. Even though Arthur had (*all ready,* *already*) gone to the grocery store once today, he had to go back because he was missing an ingredient.

1. Why don't we (*accept, except*) the seventh-graders who apply to our club so that we can increase our membership?

2. What do you think would be the (*effect, affect*) of combining hydrogen and oxygen?

3. The living room has warmed up (*somewhat, some*), but Leah still feels comfortable in a sweater and heavy socks.

4. Some of the most expensive cheeses smell (*bad, badly*).

5. I have (*fewer, less*) money in the bank than Carmelita has because she is very good at saving.

6. Did you know that Mrs. Lawless (*used to, use to*) live in Ireland?

7. Amit is going to (*bring, take*) his new videotape of *Never Cry Wolf* to Janet's party.

8. Before there was anesthesia, doctors (*could, couldn't*) hardly do surgery at all.

9. The basketball center hurt (*himself, hisself*) at the end of the first half of the championship game.

10. It's (*kind of, rather*) sad that black-and-white movies are seldom made these days.

11. Licking one paw, the snow leopard stared at us from within (*its, it's*) icy den.

12. In the middle of January, we felt (*like, as though*) warm weather would never return.

13. The lioness holds a (*real, very*) important responsibility in the pride.

14. The baby bird flapped its wings tentatively and (*than, then*) grew brave enough to fly out of the nest.

15. The city of Sydney, Mr. Wilkinson's first home, is a long (*way, ways*) from here.

16. (*This here, This*) chicken soup is the best meal to have when it is cold outside.

17. Firing a piece of pottery is (*when you bake it, baking it*) until the clay is hard and dry.

18. A bee will not sting (*without, unless*) you provoke it.

19. Yes, I'd love to see (*your, you're*) art portfolio if you are willing to show it to me.

20. (*Those sorts, Those sort*) of paint will not mix well with the ones on this shelf.

Review C: **Usage Glossary**

EXERCISE Two choices appear in parentheses in each of the following sentences. Circle the correct choice.

Example 1. I meant it when I told you that (you're) your) a talented singer.

1. After driving through this neighborhood where the houses look so similar, I hardly know where (*I am, I am at*) anymore.

2. Let's find out (*who's, whose*) going to organize the school newspaper staff next year.

3. By the end of the summer, I am determined to (*teach, learn*) myself how to steer this canoe.

4. The Johnstown Flood was a (*real, very*) tragic event in U.S. history.

5. My family (*use to, used to*) live near the beach.

6. Dr. Martin Luther King, Jr., is the leader (*that, which*) everyone remembers from the civil rights marches of the 1960s.

7. Clay has misplaced (*a real, an extremely*) important piece of paper.

8. Luis (*had ought, ought*) to finish this project before he starts the next one.

9. Jerry practiced his guitar chords every night, just (*like, as*) his teacher had encouraged him to do.

10. Carla is proud of her younger brother Joey for doing so (*good, well*) at his new job at the software company.

11. I was so hungry last night that I could (*of, have*) eaten the whole batch of pasta myself.

12. Keith has read (*alot, a lot*) of stories by his favorite science fiction author, but the tale he likes best of all is the one about the man with tattoos that come to life.

13. My best friend can sometimes seem blunt, but I am glad that she is (*an, a*) honest person.

14. Lauretta's shin stung when the tennis ball hit it, but after a minute or two it felt (*allright, all right*).

15. All of the United States is in North America (*accept, except*) Hawaii.

16. When the cast and crew were (*all ready, already*), the stage manager drew back the curtain.

17. This (*isn't, ain't*) the spiciest salsa I have ever tried, but it tastes good with the meal.

18. Maurice accidentally stepped on the back of my shoe, and the shoe flew (*off, off of*) my foot.

19. Why do your cats Princess and Wallflower always go off to the corner by (*theirselves, themselves*) when it is raining outside?

20. Could you and I (*try to, try and*) visit my old friend Jason in Seattle this summer?

Proofreading Application: Video Script

Good writers are generally good proofreaders. Readers tend to admire and trust writing that is error-free. Make sure that you correct all errors in grammar, usage, spelling, and punctuation in your writing. Your readers will have more confidence in your words if you have done your best to proofread carefully.

Because we live in a multimedia world, you will probably have the opportunity to compose scripts for video presentations. Although your words will be heard, not read, you still need to write and proofread your script. Usage errors, even when heard, always make a poor impression. Your audience may focus on the usage errors and miss the message or information you are trying to convey.

PROOFREADING ACTIVITY

Find and correct the common usage problems. Use proofreading symbols to make your corrections.

Example   The reason we are making this video is ~~because~~ we want to
                                                   ^that

introduce you to the computer lab at Mary Taylor Middle

We are very proud of these here computers. We want you to treat

them good because we have waited a long time for them.

Do not slam the mouse onto the desk or smack you're CPU! There

delicate and expensive. We don't want any of them busted. You hadn't

ought to thump the keys on the keyboards either. Anyone whose caught

doing so will find himself or herself in serious difficulty. In fact,

he or she may be setting out in the hall for the rest of the period.

You aren't permitted to take any drinks or food when you come

into the lab either. The computers they are here for everyone, so

have fun, but obey the rules!

Literary Model: Narrative

... sometimes on the water you could see a spark or two—on a raft or a scow, you know; and maybe you could hear a fiddle or a song coming over from one of them crafts. It's lovely to live on a raft. We had the sky up there, all speckled with stars, and we used to lay on our backs and look up at them, and discuss about whether they was made or only just happened—Jim he allowed they was made, but I allowed they happened; I judged it would have took too long to *make* so many. Jim said the moon could a *laid* them; well, that looked kind of reasonable, so I didn't say nothing against it. ...

—from *Adventures of Huckleberry Finn* by Mark Twain

EXERCISE A Carefully study the excerpt, and underline only those errors in standard usage covered in Chapter 12.

EXERCISE B Describe the character in this narrative. Does he sound as if he could be a real person? How does Twain's use of nonstandard elements help you to see the character? Use specific examples.

_____

_____

_____

_____

_____

_____

for **CHAPTER 12: A GLOSSARY OF USAGE**   *pages 264–78*

Literary Model (continued)

EXERCISE C   Write a brief narrative that portrays a realistic character. Use nonstandard usage, creative spellings, or any other appropriate device to relate to the reader the way your character sounds.

_____

_____

_____

_____

_____

_____

_____

_____

_____

_____

_____

_____

_____

_____

_____

EXERCISE D   Describe your character. What devices did you use to create this character? Would your character be as believable if you had used standard English? Explain your answer.

_____

_____

_____

_____

_____

Writing Application: Announcement

Many writing situations call for formal usage: letters to employers or businesses, essays for class, and applications for special programs and awards. For some writing situations, however, informal usage is actually preferable. When you want to make readers laugh by imitating comic language, when you know that formal usage will sound too serious, or when you want to re-create the sound of speech, do not be afraid to use a less formal diction. Remember, though, that even informal writing should not include nonstandard English unless there is a specific reason to do so.

FORMAL AND SERIOUS	We sincerely hope that both of you will again grace us with your presence.
INFORMAL	You guys come back soon, okay?
NONSTANDARD	I ain't gonna be happy if you guys don't come back soon.

WRITING ACTIVITY

Every morning in schools around the country, students hear announcements about upcoming activities. This week, you must make an announcement about an upcoming event. As you write your announcement, keep in mind the difference between informal writing and writing that contains usage errors. Write the announcement for the event as you think your classmates would enjoy hearing it. Be comical, be colloquial, be jazzy—and be sure to check the content with the principal before you go on the air.

PREWRITING   Brainstorm ideas for what you want to announce, and then choose the one topic you will cover. Then, gather all pertinent information about the event: time, place, cost if any, and so on. Keep in mind that regardless of tone and level of formality, your announcement needs to have its facts right and complete. Double-check your facts, or you may embarrass yourself.

WRITING   Morning announcements must be brief—students are waiting to get on with the day's work. Draft several versions of the announcement, looking for ways to make your announcement stand out from the others. How will you get students' attention? How will you keep it? Whatever solutions you come up with, be careful that the vital information about the event does not get lost in lively, entertaining writing.

REVISING   Read the best versions of your announcement to several friends. Listen to their feedback. Can they repeat to you the *when, where,* and *how* of the event? Which version do they like best, and why? Consider their comments as you make your final revisions.

PUBLISHING   Check your announcement for errors in spelling and punctuation. Errors may make you stumble while reading, especially if you are already a bit nervous. Practice your delivery several times before you read the announcement over the PA system. You may also want to publish the written announcement in the school paper or post it on a bulletin board.

EXTENDING YOUR WRITING

If you enjoyed this exercise, you could develop it into a longer writing project. For a journalism class or for the yearbook, attend the event you announced. Interview participants, jot down what you observe, take photos, and then write up the event for publication.

Choices: Investigating Capital Letters

Here's your chance to step out of the grammar book and into the real world. You may not realize it, but examples of mechanics appear in your life every day. The following activities challenge you to see how capital letters function in the world around you. Do the activity below that suits your personality best, and then share your discoveries with your class.

GEOGRAPHY

A Mixed Bag

Americans have diverse ancestries. In your own classroom you may find people with ties to many places around the world. How many? Find out. Hand out a slip of paper to everyone in the class, and ask each person to write down the native country or countries of their ancestors. Then, get a copy of a world map and record your classmates' ancestries on it.

FOREIGN LANGUAGES

When in Rome

Research this question: Do all languages have capital letters? Research capitalization use in a few languages other than English, and report your findings to the class. Provide relevant examples of these languages if you can.

COMPUTERS

A Font for Every Purpose

Computers have made a variety of wonderful fonts available to the general public. If you have access to a computer, you may be able to find hundreds of fonts. Pick at least ten of the coolest ones, and print them out. Make sure that the fonts you choose represent a variety of uses of capital letters. (Not all fonts use lowercase letters.) Next to each of your fonts, identify two or three appropriate situations for using this particular design. Post your fonts on the classroom wall.

HISTORY

Seven Wonders

Can you name all Seven Wonders of the Ancient World? Few people can. Find out about these structures, and prepare a short description of each one, making sure to capitalize correctly. Find illustrations if you can. Finally, prepare a brief presentation on the Seven Wonders, and share it with your class.

RESEARCH

Illuminated Manuscript

Go to the library and find a copy of a page or two from the *Book of Kells*, a gospel manuscript that is hundreds of years old. Show the class how this beautiful manuscript uses capital letters. Using your source material as a model, draw or paint your own illustration of script from the *Book of Kells*. Post your artwork in the classroom, along with a paragraph or two giving background information about this manuscript.

DESIGN

What's on the Menu?

You are the owner of a new restaurant. The trademark of your restaurant is entrees inspired by places all over the world. In fact, each item on your menu is named after a city, town, or country. What are you going to put on the menu—Boston baked beans or Vietnamese spring rolls, perhaps? As you design a menu for your new business, make sure that you include at least a dozen proper adjectives or nouns. You may want to look over international cookbooks for ideas. If you have access to a computer, you can make your menu look professionally printed. If you don't have access, that's fine—lots of fancy menus are hand printed.

WRITING

New Year's Eve

Before long, you'll be looking at another new year and people are going to be asking you, "What are your New Year's resolutions?" Think about the things that you would like to change in your life. Then, pick out ten of them. Write them down, using the format that follows: "Resolved: _____." Make sure that you capitalize the first word in the expression that follows each colon.

First Words and *I* and *O*

MECHANICS

13a. Capitalize the first word in every sentence.

Capitalize the first word of a directly quoted sentence.

    EXAMPLE   **S**he said, "**I**t will be hard to go home after this fun vacation."

13b. Capitalize the pronoun *I*.

    EXAMPLE   Ira said that **I** was the best dancer in the show.

13c. Capitalize the interjection *O*.

    EXAMPLE   Guide and direct us, **O** Lord.

13d. Capitalize the first word in both the salutation and the closing of a letter.

    EXAMPLES   **D**ear Mr. Novato: **S**incerely,

EXERCISE A   In each sentence below, cross out any word that has an error in capitalization and write the corrected word above it.

               A

Example 1. ~~a~~ love for reading is a great thing to develop.

1. When i was eight years old, my grandmother came to live with my family.

2. She always used to say, "great books need to be read often."

3. Every night after dinner, my grandmother and i would settle down to read.

4. On some evenings she'd say something like "o, great bookcase! What do you have for us?"

5. then she'd close her eyes and pick the first book that she touched.

EXERCISE B   In each item below, cross out any word that has an error in capitalization and write the corrected word above it.

              Recently

Example [1] ~~recently,~~ I've become interested in the great naturalist John Muir.

[6] dear Annika,

  [7] how are you? I just received your last letter. [8] as always, I enjoyed hearing your stories.

[9] I appreciated your description of your favorite book, so I thought i'd tell you about a great

book I just read. [10] it's a biography of John Muir, who founded the Sierra Club. [11] A man who

fought hard to protect the wilderness, Muir once said, "climb the mountains and get their good

tidings." [12] After reading about him, i am eager to climb a mountain myself. [13] I haven't

climbed a real mountain yet, but i do like to improve my skills on indoor climbing walls. [14] maybe

one day we could take a trip to a mountain together. Till then, I guess we'll settle for writing letters.

                                          [15] your friend,

                                          Anna

                                         HOLT HANDBOOK | Second Course

Proper Nouns A

13e. Capitalize proper nouns.

(1) Capitalize the names of persons and animals.

Capitalize initials in names and abbreviations that come before or after names. For names that contain more than one part, capitalization may vary.

EXAMPLES	Franklin **D. R**oosevelt	**Sh**ep
	Willem **de K**ooning	Walter **de la M**are
	Ms. Margaret **H**alloway	Katie Brown, **M.D.**

EXERCISE A Circle all letters that should be capitalized in the following sentences.

Example 1. The professor named Jerald (m)iddleton seems to know everything there is to know

about (w)illiam (s)hakespeare.

1. Is there anyone in this class who can tell us Booker t. washington's middle name?

2. I loved the picture Alex just sent us that shows her two cats, pumpkin and snowball.

3. Her daughter's favorite essay was written by Dr. Martin luther King, jr.

4. If you are looking for a good dentist, you may want to try Joseph Dawes, d.d.s.

5. The newspaper story announced the company's new chief financial officer: shawn t. moddes.

6. When I get my first dog, a sheltie, I will name her lassie.

7. The directions say to turn left at the street just after the sign that says "Marcia Ford, M.d."

8. While at her friend Mandy's house, Suzi felt awkward every time mandy's mother called out,

"Here, susie!" and the family's poodle came running.

9. Did the magazine article you read quote Herbert Martin, sr., or Herbert Martin, jr.?

10. When she was in high school, Jackie Joyner-kersee was on the basketball, volleyball, and

track teams.

EXERCISE B For each of the following types of common nouns, provide a corresponding proper noun. Be sure to capitalize each proper noun correctly.

Example _____Rebecca Lobo_____ **1.** name of a professional basketball player

_____**11.** pet

_____**12.** teacher

_____**13.** U.S. president

_____**14.** person in your class (include first name, middle initial, and last name)

_____**15.** doctor (followed by appropriate abbreviation)

Language and Sentence Skills Practice

MECHANICS

Proper Nouns B

MECHANICS

13e. Capitalize proper nouns.

(2) Capitalize geographical names.

EXAMPLES   the **G**ulf of **M**exico   the **S**outhwest   **P**rince **W**illiam **F**orest
Fifty-**f**irst **S**treet [The second part of a hyphenated street number is not
capitalized.]

(3) Capitalize the names of planets, stars, constellations, and other heavenly bodies.

EXAMPLES   **N**eptune   **P**olaris   **G**reat **N**ebula

EXERCISE A   For each item, write a *C* next to each common noun and a *P* next to each proper noun.

Example   ___*P*___ **1.** Cassiopeia

_____ **1.** the Milky Way   _____ **6.** Ursa Minor

_____ **2.** a constellation   _____ **7.** the large continent

_____ **3.** the Indian Ocean   _____ **8.** Mediterranean Sea

_____ **4.** a beautiful ocean   _____ **9.** a still, silent lake

_____ **5.** the southwest peak   _____ **10.** Pikes Peak

EXERCISE B   Circle all letters that should be capitalized in the following sentences. Draw a slash (/)
through any incorrectly capitalized letters.

Example **1.** A ~~C~~onstellation called the (s)outhern (c)ross appears on (a)ustralia's flag.

11. Does your Uncle live in a suburb of washington, d.c., or in the city itself?

12. Reginald says to turn left on Thirty-Seventh street.

13. The only constellation Shannon can recognize immediately is orion.

14. The main business district of Omaha, nebraska, lies near the missouri river.

15. The freshwater Lakes that empty into this river are known as the great lakes.

16. Sharing its name with a mythological god, pluto is the smallest planet in our solar system.

17. A certain species of wild monkey has been living on the famous rock of gibraltar for hundreds
of years.

18. To go from austin to san antonio, he gets on interstate 35 and starts driving south.

19. My cousins have lived on peachtree lane in atlanta, georgia, for three years.

20. The largest ice cap in iceland, vatna glacier, covers more than three thousand square miles.

Proper Nouns C

13e. Capitalize proper nouns.

(4) Capitalize the names of teams, organizations, institutions, and government bodies.

EXAMPLES   **K**ansas **C**ity **C**hiefs   **F**uture **T**eachers of **A**merica

(5) Capitalize the names of historical events and periods, special events, holidays, and other calendar items.

EXAMPLES   **M**alta **C**onference   the **S**ixties   **S**pringfield **S**ummer **F**air

EXERCISE A   Circle all letters that should be capitalized in the following sentences.

Example 1. I love to watch the city's fireworks display every year on the (f)ourth of (J)uly.

1. Will the post office be closed on columbus day this year?

2. How many schools in the United States have the name trinity college or trinity university?

3. The committee decided that the new school's teams would be known as the lincoln high panthers.

4. To punish the colonists for the rebellion known as the boston tea party, England passed a series of laws that the colonists called the intolerable acts.

5. Can you name the country where the matches of the next world cup will be played?

6. My neighbor helped organize the parade for veterans day.

7. Are you going to New Orleans during mardi gras?

8. Next september a friend of Joe's will begin attending the university of redlands in California.

9. The equal employment opportunity commission is known for combating workplace discrimination.

10. Aretha's mom has been working downtown at the department of insurance for seven years.

EXERCISE B   For each of the following common nouns, provide a corresponding proper noun. Be sure to capitalize each proper noun correctly.

Example   ___*Labor Day*___   **1.** holiday

_____ **11.** professional baseball team

_____ **12.** historical period

_____ **13.** historical event

_____ **14.** government body

_____ **15.** organization

Proper Nouns D

13e. Capitalize proper nouns.

(6) Capitalize the names of nationalities, races, and peoples.

EXAMPLES **O**jibway   **E**uropean   **C**hinese   **C**aucasian

(7) Capitalize the names of religions and their followers, holy days and celebrations, sacred writings, and specific deities.

EXAMPLES **R**oman **C**atholics   **H**anukkah   **R**ig-**V**eda   **A**llah

MECHANICS

EXERCISE A In the items below, write a *C* next to each common noun and a *P* next to each proper noun.

Example ___C___ **1.** nationality

_____ **1.** British

_____ **2.** land

_____ **3.** Germans

_____ **4.** deity

_____ **5.** Koran

EXERCISE B Circle all letters that should be capitalized in the following sentences.

Example 1. Have you ever taken part in a ⓟassover ⓢeder?

6. In Greek mythology, hermes is the cunning messenger of the gods known for his winged shoes and hat.

7. Brooke and Paige just bought tickets to see their favorite celtic band play on Saturday night.

8. Lauren's mom prepared a wonderful selection of food for the first night of rosh hashana.

9. The supreme deity of the Muslim religion, islam, is allah.

10. My two favorite dishes at that thai restaurant are ginger shrimp and cashew chicken.

11. We watched a video about the history of polynesian new zealanders, known as maoris.

12. As we drove down the street, we admired the architecture of the episcopal church to our left and the baptist church to our right.

13. When Corey visited India, she learned more about hinduism, which is the country's principal religion.

14. african culture was influenced by the egyptians, who provided Africa with its earliest civilizations.

15. One reason that Kevin is learning hebrew is to increase his understanding of the torah.

Proper Nouns E

13e.   Capitalize proper nouns.

(8) Capitalize the names of buildings and other structures.

    EXAMPLES   **G**lobe **T**heatre   **O**akwood **H**igh **S**chool   **B**rooklyn **B**ridge

(9) Capitalize the names of monuments, memorials, and awards.

    EXAMPLES   **J**efferson **M**emorial   **T**omb of the **U**nknown **S**oldier   **N**ewbery **A**ward

MECHANICS

EXERCISE A   In the items below, write a *C* next to each common noun and a *P* next to each proper noun.

    Example   _ *C* _   **1.** bridge

_____ **1.** Big Ben

_____ **2.** church

_____ **3.** L. C. Anderson High School

_____ **4.** Majestic Theater

_____ **5.** medal

EXERCISE B   Circle all letters that should be capitalized in the following sentences.

    Example 1. The (a)rc de (t)riomphe in Paris stands above France's (t)omb of the (u)nknown (s)oldier.

6. I just noticed that construction is finally underway for atkins elementary school.

7. Did you know that the design for France's eiffel tower was chosen from a contest?

8. Tanya watched the country music awards on TV last night, but I decided to read.

9. The handprints of celebrities appear in concrete at mann's chinese theatre in Hollywood.

10. In 1940, William Saroyan, a writer whose work celebrates life, turned down a pulitzer prize for a play that he said was "no more great or good" than anything else he had written.

11. When we saw a show at the paramount theater last Wednesday, we parked across the street at the covington hotel's parking garage.

12. In Washington this past summer, Kira saw the white house and the lincoln memorial.

13. Once called the tokyo imperial museum, the tokyo national museum showcases Japanese calligraphy, paintings, swords, pottery, and many other kinds of art.

14. Suddenly, a booming voice came over the loudspeaker announcing that Mr. Romano had won our school district's educator of the year award.

15. The shape of the sydney opera house is hard to forget!

Language and Sentence Skills Practice   **263**

Proper Nouns F

MECHANICS

13e. Capitalize proper nouns.

(10) Capitalize the names of trains, ships, aircraft, and spacecraft.

EXAMPLES **S**unset **L**imited   **A**jax   **E**nola **G**ay   **A**pollo 12

(11) Capitalize the names of businesses and the brand names of business products.

EXAMPLES **C**ontinental **A**irlines **H**ertz   **S**aucony shoes **S**tetson hat

EXERCISE A In the items below, write a *C* next to each common noun and a *P* next to each proper noun.

Example ___*P*___ **1.** *Hill Country Flyer*

_____ **1.** train

_____ **2.** USS *Lexington*

_____ **3.** company

_____ **4.** Kraft

_____ **5.** *Sputnik*

EXERCISE B Circle all letters that should be capitalized in the following sentences.

Example **1.** Every time Angela goes to ⓐpollo's ⓒafe, she orders the same thing: pasta primavera.

6. When the British ship *Carpathia* reached the *titanic* at 4:00 in the morning, just over seven hundred people were rescued.

7. The primary corporation that provides bus travel among cities in the United States and Canada is greyhound lines, inc.

8. Uncle Carlo was thrilled when he got the chance to unveil the sign at his brand-new store, cornerstone books.

9. Charles Lindbergh's plane, *spirit of st. louis,* had the most advanced aircraft instruments available in the late 1920's.

10. When my Australian friend Fiona says "nestlé," she pronounces the name of this company as if it rhymes with the word *wrestle.*

Proper Adjectives and Names of School Subjects

13f. Capitalize proper adjectives.

A *proper adjective* is formed from a proper noun and is capitalized.

PROPER NOUN	PROPER ADJECTIVE
Germany	a **G**erman scientist
Kansas City	a **K**ansas **C**ity landmark
Mexico	a **M**exican artist
William Shakespeare	a **S**hakespearean play

13g. Do not capitalize the names of school subjects, except course names followed by numerals and languages.

EXAMPLES   After lunch I go to **F**rench class and then to **a**rt and then to **A**lgebra I.

EXERCISE A   In each sentence below, draw a slanting line through any error in capitalization and write the letter correctly above the error.

Example 1. My new classes are ^{S}spanish and home economics.

1. Our junior high offers french, spanish, and russian courses.

2. The Chunnel connects England and France by way of the english Channel.

3. Shakespeare was the most famous of the elizabethan playwrights.

4. We studied the sculpture of Rodin in my Art History course.

5. The canadian and mexican nations are two nations on the north american continent.

6. I am taking an american history course as well as chemistry I.

7. The United States bought the alaskan region from the russian government.

8. Are you going to take government II in summer school?

9. Must you complete algebra II before you can take a geometry class?

10. In Mrs. Bard's Geography class this semester, we will focus on african and asian countries.

EXERCISE B   For each proper noun, give a corresponding proper adjective. For each proper adjective, give a corresponding proper noun. You may consult a dictionary.

Example 1. Turkey _____*Turkish*_____

11. Texas _____

12. Celt _____

13. Japan _____

14. Jewish _____

15. Scandinavia _____

Language and Sentence Skills Practice

Proper Nouns and Adjectives A

MECHANICS

13e. Capitalize proper nouns.

EXAMPLES	Hal **K. M**oss, **M.D.**	**L**ebanon	**U**ranus	**B**oston **C**eltics
	February	**A**ustralia	the **K**oran	the *Enterprise*

13f. Capitalize proper adjectives.

EXAMPLES	**F**rench	**C**ornish	**S**outh **A**merican	**E**uropean

13g. Do not capitalize the names of school subjects, except course names followed by numerals and languages.

EXAMPLES	**A**merican **h**istory	**G**eometry I	**a**rt class	**G**erman

EXERCISE A In each sentence below, draw a slanting line through any error in capitalization and write the letter correctly above the error.

Example 1. Amy signed up to take ~~s~~wahili as her elective.
                                       S

1. I'd prefer to have lunch rather than dinner at bombay grill tomorrow.

2. On May 7, 1915, the british passenger Ship *Lusitania* sank after being hit by a german torpedo.

3. Do you remember when David hyde Pierce won the funniest male actor award at the TV guide Awards?

4. After attending acting 101, aaron became even more outgoing than he had been in the first place.

5. Even though she says she wants to try something new, Kara orders enchiladas every time she goes to a mexican Restaurant.

EXERCISE B For each proper noun, give a corresponding common noun. For each common noun, give a corresponding proper noun.

Example 1. continent _____*Antarctica*_____

6. Norway _____

7. singer _____

8. Physics II _____

9. building _____

10. Houston Comets _____

Proper Nouns and Adjectives B

13e. Capitalize proper nouns.

    EXAMPLES Ms. Alice Arkeketa   Twenty-third Street   Mars   Bureau of the Interior
                    Zoroastrianism   Mayflower Hotel   Purple Heart   Banana Republic

13f. Capitalize proper adjectives.

    EXAMPLES Canadian Socratic   Israeli   Marxist

13g. Do not capitalize the names of school subjects, except course names followed by numerals and languages.

    EXAMPLES Auto Mechanics I   English literature   government   Russian

MECHANICS

EXERCISE A In the items below, write a *C* next to each common noun and a *P* next to each proper noun.

Example _P_ **1.** Hillcrest Lane

_____ **1.** highway

_____ **2.** New York City

_____ **3.** French Literature 305

_____ **4.** Avenue F

_____ **5.** general

EXERCISE B In each sentence below, draw a slanting line through any error in capitalization and write the letter correctly above the error.

Example 1. Though Kleenex is a Brand Name, many people use this word when referring to any facial tissues.

6. The author of the controversial Magazine article was pat frost, m.d.

7. Earth is the fifth largest planet in the Solar System, and it is the third farthest away from the sun.

8. An architectural masterpiece that includes elements of greek and roman design, st. paul's cathedral stands in london, england.

9. Many Churches observe ash Wednesday by using ashes of palms burned after the previous year's palm sunday service.

10. Because his Poems mimic human thought, the works of the american poet john ashbery often do not have a logical beginning, middle, or end.

Titles Used with People

13h.   Capitalize titles.

(1) Capitalize a person's title when the title comes before the person's name.

Generally, a title used alone or following a person's name is not capitalized, especially if the title is preceded by *a*, *an*, or *the*. However, a title used alone in direct address is usually capitalized.

EXAMPLES	**C**aptain Nemo	**D**r. Lo	**M**s. Kohari	the **c**olonel
	How are you, **L**ieutenant?		What did the **l**ieutenant say?	

(2) Capitalize a word showing a family relationship when the word is used before or in place of a person's name, unless the word follows a possessive noun or pronoun.

EXAMPLES	That's **M**om.	That's my **m**om.
	Aunt Toski	Una's **a**unt Toski

EXERCISE A   Two choices appear in parentheses in each of the following sentences. Circle the choice that has correct capitalization.

Example 1. We have to wait only fifteen more minutes until (*Uncle Marshall's*, *uncle Marshall's*) plane arrives from Minneapolis!

1. After a tense campaign, the Latin Club finally elected its next (*President, president*).

2. What day of the week will (*Dr. Karnik, dr. Karnik*) be taking another look at Catherine's sprained ankle?

3. If you want an opinion about crime in this town, just ask (*Constable Taylor, constable taylor*).

4. Serena's (*Sister Amy, sister Amy*) used to be a conductor of the Seattle Girls' Choir.

5. Our next-door neighbor was the (*Mayor, mayor*) of Des Moines over twenty years ago.

EXERCISE B   In each sentence below, draw a slanting line through any error in capitalization and write the letter correctly above the error.

Example 1. My M̶om's insisting that I go to the D̶octor.
                    m   *d*

6. The leader of the service this morning will be rabbi Schmidt.

7. If you ever get the chance to watch a trial at the Supreme Court, you will likely be impressed with the Justices and their knowledge of each case.

8. Signs all around town urged voters to reelect judge Perez.

9. The candidates thanked professor Sherman for arranging the round-table discussion.

10. Marta's Brother Marcus says he owes his interest in chemistry to professor Frazee.

MECHANICS

Titles of Works

13h. Capitalize titles.

(3) Capitalize the first and last words and all important words in titles and subtitles.

> **EXAMPLES** "**M**ild **A**ttack of **L**ocusts"   *The Boston Globe*   *The Nutcracker Suite*
> "**C**hapter 5: **A L**ook into the **F**uture"   *Cats*   *Dateline*
> "**H**ome on the **R**ange"   *Star Trek III: The Search for Spock*

EXERCISE A In the items below, place a check mark next to each title with correct capitalization.

Examples ____✓____ **1.** *A Separate Peace*

_____ **2.** *Yankee Thunder: the Legendary Life of Davy Crockett*

_____ **1.** "Golden Door: A Nation Of Immigrants"

_____ **2.** *Who's The Boss?*

_____ **3.** *The Return of the Native*

_____ **4.** "Section Four: Sound Effects"

_____ **5.** *Hagar the Horrible*

EXERCISE B In each sentence below, draw a slanting line through any error in capitalization and write the letter correctly above the error.

Example 1. Lynne recommended that I buy a CD called *Ten Year ₙnight* by Lucy Kaplansky.

6. Have you ever seen the TV show *the Dukes Of Hazzard*?

7. The ending of *Where The Red Fern Grows* is too sad for Rita to read more than once.

8. My mother's favorite song on her *shine* CD is "Letters To Katharine."

9. Today's *Mother Goose & Grimm* Comic Strip features the dog gnawing on its owner's shoes.

10. At Shelly's house we played *Asteroids hyper 64* for twenty minutes, then went outside and took a walk.

11. The April issue of *Reader's digest* contains an article by Connie Chung.

12. She saw James Stewart in the play *harvey* at the Lillian Beaumont Theater.

13. Aunt Helen gave me a copy of the book *Pride And Prejudice*.

14. Have you seen the play *evita*, the story of Eva Peron?

15. Your assignment for next week is to read "Chapter 18: The Power Of The People."

Language and Sentence Skills Practice   **269**

MECHANICS

Titles A

13h. Capitalize titles.

(1) Capitalize a person's title when the title comes before the person's name.

   EXAMPLES **S**enator Bradley   the **s**enator   How are you, **S**enator?

(2) Capitalize a word showing a family relationship when the word is used before or in place of a person's name, unless the word follows a possessive noun or pronoun.

   EXAMPLES **U**ncle Kele   Len's **u**ncle   **D**ad   my **d**ad

(3) Capitalize the first and last words and all important words in titles and subtitles.

   EXAMPLES *Star Wars: Return of the Jedi*   **T**reaty of **V**ersailles

EXERCISE A In the items below, place a check mark next to each word group with correct capitalization.

Examples _____ **1.** *The Principles Of Aikido*

     ___✓___ **2.** *To Kill a Mockingbird*

_____ **1.** "Chapter 2: Lawns and Gardens"

_____ **2.** my uncle Ken

_____ **3.** *Tokyo extreme Racer*

_____ **4.** *Death of a Salesman*

_____ **5.** New Hampshire's Governor

EXERCISE B In each sentence below, draw a slanting line through any error in capitalization and write the letter correctly above the error.

Example 1. How do you pronounce the word *live* in Lyle Lovett's album *Live In Texas*?

6. "Casey at the bat" may be the most famous baseball poem ever written.

7. Jerome enjoyed the Columbia Symphony Orchestra's version of Aaron Copland's *Appalachian spring.*

8. Do you think we could talk uncle Jerry into renting *A League Of Their Own* with us tonight?

9. Even though it is short, The Gettysburg address effectively describes president Lincoln's vision of American democracy.

10. I would love to get the chance to see the Broadway play *The lion King*, and then compare it to the movie.

Titles B

13h.   Capitalize titles.

(1) Capitalize a person's title when the title comes before the person's name.

EXAMPLES   **G**overnor Benally   the **g**overnor   How are you, **G**overnor?

(2) Capitalize a word showing a family relationship when the word is used before or in place of a person's name, unless the word follows a possessive noun or pronoun.

EXAMPLES   **C**ousin Abdul   Otis's **c**ousin   **G**randma   my **g**randma

(3) Capitalize the first and last words and all important words in titles and subtitles.

EXAMPLES   *The Messiah*   the *Post-Dispatch*   *A Tale of Two Cities*   "**T**he **G**ift of the **M**agi"

EXERCISE   In each sentence below, draw a slanting line through any error in capitalization and write the letter correctly above the error.

Example 1.   "A Tragedy Revealed: a̸ Heroine's Last Days" tells the story of Anne Frank.
(A written above the a)

1. James Whistler's oil painting *Miss Cicely Alexander: harmony In Gray and Green* is realistic and striking.

2. Who do you think will become the next Governor of Minnesota?

3. The group of young Soldiers addressed colonel Ezba with a great deal of respect.

4. How many recipes have you cut out of this issue of *Cooking light* magazine, grandmother?

5. *Car Wheels on A Gravel Road* by Lucinda Williams is a CD that aunt Shelby listens to constantly.

6. The Professor who teaches Jake's genetics class recommended that the students read the book *jurassic Park.*

7. Playing forcefully, the violin soloist amazed the audience with her performance in the production of Vivaldi's *the four seasons*.

8. What time will aunt mary and uncle theo be coming to dinner this Friday?

9. I find Walt Whitman's poem "o captain! my captain!" rather inspiring.

10. Whenever she gets the chance, Stacy's Aunt Thera reads *the New York Times*.

Review A: **Capitalization**

EXERCISE A In each group of words below, draw a slanting line through any error in capitalization and write the letter correctly above the error.

Example 1. delivering the *San Francisco chronicle* in berkeley
   (C above chronicle, B above berkeley)

1. queen elizabeth II of great britain

2. the capital of missouri, jefferson city

3. 327 east seventy-second street, new york, new york

4. a Summer vacation in the mountains

5. the largest newspaper in the state of alabama

EXERCISE B In each sentence below, draw a slanting line through any error in capitalization and write the letter correctly above the error.

Example 1. On our trip to Washington, D.C., we saw the Lincoln memorial.
   (C above c, M above memorial)

6. Of all of Harrison Ford's movies, i like *Raiders of The Lost Ark* the best.

7. Which song begins with the words "o beautiful, for spacious skies"?

8. You will be a fine member of the staff of Carnegie hospital, doctor.

9. The Golden Gate bridge is in San Francisco.

10. Drive West on Route 66.

11. Many texans cheer for the football team at the University of Texas.

12. Next winter we will visit my Grandmother in South Carolina.

13. The author Nadine Gordimer won a nobel prize in 1991.

14. Nova Scotia and New Brunswick are separated by the bay of fundy.

15. Brazil covers nearly half of the south american continent.

16. The United States celebrates its independence from england on the fourth of july.

17. The planet mercury is closer to the sun than is our own planet, earth.

18. Ernest hemingway wrote a book titled *the old man and the sea.*

19. The irish poet william butler yeats wrote "the wild swans at coole."

20. First-year students at houston high school must take algebra I.

Review B: **Capitalization**

EXERCISE A   In each group of words below, draw a slanting line through any error in capitalization and write the letter correctly above the error.

Example 1. a new Huffy Bicycle

1. new hampshire's largest city, manchester

2. the Western side of Pyramid lake

3. a member of the united states congress

4. the *miami herald*, a large city newspaper

5. 803 south Fifteenth avenue, Wishtree, arkansas

EXERCISE B   In each sentence below, draw a slanting line through any error in capitalization and write the letter correctly above the error.

Example 1. The first time I saw a lion was at the San Diego zoo.

6. Which Shakespeare character said "all the world's a stage"?

7. The poem begins "once upon a midnight dreary . . ."

8. In my art history class i saw a print of one of Dürer's etchings.

9. Toronto is the Canadian city closest to Niagara falls.

10. Wittenberg university is in the state of Ohio.

11. The german flag has three stripes—a red one, a gold one, and a black one.

12. In what year or years did Jack Nicholson win an academy award?

13. Last Summer I went swimming in Lake Erie.

14. farmers in the midwest grow most of the nation's wheat.

15. The Vikings were scandinavian explorers and adventurers.

16. Did you see the movie *planet of the apes*?

17. Mia and i enjoyed the french movie *the return of martin guerre*.

18. sophomores at harrington high school must take world history I.

19. When did you purchase your boat, The *Sandpiper*, captain?

20. College students really enjoy the dartmouth winter carnival.

Review C: **Capitalization**

EXERCISE In each sentence below, draw a slanting line through any error in capitalization and write the letter correctly above the error.

Example 1. Where did ~~m~~(M)om set my copy of *Great ~~e~~(E)xpectations*?

1. Are you referring to the amy Shook who is a computer programmer in san Francisco?

2. One of my favorite CDs of all time is Sarah McLachlan's *surfacing*.

3. The tourist stood in front of a map on the wall at grand central station.

4. When you get to the day-care center called here we grow, ask for the director, whose name is melissa mallett.

5. According to legend, those who kiss the famous blarney stone, located near cork, ireland, will gain the ability to persuade others.

6. When their older sister graduated with two master's degrees, Beth and sally congratulated her by sending her a letter addressed to ellen Sharp, m.a., M.B.A.

7. What did aunt Tamisha think of the 1999 version of *a Midsummer Night's Dream*?

8. The reverend Michael Hunn, a chaplain at kent high school, coaches baseball.

9. The photography in *a River Runs Through It* made Maria's Mother want to visit Montana.

10. One of the history teachers from my sister's Middle School came in yesterday and showed us slides from his trip to santiago, the capital city of chile.

11. Our friend katie brown dreamt that she bought a tiny monkey and named him pepe.

12. Marcus Aurelius, who became Emperor of rome in A.D. 161, is associated with the Golden Age of rome.

13. Muted pinks and purples dominate Paul Ladnier's work *granby snow scene*.

14. After your Mom turns left, look for the sign that reads, "Isabel Price, d.d.s."

15. Was the USS *nimitz* named for the World War II U.S. admiral chester nimitz?

16. Gemma recommends the Web site of the Women's Sports foundation.

17. Julie loved her tour of the alhambra, a palace in granada, Spain.

18. Sharla's Mom is an English teacher at the local Middle School.

19. Missy's Uncle Bruce says that he always enjoys reading *The New Yorker*.

20. Dorothy jeakins won an oscar for her costume designs in *joan of arc*.

MECHANICS

Proofreading Application: Web Page

Good writers are generally good proofreaders. Readers tend to admire and trust writing that is error-free. Make sure that you correct all errors in grammar, usage, spelling, and punctuation in your writing. Your readers will have more confidence in your words if you have done your best to proofread carefully.

Electronic card files are a helpful way for writers to display messages on a Web page. With the use of buttons, the author of a Web page links the viewer from the page's main section to secondary ones. Many of these secondary sections, or electronic card files, contain photographs with captions. In order to be taken seriously, Web page authors should use correct capitalization.

PROOFREADING ACTIVITY

Each item below is a photo caption in one Web site's electronic card files. Find and correct each capitalization error. Use proofreading symbols to make your corrections.

Example 1. New York is sometimes known as the Empire state.

1. New York serves as a major trade center in north america.

2. In search of a larger role in America's Trade, New York built the Erie canal.

3. immigrants from every part of the world have come to New York.

4. Italian, Irish, Chinese, and Hispanic immigrants—as well as Russian jews—figure prominently in New York's history.

5. Many immigrants have passed by the statue of Liberty on Liberty Island.

6. New York's transportation system, which includes John F. Kennedy International airport, also contributes to the state's trade success.

7. The Metropolitan museum encourages businesses to trade in this great city.

8. Columbia university draws some of the finest minds in the world.

9. Sites such as Niagara falls harness New York's rich natural resources.

10. Those who walk on Wall street experience a sophisticated culture that has taken Centuries to create.

Literary Model: Poetry

Southbound on the Freeway
by May Swenson

A tourist came in from
Orbitville, parked in the air, and said:

The creatures of this star
are made of metal and glass.

Through the transparent parts
you can see their guts.

Their feet are round and roll
on diagrams or long

measuring tapes, dark
with white lines.

They have four eyes.
The two in back are red.

Sometimes you can see a five-eyed
one, with a red eye turning

on the top of his head.
He must be special—

the others respect him
and go slow

when he passes, winding
among them from behind.

They all hiss as they glide,
like inches, down the marked

tapes. Those soft shapes,
shadowy inside

the hard bodies—are they
their guts or their brains?

I'm Nobody
by Emily Dickinson

I'm Nobody! Who are you?
Are you Nobody too?
Then there's a pair of us!
Don't tell! they'd banish us, you know!

How dreary to be Somebody!
How public—like a Frog—
To tell your name the livelong June
To an admiring Bog!

EXERCISE A One of these two poems follows a capitalization rule that applies only to poetry, while the other follows rules that apply to most sentences.

1. Which poem breaks traditional rules of capitalizing nouns?

   _____

   _____

   _____

2. How does Dickinson's method of capitalizing affect your reading of her poem? Does it create a particular style?

   _____

   _____

   _____

   _____

   _____

   _____

Literary Model (continued)

3. How does Swenson's method of capitalizing affect your reading of her poem? Does it create a particular style?

_____

_____

_____

EXERCISE B   Write a poem of at least ten lines. Use capitalization either to create a distinct style or to cause a reader to respond to certain words.

_____

_____

_____

_____

_____

_____

_____

_____

_____

EXERCISE C

1. Explain the method of capitalizing that you used in your poem.

_____

_____

_____

2. Do you think it would be effective to break traditional rules of capitalization in other forms of writing—for example, in book reports, essays, or business letters? Explain your answer.

_____

_____

_____

_____

Language and Sentence Skills Practice

MECHANICS | Language in Context: Writing Application

for **CHAPTER 13: CAPITAL LETTERS**   *pages 288–95*

Writing Application: Brochure

"Capitalize all proper nouns" sounds easy enough, and writers rarely forget to capitalize people's names. Looking through Rule 13e, however, you will see that many other proper nouns require capitalization. Keep in mind that names of *specific* people, places, and things are usually capitalized.

EXAMPLE   **H**al **R**odgers, pitcher for the **D**usty **D**ervishes, honed his pitching skills while attending **H**eather **H**ills **H**igh **S**chool back in his hometown of **D**ecatur, **I**owa.

WRITING ACTIVITY

Prepare a brochure for students in your school that features a school club or community organization. Explain the purpose of the organization, and give examples of its activities. If you'd like, include quotations from members about their experience with the organization.

PREWRITING   Go to at least one meeting of the organization that you have chosen. Find out about the group's goals, achievements, regular activities, and special events. Interview a few people associated with the group, and write down some of their responses; you may use one or more of those responses as quotations in your brochure. Be sure to write down important information such as leaders of the group, times when the group meets, and where the group's meetings take place.

WRITING   Decide how to organize your brochure. Write at least five short paragraphs that will be the text of your brochure. Determine whether or not your brochure will include artwork or photos, and design your piece accordingly.

REVISING   Read over your text, and make sure you have followed all rules of capitalization. Also, think about the overall organization of your writing—have you covered all the important parts of the club you are profiling? Rearrange anything that seems out of place, and add any details you may have missed in your first draft.

PUBLISHING   Using a computer or your own artistic talents, design your brochure's layout—arrange the text and illustrations in an appealing way. Double-check the accuracy of information you have included, concentrating on the spelling and capitalization of all specific names. Then, create your brochure. Once you have turned your ideas into a brochure, you will be able to share your favorite school club with others.

EXTENDING YOUR WRITING

If you enjoyed this exercise, you could develop it into a larger writing project. Get together with one or two classmates, and combine your brochures into a catalog. First, write an introduction for your catalog, explaining why people should be interested in the clubs your catalog features. Then, come up with an interesting way to bring your brochures together. Make sure the descriptions of organizations in your catalog fit together in a coherent and interesting way.

Choices: Examining Punctuation Marks

Here's your chance to step out of the grammar book and into the real world. You may not notice punctuation marks, but you and the people around you use them every day. The following activities challenge you to find a connection between punctuation marks and the world around you. Do the activity below that suits your personality best, and then share your discoveries with your class. Have fun!

ETYMOLOGY

Just the Essentials

In this chapter you have been studying essential and nonessential phrases and clauses. What does *essential* really mean? Look up the word in a good dictionary, and find out its root and the original meaning of the root. Ask yourself what other words use this same root. Look up these words and their meanings. Then, prepare a poster in which you show the words growing from the root.

STUDY AIDS

Make a Connection

In order to use commas correctly, you need to be able to identify subjects, verbs, adjectives, and other elements of a sentence. Help your classmates make the connection between these grammatical elements and punctuation. Make a chart or illustration that shows how these elements function together. How you do it is up to you, but whatever you do, make the punctuation marks large enough to stand out in your illustration.

REAL LIFE

You Say Tomatoes

The end mark called a period in American English is not so named in England. What do the British call periods? Find out, and tell the class. See if you can also find out how the two terms evolved.

TECHNOLOGY

Dot Com

You've probably heard *dot*, not *period*, when people refer to Internet addresses. If you surf the Net, explain to your classmates why the Net uses *dot* instead of *period*. Explain the function of dots on the Internet, and show how they are used.

WRITING

To Each His or Her Own

Give your classmates a chance to use colons. Prepare a handout. Your handout will be a questionnaire, but it won't have questions. Instead, you'll write incomplete sentences. To be completed, each sentence will require a series, such as "My favorite three people are as follows: _____" or "Three things that I love to eat are _____." Each student must decide whether or not to insert a colon before he or she finishes filling in each blank. Notice that not all of your sentences need to use colons. Be sure to use several methods of introducing a series. Check your textbook for details. Let your classmates keep your questionnaire to put into their journals.

ART

All Your Ducks in a Row

On notebook-sized paper, draw a giant semicolon or colon. Inside the mark, write the rules that apply to it and an example for each rule. Don't stop now! Make your illustration look sharp! How? Use colors and different-sized markers or pens, and maybe add a smaller drawing or two.

CREATIVE WRITING

My Secret Life

Write a journal entry for a semicolon. Consider the following possibilities. Is it possible that semicolons have psychological problems? After all, their name implies they are only half a thing. Perhaps they labor under a feeling of inferiority. It's possible that they try to make themselves feel better by exerting their power over defenseless independent clauses. What do you say? Be as creative as you can in your journal entry.

Language and Sentence Skills Practice   **279**

End Marks

An _end mark_ is a mark of punctuation placed at the end of a sentence.

MECHANICS

14a. Use a period at the end of a statement (or declarative sentence).

> **EXAMPLE** The manatee is also called a sea cow.

14b. Use a question mark at the end of a question (an interrogative sentence).

> **EXAMPLE** Have you ever seen a manatee?

14c. Use an exclamation point at the end of an exclamation (an exclamatory sentence).

> **EXAMPLE** That's amazing!

14d. Use a period or an exclamation point at the end of a request or a command (an imperative sentence).

> **EXAMPLES** Please read this book about manatees. [a request]
>
> Give me that book right now! [a command]

EXERCISE In the following sentences, add periods, question marks, and exclamation points where they are needed.

Example 1. Look at this amazing photograph!

1. Do you know where Sanibel Island is

2. Sometimes you can see manatees off the coast

3. Did you know they are endangered

4. Please give me that book about endangered species

5. What wonderful photos it contains

6. I'd like to learn more about endangered species

7. Will you teach me what you've learned

8. What an exciting book this is

9. I have learned a lot about animals from this book

10. Can you recommend some other good books

Abbreviations

14e. Many abbreviations are followed by a period.

EXAMPLES   Joel H. Fairweather   M. E. Gadski   Ms.   Jr.   Ph.D.   N.Y.   Ark.
Co.   Inc.   Corp.   A.M.   P.M.   B.C.   A.D.   Ave.   St.   Rd.

An *acronym* is a word formed from the first (or first few) letters of a series of words.

EXAMPLES   MADD   ZIP   OPEC   CAD   DOS   RAM

Abbreviations for government agencies and some widely used abbreviations are written as acronyms.

EXAMPLES   FBI   CD   NFL   ABC

Abbreviations for units of measure are usually written without periods. However, you should use a period with the abbreviation *in.* (for *inch* or *inches*) to distinguish it from the word *in.*

EXAMPLES   km   ml   ft   tsp

EXERCISE A   Insert periods where appropriate in the following sentences.

Example 1. I read a biography of C. S. Lewis.

1. Mrs Walsh is the principal of Westdale Elementary School.

2. Have you met Dr Richards?

3. Zechariah Hoyt, Jr, wrote the prize-winning essay on ocelots.

4. Mr and Mrs Bertinot are joining us for dinner tonight.

5. Mr A D Mannion will be playing drums with the band tonight.

EXERCISE B   On the line provided, write the abbreviation or acronym for the word or phrase.

Example   _____FBI_____ **1.** Federal Bureau of Investigation

_____ **6.** ounce

_____ **7.** pound

_____ **8.** yard

_____ **9.** National Aeronautics and Space Administration

_____ **10.** Public Broadcasting Service

_____ **11.** teaspoon

_____ **12.** centimeter

_____ **13.** Central Intelligence Agency

_____ **14.** Individual Retirement Account

_____ **15.** feet

MECHANICS

End Marks and Abbreviations

14a.	Use a period at the end of a statement (or declarative sentence).
14b.	Use a question mark at the end of a question (an interrogative sentence).
14c.	Use an exclamation point at the end of an exclamation (an exclamatory sentence).
14d.	Use a period or an exclamation point at the end of a request or a command (an imperative sentence).

EXAMPLES   I'd like to go.   Will you be going?   Hurry!   Come with me.

| **14e.** | Many abbreviations are followed by a period. |

EXAMPLES   J. R. Ewing   Rev.   Nebr.   P.M.   St.   Ltd.
               HUD   CIA   lb

EXERCISE A In each of the following sentences, add periods, question marks, and exclamation points where needed.

Example 1. Did you see Mrs. Hanson in the hallway?

1. What a wonderful day this is

2. Watch out for that hole, Mr Willis

3. The meeting is at 2:00 this afternoon

4. Is Dr Winston in today

5. James Koenecke, Sr, is speaking to our class

6. Have you read anything by F Scott Fitzgerald

7. How magnificent the dove's wings are

8. Did Mrs Evans once work for the FBI

9. The plane is about to take off, so hurry up

10. Our class did research on the life of John F Kennedy, Jr

EXERCISE B Add periods, question marks, and exclamation points where they are needed in the following sentences.

Example 1. Did you speak with Walter Griffey, Jr.?

11. Will Mr and Mrs Walton be coming to the play

12. Watch out for that car

13. Are we going to hear Ms Sills sing again

14. They were advised to speak with a specialist in internal medicine

15. What lovely roses Mrs Greene grows

Commas with Items in a Series

MECHANICS

14f. Use commas to separate items in a series.

EXAMPLES   His pocket was full of pennies, nickels, and dimes. [nouns]

The coins were small, shiny, and numerous. [adjectives]

Counting, rolling, and depositing the coins took all day. [gerunds]

Daphne knew where the bank was, how late it was open, and how we could get there. [subordinate clauses]

I counted the money, Daphne put it in the envelope, and we left. [short independent clauses]

14g. Use commas to separate two or more adjectives preceding a noun.

EXAMPLE   This adorable, cuddly puppy is available for adoption.

EXERCISE A   In the following sentences, insert commas where they are needed.

Example 1. Tony worked at a mint so that he could learn how money is made, where it is stored, and how the new counterfeit-proofing measures work.

1. He examined studied and took notes on the history of paper money.

2. On U.S. bills are portraits of Washington Lincoln and Hamilton.

3. I read a well-written interesting article about the designs on the corners of bills.

4. At the mint, Tony watched the complicated intricate processes of taking bills off the assembly line and packing the money.

5. He doesn't know who determines when money is too old to use where it goes or how it is replaced.

EXERCISE B   In the following paragraph, insert commas where they are needed.

Example [1] My French teacher got to hear, speak, and learn some French this summer.

[6] Mr. Carrillo took an interesting adventurous trip to Europe. **[7]** He flew to France traveled overland to Spain and took a boat to England. **[8]** He traveled in the air by land and on the water. **[9]** Visiting cathedrals eating pastries and seeing palaces were his favorite activities. **[10]** The trip was educational enjoyable and memorable.

Commas with Compound Sentences

14h. Use a comma before a coordinating conjunction (*and, but, for, nor, or, so,* or *yet*) when it joins independent clauses in a compound sentence.

> **EXAMPLES**   The children must go to bed early**, or** they will be tired in the morning.
>
> The sky was dark and cloudy**, but** the sun was still out.

When the independent clauses are very short, the comma before *and, but,* or *or* is sometimes omitted.

> **EXAMPLE**   I'm ready but Paul isn't.

EXERCISE A   In the following sentences, insert commas where they are needed.

Example 1. I'm interested in sound**,** so I recently read several books about it.

1. The books were informative but I learned even more in my science class.

2. Big speakers called woofers make low sounds and small speakers called tweeters make high sounds.

3. Sound comes from something moving yet you can't always see the movement.

4. Air carries vibrations to your ears and then you hear sounds.

5. Most hearing-impaired people can hear some sounds and they can feel the vibrations.

EXERCISE B   In the following sentences, insert commas where they are needed.

Example 1. I thought I left my jacket on the porch**,** but it's not there.

6. I wrote a short book about butterflies and Joshua drew the illustrations.

7. If possible, Salim will meet Beula on Tuesday or he will meet her on Friday.

8. Field hockey is an exciting team sport but soccer is my all-time favorite sport.

9. I couldn't make it to the scout meeting so I called the troop leader to tell him.

10. I submitted my best paintings and drawings to the annual art contest but another student in my class won first prize.

MECHANICS

Commas with Interrupters A

14i. Use commas to set off an expression that interrupts a sentence.

(1) Use commas to set off nonessential participial phrases and nonessential subordinate clauses.

Do not set off *essential* (or *restrictive*) phrases or clauses.

EXAMPLES   My aunt, **having been in school for five years,** is now an architect. [nonessential phrase]

Those years **that she spent in school** have prepared her well. [essential clause]

(2) Use commas to set off nonessential appositives and nonessential appositive phrases.

EXAMPLES   My best friend, **Ramona Suarez,** came here from Mexico. [nonessential]

My brother **Samuel** is the oldest of my brothers. [essential]

EXERCISE   In the sentences below, identify each underlined phrase or clause by writing above it *E* for *essential* or *NE* for *nonessential.* Insert commas where they are needed.

Example 1. Our nation, made up mostly of immigrants and their descendants, is one of the largest in the world.

1. The United States' unique mix of ideas and cultures which come from all over the world has helped to make this nation diverse and interesting.

2. The contributions made by immigrants have included inventions and business ideas.

3. One group that has contributed a great deal is Hispanic Americans.

4. Hispanic Americans many of whom are bilingual have roots in various countries.

5. This group one of the fastest-growing minorities has enriched this nation.

6. Many Mexican Americans answering the United States' call for migrant workers arrived several decades ago.

7. These workers who were paid poorly strengthened the U.S. economy.

8. Unions that they later formed helped them earn better wages.

9. Studying diversity which one can find in abundance in the United States is helpful in understanding sociological trends within a country.

10. Many Americans who are bilingual are able to get better-paying jobs than those who speak only one language.

NAME CLASS DATE

Commas with Interrupters B

14i. Use commas to set off an expression that interrupts a sentence.

(3) Use commas to set off words of direct address.

EXAMPLES When did you get here**,** Aiyana? That notebook**,** Jeff**,** is mine.

(4) Use commas to set off parenthetical expressions.

A *parenthetical expression* is a remark that adds information or shows a relationship between ideas.

EXAMPLES That vase**, I believe,** dates from the twelfth century.

On the other hand, it may not be as old as I think.

MECHANICS

EXERCISE Add commas where necessary in the following sentences.

Example 1. This tree, in my opinion, is the most beautiful in the yard.

1. Dr. Phillips should I make an appointment with you next week?
2. The race therefore was equally challenging to all the contestants.
3. Are you going to join us for tea Mrs. Collins?
4. The rowers of course were exhausted after the three-hour race.
5. Small dogs for example can be great pets for the elderly.
6. The students generally speaking enjoy a great deal of variety in the lesson plans.
7. Have you read this article yet Janet?
8. Mrs. Wyatt is this painting yours?
9. Those antiques by the way are mostly forgeries.
10. The mayor on the other hand disagreed with the committee's decision.

Commas with Introductory Elements

| **14j.** | Use a comma after certain introductory elements. |

(1) Use a comma to set off a mild exclamation such as *well, oh,* or *why* at the beginning of a sentence. Other introductory words, such as *yes* and *no,* are also set off with commas.

EXAMPLES   **Oh,** I see.   **Yes,** she has that book.

(2) Use a comma after an introductory phrase or clause.

EXAMPLES   **At the bend in the road,** turn right. [two prepositional phrases]
Signaling carefully, she changed lanes. [participial phrase]
To water the garden, use the sprinkler. [infinitive phrase]
When the artists painted, they followed several rules. [adverb clause]

MECHANICS

EXERCISE A In the following sentences, insert commas where they are needed. If a sentence is already correct, write *C* to the left of the item number.

Example   1. On the shores of the Nile, a great civilization was born.

1. No the Egyptians were not just farmers.

2. Concerned with the afterlife Egyptian rulers built great tombs for themselves.

3. Built for monarchs and nobles many great stone tombs contained supplies for use in the afterlife.

4. While he was alive the king had his picture painted.

5. On the wall of his tomb a picture shows the king hunting.

6. Well it shows how the king once hunted.

7. When I saw the jewels I thought the kings were rich.

8. Why they believed they could take jewels to the next life.

9. Based on things found in tombs the assumption can be made that they believed they could take almost everything!

10. In Egypt great riches have been found in these tombs.

EXERCISE B In the following paragraph, insert commas where they are needed.

Example   [1] During the years of the Middle Ages, beekeeping was an important part of village life.

[11] Known as the beeward the village beekeeper kept the hives. **[12]** Before sugar was readily available the only sweetener people had was honey. **[13]** By supplying beeswax the beewards also met another key need of that time—they provided a raw material for making wax candles.

[14] For most people in those days cheaper candles were made from tallow. **[15]** Extracted from animal fat tallow was also used to make soap.

Language and Sentence Skills Practice

Using Commas

14f.	Use commas to separate items in a series.
14g.	Use commas to separate two or more adjectives preceding a noun.
14h.	Use a comma before a coordinating conjunction (*and, but, for, nor, or, so,* or *yet*) when it joins independent clauses in a compound sentence.
14i.	Use commas to set off an expression that interrupts a sentence.
14j.	Use a comma after certain introductory elements.

EXERCISE Insert commas where they are needed in the following sentences.

Example 1. Mrs. Rogers, by the way, will be the substitute teacher next week.

1. We brought sandwiches fruit and drinks to the picnic.

2. The cold humid weather took everyone by surprise.

3. I studied all week for the test yet I didn't feel prepared.

4. Oh I should mention that we finished the project last night.

5. The jurors on the other hand did not understand the testimony.

6. The coach made a list of drills posted them on the bulletin board and asked her team members to practice the drills daily.

7. John joined the baseball team Marta joined the soccer team and Juanita joined the basketball team.

8. It was a long slow climb to the top of the mountain but we made it.

9. Keeping an eye out for danger the squirrel nibbled on sunflower seeds.

10. My best friend who is from Tacoma is the first violinist in our band.

Conventional Uses of Commas

14k. Use commas in certain conventional situations.

(1) Use commas to separate items in dates and addresses.

EXAMPLES On December 17, 1903, in Kitty Hawk, North Carolina, modern aviation was born.

The aviator's address is 12 Sky Lane, Rocketville, IN 46208.

(2) Use a comma after the salutation of a personal letter and after the closing of any letter.

EXAMPLES Dear Andrés,   Yours truly,

EXERCISE The following letter is missing commas. Insert commas where they are needed.

Example The next class field trip will take place on Tuesday, March 20, 2001.

18 Varnum Street

Charlottesville VA 22901

January 29 2001

Dear Angela

   I was delighted to read your last letter, and I'm happy to know that you are doing well.

Things are going well here in good old Charlottesville Virginia and I miss you.

   Last month on Friday December 16, our class went to the National Air and Space Museum in

Washington D.C. On the way we stopped in Manassas Virginia for a snack and a stretch break.

   At the museum, we saw an exhibit on the history of flight, and I learned about the first member

of the Caterpillar Club, Harold Harris. He bailed out of a plane at McCook Field Dayton Ohio and

became the first member of a club that is made up of people saved by a parachute! The exhibit

was all so interesting.

   I remember you asked me for Mrs. DeLillo's address. She is at Sunnybrook Nursing Home

Greystone Road Blacksburg VA 24060. She went there sometime in November 2000. I guess you

know that she is scheduled for surgery on Tuesday February 7. I know she would be happy to

hear from you. You could tell her about your vacation in Paris France. Her birthday is February

23 1933. Did you know that she was born in Biloxi Mississippi? I hope to hear from you soon.

Your friend

Yoko

MECHANICS

Comma Review A

14f.	Use commas to separate items in a series.
14g.	Use commas to separate two or more adjectives preceding a noun.
14h.	Use a comma before a coordinating conjunction (*and, but, for, nor, or, so,* or *yet*) when it joins independent clauses in a compound sentence.
14i.	Use commas to set off an expression that interrupts a sentence.
14j.	Use a comma after certain introductory elements.
14k.	Use commas in certain conventional situations.

EXERCISE   Insert commas where they are needed in the following sentences.

Example 1. The younger, more delicate kittens, on the other hand, will be adopted out to
families who already have at least one cat.

1. The costly fragile items will be moved first.

2. In a box under the coffee table you will find the books that you requested.

3. Well I'm not sure I would go on that trip if I were you.

4. The audience members by the way have never seen a musical production like this one.

5. Dr. Gravatz are you ready for your next patient?

6. The singers learned the music memorized the words and rehearsed the songs daily.

7. We asked how to solve the problem how to indicate the answer and where to print the results.

8. Joanna Killeen was born on November 10 1961.

9. Jeffrey Hellmer a world-class pianist studied in Rochester New York.

10. Barney doesn't play trombone nor does he play trumpet.

MECHANICS

Comma Review B

14f.	Use commas to separate items in a series.
14g.	Use commas to separate two or more adjectives preceding a noun.
14h.	Use a comma before a coordinating conjunction (*and, but, for, nor, or, so,* or *yet*) when it joins independent clauses in a compound sentence.
14i.	Use commas to set off an expression that interrupts a sentence.
14j.	Use a comma after certain introductory elements.
14k.	Use commas in certain conventional situations.

EXERCISE Insert commas where they are needed in the following sentences.

Example 1. We know jays, for example, visit our feeder, but we can't identify the other birds.

1. The amusement park had roller coasters carousels and pony rides.

2. I'm not sure if I would like this music so I will make a decision later.

3. I went to see the opera *Madama Butterfly* but I didn't understand everything.

4. The book you're reading by the way is by my favorite author.

5. Craig moved to 3145 Palmer Avenue Knoxville Tennessee.

6. Marcos did you hear my question?

7. Having stayed up most of the night the boys were very tired in the morning.

8. We planted the seeds watered them daily and watched them grow.

9. Kenneth Rutter who is my first cousin teaches horseback riding.

10. Katerina on the other hand is a skilled graceful skater.

11. We will be in Lima Ohio for one day and then we go on to New York.

12. Is it true Vinnie that you've already finished your research paper?

13. I looked all over the living room dining room and kitchen for the cat's toy.

14. I'm leaving so why don't you leave with me?

15. Jason don't forget to reserve the room.

16. Trisha and Karen are in the same classes for English Spanish and math.

17. It was a slim green leather volume.

18. Dear Kathryn

19. While you clear the table I'll start washing the dishes.

20. I'll always remember June 10 2000 as the day we moved into our new house.

MECHANICS

Semicolons A

14l. Use a semicolon between independent clauses in a sentence when they are not joined by *and, but, for, nor, or, so,* or *yet.*

  EXAMPLE   Cotton is grown in the South; it is cultivated for its fibers.

14m. Use a semicolon between independent clauses that are joined by a conjunctive adverb or a transitional expression.

  EXAMPLE   Cotton did not do well when planted in the same fields each year; **consequently,** crop rotation was eventually instituted.

14n. A semicolon (rather than a comma) may be needed to separate independent clauses joined by a coordinating conjunction when the clauses contain commas.

  EXAMPLE   Cotton is a low, bushy plant, by the way; and its fibers, which are attached to the seeds, are contained in a boll.

EXERCISE   In the following sentences, add semicolons where they are needed.

Example 1. In home economics we have been studying fabrics; wool is one of my favorites.

1. Wool is a great fabric for cold weather it keeps me warm even when it gets wet.

2. My wool sweater is soft, warm, and comfortable it was hand-knit in Norway.

3. Wool must be cut from the sheep, carded, spun, and dyed nevertheless, the result is worth the effort.

4. I like to wear wool for skating, sledding, and hiking however, my sister, who is allergic to wool, never wears it at all.

5. I also like to wear rayon and other synthetic materials therefore, I buy many different types of fabrics.

6. Nylon is a strong material however, I always seem to get runs in my nylon hose.

7. Some people prefer to wear cotton my father thinks it's the most comfortable material.

8. I like denim in fact, several of my jackets are made of denim.

9. I have bought wool sweaters for my brother, my mom, and my grandfather and my grandmother, a lady with excellent taste, once sent me a wool vest for my birthday.

10. I have learned a lot about fabrics I will be able to make informed decisions about what kinds of material to buy.

Semicolons B

14l. Use a semicolon between independent clauses in a sentence when they are not joined by *and*, *but*, *for*, *nor*, *or*, *so*, or *yet*.

> **EXAMPLE**   We left the park at dusk; it was too dark to look for the lost ball.

14m. Use a semicolon between independent clauses that are joined by a conjunctive adverb or a transitional expression.

> **EXAMPLE**   Joe loaded the camera incorrectly; **as a result,** one roll of film was ruined.

14n. A semicolon (rather than a comma) may be needed to separate independent clauses joined by a coordinating conjunction when the clauses contain commas.

> **EXAMPLE**   The debate team includes Jorge, Cindy, and Vladimir; and Martin, Cindy's brother, is an alternate.

MECHANICS

EXERCISE   In the following sentences, add semicolons where they are needed.

Example 1. Last night was a big night; I got an award for basketball.

1. The sports banquet began an hour late the delay was due to the storm.

2. Some roads were flooded consequently, people had to detour.

3. Sanjay was in charge of the program his expression showed concern.

4. Marielle, the coordinator, was eager to begin the speeches, awards presentations, and banquet but the guest speaker, who was flying in from Chicago, had not arrived.

5. The guest, our sponsor, and Coach Zeff were late all three were to present awards.

6. Umeko's dad had planned to leave early nevertheless, he agreed to lead a discussion.

7. Spring storms can cause a lot of destruction indeed, homes have been washed away.

8. Finally, our guest of honor arrived he was soaked but smiling.

9. The applause was deafening it sounded like a roar of thunder!

10. After the speeches, Ms. Weinberg brought out the awards the coach presented them to all the participants in athletic programs.

Colons

14o. Use a colon before a list of items, especially after expressions like *as follows* or *the following*.

> **EXAMPLE**   Please report to me on the following days**:** Monday, Tuesday, and Friday.

14p. Use a colon before a statement that explains or clarifies a preceding statement.

> **EXAMPLE**   I agree with what Mrs. Chan said**:** "Tell the truth and you will be happy."

14q. Use a colon before a long, formal statement or quotation.

> **EXAMPLE**   It was left to me to state the conclusion**:** "It is clear from what we have heard here tonight that this pipeline should never be built. Our lives and the lives of our children and of their children for generations to come depend on preserving the supply of clean water."

14r. Use a colon in certain conventional situations.

(1) Use a colon between the hour and the minute.

EXAMPLES   11**:**05 A.M.   8**:**30 P.M.

(2) Use a colon after the salutation of a business letter.

EXAMPLES   Dear Ms. Acevedo**:**   To Whom It May Concern**:**

(3) Use a colon between chapter and verse in Biblical references and between titles and subtitles.

EXAMPLES   John 3**:**16   Psalms 3**:**5   *Light**:** Medicine of the Future*

EXERCISE   In the following sentences, add colons where they are needed.

Example 1. We are reading *The Environment***:** *Whose Responsibility?*

1. Our teacher introduced Mr. Burkhardt "It is my honor and my pleasure to introduce Mr. Steve Burkhardt. He is a close friend, a mentor, and an accomplished scientist. Please welcome him."

2. Mr. Burkhardt told us something important We must save the elephants.

3. He also told me the following items are valued by some people elephant meat, elephant tusks, elephant hides, and elephant hair.

4. I read this fact The elephant is on the world's endangered species list.

5. Is the elephant mentioned in Genesis 1 24?

6. My concerns are as follows The herds are disappearing, illegal killing is continuing, and the rural people of Africa still need these elephants to survive.

7. I always remember what is written in Leviticus 19 17–18.

8. We will listen to a lecture at 8 30 P.M.

9. My father always taught me this Respect life in every form.

10. We will learn more about elephants in tomorrow's lecture, which begins at 9 00 A.M.

Review A: End Marks and Abbreviations

EXERCISE   Add periods, question marks, and exclamation points where they are needed in the following sentences.

Example 1. What a wonderful poem you've written, Dr. Wesley!

1. Was the letter addressed to 3212 Willis Drive

2. I received a package from St Louis this morning

3. Are you meeting with Ms Wilkinson this afternoon

4. How beautiful that song was

5. Did you hear the speech by T J Townsend

6. William McLean, Jr, is my guitar teacher

7. We'll see you for lunch tomorrow

8. Please send the money order as soon as possible

9. Are Mr and Mrs Gutierrez coming to the celebration

10. My aunt just took a research job at Plastic Innovations, Inc

11. My VCR was mailed from Boston last Friday

12. The CIA offered Mr Lemoine a job in data security

13. What an amazing film that was

14. Did Dr Cameron write this article about spiders

15. Watch out for that motorcycle

16. Save the postcard from Memphis for the scrapbook

17. Robert Corley, Sr, will be the new advisor for our school's college-bound program

18. Was the order mailed to Worthy Collections, Ltd

19. How precious that baby looks today

20. Is Mr Cambridge still scheduled for 2:45 this afternoon

MECHANICS

Review B: **Commas**

EXERCISE Insert commas where they are needed in the following sentences.

Example 1. I have aunts, uncles, and cousins in Phoenix, Arizona.

1. We stayed up too late last night so we were unable to wake up at 6:00 A.M.

2. The small shy puppy walked slowly into the room.

3. My mother usually packs oranges apples or peaches with our lunches.

4. We copied our notes over made study cards and called out questions to each other.

5. After getting busy signals for nearly an hour the customer gave up trying to call.

6. Looking in every place he could think of the young boy continued to search for his baseball glove.

7. Our family moved from Tempe Arizona to San Diego California.

8. I asked the salesclerk which computer I should buy which printer was best and which monitor would be most practical.

9. The coach was not upset about the loss nor was he discouraged.

10. Siamack is a composer of classical music and Shekoufeh is a jazz pianist.

11. Should we stay home and clean go shopping for clothes or mow the lawn?

12. Glover Gill a composer of modern classical music celebrated his forty-second birthday on March 20 2000.

13. Yes Janelle says that she enjoys the long warm summers in Pensacola Florida.

14. Kendra will be visiting us this summer I believe.

15. The children were quite tired for they had played kickball for several hours.

16. We sent my aunt's gift to 302 Main Street Port Allen Louisiana.

17. The author brainstormed made an outline and then wrote her essay.

18. After we put the dishes away Irena showed us photographs from her trip to Los Angeles California.

19. I went walking in the dark cold moonless night.

20. My best friend from kindergarten Joanna still lives in my neighborhood.

MECHANICS

Review C: Semicolons and Colons

EXERCISE Insert semicolons and colons where they are needed in the following sentences.

Example 1. The speaker hasn't arrived; therefore, the meeting will be postponed until 8:00 P.M.

1. Indira wanted to become an engineer nevertheless, she continued to study literature.

2. Terrence, the captain, flew the plane and Robert, the first officer, contacted the control tower for landing instructions.

3. The pastor explained Zechariah 9 9 to our study group.

4. Our teacher grew up in Wyoming however, she studied in Montana.

5. My grandfather's rule of thumb was this Treat others fairly, honestly, and respectfully.

6. The movie doesn't start until 3 30 P.M. nevertheless, it's a good idea to arrive early.

7. María is the best tennis player in our class in fact, she is the best in our entire school.

8. We read scary stories for half the night as a result, we were too frightened to sleep.

9. At 8 00 P.M., the guests will arrive we should get ready to greet them.

10. Carmen hopes to become a veterinarian consequently, she is studying hard in science class.

11. The clouds are beginning to move off to the east perhaps the afternoon will be sunny.

12. For a pleasant train ride, remember to bring the following items a good book, some healthful snacks, and a small pillow.

13. Nakai is a serious swimmer you can find him at the pool almost every morning.

14. The mayor made her priorities quite clear "I will not rest until this city's traffic problems have improved. I will not stop for breath until we have doubled the size of our police department. I will not let up until our schools are no longer in crisis."

15. The letter began, "Dear Ms. Kimball Thank you for your prompt response to our inquiry."

16. The book is titled *Great Danes A Complete Breed Profile* it contains helpful information on nutrition, training, and temperament.

17. Already the drought has affected three states Texas, Oklahoma, and Kansas.

18. Justin lined up the ingredients for his salad lettuce, radishes, tomatoes, and onion.

19. Edwina is driven by a great dream She hopes to one day pilot a space shuttle.

20. Lunch will be served at 1 00 the menu includes chicken enchiladas, Spanish rice, and fajitas.

MECHANICS

Review D: End Marks, Abbreviations, Commas, Semicolons, and Colons

MECHANICS

EXERCISE   Correct the following paragraphs, adding periods, question marks, exclamation points, commas, semicolons, and colons where they are needed.

Example   [1] When our history class visited Gettysburg, Pennsylvania, we gained a new understanding of the Civil War.

[1] Have you ever visited Gettysburg Pennsylvania [2] This place is the scene of one of the greatest battles of the Civil War consequently, many people have heard of Gettysburg. [3] Defending their beliefs and their honor the soldiers of the North and the South fought one of the bloodiest battles in history there [4] They fought for their generals their fellow soldiers and their way of life

[5] Visiting the battlefield today one is struck by the calm peaceful atmosphere however, on the three days of July 1 2 and 3 1863 it was different [6] What a scene of suffering it was [7] On this beautiful expanse of green soldiers fought were wounded and gave their lives

[8] General Robert E. Lee who was known as a great military strategist seems to have failed at Gettysburg. [9] He positioned Pickett's brigade across an open field from the Union Army [10] The brigade was defenseless and the Union Army positioned on a hill with many trees had its cannons ready [11] Marching courageously across that field most of Pickett's fifteen thousand troops fell.

[12] Some people blame this loss on two commanders General J E B Stuart who was in charge of the cavalry and General Longstreet who was Lee's second in command. [13] Involved in skirmishes for supplies General Stuart and the cavalry did not reach Gettysburg on time [14] Because the cavalry was needed to back up the foot soldiers the cavalry's failure to arrive contributed to the loss [15] Others blame the defeat on General Longstreet they say he was indecisive and ineffective

[16] People continue to study this battle to this day indeed it is one of the most interesting battles of the war. [17] Enthusiasts also stage reenactments of this and other Civil War battles. Will it ever end

[18] If you are interested you can visit Gettysburg [19] For information about this historic site you can write to Gettysburg National Military Park Gettysburg PA 17325 [20] Go there someday It will be well worth the trip

Proofreading Application: Invitation

Good writers are generally good proofreaders. Readers tend to admire and trust writing that is error-free. Make sure that you correct all errors in grammar, usage, spelling, and punctuation in your writing. Your readers will have more confidence in your words if you have done your best to proofread carefully.

There is one particular kind of writing that you want to proofread especially carefully—party invitations! Sooner or later, you will be giving a party. You don't want to be sitting all alone with a dozen balloons and no guests. Your guests do not want to be driving aimlessly around on the wrong day, in the wrong neighborhood, or maybe even in the wrong town. Pay attention to where you put those end marks, commas, semicolons, and colons in a party invitation.

PROOFREADING ACTIVITY

Find and correct the errors in end marks, commas, semicolons, and colons. Use proofreading symbols to make your corrections.

Example What costume will you be wearing.

```
Friends

Break out the face paint dust off those sequins, and find that old
rainbow-colored wig! Dress up as an elephant a rock star, a head of
lettuce, or an elf! We will have: live music, plenty of food, and
contests! Yes that's right; we're having contests.

If you have always dreamed of being a rock star this party could be
your big break! We are having a karaoke contest, contestants will be
singing their favorite songs on stage.

The following fabulous prizes will be offered, a genuine live gold-
fish, an authentic 45 RPM record, and an original sculpture by my
five-year-old sister.

Be at 9746 W Santana Ave. on Saturday, July 12. The fun starts at
11 00 A.M., but it's got to end at 3 00 P.M..
```

Literary Model: Novel

MECHANICS | Language in Context: Literary Model

> Oh! but he was a tight-fisted hand at the grindstone, Scrooge! a squeezing, wrenching, grasping, scraping, clutching, covetous old sinner! Hard and sharp as flint, from which no steel had ever struck out generous fire; secret, and self-contained, and solitary as an oyster. The cold within him froze his old features, nipped his pointed nose, shriveled his cheek, stiffened his gait; made his eyes red, his thin lips blue; and spoke out shrewdly in his grating voice.
>
> —from *A Christmas Carol* by Charles Dickens

EXERCISE A   Read the description of Scrooge, paying special attention to the use of commas. Then, indicate with check marks which rules in the use of commas were being followed.

_____ Use commas to separate words in a series.

_____ Use commas to separate phrases in a series.

_____ Use commas to separate clauses in a series.

_____ Use commas to separate two or more adjectives that come before a noun.

_____ Use commas to set off nonessential subordinate clauses.

_____ Use commas to set off nonessential participial phrases.

EXERCISE B   The reader encounters this description of Scrooge soon after he first appears in the novel. In a small amount of text, the author has provided a great deal of information about the character by using grammatical structures that require commas. What is your reaction to this technique?

_____

_____

_____

_____

_____

_____

_____

_____

_____

_____

NAME _____ CLASS _____ DATE _____

Literary Model (continued)

MECHANICS | Language in Context: Literary Model

EXERCISE C Write a brief description of a character that might appear in a work of fiction. Include several of the following in your description: words, phrases, or clauses in a series; two or more adjectives that come before a noun; nonessential subordinate clauses or participial phrases.

_____

_____

_____

_____

_____

_____

_____

_____

_____

_____

_____

EXERCISE D

1. What is a possible result of commas being overused in an author's description of a new character?

_____

_____

_____

_____

2. Read your character description. Do you believe you have overused commas? Support your answer.

_____

_____

_____

_____

Writing Application: Letter

Commas frequently divide a sentence into smaller parts so that readers perceive each part both alone and within the whole sentence. Often, when we speak, we insert tiny pauses or breaths between sentence elements so that the whole sentence is not heard as one blur of sound. These breaks are especially helpful in separating items in a list. Read the following sentences aloud, pausing ever so briefly at the commas in the second version.

BLURRED MEANING The drill team members purchased new skirts red-and-blue pompoms mega-phones with their names inscribed on them white boots with tassels and scrunchies for their hair.

CLEAR MEANING The drill team members purchased new skirts, red-and-blue pompoms, mega-phones with their names inscribed on them, white boots with tassels, and scrunchies for their hair.

The first sentence is very difficult to read without the commas separating the items in the list.

WRITING ACTIVITY

Your best friend's birthday is coming up, and friends are asking what presents he or she might like. Write a form letter listing items that you know the friend would enjoy and explaining why he or she would like to find them inside a brightly wrapped box. Use commas to separate items in series.

PREWRITING Give some thought to what your friend might most enjoy so that you can produce a specific and helpful selection for your generous friends. Be exact: "I know my friend would like some CDs" might suggest anything from Bach to the latest musical trend.

WRITING This writing occasion calls for a light, happy tone—after all, you are celebrating! It also calls for organization. Do not simply toss out suggestions; instead, categorize them and paragraph them. You might imagine how a mall is laid out, with different stores specializing in different goods. Also, try to convince your readers that these gifts will be hits, based on your knowledge of your best friend. You might list (using those helpful commas again) your friend's characteristics, and then tie them in with the gift list.

REVISING Have a classmate read your letter out loud, pausing briefly between items in series. Have you placed commas correctly? Ask your reader to point out any sentences that are confusing. Can he or she make suggestions to help you make your meaning clearer?

PUBLISHING Check your letter for errors in spelling and punctuation. Then, make copies of the letter and hand them out to friends who might be interested in these gift ideas.

EXTENDING YOUR WRITING

If you enjoyed this exercise, you might want to develop it into a longer writing project. For an English class, you could write a personal narrative about a special gift that you either gave or received. For social studies, you could explore the traditions that surround birthdays in various cultures.

Choices: Exploring Punctuation

Here's your chance to step out of the grammar book and into the real world. You may not notice marks of punctuation, but you and the people around you use them every day. The following activities challenge you to find a connection between punctuation and the world around you. Do the activity below that suits your personality best, and then share your discoveries with your class. Have fun!

WRITING

Tour de Force

Make a list of all the punctuation marks that you have studied in this section. Then, write your masterpiece—a poem, a short essay, or some other piece of writing. In your piece, use each and every mark of punctuation that you have learned. Consider writing a personal letter. Few forms of writing offer a writer as much freedom as a letter.

REPRESENTING

Red Vinyl Chairs

Use the names of organizations and businesses to show your classmates how to form the possessive case. Compile a list of ten names of organizations and businesses from your hometown. Then, form the possessive of each name. To form the possessive of a certain organization's or business's name, you will need to think of products or objects associated with that organization or business. For example, if your town had a diner named Munchees, you could list on your poster "Munchees' red vinyl chairs." Put the list of possessives on posterboard, and decorate your poster with illustrations or photographs (with you and your pals in them, of course). Ask your teacher for permission to display the poster in the classroom.

MATHEMATICS

Closing Statements

How do mathematicians use brackets? Find or create some examples of equations that use brackets. Write your equations on the chalkboard, and explain the function of brackets to your classmates. In your research, you may also find some other ways that mathematicians enclose statements. If you do, go ahead and show these to your classmates as well.

REAL LIFE

In the Cafeteria

Ordinary, everyday conversation is full of breaks in thought and interruptions. With permission, tape a conversation (maybe one in the cafeteria—if you can hear it). Then, write down the conversation and punctuate it, using dashes where appropriate, of course. Put your punctuation to the test by showing the written version of the conversation to the class and listening to your classmates' suggestions.

REAL LIFE

In Old Mexico

In English-speaking countries, last names are sometimes hyphenated to show either a woman's maiden name and her married name or to show the family names of two lines of descent. How are surnames handled in Mexico? Find out and tell your classmates.

HISTORY

1776

Do you know what happened in 1776? Of course you do. It's one of the dates that every American should know. Create a list of what you consider to be the most important dates in world and American history. Ten should be enough. Then, write sentences using each date in parentheses. At the bottom of a sheet of paper, list your sentences in chronological order, and number them from one to ten. At the top of the sheet of paper, draw a time line that covers the dates in your sentences. At the appropriate places on the time line, place numbers that represent the sentences you wrote. Ask your history teacher if you can display your time line in his or her classroom.

Underlining (Italics) A

15a. Use underlining (italics) for titles and subtitles of books, plays, periodicals, works of art, films, television series, and long musical compositions and recordings.

Underline (italicize) an article at the beginning of a title only if it is officially part of the title.

EXAMPLES   ***The Little Prince*** [book]   ***Hamlet*** [play]
Reader's Digest [periodical]   ***Mona Lisa*** [work of art]
Mrs. Doubtfire [film]   ***Dateline*** [television series]
The Nutcracker Suite [long musical composition]

EXERCISE   In each of the following sentences, underline the word or word group that should be italicized.

Example 1. We watched the video <u>Bambi</u> with my little sister and her friends.

1. Have you read the latest issue of <u>Sports Illustrated</u>?

2. Our class just finished acting out a scene from <u>Romeo and Juliet</u>.

3. I have read <u>The Pearl</u> by John Steinbeck.

4. One of my favorite paintings is <u>Christina's World</u>.

5. Did you read that story in the <u>Chicago Tribune</u>?

6. Copland's composition <u>Appalachian Spring</u> has become a classic.

7. Is <u>Newsweek</u> the most popular weekly newsmagazine?

8. I borrowed a copy of the Dickens classic <u>A Tale of Two Cities</u>.

9. <u>Mister Rogers' Neighborhood</u> is a children's series on PBS.

10. Do you know what the myth of Prometheus has to do with <u>Frankenstein</u>, Mary Shelley's famous book?

11. Is there a film version of <u>The Hobbit</u>?

12. Picasso's painting <u>Guernica</u> is a powerful antiwar statement.

13. Did you see the article about me in the <u>Ann Arbor News</u>?

14. My favorite old television show is <u>Gilligan's Island</u>.

15. The final scene of the opera <u>La Bohème</u> made Mimi cry.

16. Darryl's subscription to <u>Boys' Life</u> has expired.

17. The Drama Club is presenting Arthur Miller's play <u>The Crucible</u>.

18. The Humphrey Bogart film <u>Casablanca</u> also features Ingrid Bergman.

19. Is <u>Alice's Adventures in Wonderland</u> your favorite book?

20. Has this week's <u>Time</u> magazine arrived yet?

Underlining (Italics) B

15b. Use underlining (italics) for names of ships, trains, aircraft, and spacecraft.

EXAMPLES   *Queen Mary* [ship]   *Orient Express* [train]
               Flyer [plane]   *Discovery* [spacecraft]

15c. Use underlining (italics) for words, letters, and numerals referred to as such.

EXAMPLES   The *s* is doubled twice in the word *Mississippi.*
               Was the last number *3* or *4*?

EXERCISE In the following sentences, underline each word, word group, letter, and number that should be italicized.

Example 1. Do you know the history of the word <u>career</u>?

1. Parts of the Titanic were found by the underwater craft Alvin.

2. Jane has never had trouble spelling the word ambidextrous.

3. Is it correct to write one l or two in the word traveling?

4. Do you use the word very too often when you write?

5. The English-speaking woman had trouble pronouncing the rr sound in Spanish.

6. The number 14 is lucky for me.

7. The Stourbridge Lion is the name of a train that was built in England.

8. Henry's u's sometimes look like v's.

9. In 1830, the locomotive Tom Thumb raced a horse. Do you know which one won?

10. Katy pointed out the difference between the words emigrate and immigrate.

11. Columbus's three ships were the Niña, the Pinta, and the Santa Maria.

12. Charles Lindbergh crossed the Atlantic in the plane the Spirit of St. Louis.

13. How many i's are in the name Illinois?

14. From what language does the word veranda originally come?

15. This spring we are going to ride the train the City of New Orleans.

16. Is the number 17 a prime number?

17. If I had a spaceship, I'd call it the Starseeker.

18. How many times does the word blend appear in the recipe?

19. The fishing boat the Andrea Gail was lost at sea in 1991.

20. How old is the word uranium?

MECHANICS

Underlining (Italics) C

15a.　Use underlining (italics) for titles and subtitles of books, plays, periodicals, works of art, films, television series, and long musical compositions and recordings.

　　　EXAMPLES　*Star Trek: Voyager*　　*Toy Story*

15b.　Use underlining (italics) for names of ships, trains, aircraft, and spacecraft.

　　　EXAMPLES　*Graf Zeppelin*　　*Lusitania*

15c.　Use underlining (italics) for words, letters, and numerals referred to as such.

　　　EXAMPLE　Some people consider the number *13* unlucky.

EXERCISE A　In the following sentences, underline each word, word group, letter, and number that should be italicized.

Example 1. Last weekend Henry read Steinbeck's novel The Pearl.

1. The teacher asked, "Who has read the novel A Day No Pigs Would Die?"

2. In 1620, the Mayflower sailed for America.

3. The word ostracism has an interesting history.

4. After springing leaks, the ship Speedwell had to return to England.

5. The word occurrence has two r's and three c's.

6. Do you know who flies aboard Air Force One?

7. Today, we learned about the airship Hindenburg.

8. Is that a 5 or a 6? If it's a 6, then your answer is correct.

9. The New York Sun was started by Benjamin H. Day.

10. Jamie wrote an essay about the samurai in the book The Sign of the Chrysanthemum.

EXERCISE B　In the following sentences, underline each word, word group, letter, and number that should be italicized.

Example 1. The Smiths subscribe to National Geographic.

11. Kevin is a devout fan of the original Star Trek television series.

12. Tamika has a part in the play Antony and Cleopatra.

13. The number 20 has two 10's.

14. The art class studied a replica of The Thinker, a famous sculpture by Rodin.

15. Please define the words itinerary, transitory, and ephemeral.

Quotation Marks A

MECHANICS

15d.	Use quotation marks to enclose a *direct quotation*—a person's exact words.
15e.	A direct quotation generally begins with a capital letter.
15f.	When the expression identifying the speaker interrupts a quoted sentence, the second part of the quotation begins with a lowercase letter.
15g.	A direct quotation is set off from the rest of the sentence by a comma, a question mark, or an exclamation point, but not by a period.
15h.	A period or a comma is placed inside the closing quotation marks.
15i.	A question mark or an exclamation point is placed inside the closing quotation marks when the quotation itself is a question or an exclamation. Otherwise, it is placed outside.

EXAMPLES   "Where," asked Charles, "can I find a pen like that?"

Then Rosa said, "What a great backpack that is!"

Did you hear him say, "This is not my country"?

EXERCISE A In the following sentences, add quotation marks where they are needed. Then, triple underline any letters that should be capitalized but are not.

Example 1. Joel said, "what a beautiful night it is!"

1. Pang asked, is that the crescent moon?

2. I think it's the first quarter, I replied.

3. The moon will be full on March 22, he added.

4. I asked, how do you know the date?

5. He said, the phases of the moon are shown on my calendar.

EXERCISE B In the following sentences, add punctuation marks where they are needed. Then, triple underline any letters that should be capitalized but are not.

Example 1. "Today is Friday," said Miss LaSpina. "it's time to check our experiments."

6. Look at mine Wyatt said it's beginning to grow a new leaf

7. That said Miss LaSpina is looking great

8. What happened to mine asked Robert did it get enough light

9. I'm not sure said Velma that I gave it enough water.

10. Did you just say, "i'm a big fan of reptiles and arachnids"

Quotation Marks B

15j.	When you write dialogue (conversation), begin a new paragraph each time the speaker changes.
15k.	When a quotation consists of several sentences, place quotation marks only at the beginning and at the end of the whole quotation.
15l.	Use quotation marks to enclose titles and subtitles of short works such as short stories, poems, essays, articles, songs, episodes of television series, and chapters and other parts of books.

> **EXAMPLES**   "The Scarlet Ibis"   "The Circular Ruins" [short stories]
>
> Mary asked, "Do you think that we can go to the parade on Sunday? I heard that Shelly will be there."
>
> "Sure we can," answered Mary's mother.

EXERCISE A   In the following dialogue, add punctuation marks where they are needed. Also, insert a paragraph symbol (¶) where each new paragraph should begin, and put a slash mark through any letter that is capitalized but should not be.

Example [1] ¶ " I hope," said Meagan, " Ⱦhat we don't get lost."

[1] The trail guide said Watch for the blue markers. [2] Where can we find them Kristy asked.

[3] Usually, you will find them on trees, he replied, But sometimes they are on rocks. [4] It

depends on the terrain. [5] Just don't go very far without having one in view. [6] Can you show

us asked David What one looks like [7] Yes said the guide. There is a blue marker on the right-

hand post of that sign over there. [8] If, during your hike, you can't find where the next marker is,

retrace your steps to the previous marker. Then, try to find the trail again. [9] Are there any

questions [10] Yes, I have one, replied Ángel. Do we have to go

EXERCISE B   In the following sentences, add quotation marks where they are needed.

Example 1. The students in Mr. Robling's class read Edgar Allan Poe's poem " The Raven."

11. My brother can play the song Greensleeves on the guitar.

12. Piri Thomas wrote the short story Amigo Brothers.

13. My favorite chapter in our history book is The Age of Revolution.

14. The students couldn't help laughing as they read the poem Jabberwocky.

15. Ernest Hemingway's short story A Day's Wait has a surprise ending.

Quotation Marks C

15j.	When you write dialogue (conversation), begin a new paragraph each time the speaker changes.
15k.	When a quotation consists of several sentences, place quotation marks only at the beginning and at the end of the whole quotation.
15l.	Use quotation marks to enclose titles and subtitles of short works such as short stories, poems, essays, articles, songs, episodes of television series, and chapters and other parts of books.

EXAMPLES   "Daddy"   "Channel Firing" [poems]

Doug said, "I learned a lot in history class yesterday. Mrs. Lane really knows how to make history interesting."

"I learned a lot, too," replied Janet.

MECHANICS

EXERCISE A   In the following dialogue, add punctuation marks where they are needed. Also, insert a paragraph symbol (¶) where each new paragraph should begin, and triple underline any letters that should be capitalized but are not.

Example [1] ¶ "I think," replied Rico, "we should build a clubhouse." [2] ¶ "That's a good

idea. where should we build it?" asked Sara.

[1] Well said Rico we could build it in Freddy's back yard. [2] My yard is large enough, but I don't

have any building materials replied Freddy. [3] Sara said that is a problem. [4] Wait! interjected

Rico. We have all the materials we need right here. [5] look around you. [6] I don't see any build-

ing supplies said Freddy. [7] I don't see any either said Sara. What are you talking about [8] Look

at all of these boxes said Rico. There must be twenty of them. [9] Oh, I see. Instead of using wood

for the walls and roof said Sara we can use cardboard. [10] Freddy said why didn't I think of that?

We can even paint the cardboard.

EXERCISE B   In the following sentences, add quotation marks where they are needed.

Example 1. Shel Silverstein wrote a poem called "In Search of Cinderella."

11. Jack London uses irony in his story To Build a Fire.

12. Gaspar Sanz wrote a beautiful song called Canarios. Have you heard it?

13. For homework, please read the poem I Am of the Earth.

14. The poem is in a chapter titled This Old Earth.

15. Rosa named her essay Hawthorne and Puritanism.

Quotation Marks D

15m. Use single quotation marks to enclose a quotation within a quotation or a title of a short work within a quotation.

EXAMPLES   "Why were you late turning in your report?" Tamisha asked.

Meredith answered, "I don't know. I had listened to various versions of 'The Highwayman.' I was even looking forward to writing the report. But then, all of a sudden, it was due the next day, and I hadn't written it."

"Did you say, 'I was even looking forward to it'?" asked Tamisha.

"Yes," replied Meredith. "I enjoy writing."

EXERCISE   In the following sentences, add quotation marks where they are needed.

Example 1. Anna said, "Thank you for including me in your article 'Young Musicians to Keep Watching.'"

1. Steve blurted out, "My favorite song of all time is Sittin' on the Dock of the Bay."

2. "Did you see last night's episode The Klingons Return?" asked Tammy.

3. "Yes, I do read poetry," replied Ellen, "and Langston Hughes is my favorite poet. I especially like his poem Harlem."

4. Eddy said, "You might be interested in knowing that I sent my essay The Best Music of the Millennium to a magazine publisher."

5. "Do you know which character said, Uneasy lies the head that wears the crown?" asked Robert.

6. "We heard Mr. Johnson singing the song My Girl while mowing his lawn," said Gina.

7. "Did Mrs. Kay say, There will be no homework tonight?" asked Theresa.

8. "The guitar virtuoso Julian Bream recorded a beautiful version of the song Leyenda," said Carlos.

9. "Please read the poem Mama Is a Sunrise tonight," said Mr. Clark.

10. "Which character said," asked Lee, "To be or not to be?"

MECHANICS

Quotation Marks E

15d–m.   Use quotation marks and other marks of punctuation appropriately.

EXAMPLE   "I'm sure that we have homework tonight. Didn't you hear Mrs. Lee tell us?" asked Steve.

"No, I didn't hear anything about homework," replied Alice. "Mrs. Lee said that we would read during class tomorrow."

"She said," responded Steve, " 'For homework, please begin reading the story on page fifty-two.' "

"Oh, I remember now," said Alice. "We're supposed to read pages fifty-two through fifty-five of 'To Build a Fire.' "

EXERCISE A   For each of the following sentences, add punctuation marks where they are needed.

Example 1.   "Who wrote the song 'Moon River'?" asked Carla.

1. I believe that Dr. Morris said Finish reading the novel tonight replied Rebecca.

2. Have you Jill asked seen my notebook?

3. The doctor replied Take two of these tablets once a day. You should feel better in a week or so.

4. I like to see it lap the miles is a famous first line in poetry, Mrs. Gomez remarked.

5. Who said The play's the thing? asked Jerry.

EXERCISE B   In the following dialogue, add punctuation marks where they are needed. Also, insert a paragraph symbol (¶) where each new paragraph should begin.

Example [1] ¶ "Did Mrs. Phillips say, 'Be sure to study Poe for tomorrow's test'?" asked Tamara.

[6] Yes replied Peter she did say that she wants us to study Poe. **[7]** I have notes from the lecture on Poe's use of rhythm in the poem The Raven said Tamara. **[8]** Jeff responded That's good. I was absent that day. **[9]** We also need to study Hawthorne. I bet she'll ask us about the symbolism in the story The Minister's Black Veil said Gail. **[10]** Okay, here's the plan remarked Tim. Gather all of your notes, and we'll meet in the library at 6:00 P.M. to study.

Apostrophes A

15n. To form the possessive case of a singular noun, add an apostrophe and an *s*.

A proper noun ending in *s* may take only an apostrophe to form the possessive case if the addition of *'s* would make the name awkward to pronounce.

  EXAMPLES a day's pay   James's bookbag   Odysseus' journey

15o. To form the possessive case of a plural noun ending in *s*, add only the apostrophe.

To form the possessive of a plural noun that does not end in *s*, add an apostrophe and an *s*.

  EXAMPLES the Smiths' house   the students' lockers   men's clothing   people's rights

EXERCISE Form either the singular possessive or the plural possessive of each of the following items by adding an apostrophe or an apostrophe and an *s* where needed. Write your answers on the lines provided.

Example _____*boy's mittens*_____ **1.** boy mittens (*singular possessive*)

_____ **1.** teachers books (*plural possessive*)

_____ **2.** Davis desk (*singular possessive*)

_____ **3.** teenagers magazines (*plural possessive*)

_____ **4.** tree branches (*singular possessive*)

_____ **5.** Pattersons dog (*plural possessive*)

_____ **6.** girls lunches (*plural possessive*)

_____ **7.** mice cheese (*plural possessive*)

_____ **8.** cities lights (*plural possessive*)

_____ **9.** cars engines (*plural possessive*)

_____ **10.** chair legs (*singular possessive*)

_____ **11.** workers duties (*plural possessive*)

_____ **12.** CD marketability (*singular possessive*)

_____ **13.** foxes homes (*plural possessive*)

_____ **14.** restaurants atmosphere (*plural possessive*)

_____ **15.** Lewis invention (*singular possessive*)

_____ **16.** day wait (*singular possessive*)

_____ **17.** hood ornament (*singular possessive*)

_____ **18.** Hercules strength (*singular possessive*)

_____ **19.** Jill house (*singular possessive*)

_____ **20.** bands songs (*plural possessive*)

Apostrophes B

15p. Do not use an apostrophe with possessive personal pronouns.

    EXAMPLES   Is that **theirs** or **ours**?   Bring me **my** book.

15q. To form the possessive case of some indefinite pronouns, add an apostrophe and an *s*.

    EXAMPLES   somebody's boots   everyone's chance

EXERCISE Add apostrophes where necessary in each of the following items. Place each apostrophe in an upside-down caret mark to show exactly where the apostrophe should be. If a sentence is already correct, write *C* to the left of the item number.

Example 1. Someone's book was left on the table.

1. I left my book at home. Will you let me borrow yours?

2. Anybodys guess is as good as mine.

3. I have my sandwich right here. Where is yours?

4. Are you saying that this is nobodys chair?

5. John's performance was good, but hers was a little better.

6. I need a wallet for this next magic trick; anyones wallet will do.

7. My book cover is pristine, but yours looks as if it has been dragged behind a car.

8. Somebodys track shoes were left on the patio last night.

9. Although my science project is good, yours is better.

10. Is this newspaper theirs or ours?

MECHANICS

Apostrophes C

15n. To form the possessive case of a singular noun, add an apostrophe and an *s*.

 EXAMPLES Emilio's father   a week's time

15o. To form the possessive case of a plural noun ending in *s*, add only the apostrophe.

 EXAMPLES the players' goals   the Joneses' car

15p. Do not use an apostrophe with possessive personal pronouns.

 EXAMPLES **our** jobs   **his** schedule

15q. To form the possessive case of some indefinite pronouns, add an apostrophe and an *s*.

 EXAMPLES nobody's notebook   anyone's breakfast

EXERCISE A Form both the singular possessive and the plural possessive of each of the following items by adding an apostrophe or an apostrophe and an *s* where needed. Write your answers on the lines provided.

Example _____ book's; books' _____ **1.** book

_____ **1.** raft   _____ **11.** bird

_____ **2.** monkey   _____ **12.** mayor

_____ **3.** teacher   _____ **13.** country

_____ **4.** Jackson   _____ **14.** chair

_____ **5.** tooth   _____ **15.** hand

_____ **6.** goose   _____ **16.** horse

_____ **7.** student   _____ **17.** calf

_____ **8.** baby   _____ **18.** helicopter

_____ **9.** giraffe   _____ **19.** window

_____ **10.** boat   _____ **20.** garage

EXERCISE B Add apostrophes where necessary in each of the following items. If a sentence is already correct, write *C* to the left of the item number.

Example 1. Someone's bicycle will do as well as yours.

21. Nobodys test score was perfect.

22. Although his story was well written, hers was better.

23. Somebodys shoes were left in the rain.

24. Ms. Spencer was impressed by everybodys enthusiasm.

25. No ones skills will be able to replace hers.

Apostrophes D

15r.   To form a contraction, use an apostrophe to show where letters or numerals have been omitted.

EXAMPLES	I am	I'm	is not	isn't
	he will	he'll	of the clock	o'clock
	do not	don't	1999	'99

Do not confuse contractions with possessive pronouns.

CONTRACTIONS	POSSESSIVE PRONOUNS
Who's coming with us?	**Whose** jacket is this?
It's your turn.	The dog buried **its** bone.

EXERCISE A   Rewrite each of the following groups of words as a contraction.

Example 1. she will ___*she'll*___

1. should not _____   **6.** she had _____

2. he is _____   **7.** were not _____

3. will not _____   **8.** I have _____

4. they are _____   **9.** who is _____

5. it is _____   **10.** you are _____

EXERCISE B   Study the underlined word in each sentence below. If the word is incorrect, cross it out and write the correct form above it. If the word is already correct, write C above it.

Example 1. The prize is rightfully ~~there's.~~ *theirs*

11. Joel is not sure <u>who's</u> hat that is.

12. Was it your grandmother who knit <u>your</u> sweater?

13. <u>Theirs</u> the diner I was telling you about.

14. <u>Who's</u> in charge of the dues?

15. I fed the stray cat, but I didn't know <u>it's</u> name.

16. He was wondering whether <u>your</u> his friend or not.

17. The best entry in the contest was <u>theirs</u>.

18. Look outside to see whether <u>its</u> raining.

19. Was it <u>they're</u> dog that was missing?

20. <u>They're</u> not going to the dance on Saturday.

MECHANICS

Apostrophes E

MECHANICS

15s. Use an apostrophe and an *s* to form the plurals of letters, numerals, and symbols, and of words referred to as words.

> **EXAMPLES**   The word has two *r*'s in it.
> Enrico's *T*'s looked like *7*'s.
> Rap music became popular in the 1980's.
> Sharon uses too many *and*'s to join ideas in her writing.

EXERCISE   In each of the following sentences, add apostrophes where they are needed. Place each apostrophe in an upside-down caret mark to show exactly where the apostrophe should be.

Example   1. There are three *Sams* in my class.

1. When *&*s appear in company names, you should write *&*s instead of *and*s.

2. When you are proofreading, look for all the *very*s, *nice*s, and *good*s, and try to replace them.

3. The 1940s was an era of big bands and dance music.

4. He said that only 7s and 5s were in his telephone number.

5. I always think there are two *c*s in *vacuum*, but there is only one.

6. Does the child know his *ABC*s yet?

7. The teacher told them to mind their *p*s and *q*s.

8. Do many newspaper writers begin sentences with *Or*s and *But*s?

9. The young child confused his *s*s and *z*s.

10. He adds extra loops to the tops and bottoms of his 3s.

11. Sitcoms were very popular on television during the 1950s.

12. Mr. Ramirez asked the student to stop giving him *maybe*s.

13. *Cancelled* can be spelled with two *l*s or one.

14. He sometimes uses +s when he should be writing *and*s.

15. Look for *so*s in your writing, and ask yourself whether you should be writing *therefore*s or other words instead.

16. Television miniseries became popular during the 1970s.

17. Can you count to 100 by 2s?

18. Many compromises were made between the North and the South during the 1840s and 1850s.

19. Young children sometimes confuse 6s and 9s.

20. Always cross your *t*s and dot your *i*s.

for **CHAPTER 15: PUNCTUATION**   `pages 352–57`

Apostrophes F

15n.	To form the possessive case of a singular noun, add an apostrophe and an *s*.
15o.	To form the possessive case of a plural noun ending in *s*, add only the apostrophe.
15p.	Do not use an apostrophe with possessive personal pronouns.
15q.	To form the possessive case of some indefinite pronouns, add an apostrophe and an *s*.
15r.	To form a contraction, use an apostrophe to show where letters or numerals have been omitted.
15s.	Use an apostrophe and an *s* to form the plurals of letters, numerals, and symbols, and of words referred to as words.

EXERCISE   Rewrite each of the following sentences, inserting apostrophes where necessary.

Example 1. Katys father said its a good day to travel.   *Katy's father said it's a good day to travel.*

1. Whos going to rescue that little girls kitten? _____

_____

2. Didnt Sam say that you must be ready to go on a moments notice? _____

_____

3. Last months meeting didnt go as well as wed planned. _____

_____

4. Both cars tires should be replaced. Im surprised that neither of the cars has had a blowout yet.

_____

5. Whose books are these? Arent these books theirs? _____

_____

6. More often than not, the teachers lounge is a place for working, not for lounging. _____

_____

7. "Dont worry. The schools computer lab isnt in danger of losing its funding," he said. _____

_____

8. The cars visor helps protect the dashboard from the suns heat. _____

_____

9. The dentist exclaimed, "Your teeths enamel isnt indestructible!" _____

_____

10. The boys box of markers wasnt on the table where theyd left it. _____

_____

Language and Sentence Skills Practice

MECHANICS

Hyphens

15t. Use a hyphen to divide a word at the end of a line.

> **EXAMPLE** After a long search, he found the specific information he needed in the en-
> cyclopedia.

15u. Use a hyphen with compound numbers from *twenty-one* to *ninety-nine* and with fractions used as modifiers.

> **EXAMPLES** thirty-six tickets   one-fourth cup of flour   twenty-second row

15v. Use a hyphen with the prefixes *all–*, *ex–*, *great–*, and *self–* and with the suffixes *–elect* and *–free* and with all prefixes before a proper noun or proper adjective.

> **EXAMPLES** all-important   self-starter   fat-free   meso-American

15w. Hyphenate a compound adjective when it precedes the noun it modifies unless one of the modifiers ends in *–ly*.

> **EXAMPLES** a world-famous athlete   a fully formed sentence

EXERCISE Draw vertical lines to indicate all the places each item can be correctly divided at the end of a line. If an item cannot be divided, draw no lines.

Example 1. great|grandmother

1. open
2. brother-in-law
3. educate
4. strayed
5. fast-moving film
6. fascinating
7. looked
8. twelve-year-old
9. usually
10. forget-me-not

11. fifty-seven varieties
12. elephant
13. movie
14. self-improvement tape
15. two-thirds majority
16. cat
17. pre-Columbian culture
18. sugar-free snack
19. pencil
20. bandwidth

MECHANICS

Parentheses, Brackets, and Dashes

15x. Use parentheses to enclose material that is added to a sentence but is not considered of major importance.

    EXAMPLE   My brother is in the youngest group **(**ages five and six**)** in soccer.

15y. Use brackets to enclose an explanation or added information within quoted or parenthetical material.

    EXAMPLE   Professor Margulies told us, "His **[**Sigmund Freud's**]** theory of the id, ego, and superego was a starting point for many subsequent psychoanalytical theories."

15z. Use a dash to indicate an abrupt break in thought or speech.

    EXAMPLE   We're going to—you'll never guess—a small island in the Pacific.

EXERCISE Rewrite each of the following sentences on the lines provided, adding parentheses, dashes, and brackets where necessary.

Example 1. Ralph Waldo Emerson 1803–1882 was a transcendentalist.

    Ralph Waldo Emerson (1803–1882) was a transcendentalist.

1. That building excuse me, the one on Fifth Street needs to be renovated.

_____

_____

2. Theodore Roosevelt 1858–1919 was the twenty-sixth president of the United States.

_____

_____

3. The florin pronounced flôr'in is the name of a gold coin that was used in medieval Florence.

_____

_____

4. Tiffany began, "At the end of the novel, the main character but I don't want to ruin the surprise."

_____

_____

5. Dr. Brown said, "Plato 427?–347 B.C. was one of history's greatest thinkers."

_____

_____

MECHANICS

Review A: Italics and Quotation Marks

EXERCISE   Rewrite the following sentences, adding quotation marks, underlining for italics, and other punctuation marks where they are needed. Be sure to correct any errors in capitalization.

Example 1. What Henry asked Is the definition of the word clandestine   *"What," Henry asked, "is the definition of the word clandestine?"*

1. Todd asked can you explain the answer to the fourth problem? _____

   _____

2. They often confuse the words affect and effect said Diana. _____

   _____

3. Pedro my sister added Went to the all-state competition in Concord. _____

   _____

4. Have you read asked Daryll the article The Undersea War, which is about the sinking of

   the Lusitania? _____

   _____

5. I saw that sculpture at the museum said Kathie it was next to Stuart Davis's painting

   Swing Landscape. _____

   _____

6. When you read Native Son asked Troy did you know how it would end? _____

   _____

7. Did Jeb say watch 60 Minutes tomorrow night Zoe asked. _____

   _____

8. I saw that article about Apollo 17 in Smithsonian magazine said Mamie. _____

   _____

9. Is the r doubled in the word occurring Phil and Aki asked we can't seem to remember. _____

   _____

10. Lucía, please read the short story Rip Van Winkle for homework said Mrs. James. _____

   _____

Review B: **Apostrophes**

EXERCISE Rewrite the following sentences, adding apostrophes where they are needed. Be sure to correct any mistakes in the use of possessive pronouns.

Example 1. I didnt think youd be able to finish the Johnsons lawn so soon. Who's lawn mower did you use? *I didn't think you'd be able to finish the Johnsons' lawn so soon. Whose lawn mower did you use?*

1. Lets plan a trip to the mountains in 03. _____

2. Wheres the dogs bowl? Henrys mom said that she couldnt find it. _____

3. Ive got a plan to finish my paper by ten. I can use Daviss computer to conduct my research.

4. Theres the woman who's sons showed me their pool. _____

5. Jane said that she can't fix his cars transmission tonight; she needs to fix her's first. _____

6. Dont use too many *really*s when youre speaking in Ms. Fuentes class. _____

7. Everyones face lit up when the teacher announced the results of this years fund-raiser. _____

8. I don't know whos coming to my mother-in-laws house next week. _____

9. No one is quite sure whether the two girls cat is still in the tree. _____

10. He isnt sure who owns those bikes, but hes sure they arent their's. _____

MECHANICS

Review C: Hyphens, Parentheses, Brackets, and Dashes

EXERCISE   Rewrite each of the following sentences on the lines provided, adding parentheses, dashes, brackets, and hyphens where necessary.

Example 1. The small town sheriff Andy Taylor he was portrayed by Andy Griffith was a popular television character for many years. *The small-town sheriff Andy Taylor (he was portrayed by Andy Griffith) was a popular television character for many years.*

1. The well known film director Alfred Hitchcock 1899–1980 made many popular movies. ____

_____

2. The burning question who would be blamed for the crime? was the talk of the town for almost twenty two days. _____

_____

3. The word *extrinsic* ek strin'sik means "not inherent." _____

_____

4. Mrs. Miller continued, "Sir Winston Churchill 1874–1965 had a great impact on world history." _____

_____

5. "Gary, please wash the dog oh, and the cat, too before your great aunt Edna gets here. She's allergic to animal dander," said his mother. _____

_____

6. Mrs. Shaw she's my history instructor told me about the hard fought Battle of Marathon. ____

_____

7. Henry began, "The answer to riddle thirty eight is but, wait, I'll let you solve it for yourself."

_____

8. "Amelia Earhart 1898–1937," said the professor, "was a pioneer in aviation." _____

_____

9. Highwaymen people on horseback who robbed travelers were quite common in centuries past.

_____

10. Guam gwäm is an island on the Pacific Ocean. _____

_____

Review D: **All Marks of Punctuation**

EXERCISE Rewrite the following record of a class discussion, correcting punctuation and capitalization where needed. Be sure to insert a paragraph symbol (¶) where each new paragraph should begin.

Example [1] What do you think Mrs. Caldwell will talk about today asked Juanita. [2] I dont
know responded Jill. Why dont you suggest a topic

[1] ¶ "What do you think Mrs. Caldwell will talk about today?" asked Juanita. [2] ¶ "I
don't know," responded Jill. "Why don't you suggest a topic?"

[1] Tell us about the struggle for womens rights Juanita requested. [2] Mrs. Caldwell said where should I begin? [3] Lets start suggested Paul with Jane Addams' work during the 1880s in Chicagos well known Hull House. [4] After all Paul continued didnt one historian say In the settlement houses women became a force for change? [5] Well, said Mrs. Caldwell, it was in the late 1880s that womens suffrage was granted in Wyoming, Idaho, Utah, and Colorado. [6] Wasnt another important reformer Ida B. Wells-Barnett? asked another student. [7] Yes said Karen. She not only organized the National Association of Colored Women in 1896, but she also fought for other peoples rights. [8] The modern womens movement interjected Jill is also interesting.
[9] Mrs. Caldwell began Yes, it might be said to have begun with Betty Friedans book The Feminine Mystique. In the book, she writes but, wait, well save that for another time.
[10] Anyway, the word feminist was revived, and new emphasis was placed on receiving equal pay for equal work.

for **CHAPTER 15: PUNCTUATION**   *pages 342–62*

Proofreading Application: Advertisement

Good writers are generally good proofreaders. Readers tend to admire and trust writing that is error-free. Make sure that you correct all errors in grammar, usage, spelling, and punctuation in your writing. Your readers will have more confidence in your words if you have done your best to proofread carefully.

Whenever you write about authors or artists and their works, you will be using italics or quotation marks as well as apostrophes. You may well find yourself using hyphens, parentheses, brackets, and dashes when you write about literature.

PROOFREADING ACTIVITY

Find and correct the errors in italics, quotation marks, apostrophes, hyphens, parentheses, brackets, and dashes. Use proofreading symbols to make your corrections.

Example We're celebrating Black History Month!

We've gathered some of the most famous Black Americans' together in one place. Twenty five of these great writers, artists, scientists, and public officials—well, actually, our students will be impersonating them—will be appearing live on our stage. The author of the book "Life and Times of Frederick Douglass," Frederick Douglass (as portrayed by Justin Campbell) will be on hand to talk about his experiences. You'll have a chance to hear Maya Angelou (as portrayed by Nicole Parker. Miss Parker will read Angelou's essay *New Directions*. Numerous examples of African and African American art will be on display; approximately one-third of the exhibit features works by Romare Bearden. Nigel Nokimbe yes, he really was born in Kenya has a wonderful slide show of his hometown. African music will be played on the kalimba also known as the *mbira*. Several local artist's paintings, sculpture, and cloth will be available for sale. The show begins at 6:30 P.M. on Friday, February 18, at W. Recreation Center, 14 Park Road. (Additional parking will be available at Gus's Groceries [1115 Park Road.)

Literary Model: Using Contractions in a Short Story

> I don't have much work to do around the house like some girls. My mother does that. And I don't have to earn my pocket money by hustling; George runs errands for the big boys and sells Christmas cards. And anything else that's got to get done, my father does. All I have to do in life is mind my brother Raymond, which is enough. . . .
>
> I'm standing on the corner admiring the weather and about to take a stroll down Broadway so I can practice my breathing exercises, and I've got Raymond walking on the inside close to the buildings, . . . and he plays like he's driving a stage coach which is OK by me so long as he doesn't run me over or interrupt my breathing exercises, which I have to do on account of I'm serious about my running, and I don't care who knows it.
>
> —from "Raymond's Run" by Toni Cade Bambara

EXERCISE A

1. Write the six contractions that appear at least once in the original passage.

_____

2. Rewrite the second paragraph, replacing each contraction with the two words from which the contraction was formed.

_____

_____

_____

_____

_____

_____

EXERCISE B

1. Read the excerpt again. What effect on the reader does the author's use of contractions create? Support your answer with information from the excerpt.

_____

_____

_____

Literary Model (continued)

2. Would it matter if the author did not use contractions in the excerpt? Why or why not?

_____

_____

EXERCISE C   Using the excerpt of "Raymond's Run" as a model, write a short narrative. Create an interesting character who narrates from the first-person point of view. Include contractions in your narrative to create a believable voice for your character.

_____

_____

_____

_____

_____

_____

_____

_____

_____

_____

_____

_____

EXERCISE D

1. Choose two of the sentences you wrote that contain contractions. Rewrite them, replacing each contraction with the two words from which the contraction was formed.

_____

_____

2. What effect would the elimination of all the contractions have on your narrative? Explain.

_____

_____

_____

Writing Application: Memo

Sometimes punctuation enables readers to find bits of information in a sentence quickly. When writers mark the names of articles, musical compositions, works of art, stories, and so on by placing them in italics or quotations, the writers eliminate confusion and help readers comprehend the sentence with ease.

UNCLEAR   Lunch on the Lawn is my favorite Manet painting.

CLEARER   *Lunch on the Lawn* is my favorite Manet painting.

At first reading, the reader might think that the writer enjoyed going on picnics! Italicizing the title allows readers to take in the painting's name as a unit.

WRITING ACTIVITY

You are on the committee responsible for planning your school's Valentine's Day dance, and your job is to decide on three songs to be played and three poems to be displayed at the dance. Write a memo to the other committee members and sponsoring teachers in which you present and explain your choices. Correctly mark the titles of the poems (and the book or books in which the poems appear) as well as the titles of the songs.

PREWRITING   Brainstorm a list of possible songs and poems, based on personal experience. Also, interview classmates to get their comments about your selections. Write these comments down in the form of quotations. You will use the quotations as support when you write your memo. Then, examine your list and decide which three songs and three poems would best fit the atmosphere of a Valentine's Day dance. Explain your choices to yourself before you try to explain them to the committee.

WRITING   You can structure this memo in various ways. Perhaps you could discuss all of the poems and then all of the songs. If certain songs can be paired with certain poems, perhaps you will write three paragraphs, each containing a song-poem pair. Sketch several possible outlines so that you can choose the best order of presentation. Avoid clumping your ideas on all six choices in one confusing, overloaded paragraph. Also, as support for your choices, include at least two of the quotations you gathered from your classmates.

REVISING   Let a friend read the memo. Then, ask whether the reasons behind your choices are clear. The memo should not read like a list of titles! Strong transitions between suggestions will also keep the memo from sounding like a list.

PUBLISHING   Check your writing for errors in grammar, usage, spelling, and punctuation. Be sure that you have spelled and marked the titles correctly and that you have properly punctuated the quotations you used. With your teacher's permission, post your memo in the classroom, alongside those your classmates have written. Let the class decide which memo is most persuasive.

EXTENDING YOUR WRITING

You may wish to develop this writing exercise into an essay. You could analyze several poems to see how different poets express similar ideas. You could compare and contrast a poem and a song written on the same subject or theme. You could even explore the question of why some teens enjoy song lyrics but do not enjoy poetry.

Choices: Exploring Spelling

Here's your chance to step out of the grammar book and into the real world. You may not notice mechanics, but you and your friends use spelling every day. The following activities challenge you to find a connection between spelling and the world around you. Do the activity below that suits your personality best, and then share your discoveries with your class. Have fun!

COMPUTER GAMES

Anagrams and Crosswords

A number of computer programs create word games based on the words of your choice. If you have access to such a program, print out a word game for a list of words that you misspell most often. Give copies to your class.

HISTORY

A First Time for Everything

Once upon a time, dictionary entries were not written in alphabetical order. Yikes! Of course, that was a long time ago. By the way, when and where was the first dictionary written? The first English dictionary? The first American dictionary? Find out. While you're in the library and looking at a book about dictionaries, find out a little more about them. Make a time line that shows your classmates what you have discovered.

TECHNOLOGY

In the Spotlight

Certain letter combinations are known for causing spelling problems. Survey your classmates for the top twenty spelling errors. If you have access to a computer and printer, type in these words, formatting the troublesome letters in a larger font. For instance, the word *believe* might be printed in small letters except for the letters *ie*, which would be large. Pass out copies of your list to your classmates. If you don't have a printer, handwrite the list on poster board and hang it in the classroom.

GAME

Amaze Everyone

Create a maze game. The only way through the maze is to follow the correctly spelled words. Most of the words will be misspelled and will lead nowhere. Use graph paper to compose your maze. Write the correct words first, and then anything goes! Words can go up, down, or sideways. When you've written in all the words, draw walls for your maze. Give copies to your classmates.

STUDY AID

Weigh Eight Beige Sleighs

You'll remember those *ei* and *ie* words more easily if you categorize them. You know how to spell *eight*, right? If you can pair *eight* with *weigh*, *beige*, and *sleigh* in your mind, you'll never misspell them. Look at a list of words that use, for instance, *ei*, and then make up a silly sentence that uses only these words. Write five such sentences on a poster, and ask to hang it in the classroom.

WRITING

You're the Tops

Ben Franklin, man of wide interests that he was, had more than a little to say about English spelling. Find and read Ben Franklin's suggestions. Then, write your own proposal for the reformation of English spelling and top his!

TECHNOLOGY

The Principal's Principles

Homonyms can cause problems for computers, as well as students. Type a paragraph that misuses several homonyms. Then, run a word processor's spellchecking program. How well did it do? Report your findings to the class.

Good Spelling Habits

You can improve your spelling by using the following methods.

(1) Pronounce words correctly.
(2) Spell by syllables.
(3) Use a dictionary.
(4) Keep a spelling notebook to list and review difficult words.
(5) Proofread for careless spelling errors.

EXERCISE   Cross out each misspelled word in the sentences below. Then, above the word, write it correctly. If a sentence contains no error, write *C* after the sentence. Use a dictionary if you need it.

Example 1. With her wise decision, Nilda proved she has great ~~strenth~~ *strength* of character.

1. Germaine decided to write about South America insted of about factory strikes.

2. After he bilt his cabin in the woods, Henry David Thoreau tried to live a simple life.

3. That is eazy for an acrobat who is strong and flexible.

4. The fire cheif came to the school to review our fire emergency procedures.

5. Many wimen today have careers that their mothers would not have imagined.

6. At the last minit, the cavalry rode in and defended the fort.

7. The hotel simply could not accommodate any more guests for the holiday weekend.

8. Hidden above the ceeling in an old London townhouse was a dress covered with precious gems that had once belonged to a queen.

9. "Your reputation precedes you, sir," said the major to the young officer.

10. After my first day skiing, there wasn't a muscle in my body that wasn't sor.

11. The wagon train leaders may have had to gess which route was the safest.

12. When Charlene was in the mountins, she saw a cougar.

13. Tho flavored yogurt tastes good, it has more calories than plain yogurt has.

14. Over seven thousand women soldeirs from the United States were in Vietnam during the war.

15. Lawrence of Arabia would tair across the desert sand, his robe whipping in the wind.

16. After a long airplane ride, you will probably be tired.

17. My mother wants to live in the contry, but Dad prefers city life.

18. A coff is the body's way of clearing your lungs.

19. There is one more hour until the end of the year.

20. Four large juices will probly be enough for the group of friends.

MECHANICS

ie and *ei*

16a. Write *ie* when the sound is long *e*, except after *c*.

    EXAMPLES bel**ie**f, f**ie**rce, rec**ei**pt   **EXCEPTIONS** **ei**ther, n**ei**ther, l**ei**sure

16b. Write *ei* when the sound is not long *e*, especially when the sound is long *a*.

    EXAMPLES n**ei**ghbor, forf**ei**t, w**ei**ght   **EXCEPTIONS** anc**ie**nt, consc**ie**nce, fr**ie**nd

MECHANICS

EXERCISE A Cross out the misspelled word in each sentence below. Then, above the crossed-out word, write the word correctly.

neighborhood
Example 1. All the streets in this ~~nieghborhood~~ are named after U.S. presidents.

1. The nurse applied an elastic bandage to releive the pressure on the knee.

2. A viel of secrecy surrounded the plans for the ice carnival.

3. Some people practice deciet because they don't have much self-confidence.

4. The United States has spent about three billion dollars on foriegn aid this year.

5. A small peice of rock fell to the ground.

6. Sitting Bull was a Sioux cheif who united his people in a struggle for survival.

7. Feild mice eat grain, so farmers consider them pests.

8. Neither LaToya nor Shanique could find the reciept.

9. Each teacher nominated a student for the Outstanding Acheivement award.

10. The truck driver skillfully backed his rig into the recieving dock.

EXERCISE B The following paragraphs contain words with missing letters. Add the letters *ie* or *ei* to complete each word correctly.

Example [1] How much does a cutter w__*ei*__ gh?

A cutter is a type of horse-drawn **[11]** sl_____ gh. In the 1800s in America, the cutter was an

[12] effic_____nt means of travel across **[13]** f_____lds and roads in snowy weather. The cutter is

[14] lightw_____ght and open in design, usually seating two people. Some cutters feature a sec-

ond, removable seat for two additional **[15]** fr_____nds or family members.

Once travel by automobile was **[16]** ach_____ved, cutters gradually became less common.

Today some people **[17]** bel_____ve cutters to be a fun alternative to the automobile. Some owners

use **[18]** th_____r cutters to give old-fashioned cutter rides. They **[19]** rec_____ve additional

income by selling tickets for rides in the cutter. You can probably imagine a cutter with bells

jingling on the horse's **[20]** r_____ns during winter festivities.

–cede, –ceed, and –sede

16c. In English, the only word ending in *–sede* is *supersede*. The only words ending in *–ceed* are *exceed*, *proceed*, and *succeed*. Most other words with this sound end in *–cede*.

EXAMPLES con**cede**, inter**cede**, pre**cede**, re**cede**

EXERCISE A In each of the following sentences, underline the word in parentheses that is spelled correctly.

Example **1.** I *(conceed, concede)* that you are right.

1. The new sales strategy *(superseeds, supersedes)* the old one.

2. Some people wonder if any state will ever again *(seceed, secede)* from the union.

3. Nate *(conceded, conceeded)* the winning point to Zeina.

4. A flash of lightning *(preceeds, precedes)* a crash of thunder.

5. Looking at his grandfather, Noel wondered if his own hairline would someday *(receed, recede)*.

6. Some people say that to *(succeed, succede)* in life means to be happy with yourself.

7. After pausing to answer a question, Bettina *(proceeded, proseeded)* with her speech.

8. "You have *(exceded, exceeded)* my highest expectations," Ms. Khuu said to me.

9. Your guidance counselor can *(intercede, interceed)* on your behalf.

10. I have *(succeeded, sucseded)* in earning the money I need for the trip!

EXERCISE B Most of the sentences below contain a misspelled word ending in *–cede*, *–ceed*, or *–sede*. Cross out any word that is misspelled. Then, above the crossed out word, write the word correctly. If the word ending in *–cede*, *–ceed*, or *–sede* is spelled correctly, write *C* above it.

Example **1.** We will now ~~prosede~~ proceed to the playing field.

11. After the flood waters reseded, we could play again on the banks of the river.

12. "If you want to succede at the kickball game, listen to the rules," said Esteban.

13. My new kickball game rules superceed the old ones.

14. If there is a dispute, I will interceed to resolve it.

15. The number of players on one team cannot exsede seven.

16. The assignment of a player to the position of kicker presedes all else.

17. No player is allowed to intercede when the kicker has the ball.

18. If you interrupt the kicker, you conceed a point to the opposing team.

19. The amount of time a ball is in play must exceed sixty seconds, or it is a "dead ball."

20. When the teams have taken their places, we'll prosede.

Language and Sentence Skills Practice   **331**

MECHANICS

NAME _____ CLASS _____ DATE _____

for **CHAPTER 16: SPELLING** `page 372`

Prefixes

16d. When adding a prefix to a word, do not change the spelling of the word itself.

    EXAMPLES im + prove = **im**prove   dis + solve = **dis**solve

EXERCISE A For each item below, add the prefix given to form a new word. Write the new word on the lines provided.

Example 1. mis + spell = _____*misspell*_____

1. mis + understand = _____

2. pre + wash = _____

3. im + possible = _____

4. over + cook = _____

5. in + appropriate = _____

6. over + run = _____

7. dis + cover = _____

8. il + legible = _____

9. un + natural = _____

10. re + new = _____

EXERCISE B On the line provided, write the word given in parentheses, adding the prefix given.

Example 1. Somsay carefully _____*rearranged*_____ the glass figurines. (*re + arranged*)

11. At eight o'clock each morning, Somsay _____ the store's front door. (*un + locks*)

12. Somsay then _____ the list of tasks that the manager has left him. (*re + views*)

13. Today he must _____ the display in the front window. (*dis + assemble*)

14. After he _____ the old items, he will arrange a new display. (*re + moves*)

15. The new display will _____ upon the old one. (*im + prove*)

16. To _____ accuracy, he counts the cash for the register twice. (*en + sure*)

17. He arranges several turquoise rings in a _____ in a small glass case. (*semi + circle*)

18. Several pairs of earrings have been _____, and he rearranges them. (*mis + matched*)

19. During his morning break, Somsay _____ a sandwich to eat. (*un + wraps*)

20. He _____ the can of juice in the refrigerator, preferring water instead. (*dis + regards*)

332   HOLT HANDBOOK | Second Course

Suffixes A

16e. When adding the suffix −*ly* or −*ness* to a word, do not change the spelling of the word itself.

EXAMPLES	careful + ly = careful**ly** calm + ness = calm**ness**
EXCEPTIONS	For words that end in *y* and have more than one syllable, change the *y* to *i* before adding −*ly* or −*ness*.
	merry + ly = merr**ily** busy + ness = bus**iness**

EXERCISE A   For each item below, add the suffix given to form a new word. Write the new word on the lines provided.

Examples 1. natural + ly = _____*naturally*_____

2. silly + ness = _____*silliness*_____

1. quick + ly =   _____

2. open + ness =   _____

3. rare + ly =   _____

4. cheery + ly =   _____

5. gritty + ness =   _____

EXERCISE B   Most of the following sentences contain a misspelled word ending in −*ly* or −*ness*. Cross out each misspelled word. Then, above it, write the word correctly. If a sentence contains no error, write *C* after the sentence.

Example 1. The weary traveler ~~resolutly~~ *resolutely* put one foot before the other.

6. Was this trek through the desert an act of pure crazyness, the traveler wondered.

7. The vastness of the desert was almost overwhelming.

8. The barreness of the land was evident in the brownish tinge of the few surviving plants.

9. The sun shone hottly from above, evaporating all traces of moisture.

10. The driness of the soil prohibited seeds from germinating.

11. Prickly thorns protruded from various kinds of cactuses.

12. The lone human traveler sought to ease his dizzyness with a few sips of precious water.

13. Lizards eyed the human intruder with waryness.

14. A far-off speck on the horizon gradualy became clear as he approached it.

15. He could barly contain his happiness as he recognized the green of an oasis.

MECHANICS

Suffixes B

16f.   Drop the final silent *e* before adding a suffix beginning with a vowel.

    EXAMPLES   age + ing = **ag**ing   freeze + able = **freez**able

    EXCEPTIONS   Keep the final silent *e* in a word ending in *ce* or *ge* before adding a suffix beginning
                with *a* or *o* (as in tra**ceable**) and in the words dy**eing** and mil**eage**.

16g.   Keep the final silent *e* before adding a suffix beginning with a consonant.

    EXAMPLES   place + ment = plac**e**ment   face + less = fac**e**less

    EXCEPTIONS   **nin**th, **tru**ly, **awf**ul, **argu**ment, **judg**ment, **wholl**y

MECHANICS

EXERCISE A   For each item below, add the suffix given to form a new word. Write the new word on the
lines provided.

    Examples 1. move + able = _____*movable*_____

               2. awe + ful = _____*awful*_____

1. grace + ful = _____

2. salvage + able = _____

3. dye + ing = _____

4. engage + ment = _____

5. saxophone + ist = _____

EXERCISE B   Most of the following sentences contain a misspelled word. Cross out each misspelled
word. Then, above it, write the word correctly. If a sentence is already correct, write *C* after it.

                                      narration

Example 1. I listened in fascination to Natalie's ~~narrateion~~ of the events.

6. Natalie and her friends had gone scuba diveing in clear, warm water.

7. They had gone only about ninty feet out from the shoreline.

8. Underwater, they watched a graceful manta ray swim by.

9. They examined a lovly, multicolored coral reef and other underwater sea life.

10. Hovering in the water a short distance away, a whiteish cloud of objects appeared.

11. Natalie immediately launched an investigateion of the mysterious white cloud.

12. Trained divers, Natalie and her friends knew they should approach carfully.

13. Moving closer, they saw that the "white cloud" was a mass of clear, floating objects.

14. The round, clear shapes became recognizeable; they were jellyfish!

15. Natalie and her friends immediatly swam quickly in the opposite direction.

Suffixes C

16h. For words ending in *y* preceded by a consonant, change the *y* to *i* before any suffix that does not begin with *i*.

    EXAMPLES   fancy + ful = fanc**iful**   scurry + ing = scurr**ying**

16i. For words ending in *y* preceded by a vowel, keep the *y* when adding a suffix.

    EXAMPLES   play + ing = pla**ying**   deploy + able = deplo**yable**
    EXCEPTIONS   day + ly = da**ily**   pay + ed = pa**id**
                     lay + ed = la**id**   say + ed = sa**id**

MECHANICS

EXERCISE A   On each blank, write the word formed by joining the word and the prefix given in parentheses.

Example 1. My grandparents are opening a new ____*business*____ on State Street. (*busy + ness*)

1. Grandpa helped install a _____ belt in the warehouse. (*convey + or*)

2. The _____ is caused by the open warehouse doors. (*breezy + ness*)

3. Grandma and Grandpa are _____ about their plans for the future. (*joy + ful*)

4. Those trucks are _____ the first shipments of merchandise. (*carry + ing*)

5. They approach the entire endeavor with great _____. (*enjoy + ment*)

EXERCISE B   Most of the following sentences contain a misspelled word. Cross out each misspelled word. Then, above it, write the word correctly. If a sentence is already correct, write C after it.

Example 1. Kylie arrived at the stables early; ~~tardyness~~ *tardiness* was not tolerated.

6. Kylie easly found the grooming supplies in the tack room.

7. She was paying for these horseback riding lessons herself.

8. So far, she had enjoied every lesson with Cowboy, her assigned horse.

9. Without hurrying, she combed Cowboy's coat with the currycombs.

10. When she bent to pick Cowboy's hoof, she sayed firmly, "Hoof!"

11. Cowboy lifted his foot dutyfully.

12. After picking dirt and gravel from the hooves, Kylie layed a blanket across Cowboy's back.

13. She carryed the saddle and bridle into the stall and put them on Cowboy as well.

14. When she finally rode Cowboy outdoors, she felt as though she were fliing.

15. Cowboy obeyed every command.

Suffixes D

| **16j.** | Double the final consonant before adding a suffix beginning with a vowel if the word (1) has only one syllable or has the accent on the last syllable and (2) ends in a single consonant preceded by a single vowel. |

EXAMPLES   bat + ed = ba**tt**ed   run + er = ru**nn**er   begin + ing = begi**nn**ing

Otherwise, the final consonant is usually not doubled before a suffix beginning with a vowel.

EXAMPLES   pitch + er = pit**ch**er   cheer + ed = chee**r**ed   open + ing = ope**n**ing

MECHANICS

EXERCISE A   For each item below, add the suffix given to form a new word. Write the new word on the lines provided.

Examples 1. trot + ed = ___trotted___

2. sweep + ing = ___sweeping___

1. inform + ed = _____

6. stun + ing = _____

2. slam + ing = _____

7. special + ist = _____

3. tap + ed = _____

8. forgot + en = _____

4. contort + ing = _____

9. horticultural + ist = _____

5. program + er = _____

10. step + ed = _____

EXERCISE B   In each of the following sets of expressions, one expression contains a spelling error. On the line provided, write the letter of the expression containing the error. Then, write the expression correctly.

Example 1. a. reliving the memories   **b.** sitting in the sun   **c.** diging a ditch

_____ c. digging a ditch _____

11. a. startting to go   **b.** humming a tune   **c.** relaxed by the lake

_____

12. a. weeded the lawn   **b.** resubmited the paper   **c.** plotted against them

_____

13. a. dropped the ball   **b.** draining the pool   **c.** his thining hairline

_____

14. a. stopping traffic   **b.** prefered customers   **c.** renewable prescription

_____

15. a. forbidden fruit   **b.** a dimmer switch for the lights   **c.** centerred on the page

_____

Spelling Rules Review A

16a. Write *ie* when the sound is long *e*, except after *c*.

16b. Write *ei* when the sound is not long *e*, especially when the sound is long *a*.

16c. In English, the only word ending in *–sede* is *supersede*. The only words ending in *–ceed* are *exceed, proceed,* and *succeed.* Most other words with this sound end in *–cede*.

16d. When adding a prefix to a word, do not change the spelling of the word itself.

16e. When adding the suffix *–ly* or *–ness* to a word, do not change the spelling of the word itself.

EXAMPLES   fie**ld**, w**ei**gh, con**cede**, **un**natural, joyful**ly,** dark**ness**

MECHANICS

EXERCISE A   In each of the following sentences, underline the word in parentheses that is spelled correctly.

Example 1. Do you (<u>believe</u>, beleive) in miracles?

1. The childcare worker's (kindlyness, kindliness) was soothing to the young child.

2. I am absolutely certain that I will (succeed, succede) at my goals.

3. That line of reasoning is (illogical, ilogical).

4. The (cheif, chief) of police met with the mayor.

5. The (wetness, wettness) of the weather prevented us from going outside.

EXERCISE B   Most of the following sentences contain a misspelled word. Cross out any misspelled word. Then, above it, write the word correctly. If a sentence is already correct, write C after it.

Example 1. Roberto will install the new ~~cieling~~ fan.
                                                   ceiling

6. The opposing team does not have enough players present; they will forfiet the game.

7. The lake has receeded several feet from the high-water mark.

8. The hikers carried thier own equipment for the week-long trek.

9. The ferociously barking dog unerved Esther.

10. I suffered shortness of breath after rushing across campus.

11. The wrist corsage that Tina is wearing is lovly.

12. Why don't we work on our science homework together?

13. This shipment excedes the weight limit and must be unloaded.

14. The toughness of the meat discouraged me from eating all of it.

15. Farid casualy said hello to Phoebe.

Language and Sentence Skills Practice   **337**

Spelling Rules Review B

| **16f.** | Drop the final silent *e* before adding a suffix beginning with a vowel. |

| **16g.** | Keep the final silent *e* before adding a suffix beginning with a consonant. |

| **16h.** | For words ending in *y* preceded by a consonant, change the *y* to *i* before any suffix that does not begin with *i*. |

| **16i.** | For words ending in *y* preceded by a vowel, keep the *y* when adding a suffix. |

| **16j.** | Double the final consonant before adding a suffix beginning with a vowel if the word (1) has only one syllable or has the accent on the last syllable and (2) ends in a single consonant preceded by a single vowel. |

EXAMPLES remov**al**, aw**e**some, duti**ful**, pa**y**er, scru**bb**ing

EXERCISE A For each item below, form a new word by joining the word and the prefix given.

Example 1. easy + ly = _____*easily*_____

1. spine + less = _____
2. pine + ing = _____
3. courage + ous = _____
4. pollute + ant = _____
5. begin + er = _____

EXERCISE B Most of the following sentences contain a misspelled word. Cross out any misspelled word. Then, above it, write the word correctly. If a sentence is already correct, write *C* after it.

Example 1. Charles mended the ~~lineing~~ *lining* of his formal suit coat.

6. One runner droped out of the race because of a sprained ankle.
7. Several students are shareing a table during lunch.
8. The camp counselors planned numerous activities for the campers' amusement.
9. The chicken flapped its wings but did not fly.
10. Dad is frying fish; I already fryed the potatoes.
11. The eighth-graders are prepareing for the Eighth-Grade Picnic.
12. What is the scaryest movie you've ever seen?
13. Please use ink to fill out this application for employment.
14. I submited one of my poems to a poetry contest.
15. Carefully, I ensured that the poster was centerred on the bulletin board.

NAME _____ CLASS _____ DATE _____

for **CHAPTER 16: SPELLING**   pages 376–77

Plurals A

16k. To form the plurals of most nouns in English, add *s*.

16l. For nouns ending in *s, x, z, ch,* or *sh*, add *es*.

| SINGULAR | shoe | bow | Alcott | mix | lunch | Martinez |
| PLURAL | shoe**s** | bow**s** | Alcott**s** | mix**es** | lunch**es** | Martinez**es** |

16m. For nouns ending in *y* preceded by a vowel, add *s*.

16n. For nouns ending in *y* preceded by a consonant, change the *y* to *i* and add *es*.

SINGULAR	tray	boy	Farley	cherry	copy
PLURAL	tray**s**	boy**s**	Farley**s**	cherr**ies**	cop**ies**
EXCEPTIONS	For proper nouns, add *s*.				
	Kennedy—Kennedy**s**				

EXERCISE A Spell the plural form of each of the following words. Write on the line provided.

Example 1. history _____*histories*_____

1. ash _____
2. bunny _____
3. Murry _____
4. refrigerator _____
5. box _____
6. infirmary _____
7. Perry _____
8. cranberry _____
9. grass _____
10. locker _____

EXERCISE B Cross out each misspelled word in the following sentences. Then, above the misspelled word, write the word correctly. If a sentence is already correct, write *C* after it.

Example 1. Several of these statues were made by local ~~sculptores.~~ *sculptors*

11. Our city is one of those citys that proudly display the artwork of their citizens.

12. At school, art classes are usually packed with eager learners.

13. The Rodriguezs enlisted the help of a high school student.

14. The student painted colorful murals on their restaurant walles.

15. Judges at the courthouse decorated the hallways with prints by local photographers.

16. A few boxs of pottery were requested by the owners of a bank building.

17. They created elegant displays in both the front and the side lobbies.

18. Even youngsteres are encouraged to contribute to the local art scene.

19. The kids painted their own paving tiles using small brushs and waterproof paints.

20. The tiles were used as borderes around the flower beds at their school.

Language and Sentence Skills Practice   **339**

MECHANICS

Plurals B

16o. For some nouns ending in *f* or *fe*, add *s*. For others, change the *f* or *fe* to *v* and add *es*.

SINGULAR	staff	giraffe	wolf	leaf
PLURAL	staf**fs**	giraffe**s**	wol**ves**	lea**ves**

16p. For nouns ending in *o* preceded by a vowel, add *s*.

16q. For nouns ending in *o* preceded by a consonant, add *es*.

SINGULAR	patio	cameo	potato
PLURAL	patio**s**	cameo**s**	potato**es**
EXCEPTIONS	For musical terms and proper nouns, add *s*.		
	concerto—concerto**s**	Sakamoto—Sakamoto**s**	

EXERCISE A Spell the plural form of each of the following words. Write on the line provided.

Example 1. commando _____*commandos*_____

1. tomato _____

2. alto _____

3. shelf _____

4. mosquito _____

5. gaffe _____

6. studio _____

7. reef _____

8. soprano _____

9. Scorpio _____

10. tariff _____

EXERCISE B Cross out each misspelled word in the following sentences. Then, above the misspelled word, write the word correctly. If a sentence is already correct, write *C* after it.

Example 1. ~~Rooves~~ *Roofs* on houses in my neighborhood were damaged in the hailstorm.

11. The electronics store has stereoes on sale this week.

12. These igloos are made of packed snow.

13. Rocky cliffes towered above the tiny, sandy beach.

14. The major movie studioes are releasing some great new movies!

15. Mom selected one of the carving knifes for slicing the ham.

16. Carefully, Stephen painted the torpedos that were part of the model ship.

17. Most of the wives voted to include men in their homemakers' group.

18. Jamaal likes people who don't take themselfs too seriously.

19. Carlito manages four chefs at an Italian restaurant.

20. Which of these pianoes needs tuning?

Plurals C

16r.	Some nouns have irregular plural forms.

16s.	For most compound nouns, form the plural of the last word in the compound.

16t.	For compound nouns in which one of the words is modified by the other word or words, form the plural of the word modified.

SINGULAR	child	shipwreck	sister-in-law
PLURAL	child**ren**	shipwreck**s**	sister**s**-in-law

EXERCISE A In each of the following sentences, underline the correct form of the plural in parentheses.

Example 1. Most of the old movie (<u>*drive-ins*</u>, *drives-in*) are closed now.

1. Overnight we caught two (*mouses, mice*) in the traps.

2. I'll add two more (*spoonfuls, spoonsful*) of vinegar to the salad dressing.

3. Edith writes an advice column for newlyweds and their (*parent-in-laws, parents-in-law*).

4. The (*thirteen-year-olds, thirteen-years-old*) must pay the adult admission price.

5. (*Womans, Women*) enjoyed that film more than men did.

6. Both lighthouses on the island sounded their (*fogshorn, foghorns*).

7. Piranha have sharp (*teeth, tooths*) with which they devour their prey.

8. From the hardware bin, I pulled out two (*handfuls, handsful*) of nails.

9. Please hang your wet coats on one of the (*coats rack, coat racks*).

10. We need a photo of all the class (*vices-president, vice-presidents*) for the yearbook.

EXERCISE B Each sentence below contains a spelling error. Draw a line through each error, and write the correctly spelled word above it.

Example 1. There are three blank ~~videotaps~~ *videotapes* in the cabinet.

11. My foots ached after the exhausting hiking trip.

12. There are so many teethbrushes to choose from at this grocery store!

13. How many people will attend the spring conference for editor in chiefs?

14. The waiter says there are two soup of the days; they both sound good.

15. Did you see the large, active flock of gooses at the park?

MECHANICS

Plurals D

16u. For some nouns, the singular and the plural forms are the same.

EXAMPLES Japanese, sheep, aircraft

16v. For numerals, letters, symbols, and words used as words, add an apostrophe and *s*.

EXAMPLES *9's, A's, %'s, hello's*

EXERCISE On each line provided, write the plural form of the word, numeral, letter, or symbol given in parentheses.

Examples 1. How many ___*B's*___ have you gotten in math this semester? *(B)*

2. Both male and female ___*reindeer*___ have antlers. *(reindeer)*

1. The full-color book contained photographs of various _____. *(spacecraft)*

2. I typed a line of _____ to separate two sections of my e-mail message. *(*)*

3. I practiced my oral presentation, trying to stop using so many _____. *(um)*

4. Sandy writes _____ with a curly flourish. *(2)*

5. Ms. Matson could not discern whether Alejandro had written _____ or zeros. *(O)*

6. He put the salmon in a basket with the other _____ he had caught. *(salmon)*

7. "In your formal writing," wrote Mr. Polaski, "Do not use _____." *(&)*

8. Some people believe that _____ are lucky. *(7)*

9. I used a function on the computer to find all the _____ in my paper. *(very)*

10. Hannah writes _____ before apartment numbers in addresses. *(#)*

11. "How many _____ are in the word?" asked the game show host. *(e)*

12. My phone number contains four _____. *(3)*

13. Simon is fascinated with _____, and he plans to become a pilot. *(aircraft)*

14. The culture of the _____ is both ancient and intriguing. *(Chinese)*

15. The cartoonist wrote three _____ in the speech bubble. *(?)*

16. Did any of the gymnasts score _____ at the competition? *(10)*

17. I heard a few _____ as I climbed across people's feet to get to my seat. *(ouch)*

18. My friend Irma pronounces her _____ differently than I do. *(r)*

19. There are only two red _____ on my test! *(X)*

20. Several _____ cautiously approached the water hole. *(moose)*

MECHANICS

Numbers

16w. Spell out a number that begins a sentence.

    EXAMPLE   **Two hundred fifty** teenagers have jobs at the amusement park.

16x. In a sentence, spell out numbers that can be written in one or two words. Use numerals for other numbers.

    EXAMPLES   At the amusement park, **two hundred** teenagers have jobs.
                  At the amusement park, **475** people have jobs.

16y. Spell out numbers used to indicate order.

    EXAMPLE   The Bottomless Roller Coaster is the **second** [not 2nd] most popular ride.

MECHANICS

EXERCISE A   Each of the following sentences contains an error in writing a number. Cross out each error. Then, above the error, write the number correctly.

                                       two thousand
Example 1. Our school has an enrollment of over ~~2,000~~ students.

1. There are four-hundred fifty people in our class this year.

2. 300 students were in last year's graduating class.

3. The girl who spoke at graduation was 1st in the class academically.

4. There were 1,000 people in attendance at the ceremony.

5. My cousin's school has fewer than one hundred seventy-five students.

EXERCISE B   Most of the following sentences contain an error in writing a number. Cross out each error. Then, above the error, write the number correctly. If a sentence is already correct, write *C* after it.

                                 four
Example 1. An adult llama is about ~~4~~ feet tall at the shoulder.

6. In South America, many people's 1st choice among pack animals is the llama.

7. A llama can carry a load weighing up to 60 kilos.

8. An adult llama usually weighs around 113 kilos.

9. Another pack animal, the Bactrian camel, measures about 7 feet at the top of its two humps.

10. 30 miles of travel in a day is not uncommon for this camel, which lives in Central Asia.

11. The one-humped camel, called the Arabian camel, stands about seven feet tall at the shoulder.

12. The Arabian camel can carry a rider while traveling at up to 10 miles per hour.

13. 18 hours of travel at this speed would be possible.

14. The Arabian camel was imported to Australia around one hundred fifty years ago.

15. Today, about 25,000 camels roam wild in the Australian outback.

Plurals and Numbers

| **16r.** | Some nouns have irregular plural forms. |

| **16s.** | For most compound nouns, form the plural of the last word in the compound. |

| **16t.** | For compound nouns in which one of the words is modified by the other word or words, form the plural of the word modified. |

| **16u.** | For some nouns, the singular and the plural forms are the same. |

| **16v.** | For numerals, letters, symbols, and words used as words, add an apostrophe and *s*. |

| **16w.** | Spell out a number that begins a sentence. |

| **16x.** | In a sentence, spell out numbers that can be written in one or two words. Use numerals for other numbers. |

| **16y.** | Spell out numbers used to indicate order. |

EXAMPLES child**ren**, push-up**s**, sister**s**-in-law, **deer**, *5's*, *C's*, *&'s*, *and's*
Fifty people attended the late movie, but **one hundred** attended the **first** showing.

EXERCISE A   On the lines provided, spell the plural form of each of the following words, numerals, letters, and symbols.

Example 1. *hello* _____ *hello's* _____

1. goose _____
2. $ _____
3. aircraft _____
4. *14* _____
5. bucketful _____
6. *very* _____
7. *F* _____
8. maid of honor _____
9. Sioux _____
10. eighth-grader _____

EXERCISE B   Most of the following sentences contain an error in writing a number. Cross out each error. Then, above the error, write the number correctly. If a sentence is already correct, write *C* after it.

Example 1. The cafeteria needs ~~one hundred twenty-five~~ *125* more hamburger buns.

11. I'll take the 2nd menu option, Salisbury steak.
12. 47 students voted for more vegetarian menu options.
13. The head cook promised to offer five or six vegetarian dishes during the next two weeks.
14. All four hundred fifty students said they would eat coleslaw at least once a week.
15. Only 25 students said they would not eat tofu.

Words Often Confused A

Review the Words Often Confused covered on pages 380–381 of your textbook for information on the correct spelling and usage of the following terms.

accept, except	*all ready, already*	*all together, altogether*
advice, advise	*all right*	*brake, break*
affect, effect	*altar, alter*	

MECHANICS

EXERCISE A Underline the word or word group in parentheses that correctly completes each sentence .

Example 1. I am *(all together, <u>altogether</u>)* pleased with the results of my experiment.

1. When the school bus driver applied her air *(brake, break)*, she heard a hissing noise.

2. Will you *(accept, except)* my sincere apology?

3. The bride wanted yellow flowers on the *(altar, alter)* on her wedding day.

4. My hockey gear is finally *(all together, altogether)*, and we can go now.

5. In ancient times, a person would *(break, brake)* bread with others to show trust and friendship.

6. After crashing into Frank on my skateboard, I asked, "Are you *(all right, alright)?*"

7. My *(advice, advise)* is that you wear protective gloves when using bleach.

8. To separate an egg, you *(break, brake)* the egg in the center and spill the white into a cup.

9. Did Coach Crowe *(advice, advise)* the players to drink water during the game?

10. The *(affects, effects)* of the fire were catastrophic.

EXERCISE B Most of the following sentences contain an error in word usage. Cross out each error, and write the correct word above it. If a sentence is already correct, write *C* after it.

Example 1. If we ~~altar~~ the sleeves, this shirt will fit you.
                          alter

11. A tuxedo jacket with tails creates a very formal affect.

12. On the wall of the tuxedo store hung a portrait of a bride and groom standing before an alter.

13. I like all of these tuxedos accept the pale blue one.

14. The type of cummerbund you choose effects the overall look of the tuxedo.

15. Will my black dress shoes look all right with a gray tuxedo?

16. The store clerk advised me to rent shoes in the same color as the tuxedo.

17. Thea and I will accept your and Keisha's offer to share a ride to the dance.

18. Thea has all ready gotten her Dad's permission.

19. It will be nice to arrive altogether instead of one by one.

20. Thea and Keisha will be altogether impressed when they see us in our tuxedos.

Words Often Confused B

Review the Words Often Confused covered on pages 382–384 of your textbook for information on the correct spelling and usage of the following terms.

capital, capitol	*complement, compliment*
choose, chose	*consul, council, counsel*
clothes, cloths	*councilor, counselor*
coarse, course	

EXERCISE A Underline the word in parentheses that correctly completes each sentence.

Example 1. A pale shade of blue will (<u>complement</u>, *compliment*) your eye color.

1. The dome on the (*capital, capitol*) was painted black instead of gold during World War II.

2. When I came to the fork in the path, I (*choose, chose*) the path on the left.

3. The (*coarse, course*) pink sand sparkled against the dark blue water.

4. Jonathon waxed the sports car using clean, soft (*clothes, cloths*).

5. The (*capital, capitol*) of Bulgaria is the ancient city of Sofia.

6. Columbus plotted a (*coarse, course*) west across the Atlantic.

7. My favorite (*coarse, course*) in history taught me about the ancient Greeks.

8. Becca often (*complements, compliments*) her friends on their best qualities.

9. Several of the (*councilors, counselors*) were late to the important council meeting.

10. My guidance (*councilor, counselor*) helped me find an English tutor.

EXERCISE B Using the list at the top of this page, write a word that sensibly completes each sentence.

Example 1. Dr. Patras wrapped the wound with sterile white _____*cloths*_____ .

11. A dinner will be held for the German _____ and other government personnel.

12. If you follow through with this _____ of action, you should succeed.

13. Lawyers are sometimes called _____ because they give legal advice.

14. Which city is the _____ of your state?

15. The city parks planning _____ will meet tomorrow.

16. Each team captain will _____ his or her team members.

17. Martin works as a janitor in the _____ .

18. I can't wear any of these _____ because they are all wrinkled.

19. _____ language is a turn-off to most of my friends.

20. The school nurse can give you valuable _____ regarding sports injuries.

MECHANICS

Words Often Confused C

Review the Words Often Confused covered on pages 384–387 of your textbook for information on the correct spelling and usage of the following terms.

desert, desert, dessert   lead, led, lead
formally, formerly   loose, lose
hear, here   passed, past
its, it's

EXERCISE   Underline the word in parentheses that correctly completes the meaning of each sentence below.

Example   1. The caterer served fruit and cheese for *(desert, dessert)*.

1. "There's no changing the *(passed, past)*," the aging general said with a sigh.

2. The smallest horse *(passed, past)* the others in the last few seconds of the Kentucky Derby.

3. At the reception, Rod was *(formally, formerly)* introduced to the mayor.

4. We can study at your house, or you can come over *(hear, here)*.

5. Most house paint used to have *(lead, led)* in it, but then scientists discovered that the metal could poison people.

6. Every time I *(lose, loose)* my glasses, I get so annoyed with myself.

7. When it's nighttime in the *(desert, dessert)*, the air temperature can drop forty degrees.

8. The Tungs *(formerly, formally)* lived in Tampa, but now they live in Albuquerque.

9. During times of peace our memories of *(passed, past)* wars sometimes grow dim.

10. Animals that live in the *(dessert, desert)* need protection from intense heat and cold.

11. Climbing out of the lake, the dog shook water from *(its, it's)* thick coat.

12. Mr. Castillo was *(formerly, formally)* a professional basketball player, and now he's our coach.

13. The stallion *(led, lead)* the mares through the rushing stream.

14. Check to make sure that your seat belt is not too *(lose, loose)*.

15. I would never *(desert, dessert)* a friend who needed my help or moral support.

16. Morton couldn't *(hear, here)* the park ranger's shouts over the roar of the waterfall.

17. Don't go near a dog or wild animal if *(its, it's)* foaming at the mouth.

18. In our country's *(past, passed)* there have been many challenges.

19. One cheerleader, Andrea, will *(lead, led)* all of the cheers during this game.

20. Our family hardly ever eats *(desert, dessert)* after dinner.

MECHANICS

Words Often Confused D

Review the Words Often Confused covered on pages 387–389 of your textbook for information on the correct spelling and usage of the following terms.

peace, piece	*quiet, quite*	*than, then*
plain, plane	*shone, shown*	*their, there, they're*
principal, principle	*stationary, stationery*	

EXERCISE A　Underline the word in parentheses that correctly completes each sentence below.

Example 1. I can see a great distance across the (*plain*, plane).

1. Since the breakup of the Soviet Union, (*peace, piece*) has replaced the cold war.

2. Whitney has strong (*principals, principles*); he won't gossip.

3. The children were so (*quiet, quite*) that Ms. Robles wondered what they were doing.

4. Ramona uses sheets of (*stationary, stationery*) that have her initials embossed at the top.

5. You'll find the Boy Scout uniforms on those racks over (*their, there, they're*).

6. The security guard had (*shone, shown*) us what to do in an emergency.

7. I can't believe you have grown taller (*than, then*) your father!

8. Ms. Nguyen, our (*principal, principle*), knows most of us by name.

9. Enrico has never flown in a (*plain, plane*), but he will do so on Saturday.

10. Randy was (*quite, quiet*) secretive about his plans for the party.

EXERCISE B　On the blank in each of the following sentences, write a word to complete the sentence correctly. Choose a word from the list at the top of this page.

Example 1. I used a compass to measure the angles of the _____*planes*_____ .

11. Some wars have been fought on the basis of _____ such as freedom.

12. We placed a _____ of old carpet in Rex's doghouse.

13. If you become lost, remain _____ rather than wandering aimlessly.

14. In history class, _____ reading *The Red Badge of Courage*.

15. Marguerite's eyes _____ with happiness.

16. Should I wear a _____ sweater, or should I wear something fancier?

17. I was _____ sincere when I said I would not play basketball this year.

18. Stretch your muscles and _____ begin your workout.

19. The Zellers said I could stay at _____ house while Mom is out of town.

20. Your _____ duties are clearing the tables and wiping the counters.

MECHANICS

Words Often Confused E

Review the Words Often Confused covered on pages 389–391 of your textbook for information on the correct spelling and usage of the following terms.

threw, through	*weak, week*	*who's, whose*
to, too, two	*weather, whether*	*your, you're*
waist, waste		

MECHANICS

EXERCISE A   Underline the word in parentheses that correctly completes each sentence below.

Example 1. We were (to, <u>too</u>, two) late; the bus had already departed.

1. Frankie Jean couldn't decide *(whether, weather)* to watch the scary movie.

2. Mai-Lei wrapped a colorful sash around her *(waist, waste)*.

3. Your muscles may be *(weak, week)* now, but they'll become stronger as you work out.

4. *(Who's, Whose)* the vice president of the United States?

5. Vivian wondered *(whether, weather)* it would rain this weekend.

6. "*(Your, You're)* kidding, right?" I said to Thanh.

7. Domingo accidentally *(threw, through)* away Karma's phone number.

8. Are you hungry enough *(to, too, two)* eat one of these huge bran muffins?

9. The *(whether, weather)* is perfect for playing volleyball on the beach.

10. I wasn't sure *(who's, whose)* science book it was, so I gave it to Mr. Reddick.

EXERCISE B   Most of the following sentences contain an error in word usage. Cross out each error, and write the correct word above it. If a sentence is already correct, write *C* after it.

Example 1. In the 1800's, many women wore corsets to create a tiny ~~waste~~. *waist*

11. Your invited to a masquerade party.

12. Dress so that no one will know whose inside your costume.

13. I've been designing my costume for a weak.

14. If the whether is nice, we will dance and eat outdoors.

15. My parents will be there through the entire evening.

16. The party will be next week on Friday night.

17. If you need a ride too my house, just call me.

18. Please RSVP so that we don't waste food by buying too much.

19. If your not sure about a costume, ask me for ideas.

20. I have too extra costumes that I can lend to people.

Review A: **Spelling Rules**

MECHANICS

EXERCISE A In each sentence below, add the letters needed to spell the words correctly.

Example 1. I have confidence that your plan will suc ___ceed___ .

1. The anc _____ nt bones told the scientist a story.

2. The waves re _____ de as the tide goes out.

3. Mr. Valdez is a good n _____ ghbor; he's friendly and considerate.

4. The homecoming float broke loose on the hill and began to exc _____ d the speed limit.

5. Laverne felt that she had ach _____ ved independence when her mother let her do the family grocery shopping.

EXERCISE B For each item below, write a new word as indicated.

Examples 1. beauty + ful = _____ _beautiful_

2. plural of A = _____ _A's_

6. plural of 5 = _____

7. un + likely = _____

8. plural of donkey = _____

9. silly + ness = _____

10. set + ing = _____

11. plural of goose = _____

12. trouble + some = _____

13. plural of kitty = _____

14. mis + place = _____

15. seam + less = _____

16. plural of brother-in-law = _____

17. dye + ing = _____

18. plural of beach = _____

19. race + ed = _____

20. plural of piano = _____

HOLT HANDBOOK | Second Course

Review B: **Words Often Confused**

EXERCISE   Underline the word or word group in parentheses that correctly completes the meaning of each sentence below.

Example 1. The players are (<u>all ready</u>, already) for the game.

1. The quarterback's argument did not (affect, effect) the referee's decision.

2. Roy enjoys playing all sports (accept, except) golf.

3. Each year, a statewide track meet is held in the (capital, capitol).

4. Coach Novinger will (complement, compliment) a player who deserves it.

5. For several days before the big game, none of the players ate (desert, dessert).

6. If the volleyball is low on air, (its, it's) of no use to us.

7. The Fighting Muskrats are determined not to (loose, lose) to the Laughing Hyenas.

8. Since Angela (passed, past) all her classes, she can play in the next game.

9. Our school (principal, principle) attends all of the home games.

10. The fans in the bleachers grew (quiet, quite) as Debra prepared for a free throw.

11. We will jog three miles; (than, then), we will practice lay-ups.

12. Coach Rogers told us to go to the tennis courts, and she will meet us (their, there, they're).

13. Because of the rain, I don't know (weather, whether) the golfers will be able to play.

14. "Who is (your, you're) best server?" asked a volleyball player on the other team.

15. During practice Coach often shouts, "Keep moving! Don't (waist, waste) your time!"

16. Carlos's pitches are (to, too, two) fast for most batters to hit.

17. (Who's, Whose) going to fill in for the injured player?

18. Going into the game, I felt a sense of (peace, piece) about the outcome.

19. Bryan (formally, formerly) played for a school across town.

20. The school (consul, council, counsel) has agreed to create a soccer field beside the gym.

MECHANICS

Review C: **Spelling Rules and Words Often Confused**

EXERCISE Underline the correct word or number in parentheses to complete each of the sentences below.

Example 1. Mount Everest's peak is over (29,000, <u>twenty-nine thousand</u>) feet high.

1. Winston Churchill (*led, lead*) the British through World War II.

2. Two (*armies, armys*) met on the battlefield.

3. There will be a (*breif, brief*) intermission after the second act of the play.

4. If I (*break, brake*) last year's record, I will be the fastest swimmer in the county.

5. (*Eleven, 11*) chefs graduated from the Chinese cooking school last week.

6. The artist has skillfully captured the glow of sunlight on (*sheafs, sheaves*) of wheat.

7. Ms. Raign suggested I use fewer (*reallys, really's*) in my writing.

8. Some scientists (*believe, beleive*) that the earth's atmosphere is getting warmer because of pollution.

9. Doug's (*carefullness, carefulness*) with dangerous tools is commendable.

10. There were (*5,000, five thousand*) people at the Italian festival last night.

11. (*Twenty thousand, 20,000*) years ago, there were people living on the American continents.

12. After December 2000, we (*proceeded, proceded*) to the twenty-first century.

13. New York City is the most populous city in the state of New York, but Albany is the (*capitol, capital*).

14. After the marathon, I massaged my aching (*feet, feets*).

15. A horse's (*hieght, height*) is measured in hands rather than in inches and feet.

16. There are more than (*600, six hundred*) islands in the Micronesian chain.

17. Sometimes we have cheese and fruit for (*dessert, desert*).

18. (*Whether, Weather*) the senator is reelected is up to the voters of our state.

19. "I will not (*concede, conceed*) defeat," declared the losing candidate.

20. Why does medicine usually taste (*aweful, awful*)?

Review D: **Spelling Rules and Words Often Confused**

MECHANICS

EXERCISE A   For each item below, write a new word as indicated.

Example   1. plural of thirteen-year-old = _____*thirteen-year-olds*_____

1. cry + ing = _____

2. re + view = _____

3. plural of father-in-law = _____

4. save + ing = _____

5. plural of *hello* = _____

6. plural of tooth = _____

7. semi + circle = _____

8. plural of *$* = _____

9. state + ment = _____

10. plural of *&* = _____

11. plural of jetty = _____

12. plural of knife = _____

13. plural of *@* = _____

14. mis + fortune = _____

15. begin + ing = _____

16. cheery + ly = _____

17. plural of *r* = _____

18. plural of couch = _____

19. plural of tomato = _____

20. begin + er = _____

EXERCISE B   Underline the correct item in parentheses to complete each of the sentences below.

Example   1. (550, *Five hundred fifty*) houses were without electricity during the storm.

21. The library allows patrons to check out up to *(fifteen, 15)* books at one time.

22. Lance finished the hundred-yard dash in *(third, 3rd)* place.

23. This history book covers the past *(1,500, one thousand and five hundred)* years of history.

24. *(24, Twenty-four)* cats and dogs await adoption at the pet shelter.

25. May I trade this dollar for *(4, four)* quarters?

Language and Sentence Skills Practice

353

Proofreading Application: Public Notice

Good writers are generally good proofreaders. Readers tend to admire and trust writing that is error-free. Make sure that you correct all errors in grammar, usage, spelling, and punctuation in your writing. Your readers will have more confidence in your words if you have done your best to proofread carefully.

Sooner or later, you will write a classified ad, a poster, or some other type of notice that the public will see. When you write a public notice and misspell words, your readers may doubt the worth of your service, product, or event. Help your readers trust your words; proofread carefully.

PROOFREADING ACTIVITY

Find and correct the spelling errors in the public notice below. Use proofreading symbols to make your corrections.

Example   What's more fun ~~then~~ *than* a barrel of ~~monkie~~*monkeys*s?

Family Fall Festival

Its time for the Family Fall Festival! Bring the whole family too share the fun! You'll have your pick of over thirty boothes right here at Kennedy Junior High School. Fish in our pond, get your face painted, or run our obstacle course.

We'll have music, good food, and many activitys. One of our coachs, Tom McAndry, will follow through on his promise to sit in the dunking booth! For the kids, we'll even have a peting zoo with goats, donkies, lambs, ponies, and rabbits.

All procedes from the event will go to the purchase of new books for the library's shelfs. Be their on Saturday, October 10, from 11:00 A.M. until 4:00 P.M. It's all happening here at Kennedy Junior High School at 95 Palmer Avenue.

Literary Model: Folk Tale

Back in the days when the animals could talk, there lived ol' Brer Possum. He was a fine feller. Why, he never liked to see no critters in trouble. He was always helpin' out, a-doin' somethin' for others. . . .

One mornin', as he walked, he come to a big hole in the middle of the road. Now, ol' Brer Possum was kind and gentle, but he was also nosy, so he went over to the hole and looked in. All at once, he stepped back, 'cause layin' in the bottom of that hole was ol' Brer Snake with a brick on his back.

Brer Possum said to 'imself, "I best git on outa here, 'cause ol' Brer Snake is mean and evil and lowdown, and . . . he jist might git to bitin' me." . . .

Brer Snake looked up and said, "I've been here in this hole for a mighty long time with this brick on my back. Won't you help me git it offa me?"

Brer Possum thought. . . .

He climbed into the tree, broke off the limb, and with that ol' stick, pushed that brick offa Brer Snake's back. Then he took off down the road.

—*"Brer Possum's Dilemma,"* retold by Jackie Torrence

EXERCISE A After reading the excerpt aloud, write four words that the writer has spelled using nonstandard spelling conventions. Do not include words in which an apostrophe indicates that a letter has been left out.

_____

EXERCISE B The author deliberately used some nonstandard spelling conventions in the folk tale. Why do you think she did so?

_____

_____

_____

_____

MECHANICS | Language in Context: Literary Model

Literary Model (continued)

EXERCISE C   *Dialect* is a form of speech spoken by people of a particular region or who belong to a particular group. Think of a dialect you have heard in a movie, on television, or in real life. Write one or two paragraphs spoken by a character who uses this dialect. Use nonstandard spelling conventions to help represent the dialect.

_____

_____

_____

_____

_____

_____

_____

_____

_____

_____

_____

_____

_____

_____

_____

EXERCISE D

1. Will your use of nonstandard spelling conventions benefit your reader, hinder your reader, or both? Explain your answer.

_____

_____

_____

2. In what types of writing would the use of nonstandard spelling conventions not be effective? Explain your answer.

_____

_____

_____

Writing Application: Spelling Handbook

Whenever you use a word processor to write, you can take advantage of its spellchecker. Even so, it is important to remember that *you* must make the final decision about correct spelling. If you type "four" when you meant to type "for," the spellchecker will not see the error, since both spellings are in its dictionary.

Also, the spellchecker may suggest a spelling that does not fit your sentence. Only you, the thinking writer, can decide which suggestions to follow. For example, you might instruct readers who have just had their wisdom teeth removed to rinse with "the plastic surenge from the manilla envelope." The spellchecker might change the misspelled words so that readers are told to rinse with "the plastic surgeon from the vanilla envelope." It does not recognize the nonsense of such a statement—but you do. Check your work carefully, reading every sentence aloud to listen for errors that your eyes might miss.

WRITING ACTIVITY

Working with all the other students in your English class, assemble for publication a handbook of spelling tips you have picked up over the years. Do you remember the difference between *principle* and *principal* by telling yourself that the principal is your "pal"? What memory helpers do you know? For the class spelling handbook, each student will submit two hints for spelling words correctly.

PREWRITING   You may have to spend some time thinking back to rhymes, riddles, or other word games that have helped you spell tricky words in the past. Your part of the class's project is to contribute two such spelling helpers. List as many as you can remember; then, pick your two favorites.

WRITING   Write out your two spelling hints, using wording that makes your hints clear and easy to remember. If your hints help you with the spellings of more than one word, give examples of as many of these words as possible. If you can recall the circumstances under which you learned each hint, report these circumstances to your readers.

REVISING   Spelling is hardly a favorite subject with most students, so try to counter this resistance by turning spelling problems into a little game. Word choice and tone can either encourage students to play along or make drudgery of potential fun.

PUBLISHING   Check your contributions for errors in spelling and punctuation. Then, combine them with the other students' contributions. With your teacher's permission, publish and distribute your handbook. You could also create a bulletin board with spelling tips.

EXTENDING YOUR WRITING

If you enjoyed this exercise, you could extend it into a longer writing project. Sometimes it is easier to remember a word's spelling if you know its history. For an English class, choose a word that you have trouble spelling and research its history in a good dictionary. Write up your findings, and comment on how you can use what you learned to help you spell the word correctly.

COMMON ERRORS | Language in Context: Choices

Choices: Exploring Common Errors

Here's your chance to step out of the grammar book and into the real world. You may not realize it, but examples of common errors appear in your life every day. The following activities challenge you to find a connection between common errors and the world around you. Do the activity below that suits your personality best, and then share your discoveries with your class. Have fun!

Baby Sitters and Lawn Mowers

Baby-sitting might be no big deal to you, but to a parent the care of his or her child is a really big deal. What's more, a lot of homeowners feel almost the exact same way about their lawns. Whenever you apply for a job, treat your own request seriously! Have a short typed list of your work experience. Mention your grades, the clubs you belong to, the school you attend, and anything else that makes you look good. Naturally, this list, which is your résumé, should be neat and error-free. Right now, you've got classmates and a teacher to help you perfect your résumé. Take advantage of this opportunity and write the résumé that will get you that job!

Mr. or Ms. English

Have you ever seen a cartoon description of, say, a college student? There might be an arrow labeled "empty" pointing to his or her pockets. Draw a cartoon personifying the English language. You can add labels to your cartoon to tell your audience about your character. If drawing makes you nervous, compose a collage cut from pictures in magazines.

To Fragment or Not to Fragment

Do those pesky sentence fragments drive you crazy? Well, one of the best ways to learn how to identify them is to write some yourself. In fact, go ahead and write fifteen or so sentence fragments and put them together in the form of a test. Add some complete sentences, too. Then, give your test to your classmates and have them identify each fragment and each complete sentence.

Roll the Presses

Your classmates have created some great stuff for English class! Now it's time to form a committee to choose the best of the best and publish these works in your class newsletter or Web site. Include all kinds of written materials. Be sure to give credit where credit is due. You'll also want to write a short report of interesting events that occurred since the last newsletter. Assign someone to interview your teacher and get his or her opinion of the projects. Take a few photographs as well. When you're done, you'll have something really special to help you remember this exciting year.

Agreement Rules!

What is it about subjects and verbs that makes them disagree so much? Can't they just get along? For this activity, write a dialogue between a disagreeing subject and verb. Start the dialogue out by showing how the two tend to disagree in certain instances, for example, when a prepositional phrase intervenes. As the dialogue progresses, have the subject and verb work out their problems and come to an "agreement." Then, with a friend perform your dialogue in front of the class.

Punctuation Problems

Punctuation can really confuse some people. Do your classmates and yourself a favor and compile a list of the rules for the most commonly made punctuation errors. First, ask your teacher what he or she has observed in students' writing. Then, draw up a list of the rules with relevant examples. Pass out copies to your classmates.

Sentence Fragments and Run-on Sentences A

EXERCISE Identify each of the following word groups by writing on the line provided *F* if the word group is a *sentence fragment*, *R* if it is a *run-on sentence*, or *S* if it is a *complete sentence*.

Example ___*F*___ **1.** Last Friday, after the final bell had rung.

_____ **1.** Finally finished the project we had been working on for months.

_____ **2.** Shouldn't Aunt Lucia have called the house by now?

_____ **3.** Whenever I see a full moon, my thoughts.

_____ **4.** The fog obscured the skyscrapers, a soft rain began to fall.

_____ **5.** Never had she seen so many chickens in one place!

_____ **6.** Exactly what he had wanted to happen.

_____ **7.** Quickly he ran to the fence, the horses had escaped during the night.

_____ **8.** In the middle of the night, as the howling increased, the children shivering in their beds.

_____ **9.** Do you want the fish, or would you rather have one of the pasta dishes?

_____ **10.** The telephone number to call in the event of an emergency.

_____ **11.** Holding the old book under a strong light, she could see some faint writing.

_____ **12.** Before we paint, we have a lot of preparation to do, we will have to remove all the books from the shelves.

_____ **13.** Don't forget to buy some dropcloths at the hardware store!

_____ **14.** All the dry ingredients, including flour, sugar, salt, baking powder, and baking soda.

_____ **15.** Let the bread dough rise for an hour, form it into loaves.

_____ **16.** Do you think you will enjoy either rock climbing or caving?

_____ **17.** Whether we will meet them at the theater or give them a ride in our car.

_____ **18.** When his mother returned from her errands, he borrowed the car.

_____ **19.** The accident, although frightening, was not bad, no one was hurt.

_____ **20.** We were too tired to eat much dinner, we went straight to sleep.

Sentence Fragments and Run-on Sentences B

EXERCISE On the short lines provided, identify each numbered word group as a *sentence fragment (F)*, a *run-on sentence (R)*, or a *complete sentence (S)*. Then, on the long lines provided, rewrite any sentence fragments or run-ons to create complete sentences.

Example ___R___ **1.** People in the United States can expect fireworks on the Fourth of July many other nations also have independence celebrations.

People in the United States can expect fireworks on the Fourth of July.

Many other nations also have independence celebrations.

_____ **1.** The oldest independence day celebration is on August 1 in Switzerland.

_____

_____

_____ **2.** Before that date there were three separate Swiss states they decided to form a union.

_____

_____

_____ **3.** Elephants wearing bright blankets in India's independence day parades.

_____

_____

_____ **4.** The United States gained its independence from England, Mexico won its independence from Spain.

_____

_____

_____ **5.** Imagine the celebrations in Mexico City each year its population is huge.

_____

_____

Subject-Verb Agreement A

EXERCISE A In each of the following sentences, underline the verb in parentheses that agrees in number with its subject.

Example 1. Either Corinna or Michael (<u>has</u>, have) a slide projector.

1. One of these dogs (is, are) not very well trained.

2. Every hallway in our school (look, looks) different.

3. Neither Chris nor his brother Carl (play, plays) football.

4. Unfortunately, the bouquet of flowers (have, has) wilted already.

5. Although my brother and I (are, is) the same age, he is taller than I am.

6. (Do, Does) the lights in this room seem dim to you?

7. Our cats and our dog (sleeps, sleep) on the same blanket.

8. All of the colors in that painting (appear, appears) muted to me.

9. Everyone checked out a novel; none of the biographies (were, was) chosen.

10. (Are, Is) forty-two or forty-three the correct answer?

EXERCISE B In each of the following sentences, cross out any verb that does not agree with its subject and write the correct form of the verb above the incorrect form. If the sentence is correct, write *C* after it.

Example 1. Either a mouse or some moths ~~has~~ *have* eaten a hole in my favorite jacket.

11. My brother, along with his friends Neil and Mick, play clarinet in the band.

12. Not a single one of the eggs in the carton were broken.

13. If the choir practice three more times this week, the concert will go smoothly.

14. Haven't Nathan or Christina turned in the paper yet?

15. The coaches for the team hasn't made a decision about the starting lineup.

16. Flour, along with a little yeast, olive oil, water, and salt, is the main ingredient in pizza dough.

17. Either ice-skating or sledding are fun on a cold winter's day.

18. In that classroom, neither the door nor the windows open easily.

19. A horse and wagon were the only mode of transportation at that time.

20. Either my grandmother or my mother's sisters cooks the holiday dinner.

Subject-Verb Agreement B

EXERCISE A In each of the following sentences, decide whether the underlined verb agrees in number with its subject. If the verb form is incorrect, write the correct form above it. If the verb is correct, write *C* above it.

Example 1. Each of us <u>have</u> brought lunch from home today.
has

1. The reflection of the moon on the waves <u>is</u> beautiful.

2. She occasionally <u>eat</u> chicken, but fish is her favorite choice.

3. Neither my science class nor my math class <u>have</u> difficult homework.

4. <u>Has</u> either of you boys written to your grandfather lately?

5. Both my brother and Frank, his best friend since the first grade, <u>thinks</u> that movie is great.

6. <u>Does</u> Al and his teammates expect to win the game tomorrow?

7. Justine, along with Katie and Rose, <u>go</u> to the same camp every summer.

8. Some pieces of the jigsaw puzzle <u>was</u> missing.

9. Randall and Maria, his sister, <u>are</u> certainly the fastest runners in the school.

10. In addition to a pencil, graph paper, and a ruler, what else <u>are</u> needed for this problem?

EXERCISE B In each of the following sentences, circle the subject of the underlined verb. Then, if the verb does not agree in number with its subject, write the correct form of the verb above the incorrect form. If the verb already agrees with its subject, write *C* above it.

Example 1. The teacher is concerned because (no one) in the class <u>have</u> studied.
has

11. <u>Do</u> everyone in the class understand the material?

12. Several of the students <u>have</u> asked for additional help.

13. Either Oscar's father or one of his uncles <u>have</u> offered to drive us to the movies.

14. The band <u>play</u> when the team runs onto the field.

15. The most interesting exhibit in that museum <u>are</u> the rocks and minerals.

16. Sam agreed that the rocks and minerals <u>was</u> really fascinating.

17. Where will you go to school when your family <u>move</u>?

18. She won't be able to join us unless someone <u>give</u> her a ride.

19. I think you've made a mistake; fifty-seven cents <u>is</u> the wrong change.

20. He couldn't wear the suit because the pants <u>was</u> too short.

COMMON ERRORS

Pronoun-Antecedent Agreement A

EXERCISE A   In each of the following sentences, circle the antecedent of the pronoun in parentheses. Then, underline the pronoun in parentheses that agrees with the antecedent.

Example 1. Every ⟨child⟩ should wear *(their, his or her)* hat outside today.

1. One of my brothers has forgotten *(their, his)* hat and gloves.

2. The questionnaire asked the public *(their, its)* opinions about the candidates.

3. My family is from Sioux Falls, South Dakota; can you find *(them, it)* on a map?

4. One of the birds had broken *(its, his)* wing.

5. If anyone is interested in chess, *(they, he or she)* is welcome to join our club.

6. Van, Matthew, and Erik woke up early on the morning of *(his, their)* big exam.

7. I've lost my sunglasses again; do you know where I left *(them, it)*?

8. He used blackstrap molasses because of *(its, their)* high vitamin content.

9. My sister is taking economics this semester because her degree program requires *(them, it)*.

10. Someone on the girls' basketball team spilled spaghetti sauce on *(themselves, herself)*.

EXERCISE B   In each of the following sentences, cross out any pronoun that does not agree with its antecedent. Then, write the correct pronoun above it. If the sentence is correct, write *C* after it.

Example 1. I didn't take gymnastics because ~~they~~ *it* was offered at the same time as earth

science was.

11. *Ad astra per aspera* is the motto of Kansas; it means "to the stars through hardships."

12. Many people are familiar with E. E. Cummings's poetry because of their unusual punctuation

and capitalization.

13. Denise and Emil were not happy about his and her grades on the essay test.

14. His mother bought him some nice slacks, but he refused to wear it to the awards banquet.

15. The strength of the United States lies in their people.

16. Measure three tablespoons of milk and add them to the mixture.

17. Neither of the girls remembered to bring their notebook to class.

18. The islands that make up the state of Hawaii are well known for their natural beauty.

19. I didn't watch the news last night because I fell asleep before they came on.

20. Thomas and Clive, you should congratulate yourself for a job well done.

Language and Sentence Skills Practice

Pronoun-Antecedent Agreement B

EXERCISE In each of the following sentences, circle the antecedent of the pronoun in parentheses. Then, underline the pronoun in parentheses that agrees with the antecedent.

Example 1. Until she studied *(them, it)*, she thought she didn't like physics.

1. Each of the horses is stabled in *(their, its)* own stall.

2. Max, who wanted to go to the mountains, will not be able to borrow *(their, his)* father's car this weekend.

3. If your binoculars are more powerful than mine are, please let me use *(it, them)*.

4. Everyone who plans to go to the concerts should bring five dollars for *(their, his or her)* ticket.

5. The team does warm-up exercises for fifteen minutes before each of *(its, their)* games.

6. I don't believe that either Simone or Mary colors *(their, her)* hair.

7. One of the paperback books is missing some of *(their, its)* pages.

8. The crowd showed *(their, its)* appreciation by cheering and clapping.

9. Ask Ana or Maria what *(her, their)* middle name is.

10. Both Ivan and Zeke agree *(his, their)* biology exam was harder than they thought it would be.

11. You can locate a country or a city in the atlas by looking in *(their, its)* index.

12. Neither Carlos nor Ulises likes to buy *(their, his)* lunch in the cafeteria.

13. The cat picked up *(its, his or her)* kittens, one by one, and carried them to the basket.

14. Anyone who is interested in photography should give Mr. Knight *(their, his or her)* name.

15. My mother and father went out to dinner on *(his and her, their)* anniversary.

16. Some of the apples are rotten, aren't *(it, they)*?

17. Everyone in this room needs to remind *(themselves, himself or herself)* about the need for silence during the test.

18. Do you know of anyone who lost *(their, his or her)* wallet on the bus?

19. Some of my friends like to do *(his or her, their)* science projects at the last minute, but I can't work that way.

20. Sometimes we work together on a problem in class, but this time each of us has to get the answer by *(ourselves, himself or herself)*.

Verb Forms A

EXERCISE A   In each of the following sentences, underline the correct form of the verb in parentheses.

Example 1. Have you ever (*sang, sung*) in a choir before?

1. Some pages (*tore, torn*) when I dropped the book.

2. Before she had (*written, wrote*) two pages, all the electricity in the school went off.

3. You should have (*spoke, spoken*) to your counselor about the course schedule.

4. Last weekend, my brother and I (*flew, flown*) alone to Topeka to visit our grandparents.

5. Sharon, with some help from her father, has (*builded, built*) a doghouse for Treasure, her golden retriever.

6. Although he had never (*drew, drawn*) much before, he was clearly talented.

7. Some of the peaches had (*fell, fallen*) off the trees, but plenty were left to pick.

8. Overnight, the rain had (*froze, frozen*) into a thin sheet of ice on all the roads.

9. My great-grandmother (*brung, brought*) these dishes with her when she came to America.

10. Did you (*break, broke*) your collarbone when you fell off the fence?

EXERCISE B   In each of the following sentences, choose the correct verb in parentheses.

Example 1. Please (*sit, set*) the packages on that chair.

11. None of the dogs learned how to (*sit, set*) during obedience class.

12. When the sun (*rises, raises*), we will be able to see the island.

13. As I was (*lying, laying*) down for a nap, the doorbell rang.

14. Who is responsible for (*rising, raising*) the flag every morning?

15. My glasses were (*setting, sitting*) on the table the last time I saw them.

16. Weak from her long illness, she could barely (*raise, rise*) her head off the pillow.

17. The father (*lay, laid*) his baby girl in the crib, tiptoed out of the room, and shut the door quietly.

18. She (*sat, set*) the dishes on the counter and wiped off the table.

19. They must have (*laid, lain*) in the sun too long; they both look a little sunburned.

20. Kristin and Thad had already (*raised, risen*) from their seats and were starting toward the door.

COMMON ERRORS

Verb Forms B

EXERCISE A   On the lines provided, write the correct past or past participle form of the verb given.

Example 1. *be*   Before last summer, I had never _____*been*_____ to our community's animal

care center.

1. *go*   I didn't know when I _____ there that they needed volunteers.

2. *shake*   Mr. Blumenthal _____ my hand when I said I wanted to help.

3. *take*   I had _____ care of neighborhood pets before, but the center's iguanas pre-

sented a new challenge.

4. *teach*   The trained caretakers _____ me how to prepare vegetables for the rabbits.

5. *keep*   One day I _____ a baby llama until its mother was found.

6. *bring*   Several people _____ in young squirrels that needed care.

7. *break*   A mallard duck that had _____ its wing stayed with us until it could fly.

8. *swim*   A turtle found in the parking lot _____ away when we released it at the lake.

9. *want*   Our guest monkey always _____ to be held.

10. *put*   My friend Andy Mendoza has _____ in his application to help at the center

next summer.

EXERCISE B   In each of the following sentences, underline the verb or verb phrase. Then, identify the voice of the verb by writing above it *A* if the verb is in the *active voice* or *P* if the verb is in the *passive voice*.

Example 1. These flowers <u>were brought</u> by one of my friends.
                                     P

11. Reginald doesn't remember the name of that actor.

12. That garden was planted by our class last spring.

13. On Tuesdays, the museum doesn't open until noon.

14. Unfortunately, the roof of the barn had been torn off.

15. Several techniques were demonstrated during this afternoon's art class.

16. Natalie began the application.

17. The dogs chased the mail truck for blocks.

18. All of the food at the birthday party was prepared by my mother and my aunt.

19. The choir had been practicing for weeks for the holiday concert.

20. Claire will have read over two hundred books by May.

Pronoun Forms A

EXERCISE A In each of the following sentences, underline the correct pronoun in parentheses.

Example 1. Akim read Susan, Josh, and (I, *me*) the inscription inside his ring.

1. Without (he, him) as the troop leader, we were less enthusiastic about the campout.

2. The safari guide showed (we, us) how to take better photographs.

3. The batter with the best hitting record could be (he, him).

4. Lucinda and (she, her) already bought tickets to see *Phantom of the Opera*.

5. It is (we, us) who recommend the Caesar salad.

6. The reporter asked Nan and (they, them) if the exhibit was more fun than a movie.

7. Yann and (we, us) saw three toads by the gutter spout last night.

8. The airplane to Lima, Peru, did not wait for the officer and (she, her).

9. It was baseball announcer Harry Caray (who, whom) was known for shouting "Holy Cow!"

   after a big play.

10. (We, Us) skaters have practiced at the ice rink every day.

EXERCISE B In each of the following sentences, cross out any incorrect pronoun and write the correct pronoun above it. If a sentence is correct, write *C* above it.

Example 1. He and ~~me~~ are the only returning team members this year.

11. Vincent's sisters and him visited their cousins in New Mexico last summer.

12. As the plane rolled away from the gate, Raul could see his mother waving at his brother and he.

13. Only one of we girls wants to play a percussion instrument.

14. Who should we call about the broken fire hydrant?

15. The student who won first place in the debate tournament is him.

16. Tell Melinda and her about the comedian you saw last night.

17. This is a reminder for whomever is the last person to leave the room.

18. Us biology students have a lot of homework.

19. Did you bring extra sandwiches for Michelle and I?

20. Peter told Dan and I about his plans for the summer vacation.

Language and Sentence Skills Practice **367**

Pronoun Forms B

EXERCISE In each of the following sentences, underline the correct pronoun in parentheses.

Example 1. My best friends, *(her, she)* and Ruth, are coming with us to the movies.

1. *(Who, Whom)* should have shut the windows before it rained?

2. Please remind *(we, us)* new members about the meeting.

3. Four of the students in my class, Alice, Terrell, David, and *(her, she)*, entered essays in the contest.

4. I told *(he, him)* about the program.

5. The girl who raised the most money during the fund-raising drive was *(her, she)*.

6. My mother has invited some of her relatives—my aunt Kera and my two cousins, Jim and *(she, her)*—to go to the play with us.

7. I bought *(him, he)* and Jack a cold drink.

8. When Jean calls, ask her to bring her notes with *(her, she)*.

9. If we don't reach Gabe and *(he, him)* tonight, we can tell them tomorrow at school.

10. Did either Yvonne or *(her, she)* need a ride to the rehearsal?

11. Caroline and *(me, I)* were planning a picnic, but it rained.

12. If you see Saul or Nina today, please don't tell *(he or she, him or her)* the secret.

13. Were the boys who painted the fence for your father *(they, them)*?

14. *(Her, She)* and her sister always get up early on weekends.

15. Do you have any last-minute advice for Edgar and *(I, me)*?

16. The teacher you've liked the best so far is *(who, whom)*?

17. The person who left that mess in the kitchen was either my niece or *(him, he)*.

18. By *(who, whom)* was this poem written?

19. Choose Frances and *(I, me)* to be in your project group.

20. Sit next to Marty and *(he, him)*; they've saved a place for you.

COMMON ERRORS

Comparative and Superlative Forms A

EXERCISE In each of the following sentences, underline the correct form of the adjective or adverb in parentheses.

Example 1. Both of my sisters are (tallest, <u>taller</u>) than I am.

1. Did you do (better, gooder) on the test than you expected?

2. The children walked (farther, farthest) today than they ever have before.

3. This is some of the (interestingest, most interesting) music I've ever heard.

4. I know I will follow directions (most carefully, more carefully) the next time.

5. Is the backyard (shadier, more shadier) than the front yard?

6. Of all the essays, his was by far the (more impressive, most impressive).

7. He didn't look well yesterday, but I hope he's feeling (weller, better) today.

8. Which one of the seven designs did you like (better, best)?

9. Everyone was (happier, more happier) when spring arrived at last.

10. She dances (more gracefully, gracefuller) than most dancers her age.

11. Tuesday was the (worse, worst) day I've had in a long, long time.

12. The Caesar salad Rick's mom made was the (more tasty, tastiest) I've ever eaten.

13. Which of these two dresses looks (gooder, better) on me?

14. That theater has the (less expensive, least expensive) tickets in the whole city.

15. The students finished this set of problems (more quickly, more quicker) than they had finished the previous set.

16. Which one of your dogs—Minnie or Moe—is (most obedient, more obedient)?

17. The final problem on the test took (much, more) time than any of the others.

18. We go to the park (more often, often) than we used to.

19. You put (little, less) turkey on this sandwich than you put on the other one.

20. I enjoyed that movie (more, most) than the other one we saw.

Comparative and Superlative Forms B

EXERCISE On the lines provided, write the correct positive, comparative, or superlative form of the italicized adjective or adverb.

Example 1. *desirable* Plant breeders develop vegetables with ___*more desirable*___ traits.

1. *large*   The _____ snail on land is the African snail.

2. *tiny*   Newborn opossums are much _____ than a teaspoon.

3. *good*   A recycling center operator might know the _____ way to avoid wasting resources.

4. *old*   Historians say that the _____ dice are from India and Iraq.

5. *famous*   The *Messiah* is probably George Frideric Handel's _____ work.

6. *frequently* Hummingbirds beat their wings _____ than any other bird.

7. *complex*   Please choose the _____ jigsaw puzzle out of the three. We enjoy a challenge!

8. *available*   During the late 1800s work outside the home became _____ to women than ever before.

9. *gracefully* Ballet dancers are likely to move _____ than people without formal training.

10. *dry*   The _____ weather periods on record are referred to as *droughts*.

11. *well*   Doesn't she feel any _____ than she did yesterday?

12. *lonely*   The little boy felt _____ in his new neighborhood, far away from his old friends.

13. *horrible*   Sharon left the supply closet in the art room in the _____ condition it has ever been in, Sarah.

14. *much*   Did you spend _____ time on your homework last night?

15. *soon*   The flight arrived _____ than expected.

16. *important* Please get off the phone; I'm expecting the _____ call of my life!

17. *quickly*   After the sun came out, the temperature rose _____ .

18. *little*   The _____ of all the puppies nestled close to its mother.

19. *bad*   The weather today is much _____ than it was yesterday.

20. *far*   We don't have to walk much _____ to catch the bus.

Double Comparison and Double Negatives

EXERCISE A In each of the following sentences, draw a line through any unnecessary words or parts of words to correct a double comparison or double negative.

Example 1. We couldn't barely see over the heads of the people in front of us.

1. Cole is much more taller than his brother.

2. He can't never make up his mind.

3. Ten kilometers is the most farthest I've run at one time.

4. Without a doubt, that was the worstest movie I've ever seen.

5. The construction noise was so loud that she couldn't hardly hear the radio.

6. No, thank you, I don't want no rice or potatoes with my meal.

7. We don't never have enough time to finish our work in class.

8. I hope I wake up more earlier tomorrow than I did today.

9. Of all the birds in my yard, the cardinal is my most favorite.

10. She didn't have no money to pay for her ticket.

EXERCISE B On the line provided, rewrite each of the following sentences to correct the double comparison or double negative.

Example 1. We can't paint no more murals until this wall dries. *We can't paint any more murals until this wall dries.*

11. If you keep eating apples, there won't be no more to take on the trip. _____

_____

12. Any band will perform more better with a little practice. _____

_____

13. New Hampshire is much more smaller than Alaska. _____

_____

14. There wasn't hardly anybody at the bus stop this morning. _____

_____

15. The new principals don't allow nobody without a pass in the hallway. _____

_____

COMMON ERRORS

Misplaced and Dangling Modifiers A

EXERCISE   On the lines provided, rewrite each of the following sentences to correct any dangling or misplaced modifiers. You may have to add or rearrange words to make the meaning of a sentence clear.

Example 1. The child held onto the cat who had her hair tied in pigtails. *The child, who had her hair tied in pigtails, held onto the cat.*

1. Reaching the station with only a few minutes to spare, the conductor hurried the girl into the waiting train. _____

2. Chirping and flapping their little wings, the boys admired the baby birds. _____

3. When planning a hike in rugged country, a compass and a map of the area are necessary. ____

4. The boy from Finland fixed the old porch rail that stayed with my family last summer. _____

5. To get the most out of school and my other activities, learning to manage my time was important. _____

6. While riding the bus to school last week, an accident happened right in front of us. _____

7. I heard that a mastodon skeleton had been discovered on the radio today. _____

8. The high winds scared us that were bending the trees nearly to the ground. _____

9. Weary but satisfied with our day's work, the shade of the trees was welcome. _____

10. Running down the hill near our house, my knee was hurt. _____

COMMON ERRORS

Misplaced and Dangling Modifiers B

EXERCISE On the lines provided, rewrite each of the following sentences to correct any dangling or misplaced modifiers. You may have to add or rearrange words to make the meaning of a sentence clear.

Example 1. Determined to win, four medals were awarded to the track team. *Determined to*
win, the track team was awarded four medals.

1. Traditional Navajo houses are distinctive, which are made of logs and earth. _____
_____

2. The Switzerland poster shows how spectacular the mountains are in my room. _____
_____

3. Antoine gave a pendant to his grandmother engraved with family names. _____
_____

4. Belonging to one of the Aleman twins, we will remember to return this jacket. _____
_____

5. Tired from the long bus ride home, the city-limit sign was cheered by the students. _____
_____

6. James Watt created the term *horsepower*, who invented a new kind of steam engine. _____
_____

7. Uncle John found a raccoon in his garage that was sleeping. _____
_____

8. Eager and confident, news of the first triumph was no surprise to the coach. _____
_____

9. Richard the Lion-Hearted left his kingdom to fight in the Crusades, whose brother was
Prince John. _____
_____

10. Tanya and Guy almost finished the practice quiz at the same time. _____
_____

COMMON ERRORS

Standard Usage A

EXERCISE A For each of the following sentences, determine whether the underlined word or word group is correct according to standard, formal English usage. If the word or word group is not standard, formal usage, write the correct usage above it. If the word or word group is correct, write *C* above it.

Example 1. I learned some important lessons when I ~~busted~~ my wrist. *broke*

1. One morning I noticed a kitten <u>setting</u> high in a tree.

2. I <u>should of</u> gone on about my business.

3. Instead, I acted <u>like</u> the situation required emergency action.

4. Since I <u>ain't</u> afraid of heights, I grabbed our ladder.

5. <u>That there</u> kitten was clearly frightened as I approached.

6. I decided to <u>try and</u> stand on the top step of the ladder.

7. <u>Them</u> warning labels are there for a purpose.

8. Do you know how it feels to <u>lay</u> injured on the ground?

9. The kitten managed to climb down very <u>well</u> by itself.

10. Don't climb a ladder <u>without</u> you have someone to hold it steady.

EXERCISE B On the lines provided, rewrite each of the following sentences, correcting any errors in standard, formal English usage.

Example 1. My mother she don't like dirty shoes in the house. *My mother doesn't like dirty shoes in the house.*

11. How come I had to wait a hour for you? _____

_____

12. When he wasn't excepted into the summer program, he was sort of embarrassed. _____

_____

13. The reason I don't have a jacket is because I looked all over the house, but it was nowheres.

_____

14. The teacher who use to learn us math moved to Milwaukee. _____

_____

15. They were suppose to read the book theirselves and than kind of tell how it effected them. __

_____

NAME _____ CLASS _____ DATE _____

for CHAPTER 17: CORRECTING COMMON ERRORS   pages 264–78

Standard Usage B

EXERCISE A For each of the following sentences, determine whether the underlined word or word group is correct according to standard, formal English usage. If the word or word group is not standard usage, write the correct usage above it. If the word or word group is correct, write *C* above it.

              Doesn't
Example 1. <u>Don't</u> she know that the bell rings at 8:00 A.M.?

1. I have <u>less</u> pairs of shoes than my sister has.

2. They had a private discussion <u>between</u> the three of themselves.

3. You <u>hadn't ought to of</u> left the windows open last night.

4. Please <u>bring</u> these books when you go to the library this afternoon.

5. Unfortunately, <u>it's</u> closed on Monday afternoons.

6. These <u>kind</u> of sweater is too warm for our climate.

7. He was <u>real</u> excited about the research project.

8. My aunt Nelda feels <u>bad</u> today.

9. Everyone <u>accept</u> Jerome is coming on the field trip.

10. <u>Their</u> wasn't any spaghetti left by the time I ate lunch.

EXERCISE B On the lines provided, rewrite each of the following sentences, correcting any errors in standard, formal English usage.

Example 1. I all ready know who's shoes them are. *I already know whose shoes those are.*

11. He dances real good, don't he? _____

12. We should of been able to find some seats together somewheres in the theater. _____

13. The reason you can't scarcely see through the windshield is because its covered with mud. _____

14. This here book has less pages then the one your reading. _____

15. He told me that he learned hisself to ride a bike when he was five years old. _____

Language and Sentence Skills Practice **375**

COMMON ERRORS

Capitalization A

EXERCISE A In each of the following sentences, circle any letter that should be capitalized.

Example 1. Did you call m̲rs. s̲impson about the article in the n̲ew y̲ork t̲imes?

1. Are belgium and luxembourg also members of nato?

2. Merrill longham, d.v.m., is a large-animal veterinarian; he grew up on a ranch somewhere in the west.

3. I don't know what the statue on the top of the u.s. capitol building represents.

4. The constellation *ursa major,* or the big bear, is known to many people as the big dipper.

5. The german airship *hindenburg* exploded as it was docking in lakehurst, new jersey, on may 6, 1937.

6. elizabeth II, queen of the united kingdom of great britain and northern ireland, succeeded her father, king george vi, in 1952.

7. The rocky mountains form the continental divide, which separates rivers that flow west to the pacific ocean from rivers that flow east to the atlantic ocean.

8. Although the capital city of south dakota is pierre, its largest city is sioux falls.

9. I think she lives at 4422 avenue b, which is near the intersection of wise street and the flint parkway.

10. In 1830, in a famous race between peter cooper's steam locomotive *tom thumb* and a horse, the horse won.

EXERCISE B In each of the following sentences, circle any letter that should be capitalized but is not, and draw a slash (/) through any letter that is capitalized but should not be.

Example 1. You can cash this check at any B̸ranch of the f̲irst n̲ational b̲ank.

11. The O̸fficial L̸anguage of Iran is persian, also called farsi, a language written in arabic script.

12. the taj mahal, at agra in northern india, must be one of the W̸orld's most beautiful buildings.

13. He has memorized several poems by robert frost, but his favorite is the P̸oem that begins, "whose woods these are I think I know."

14. The photography club will meet on the first wednesday of every M̸onth, except for december.

15. This semester my E̸lectives include art I and journalism I.

COMMON ERRORS

Capitalization B

EXERCISE A In each of the following sentences, circle any letter that should be capitalized but is not.

Example 1. I think ⓟeterson's ⓓrugstore is on ⓣenth ⓢtreet.

1. The winner of the newbery medal in 1999 was louis sachar's novel *holes*.

2. Most u.s. currency is printed at the bureau of engraving and printing in washington.

3. our school's team is called the callaway cardinals, our colors are red and white, and our mascot is a cardinal named cal.

4. When the new hayfield high school opened, crowding at mt. vernon high school was relieved.

5. She shook dr. michaelman's hand and said, "it's nice to meet you."

6. That restaurant serves many kinds of asian dishes, but I especially like one of their thai noodle dishes.

7. i wonder what earth looks like from the moon.

8. He lives on forty-third street, just north of the university of texas campus.

9. my family doesn't watch much tv, but we subscribe to several magazines, including *national geographic* and *time*.

10. on labor day, many afl-cio members gather for a parade and a picnic.

EXERCISE B In each of the following sentences, circle any letter that should be capitalized but is not, and draw a slash (/) through any letter that should be lowercase but is not. If the capitalization in a sentence is correct, write *C* after the sentence.

Example 1. The current Ȼountry borders of ⓝorth America are certainly not what they have always been.

11. Before 1803, the huge area called the louisiana territory belonged to spain and France.

12. The area stretched from the Mississippi river to the Rocky mountains; its northern border was Canada, and it extended all the way south to Mexico.

13. American farmers who lived West of the appalachian mountains depended on the mississippi river to ship their produce to the gulf of mexico.

14. President Jefferson, who did not wish to see France increase its influence on the north American Continent, authorized the purchase of florida and new orleans.

15. His envoys agreed to buy the whole territory from the French emperor, Napoleon I, for about fifteen million dollars.

Commas A

EXERCISE In each of the following sentences, draw a caret (∧) where any missing commas should be inserted.

Example 1. During the month before the contest∧the math team will meet every Tuesday∧

        Wednesday∧and Friday.

1. Before you begin to write your first draft make an outline of your paper.

2. My brother and John one of our cousins on our mother's side are in the same class.

3. Send the completed application form to 442 Winston Ave. Sherwood MI 40007.

4. In that building are the offices of Kelly Donohue Jr. M.D. and his father Kelly Donohue Sr. D.D.S.

5. In the middle of the night a loud clap of thunder rattled the windows.

6. On Monday May 10 we have our final exam in social studies.

7. My aunt Sara was born on Christmas day December 25 1959 in New London Connecticut.

8. On Tuesday after school the Drama Club will meet in the auditorium.

9. Ms. Masterton may I please use the telephone on your desk?

10. Laughing and shouting the children ran onto the playground.

11. Yes I think I would enjoy watching the parade from your apartment.

12. Rob Betty and Suzanne have been chosen to represent the class on the student council.

13. The banner across the hallway is really impressive but the posters look great, too.

14. Although no rain had been forecast a thunderstorm ruined our picnic.

15. My family has two dogs three cats a parrot and some goldfish.

16. You can wash the lettuce for the salad and Calvin can slice the bread.

17. When the telephone rang before dawn I sprang out of bed.

18. In the fall of 1999 we drove from Texas to Oregon camping at national parks along the way.

19. I've had this old stuffed bear since I think I was three or four years old.

20. The hikers filled their water bottles strapped on their packs and set off into the woods.

Commas B

EXERCISE A In each of the following sentences, draw a caret ($\wedge$) to show where any missing commas should be inserted. If a sentence is correct, write *C* above it.

Example 1. At elevations higher than a mile$_\wedge$most people begin to feel the effects of reduced oxygen.

1. At high altitudes tired sleepy people may also get *soroche* which means "mountain sickness."

2. However the Quechua Indians of the Andes have special body characteristics.

3. A very high mountain range in South America the Andes has a top altitude of 22,835 ft.

4. The Quechua do not live on the highest peaks but they do make their homes at altitudes of more than two miles above sea level.

5. Imagine how terribly out of breath most people would feel at that altitude!

6. How do the Quechua Indians manage to survive in an atmosphere with less oxygen?

7. Studies show the Quechua have larger chests lung capacities and hearts than other people.

8. Because this Indian group has a higher breathing rate they can take in enough oxygen.

9. On the other hand their heartbeat is slower than that of sea-level inhabitants.

10. Could it be that an extra-large amount of blood is pumped with each heartbeat?

EXERCISE B In each of the following sentences, draw a caret ($\wedge$) to show where any missing commas should be inserted and draw a slash (/) through any unnecessary commas.

Example 1. The meetings/are on Tuesday$_\wedge$March 14$_\wedge$and Wednesday$_\wedge$March 29.

11. "Zack" Michael asked "do you want to meet, at my house on Saturday morning?"

12. Noel Sandy and Tricia, have dogs but Kim, and Phil have cats.

13. Renata would you please, help me sort the recycling?

14. Put bottles, and jars, into this bin aluminum cans into that box and steel cans, into that box.

15. On September 19 2001 at 4:00 P.M. we will play our first, big game of the season.

16. If Amanda calls, while I'm in the shower, please tell her, I'll be there in twenty minutes.

17. He was after all one of my closest, friends.

18. Tired but happy after a long day in the sun the children fell asleep, in the car, on the way home.

19. She was born, in Evanston Illinois but both of her brothers, were born in Des Moines Iowa.

20. Martin along with three other students in his class was inducted, into the honor society, last year.

COMMON ERRORS

Semicolons and Colons

EXERCISE In each of the following sentences, underline each word or number that should be followed by a colon, and draw a caret mark (∧) to show where a semicolon should be inserted instead of a comma.

Examples 1. For the project, you will need the following <u>supplies</u> poster board, felt-tip pens, index cards, and a glue stick.

2. Busloads of students arrived at the theater at <u>12 00</u>, unfortunately, the movie had started at <u>11 30</u>.

1. Many people try to follow a version of the golden rule Treat others the way you want to be treated.

2. This camping equipment should be considered necessary a tent, a sleeping bag, a flashlight, and a first-aid kit.

3. The costume requires the following materials six yards of muslin, a large spool of thread, a 26-inch zipper, and two yards of inch-wide elastic.

4. Good sportsmanship is important to our coach, she says that poor losers and poor winners are both poor sports.

5. Their travel plans included stops in the following cities Milan and Venice, Italy, Munich, Germany, and Strasbourg and Paris, France.

6. Subway trains depart from this station every five minutes except between midnight and 6 00 A.M., there are only four trains every hour during that period.

7. My research paper is very ambitious, I plan to title it "The New Deal, Government Programs During the Great Depression."

8. My mother asked me to put away the clean clothes, which are lying on the bed, write a letter to my uncle, who is on a ship somewhere in the Mediterranean, and, after giving the dog a bath, clean out the garage.

9. At our school, we don't have to eat in the cafeteria, if we prefer, we can eat outside at the picnic tables or under the trees.

10. We counted all these signs between our house and the highway twenty-five stop signs, fifty street signs, sixteen billboards, three yield signs, two one-way street signs, and I don't know how many speed-limit signs.

Quotation Marks and Other Punctuation A

EXERCISE A   Rewrite each of the following sentences, adding capital letters, quotation marks, and other punctuation where needed.

Example 1. Mom, asked Alice, may I go to the movies with Erica and Mark tonight?

"Mom," asked Alice, "may I go to the movies with Erica and Mark tonight?"

1. I don't know answered Doug I've never seen anything like that before _____

_____

2. Peering into the aquarium, Doug added wow just look at the colors on its fins _____

_____

3. Could you tell us what kind of fish that is Cal asked the store manager we'd also like to know

how much it costs _____

_____

4. You'll have to buy a pair of fish, boys the manager replied and a pair costs seventy-five dollars

_____

5. Seventy-five dollars exclaimed Doug and Cal together that's a lot of money for two fish

_____

EXERCISE B   In each of the following sentences, draw a caret ($_\wedge$) to show where a hyphen should be inserted and underline any word that should be italicized.

Example 1. On her desk was a well$_\wedge$worn copy of <u>Wuthering Heights</u>.

6. Listen to the radio for the most up to date weather forecast.

7. We will read one of Shakespeare's plays this year, either The Tempest or A Midsummer

Night's Dream.

8. I had only an hour and forty five minutes to finish my research about the Titanic.

9. Priscilla's father designed the set for the Puccini opera La Bohème.

10. He described the well known book as his magnum opus, which my great grandmother told

me means "masterpiece."

COMMON ERRORS

Quotation Marks and Other Punctuation B

EXERCISE A On the lines provided, rewrite each of the following sentences, inserting quotation marks and other punctuation as necessary and correcting the capitalization.

Example 1. What does your brother think of the new high school Asked Naomi
  "What does your brother think of the new high school?" asked Naomi.

1. He likes the lockers and the band Hai said but he misses some of his friends _____

_____

2. do you think he misses me Naomi asked bluntly _____

_____

3. Gee I don't know said Hai you can always call him and ask him yourself _____

_____

4. No I'll just ask him when I see him in the hallway one day soon she responded _____

_____

5. Wow does that mean your family moved closer to the new school, too asked Hai _____

_____

EXERCISE B On the lines provided, rewrite each of the following sentences, underlining any words that should be italicized, and inserting hyphens, dashes, parentheses, and brackets where necessary.

Example 1. During the fire drill please pay attention the elevators will not work.
  During the fire drill—please pay attention—the elevators will not work.

6. During President Roosevelt's third term in office 1941–1945, the U.S. entered World War II. __

_____

7. Did you say I'm sorry to interrupt that you were going to the post office? _____

_____

8. Our town's weekly newspaper is called the Metropolitan Mirror. _____

_____

9. None of us have finished the book yet, although our papers are due in mid October. _____

_____

10. To some people, figures in the paintings of El Greco his real name was Domenikos

Theotokopoulos 1541–1614 look elongated and distorted. _____

_____

COMMON ERRORS

Apostrophes

EXERCISE In each of the following sentences, draw a caret ($\wedge$) to show where any missing apostrophes should be inserted.

Example 1. They$\wedge$re not going to reach into all those hives and remove the bees$\wedge$honey, are they?

1. That yellow umbrella left in the womens department is hers.

2. All of that clubs officers gathered in the courtyard for a yearbook picture.

3. Check your alarm clock; if its not working, take ours.

4. Coach Smiths observation was that you have a runners natural ability.

5. Dont follow advice that you wouldnt give to a good friend.

6. After a good nights sleep, Ill feel much better.

7. He doesnt use any punctuation marks except !s.

8. The team will meet on the practice field at four o clock.

9. Nadine and Natashas fathers name is Nick.

10. If youll wait until those shoes go on sale, youll really get your moneys worth.

11. The Martinezes yard is big enough for Mr. Martinezs Great Dane, Woof.

12. The sheeps pen, near the barn, is where youll find the lambs.

13. This morning well meet with the *Morning Star*s reporter, Greg Gibson, who covers school events.

14. Whos willing to volunteer for this clubs car wash on Saturday?

15. Someones coat and wallet were left in the auditorium after Thursdays performance.

16. My oldest brothers bicycles handlebars are too high for me.

17. During the late 1990s, I attended an elementary school near my grandmothers house in Abilene.

18. I cant tell whether these letters are *T*s or *J*s, can you?

19. This mornings assembly in the gym will be short; well begin by introducing the schools interim principal.

20. Shes been appointed to take Dr. Garcias place until a permanent replacement can be found.

COMMON ERRORS

All Marks of Punctuation Review

EXERCISE Revise the following letter, inserting necessary end marks, commas, semicolons, colons, apostrophes, hyphens, dashes, parentheses, and quotation marks. Underline any words that should be italicized.

Example [1] Raul's letter of application for the internship was mailed on Friday, April 12.

[1] 211 South Thirty fifth St

[2] Northumberland KS 52333

[3] April 11 2001

[4] Dr Wilma B Porter

Northumberland Public Library

[5] 557 North Main Ave

Northumberland, KS 52335

[6] Dear Dr Porter

[7] When I was at the library last week I saw a flyer advertising library internships for students [8] The school librarian Mr Dan Simpson encouraged me to apply

[9] I have worked in our schools library for three years now since I began sixth grade [10] In our library I reshelve books straighten shelves and help students locate books [11] Mr Simpson says that I am a dependable responsible and good natured worker

[12] Of course I am also an avid reader some weeks I read as many as ten books and have had a library card for ten years [13] Some of my favorite books are the following The Adventures of Tom Sawyer and any other book by Mark Twain C S Lewiss Chronicles of Narnia especially The Magicians Nephew and anything by Isaac Asimov

[14] During the summer I can work four hours a day from 10 00 A.M. to 2 00 P.M. [15] Will those hours be enough for an internship [16] My house is only a ten minute walk from the library so I will always be on time

[17] I hope you will consider me for an internship I would really like to work at the library. [18] My application is enclosed and my telephone number is 555-5301 if you need additional information [19] Thank you for your help

[20] Sincerely

Raul Cantutt

COMMON ERRORS

Spelling A

EXERCISE A In each of the following sentences, underline any misspelled word and write the word correctly above the misspelled word. If all the words in a sentence are correct, write *C* above the sentence.

Example 1. The <u>athelete</u> began a long-term <u>trainning</u> program.
(athlete) *(training)*

1. The astronaut became furyous.

2. If you complete this circuit, you may recieve a shock.

3. I found these supplys in an old-fashioned stationary store.

4. My father saw water stains on several of the cieling tiles downstairs.

5. In a tree in that feild, Shelly saw the tinyest bird she had ever seen.

6. Although Manny is a little forgettful sometimes, he is always a good freind.

7. The parade could not procede until the police had cleared the intersection.

8. The courageous sailors stayed with their damaged ship.

9. When he transfered out of our class, he needed the counselor's aproval.

10. Although we studied hard, that test was truely aweful.

EXERCISE B On the lines provided, write the plural form of each of the following words.

Example 1. success _____*successes*_____

11. opera _____

12. waltz _____

13. knife _____

14. hero _____

15. mouse _____

16. eighth-grader _____

17. six _____

18. dairy _____

19. matinee _____

20. kimono _____

COMMON ERRORS

Spelling B

EXERCISE A In each of the following sentences, two words are underlined. If either word is misspelled, write the correct spelling above it. If both words are spelled correctly, write C at the end of the sentence.

Example 1. Little Hawk made *noticeable* ~~noticable~~ progress in his efforts to track foxes.

1. Luckily, wash hung outside will continue to dry even in freezing temperatures.

2. Some industrious gymnasts maintain a dayly exercise routine of eight hours.

3. Before submitting your short story, ask one of your freinds to proofread it carefully.

4. I don't know whether van Gogh painted daisys, but my neighbor has a print of the artist's painting of sunflowers.

5. Are there fewer than forty potatos in a score?

6. If the ground rules are disobeyed, the game will be forbidden.

7. The thiefs stole the radios that students were assembling in electronics class.

8. My flute teacher says that a beginer often feels dizzy.

9. Soon we'll have to build new shelves for all the tropheys we're winning!

10. Lewis and Clark heard the echos of the horses' hooves.

EXERCISE B In each of the following sentences, underline any misspelled word and write the word correctly above it. If all the words in a sentence are correct, write C at the end of the sentence.

Example 1. No, I don't think he's *conceited* ~~concieted~~.

11. My grandmother enjoys playing dominos with the nieghborhood children.

12. The sheriffs from three counties held a news conference when they captured the thiefs.

13. Did the people in that region use oxes or horses to pull thier wagons?

14. Two of my sister-in-laws teach four-year-olds.

15. Only twelve students showed up in response to the anouncement.

16. When we were in Canada last fall, we saw at least nine moose and countless deer.

17. The Gomezs have a new litter of puppys.

18. On one of their journies, they explored these vallies.

19. Last winter was so cold that we were able to build iglooes in the backyard.

20. The team members were a little embarassed when they conceeded defeet.

Words Often Confused

EXERCISE A In each of the following sentences, underline the correct word in parentheses.

Example 1. Thunderstorms moved *(threw, through)* the area ahead of the cold front.

 1. An expert grammarian, Ms. Marcos knows the *(principle, principal)* parts of any verb.

 2. The new mayor was *(formerly, formally)* a member of the school board.

 3. It is common knowledge that the Puritans preferred *(plane, plain)* clothing.

 4. Move any of the benches that are not *(stationary, stationery)*.

 5. *(Who's, Whose)* hilarious cartoon is displayed on the bulletin board in the hall?

 6. Our usual program will not be *(shone, shown)* tonight due to this special report.

 7. Our cat Max prefers the company of *(quite, quiet)* adults to that of rowdy children.

 8. New prescription drugs must be tested to verify how they will *(affect, effect)* people.

 9. Professor Luchesi offers his expert *(advice, advise)* to first-year music students.

 10. Our new *(counselor, councilor)* says next year's student schedules are ready.

EXERCISE B In each of the following sentences, underline any incorrect word and write the correct word above it. If all the words in a sentence are correct, write *C* at the end of the sentence.

Example 1. That story certainly had an *effect* on me.

 11. My parents had all ready gone to bed by the time we arrived.

 12. I wish she would learn how to except a complement.

 13. Would you like fruit for desert?

 14. Oh, no, the dogs have gotten lose again!

 15. Of course, we could choose our courses together.

 16. When the plain past low overhead, the windows rattled.

 17. Our house is no smaller then they're house is.

 18. The largest city in a state is not necessarily it's capitol.

 19. Gabriela was all together tired of listening to well-intentioned advise.

 20. Please don't break the car quiet so fast the next time!

Spelling and Words Often Confused

EXERCISE   In each of the following sentences, underline each misspelled or misused word and write the correct word above it. If all the words in a sentence are correct, write *C* at the end of the sentence.

Example 1. When the floodwaters <u>receeded</u>, the city <u>counsel</u> surveyed the damage.
(above "receeded": receded; above "counsel": council)

1. One of our nieghbors recognized the thiefs from a poster she saw in the grocery store.

2. For my birthday, my parents gave me a set of wrenchs for my bicycle.

3. He had all ready set the table with forks, spoons, and knifes.

4. I can't tell the difference between her 2s and her 5s; do we need 2 or 5 tablespoons of flour?

5. The guest of honors at the banquet were introduced by our principle.

6. We could take her advise and altar our plans to include a side trip to Williamsburg.

7. Each of the winners was formally introduced to the audience.

8. If you loose your key, whose going to let you in?

9. Although the whether was all together unpleasant that day, we enjoyed our visit to the science museum.

10. Their are at least 7 mispelled words in you're essay.

11. After a weak's intensive practice, the sopranoes will know their part.

12. We spent only about ninty minutes at the amusement park.

13. Many public librarys have unabridged dictionarys.

14. I really don't know weather gooses like to eat potatos.

15. First the led in my pencil broke, and than my pen ran out of ink.

16. Her eyes shown with releif and gratitude when the jury brought in it's verdict.

17. Our mileage would improve if you didn't always have your foot on the break.

18. A police car preceeded the funeral procesion.

19. Unfortunatly, the movie was almost over by the time we finaly found the theater.

20. During this time of year, the salmon in that stream are protected.

Review A: **Usage**

EXERCISE A Most of the following sentences contain a subject-verb or pronoun-antecedent agreement error. If a sentence contains an agreement error, underline the incorrect pronoun or verb and write the correct word or words above it. If the sentence is correct, write *C* after it.

Example 1. One of the world's oceanographers *is* are interested in animal groups.

1. Born in Japan, Dr. Akira Okubo studies sea animals to learn about its movements.

2. Did Mesa Verde or Grand Teton National Park get their name from the French language?

3. Volcanoes, like Mt. Pinatubo and Mt. Etna, gives scientists a chance to predict eruptions.

4. Several of these curry spices are found in India and throughout the world.

5. Several cultures, including the Maya, was beginning to cultivate the cacao tree.

6. A blend of cocoa and vanilla were a favorite flavor among the Aztecs.

7. China and Sweden have switched its traffic policy and ordered vehicles to drive on the right.

8. Neither the ordinary viewer nor the art expert has the ability to explain the *Mona Lisa*.

9. Everyone in our science class has their own opinion about how to save the Amazon Rain Forest.

10. Two horns and square lips identify the white rhino of Africa.

EXERCISE B On the lines provided, rewrite the following sentences, correcting any errors in the use of modifiers.

Example 1. The grass is much more greener now than it was last summer. *The grass is much greener now than it was last summer.*

11. To design a house, knowledge about local building codes, construction techniques, and materials is important. _____

12. We don't ever have no homework in this class. _____

13. Having tripped over a rock on the sidewalk, the bag of groceries fell out of the woman's arms. _____

14. His argument was the more simply stated of all. _____

15. After the rain stopped, a rainbow was seen on his way to the store. _____

Review B: **Mechanics**

EXERCISE   On the lines provided, rewrite each of the following sentences, using capital letters and punctuation where needed, and correcting any misspelled or misused words. Underline any words that should be italicized.

Example 1. annie asked nora do you want to borrow my copy of to kill a mockingbird

"Annie," asked Nora, "do you want to borrow my copy of To Kill a Mockingbird?"

1. to apply for my passport I had to bring the following a certified copy of my birth certificate a filled out application and two photographs _____

_____

2. one of my parents signatures was also required since I am under 18 years old _____

_____

3. you should of seen the line at the passport office _____

_____

4. my mother wrote one check to the u s state department and a second check to the u.s. postal service the second check was for a processing fee _____

_____

5. are you planing to travel soon asked the clerk your passport wont be ready for 5 or 6 weaks

_____

6. no I answered were not leaveing until let me see I have the ticket right hear may 25 _____

_____

7. a woman behind us in line recomended a book called italy the real guide she said its available in any bookstore. _____

_____

8. my father is taking one flight my mother and I will go on a different plain _____

_____

9. our flight leaves at 7 00 A.M. I know I wont be able to sleep the night before and we will arrive in rome at about 8 30 P.M. the next night _____

_____

10. my mothers uncle and aunt in italy told us that their planning a big celebration because the family will be altogether again. _____

_____

COMMON ERRORS

Review C: **Usage and Mechanics**

EXERCISE In the following newspaper article, most of the punctuation and capitalization has been left out. The reporter has also made errors in usage and spelling. Revise the article, correcting any errors in agreement, the use of modifiers, punctuation, capitalization, and word spelling or usage. Use proofreading marks to make your corrections.

Example **[1]** the redmond valley intermediate school student ~~counsel~~ council met on tuesday, march 14 at 3:30 P.M.

[1] the student bodys president theo vavilis reveiwed the agenda for the class representives, which included the following items the school wide fundraiser for the library a landscaping project and the problem of noise in the cafeteria **[2]** president vavilis announced that the fund-raising committee had decided to hold a car wash at mcintoshs service station on the corner of thirty fourth street and oak street **[3]** everyone pass by that corner said president vavilis we should get alot of customers" **[4]** one of the 6th grade representatives offerred to bring a vaccuum cleaner and theo asked for more volunteres **[5]** the car wash will be from 8 00 A.M. until noon saturday march 25 **[6]** anyone who is interested in helping should put their name on the list

[7] nancy fredrickson an eighth grader than explained the landscaping plans **[8]** the area right outside the front door is a mess she exclaimed students leave trash everywhere **[9]** its all together disgusting one of the representatives agreed **[10]** some of the parents has offered to build benchs for that area nancy continued and we need donations of the following items landscaping soil lumber small shrubs flower seeds and tools **[11]** whose available to help after school next week

[12] the council spent more of the meeting discusing the noise problem in the cafeteria **[13]** every student in the school know that the acoustics in the room is bad **[14]** noise echos and bounces off the walls **[15]** in addition some students do not seem to know the meaning of the word quiet **[16]** on the other hand students look forward to seeing his or her friends during lunch period and no one want to sit threw lunch without saying a single word

[17] the council finaly decided to ask the cafeteria monitors to remove extremly loud or unruly students so that everyone else could enjoy their lunch in piece. **[18]** if these measures dont effect the noise levels said theo well have to come up with some more ideas **[19]** mr rauh the student councils sponsor said that he would take the councils suggestion to the principle **[20]** having reminded the representatives to report back to they're classes the meeting was adjourned

COMMON ERRORS

Proofreading Application: Book Report

Good writers are generally good proofreaders. Readers tend to admire and trust writing that is error-free. Make sure that you correct all errors in grammar, usage, spelling, and punctuation in your writing. Your readers will have more confidence in your words if you have done your best to proofread carefully.

Book reports are part of school life. Numerous times you will be asked to review and comment on books. Some of these books you will like and some you will not like. When you decide to criticize an author's work, be very sure that you proofread carefully. The appearance of common errors in your report will weaken your argument. As the old saying goes, "People in glass houses shouldn't throw stones."

PROOFREADING ACTIVITY

Find and correct the errors in grammar, usage, and mechanics in the following excerpt from a book report. Use proofreading symbols to make your corrections.

Example   Smythe, ~~who's~~ *whose* autobiography was recently republished, led a

privileged life.

Wilimena Calpernica Smythes autobiography Everyday Life of a

Victorian Lady describes what she calls the ordinary life of a woman

of her age. Apparently at pains to appear educated Smythe has

created a painful obstacle coarse of strange inverted sentences dot-

ted with obscure vocabulary

   Her cheif interest seem to have been gardens long, detailed

descriptions of virtually every flower in her yard begin each chap-

ter. This provides a setting for the events that follow. "What are

these events" one might understandably ask.

   The major events of the book fall into two categories the

harvestting of vegetables and the planning and attending of parties.

Peas are checked rechecked, picked, and pickled. Sterilizing jars

and assembling scores of vats of boiling water to preserve the boun-

ty of Smythe's garden. Of some interest to modern readers is the

herbs. Such as peppermint, that Smythe dries and preserves for medi-

Literary Model: Journal

Progris riport 1—martch 5 1965

Dr. Strauss says I shud rite down what I think and evrey thing that happins to me from now on. I dont know why but he says its importint so they will see if they will use me. I hope they use me. Miss Kinnian says maybe they can make me smart. I want to be smart. My name is Charlie Gordon. I am 37 yers old and 2 weeks ago was my brithday. I have nuthing more to rite now so I will close for today.

April 18

What a dope I am! I didn't even understand what she was talking about. I read the grammar book last night and it explanes the whole thing. Then I saw it was the same way as Miss Kinnian was trying to tell me, but I didn't get it. I got up in the middle of the night, and the whole thing straightened out in my mind. . . .

After I figgered out how punctuation worked, I read over all my old Progress Reports from the beginning. Boy, did I have crazy spelling and punctuation! . . .

—from *Flowers for Algernon* by Daniel Keyes

EXERCISE A Underline each misspelled word in the above entries.

EXERCISE B

1. What generalizations can you make about the spelling errors in the first entry?

_____

_____

_____

2. How do the spelling errors in the second entry compare with those found in the first entry?

_____

_____

_____

_____

From "Flowers for Algernon" by Daniel Keyes. Originally published in *The Magazine of Fantasy & Science Fiction*. Published by Bantam Books, New York, 1959.

Literary Model (continued)

EXERCISE C Using the excerpts written by the character Charlie in the novel *Flowers for Algernon* as a model, write two or three entries in a diary kept by someone who is gradually being educated and learning to spell. The writer might be a young child, an adult like Charlie, or someone who is learning English as a second language. Have the writer's spelling reflect his or her progress.

_____

_____

_____

_____

_____

_____

_____

_____

_____

_____

_____

_____

_____

_____

_____

_____

_____

_____

_____

EXERCISE D How did you decide what kinds of spelling errors to use in the entries?

_____

_____

_____

_____

_____

for **CHAPTER 17: CORRECTING COMMON ERRORS**   *pages 173–79*

Writing Application: Survey

Writing is a stricter and more rule-bound form of communication than speech. Spoken words flow by so quickly, with starts and stops and *umm*'s. We pass over, ignore, and forgive many little glitches as long as we understand the speaker generally. In writing, on the other hand, we have time to read, consider, re-read—time to see problems in grammar and to puzzle over problems in meaning. Take care not to transfer casual but incorrect agreement to your writing.

NONSTANDARD   Everyone I know plans to work on their organization's homecoming float next weekend.

STANDARD   **Everyone** I know plans to work on **his** or **her** organization's homecoming float next weekend.

STANDARD   **All** of my friends plan to work on **their** organizations' homecoming floats next weekend.

WRITING ACTIVITY

For a graphing exercise in your math class, you need to survey your classmates to determine what extracurricular activities are most popular among them. Write up your findings in a succinct paragraph; include students' comments about why they prefer the activities in which they participate. Use indefinite pronouns as you group the students by preference, but be sure that you then check agreement carefully.

PREWRITING   Generate two or three questions that will draw out of each student the information you need. Then, conduct "mini-interviews" with the students, jotting down their replies. When you have all the data in hand, decide how to organize it. You could present the numbers categorized by age of student, by type of activity, or by some other sensible plan.

WRITING   Formal diction, standard usage, and straightforward tone mark writing of this sort. Present your data in clear, simple sentences; link related information with obvious, logical transitions. Do not use students' names as you report your findings; instead, use indefinite pronouns.

REVISING   Because you are working with numbers that you can translate into percentages, you are actually writing up statistical findings. You must be quite certain that your numbers are correct. Check them carefully. Check the written report against the graph to see that they agree.

PUBLISHING   Check your report for errors in agreement. Then, print the report neatly and attach it to the graph. With your teacher's permission, post the graph and the report on the bulletin board in the classroom.

EXTENDING YOUR WRITING

If you enjoyed this exercise, you could develop it into a longer writing project. For a class in journalism, investigate how advertisements use statistics to sell products. When an ad claims that its product is twice as good, strong, fast, or effective as its competitor, where do these implied numbers come from? How do these numbers affect people reading the ad?

Symbols for Revising and Proofreading

Symbol	Example	Meaning of Symbol
≡	at Scott lake	Capitalize a lowercase letter.
/	a gift for my Ʋncle	Lowercase a capital letter.
∧	cost ^fifty^ cents	Insert a missing word, letter, or punctuation mark.
∧	by ~their~ ^our^ house	Replace something.
ℯ	What day is ~is~ it?	Leave out a word, letter, or punctuation mark.
∪	recieved	Change the order of letters or words.
¶	¶The last step is	Begin a new paragraph.
⊙	Please be patient⊙	Add a period.
∧	Yes∧ that's right.	Add a comma.

Identifying Sentence Fragments

EXERCISE A   Determine which of the following word groups are sentence fragments and which are complete sentences. If the group of words is a complete sentence, write *S* on the line provided. If the group of words is a fragment, write *F*.

Example   _____F_____   **1.** May dress as a medieval countess for the costume contest.

_____ **1.** If you think some of today's fashions are weird.

_____ **2.** You should see the clothes people wore in the Middle Ages.

_____ **3.** Patterns of floral or geometric shapes popular.

_____ **4.** Liked clothes that were half one color and half another.

_____ **5.** Might have one green leg and one red leg!

_____ **6.** People often wore heavy leather belts decorated with metal and jewels.

_____ **7.** Edges of clothing into shapes called *dagges*.

_____ **8.** Sleeves with streamers that were two or three feet long.

_____ **9.** Shoes had long toes that were padded to retain their shape.

_____ **10.** Tights of velvet or silk.

_____ **11.** When clothes were edged and lined in fur.

_____ **12.** Layers very common in medieval clothing?

_____ **13.** Was a way of displaying wealth.

_____ **14.** The more clothes a person wore, the wealthier that person was.

_____ **15.** Might wear a short-sleeved tunic over a long-sleeved tunic, with a sleeveless mantle over all.

_____ **16.** The usual head covering for men a hood with an attached shoulder cape and a long, extended point, like a tail.

_____ **17.** Women wore a neckcloth pinned to their braids, hiding their hair.

_____ **18.** On top of the head, would wear a veil, a linen crown, or a small, round hat.

_____ **19.** In the later Middle Ages, women wore jeweled metal nets over their coiled braids.

_____ **20.** Current fashions a little boring in comparison!

SENTENCES

Identifying Sentence Fragments (continued)

EXERCISE B   Determine which of the word groups in the following paragraph are sentence fragments and which are complete sentences. If a word group is a complete sentence, write *S* above its item number. If the word group is a fragment, write *F* above its item number.

Example   [1]   South Pole on continent of Antarctica.   [2] Antarctica has the highest average elevation of the seven continents.

[21] No native people on the continent of Antarctica.   [22] Because it is too cold.   [23] Although scientists and other workers live in Antarctica for about a year at a time.   [24] These people live there to study many things.   [25] The ozone layer, sleep patterns, and fish survival in subzero temperatures.   [26] Ninety-five percent of Antarctica covered with ice.   [27] Also has very high winds.   [28] Sometimes Antarctica's winds reach speeds of 200 miles per hour.   [29] Many animals in the ocean around Antarctica.   [30] One type of bird found on Antarctica is the penguin.

SENTENCES

for **CHAPTER 18: WRITING EFFECTIVE SENTENCES** | pages 439–40

Finding and Revising Sentence Fragments

EXERCISE A Some of the following word groups are sentence fragments. Others are complete sentences. If a word group is a complete sentence, write *S* on the line provided; if it is a fragment, write *F*. Then, use proofreading symbols to revise each fragment so that it contains a subject and a verb and expresses a complete thought. Change punctuation and capitalization when necessary.

Example ___*F*___ **1.** Because Denise and I like to explore our town⸮
                                                        , we spend a lot of time on our bikes.

_____ **1.** Yesterday, Denise and I to go for a bike ride.

_____ **2.** We put on our helmets for the trip.

_____ **3.** Our part of town a lot of steep hills.

_____ **4.** Saw many interesting places along the way.

_____ **5.** The breeze hit our faces as we coasted down the hills.

_____ **6.** Although going down the hills was really fun.

_____ **7.** Felt tired after pedaling up all those hills.

_____ **8.** Some hills steeper than they had looked at first!

_____ **9.** Rested and drank some water after several miles.

_____ **10.** My legs shaky.

_____ **11.** When we got up to go, suggested that we pedal home slowly.

_____ **12.** After we had taken our break.

_____ **13.** As we crested the last hill.

_____ **14.** When we waved to our friends across the street.

_____ **15.** Was my favorite part of today's trip.

_____ **16.** We decided to explore another part of town on our next bike ride.

_____ **17.** Agreed to take our next bike trip on Saturday.

_____ **18.** I wish my bike had a motor on it!

_____ **19.** Am glad my bike is modern.

_____ **20.** Early bicycles had heavy wooden frames and iron tires.

SENTENCES

Finding and Revising Sentence Fragments (continued)

EXERCISE B Some of the following word groups are sentence fragments. Others are complete sentences. If a word group is a complete sentence, write *S* on the line provided; if it is a fragment, write *F* on the line. Then, use proofreading symbols to revise each fragment so that it contains a subject and a verb and expresses a complete thought. Change punctuation and capitalization when necessary.

Example __*F*__ **1.** When one of my friends began training for a marathon, *, I decided I would train, too.*

_____ **21.** A marathon is a running event.

_____ **22.** Has a distance of approximately twenty-six miles.

_____ **23.** The race's length a historical basis.

_____ **24.** In 490 B.C., a Greek soldier from Marathon to Athens with news of a Greek victory over the Persians.

_____ **25.** Reproduces that soldier's run, although the current marathon distance is actually longer.

_____ **26.** Marathons and half-marathons in many cities.

_____ **27.** Boston and New York City both have famous marathons.

_____ **28.** Because the marathon is such a long race.

_____ **29.** Whether a marathon runner is a beginner or a seasoned veteran, should commit to months of training.

_____ **30.** Must keep their bodies strong and well rested.

SENTENCES

Identifying and Revising Run-on Sentences

EXERCISE A Decide which of the following groups of words are run-on sentences. If a word group is a correct sentence, write *C* for *correct* on the line provided. If it is a run-on sentence, use proofreading symbols to revise it by (1) making it into two separate sentences, (2) using a comma and a coordinating conjunction, or (3) using a semicolon.

Example _____ **1.** Bears can live in many different habitats these animals occupy mountains, forests, and arctic wilderness.

_____ **1.** Brown bears include the grizzly and the kodiak, the largest brown bear is the kodiak.

_____ **2.** Did you know that kodiak bears weigh as much as 1,700 pounds, they can grow to a height of ten feet?

_____ **3.** In the wild, bears can live longer than thirty years!

_____ **4.** A bear's sense of smell is more developed than its hearing or sight.

_____ **5.** Females give birth to as many as four cubs, the cubs stay with their mother two or three years.

_____ **6.** Many people are afraid of bears, encounters with bears are actually infrequent.

_____ **7.** Grizzly bears are solitary animals, they do not want to interact with people.

_____ **8.** Generally, bears attack only when they are surprised or when they are protecting their young.

_____ **9.** In bear country, people should always store food and garbage properly, bears could be attracted by the smell.

_____ **10.** Never try to outrun a bear, it can run more than thirty miles per hour!

SENTENCES

Identifying and Revising Run-on Sentences (continued)

EXERCISE B   Decide which of the word groups in the following paragraph are run-on sentences. If a word group is a correct sentence, write *C* for *correct* above the item number. If it is a run-on sentence, use proofreading symbols to revise it by (1) making it two separate sentences, (2) using a comma and a coordinating conjunction, or (3) using a semicolon.

Example **[1]** Albert Einstein was one of the greatest thinkers of the twentieth century, he changed the way people view the universe.

[11] In Munich, school was too rigid and boring for young Einstein he did not do well.

[12] However, Einstein showed a talent for mathematics, at the age of twelve, he taught himself Euclidean geometry. **[13]** After finishing secondary school, he entered the Federal Polytechnic Academy in Switzerland, he did not like the teaching methods there. **[14]** The academy frustrated him he could not learn in a way that interested him. **[15]** Einstein chose to educate himself, and he missed classes often to study physics on his own.

[16] His professors had low opinions of him, he graduated anyway in 1900. **[17]** In 1905, he published a paper on physics the University of Zürich awarded him a Ph.D. for this work.

[18] In the same year, he published four more papers that presented new thoughts on the nature of light and other important concepts. **[19]** Physicists resisted Einstein's ideas at first, eventually his general theory of relativity was confirmed through observation. **[20]** Einstein achieved international recognition, in 1921 he received the Nobel Prize in physics.

Review A: Revising Sentence Fragments and Run-on Sentences

EXERCISE A The following paragraph is confusing because it contains some complete sentences, some sentence fragments, and some run-on sentences. Identify the fragments by underlining them once. Identify the run-ons by underlining them twice. Then, rewrite the paragraph, revising all fragments and run-ons to make them complete and correct sentences.

Example Scuba diving a popular pastime. This pastime has an interesting history, humans have been underwater explorers for centuries. *Scuba diving is a popular pastime that has an interesting history. Humans have been underwater explorers for centuries.*

Scuba is an acronym The acronym stands for "**s**elf-contained **u**nderwater **b**reathing **a**pparatus." In the fifteenth century, Leonardo da Vinci designed an underwater diving suit. Functional equipment not developed until much later. Inventors in the eighteenth century designed practical devices for breathing underwater. Such as diving suits and diving bells. Wearing these suits, divers could breathe underwater, their mobility was limited. The twentieth century had Jacques Cousteau and Émile Gagnan to solve the problem. Perfected the aqualung. The aqualung is a cylinder of compressed air, the cylinder is worn on the diver's back and is connected to a mouthpiece. With an aqualung, divers have both air and mobility. Since 71 percent of the earth's surface is covered by oceans. Scuba diving opened up a whole new world.

Review A: Revising Sentence Fragments and Run-on Sentences (continued)

EXERCISE B The following paragraph is confusing because it contains some complete sentences, some sentence fragments, and some run-on sentences. Identify the fragments by underlining them once. Identify the run-ons by underlining them twice. Then, rewrite the paragraph, revising all fragments and run-ons to make them complete and correct sentences.

Example In class we learned about penguins, they are impressive creatures. Penguins can live in

extremely cold climates. *In class we learned about penguins, which are impressive*

creatures. Penguins can live in extremely cold climates.

Penguins look clumsy on land, they are graceful in the water. Their bodies are perfectly suited for swimming and diving. They a streamlined torpedo shape. Their wings are shaped like flippers penguins use them to propel themselves through the water at speeds up to thirty miles per hour. Use their webbed feet to steer. Most penguins can even swim like porpoises. Leap out of the water to breathe and then dive back in with one graceful motion. Penguins frequently need to dive deep to catch prey. Sometimes descend to depths of more than a thousand feet. Penguins special air chambers in their bodies. When a penguin dives, the chambers squeeze, air is forced into the penguin's lungs. The extra air keeps the lungs from collapsing under the water pressure. The chilly waters that penguins prefer would be too cold for most birds, penguins are insulated by waterproof feathers and a thick layer of fat. Penguins may be awkward on land, but they are perfectly suited for the water.

_____

_____

_____

_____

_____

_____

_____

_____

_____

_____

_____

_____

_____

_____

SENTENCES

HOLT HANDBOOK | Second Course

Combining Sentences by Inserting Words

EXERCISE A   Each of the following items contains two sentences. Use proofreading symbols to combine each sentence pair by taking a word from one sentence and inserting it into the other. Then, put a delete mark through the unneeded sentence. You may have to change the form of some words.

Example 1. In earlier times, people stayed indoors at night. ~~Staying indoors was normal.~~

(normally inserted above "stayed")

1. Nightfall used to leave city streets in darkness. The darkness was complete.

2. Animals in the streets were difficult to see during the night. The night was dark.

3. In the fifteenth century, some cities began to hang lanterns outside on winter nights. The cities were European.

4. Two hundred years later, New York City lit its streets with lamps hung on posts. The lamps contained oil.

5. Neither of these efforts to light the streets helped very much. These efforts were early.

6. In 1807, Pall Mall in London became the first street with gaslights. The lights were bright.

7. As gaslights spread across Europe and to the United States, more people could travel at night in a city. Travelers were safe.

8. New York began to use electric streetlights in the late nineteenth century. Electric lights have economic advantages over other light sources.

9. The introduction of these brilliant lights drastically reduced street crime in the United States. They were introduced in a gradual way.

10. In some modern cities, cameras attached to the lights help to reduce crime even further. These are video cameras.

SENTENCES

Combining Sentences by Inserting Words (continued)

EXERCISE B   Each of the following items contains two sentences. Use proofreading symbols to combine each sentence pair by taking a word from one sentence and inserting it into the other. Then, put a delete mark through the unneeded sentence. You may have to change the form of some words.

Example 1.   One popular belief is that the earliest ∧English colonists in America lived in log cabins. ~~The belief refers to colonists from England~~.

11. This idea is completely incorrect. The idea can charm people.

12. The colonists first built shelters such as huts or tents. The shelters were temporary.

13. Next, they built the kind of houses they had had in England. The construction was prompt.

14. The Pilgrims and Puritans of New England lived in houses. The houses were European-style.

15. In 1638, settlers established a colony on the Delaware River. The settlers were Swedish.

16. The log cabins in America were built by these Swedes. These log cabins were the original ones.

17. Later, German immigrants constructed log cabins in America. These immigrants were independent of the Swedish settlement.

18. In the eighteenth century, log cabins became a common sight on the western frontier. The western frontier continued to expand.

19. People began to associate this well-known symbol of frontier life with the earliest English settlers of America. These people were mistaken.

20. Regardless of where they came from, log cabins are still popular as simple places to vacation. Primitive-style cabins are appealing.

Combining Sentences by Inserting Phrases

EXERCISE A Combine each of the following pairs of sentences. Take the underlined phrase from one sentence and insert it into the other sentence. The hints in parentheses tell you how to change the forms of words. Add commas where needed. Then, put a delete mark through the unneeded sentence.

Example 1. The facsimile machine ∧*also known as a fax machine,* is on the desk beneath the window. ~~A facsimile machine is also known as a fax machine.~~

1. The fax machine is an important tool. It is a tool <u>for modern communications</u>.

2. Alexander Bain was a <u>Scottish mechanic</u>. The first patent for a facsimile machine was given in 1843 to Alexander Bain.

3. English physicist Frederick Blakewell gave the first demonstration of a working facsimile machine. The demonstration took place <u>at the 1851 World's Fair</u>.

4. In 1863, a commercial fax system was set up in France. The system <u>linked Lyon and Paris</u>. (Change *linked* to *linking*.)

5. By 1906, Germany had a fax system between Munich and Berlin. The fax system <u>sent newspaper photographs</u>. (Change *sent* to *to send*.)

6. Later, telegraph lines were used <u>as the standard means</u> of fax transmission. In the early twenties, the United States used telegraph lines to fax photographs to newspapers.

7. American researchers developed a new method. The new method <u>involved telephone lines</u>. (Change *involved* to *involving*.)

8. Further advances in the thirties allowed anyone to have newspapers faxed right to the home. Anyone who <u>owned a telephone or radio</u> could use this service. (Change *owned* to *owning*.)

9. Fax technology is <u>a wonderfully fast way to send documents</u>. Fax technology has become an important part of the business world.

10. I expect to receive an important fax. I will be receiving the fax <u>this afternoon</u>.

SENTENCES

Combining Sentences by Inserting Phrases (continued)

EXERCISE B Combine each of the following pairs of sentences. Take the underlined phrase from one sentence and insert it into the other. The hints in parentheses tell you how to change the forms of words. Add commas where needed. Then, put a delete mark through the unneeded sentence.

Example 1. The magazine article taught me about giant squids. _{some extraordinary creatures,} ~~Squids are some extraordinary creatures.~~

11. The giant squid <u>lives deep in the ocean</u>. The giant squid is a mysterious creature. (Change *lives* to *living*.)

12. For years, researchers tried in vain to see a giant squid. They tried to see one <u>in its natural habitat</u>.

13. A cephalopod is <u>a kind of mollusk</u>. The giant squid is a cephalopod.

14. The squid moves very quickly. It does so <u>by expelling a stream of water</u>.

15. A pursued squid will shoot a cloud. The cloud is made of dark ink.

16. The giant squid has eyes the size of volleyballs. The eyes <u>make it look like a sea monster</u>. (Change *make* to *making*.)

17. The giant squid is <u>a truly imposing animal</u>. The giant squid averages between twenty and forty feet in length.

18. The largest squid on record was a giant. It <u>measured sixty feet long and weighed almost a ton</u>. (Change *measured* to *measuring* and *weighed* to *weighing*.)

19. The squid's "arms" are covered with suction cups. The suction cups are what it <u>uses to catch prey</u>. (Change *uses* to *used*.)

20. The giant squid remains out of the sight of curious scientists. The squid lives <u>at depths of 700 to 3,000 feet</u>.

Creating Compound Subjects and Verbs

EXERCISE A   Use proofreading symbols to combine each of the following sentence pairs by forming a compound subject or a compound verb. Make sure your new subjects and verbs agree in number.

Example 1. Lions ~~are powerful animals.~~ Tigers are powerful animals.

(and inserted)

1. These big cats have much in common. They can also be contrasted.

2. Lions belong to the genus *Panthera*. Tigers belong to the genus *Panthera*.

3. Lions grow to a length of about eleven feet. They weigh up to 550 pounds.

4. Tigers grow up to twelve feet long. They weigh as much as 675 pounds.

5. Lions are social animals. They live in large groups.

6. Tigers prefer to be alone. They come together occasionally.

7. Tigers can live about fifteen years in the wild. Lions can live about fifteen years in the wild.

8. A tiger eats deer and cattle. It sometimes lives on frogs and fish.

9. Lions can eat more than eighty pounds of meat at a single sitting. They might go for a week without eating.

10. Concealment helps lions and tigers catch their prey. Speed helps lions and tigers catch their prey.

SENTENCES

Creating Compound Subjects and Verbs (continued)

EXERCISE B   Use proofreading symbols to combine each of the following sentence pairs by forming a compound subject or a compound verb. Make sure your new subjects and verbs agree in number.

Example 1. The world's oceans contain unique creatures, ~~The oceans~~ *and* provide a fascinating classroom for students and scientists.

11. Lionfish can injure people who touch them. Moon jellyfish can injure people who touch them.

12. The rays of a lionfish are brightly colored. They contain a strong, painful venom.

13. Moon jellyfish can grow up to eight inches wide. They have tentacles that can sting bare skin.

14. Moon jellyfish are found in oceans worldwide. Blue whales are found in oceans worldwide.

15. Blue whales can grow to a length of 100 feet. They can weigh up to 130 tons.

16. A blue whale's heart is the size of a small car. The heart can pump almost ten tons of blood.

17. Blue whales feed on tiny animals and plants called plankton. Manta rays feed on tiny animals and plants called plankton.

18. Manta rays have been called devilfish by some people. They are not dangerous to humans.

19. Dangerous beasts can be found in our oceans. Harmless creatures can be found in our oceans.

20. Like creatures on land, ocean creatures can be harmless to humans. Like creatures on land, ocean creatures usually are not harmless to one another.

SENTENCES

Forming Compound Sentences

EXERCISE A   The sentences in each of the following pairs are closely related. Make each pair of sentences a compound sentence by adding a comma and a coordinating conjunction such as *and, but,* or *or.*

Example 1. Courtney and Christa were considering vacation ideas with their aunt Betty, A hiking
            trip sounded best to them.

(handwritten: , and — inserted after "Betty")

1. Books about the Pacific Crest Trail mentioned its history and variety. Courtney, Christa, and Aunt Betty agreed to hike a section of it.

2. The Pacific Crest Trail runs from Mexico to Canada. Its five sections total 2,650 miles.

3. The trail runs through three states. Both deserts and mountains lie in its path.

4. They were excited about the trip. They were not sure where to begin their hike.

5. Courtney compiled a list of the gear they would need. Christa made a map of the route they would take.

6. Aunt Betty suggested they travel slowly. Courtney and Christa agreed.

7. They could walk ten miles each day for three days. They could spend more time enjoying the trail.

8. The trail goes through Crater Lake National Park. There is a thirty-mile segment of trail there.

9. The scenery was beautiful. The weather was overcast at first.

10. The sun came out after a few hours. The weather was perfect.

SENTENCES

Forming Compound Sentences (continued)

EXERCISE B The sentences in each of the following pairs are closely related. Make each pair of sentences a compound sentence by adding (1) a semicolon or (2) a comma and a coordinating conjunction such as *and, but,* or *or.*

Example 1. Lighthouses are a feature of coastlines, Sailors have long relied on lighthouse signals.

11. Fire was used as a light source for early lighthouses. More reliable sources of light are used today.

12. The light guides ships by night. The lighthouse itself serves as a marker by day.

13. Submerged rocks might be marked. A harbor entrance could be indicated by a lighthouse.

14. The British colonies on the North Atlantic had a vigorous sea trade. The earliest North American lighthouses were built there.

15. The first U.S. lighthouse was established in 1716 at Boston Harbor. Congress has preserved it as a monument.

16. The keepers of this lighthouse were originally paid by the city of Boston. Modern U.S. lighthouses are maintained by the United States Coast Guard.

17. In the nineteenth century, whaling and fishing were major industries in the Pacific Northwest. Lighthouses were needed to guide the ships.

18. The Pacific Northwest has a rough coastline. Engineers have built lighthouses there.

19. The Great Lakes can be almost as dangerous as the oceans. Their rough waters have caused many shipwrecks.

20. The Great Lakes support many ships. Hundreds of lighthouses have been built on the lakes' shores.

SENTENCES

Using Subordinate Clauses

EXERCISE A Combine each of the following sentence pairs. Make one sentence a subordinate clause and attach it to the other sentence. The hint in parentheses will tell you which word to use at the beginning of the subordinate clause. To make a smooth combination, you may need to delete one or more words.

Example   **1.** Sharks are ecologically important creatures, ~~They~~ *that* are also fascinating.

1. There are about 350 species of sharks. They swim the world's oceans. (Use *that*.)

2. The largest species is the whale shark. Whale sharks can grow to be fifty feet long. (Use a comma and *which*.)

3. The pygmy ribbontail catshark is a small shark. It never grows longer than ten inches. (Use *that*.)

4. Little is known about sharks' lives even by researchers. The researchers study sharks. (Use *who*.)

5. Some of the largest sharks feed near the surface. They eat tiny plants and crustaceans. (Use a comma and *where*.)

6. One shark called the wobbegong lives on the sea floor and catches small fish. The fish are lured into the shark's mouth by the waving tendrils around the wobbegong's mouth. (Use a comma and *which*.)

7. Other sharks are aggressive hunters. These sharks attack dolphins, sea lions, and giant tuna. (Use *that*.)

8. Sharks' teeth sometimes break off. The sharks attack prey. (Use *when*.)

9. A shark that attacks a human usually bites just once. The shark swims away. (Use *before*.)

10. Some people think all sharks are deadly. Many popular movies and books depict fictional shark attacks. (Use *because*.)

SENTENCES

Using Subordinate Clauses (continued)

EXERCISE B Combine each of the following sentence pairs. Make the second sentence a subordinate clause and attach it to the first sentence. The hint in parentheses will tell you which word to use at the beginning of the subordinate clause. To make a smooth combination, you may need to delete one or more words in the second sentence of each pair.

Example 1. Gravel is fragmented rock. ~~The fragmented rock~~ *that* is produced by erosion.

11. The action of rivers and oceans creates gravel. The gravel is usually worn and rounded. (Use *that*.)

12. Gravel is sometimes transported by ice. The ice protects the rock edges and leaves them sharper and less worn. (Use a comma and *which*.)

13. This sharp-edged gravel is then deposited. The ice melts. (Use *when*.)

14. Companies that produce gravel must mine it. They find natural deposits. (Use *wherever*.)

15. Most producers sort the gravel by size. Trucks, trains, or barges transport it. (Use *before*.)

16. It is important to use a high-quality gravel. A high-quality gravel will not break down easily or react with cement. (Use *that*.)

17. Concrete can expand and crack. Certain kinds of gravel react with the cement in the concrete. (Use *after*.)

18. People have depended on gravel as a building material. The Romans first used it in road construction. (Use *since*.)

19. Houses, office buildings, airports, roads, bridges, and water systems are just some of the modern structures. They require gravel. (Use *that*.)

20. For the most part, all this rock goes unnoticed by the people. These people stand, walk, and drive on it all day long. (Use *who*.)

Review B: Revising a Paragraph by Combining Choppy Sentences

EXERCISE A The following paragraph sounds choppy because it has too many short sentences. Use the methods you have learned in this section to combine some of the sentences.

Example A moon is a natural object. ~~It~~ that orbits a planet.

There are at least sixty-one moons. The moons are found in our solar system. These satellites are every bit as varied as the planets they orbit. The satellites are fascinating. For instance, both of Mars's moons have a diameter that is less than twenty miles. Two of Jupiter's moons are larger than the planet Mercury. These moons have little or no atmosphere. Most of the other moons in the solar system have little or no atmosphere. However, Titan has an atmosphere twice as dense as Earth's. Titan is Saturn's largest moon. Triton orbits Neptune. Triton orbits in the opposite direction of Neptune's rotation. Triton is not content with just one special feature. Triton is also one of the two moons that hold solar-system records. Triton is the coldest body in the solar system. Jupiter's moon Io is the solar system's most volcanically active body. Nonetheless, others have experienced even greater extremes. Uranus's moon Miranda broke into pieces in a huge collision. Miranda then drifted back together. An astronomer could spend all of his or her time just studying the moons in our solar system.

SENTENCES

Review B: Revising a Paragraph by Combining Choppy Sentences (continued)

EXERCISE B The following paragraph sounds choppy because it has too many short sentences. Use the methods you have learned in this section to combine some of the sentences.

Example There are several observatories in the United States. One of the best is in Texas.

                     , and

  You might not think of West Texas when you think of astronomy. The McDonald Observatory in the Davis Mountains is one of the best places in the United States to view the stars. The University of Texas had a minor astronomy program. William Johnson McDonald willed over one million dollars to the university in 1926. He willed the money for the construction of a large telescope. The University of Texas joined in a partnership to found McDonald Observatory. The University of Chicago joined in a partnership to found McDonald Observatory. The Davis Mountains were chosen as the observatory's location. They were chosen for their high elevation, low humidity, and remoteness. The observatory is 160 miles from the nearest large city. Several large telescopes belong to the observatory, including the Hobby-Eberly Telescope. The Hobby-Eberly Telescope is the third largest in the world. Another astronomical device is the McDonald Lunar Laser Ranging Station. The McDonald Lunar Laser Ranging Station fires a laser beam at the moon to measure its changes in motion. Perhaps the most exciting feature of the observatory is that it has several telescopes. These telescopes are public. Visitors can use them.

Revising Stringy Sentences

EXERCISE A Some of the following sentences are stringy and need revision. If a numbered item needs no revision, write *C* for *correct* on the line provided. If the item is stringy, revise it by using one of the methods you have learned.

Example _____ **1.** In the spring and summer we see many ₍bright, colorful₎ butterflies, ~~and they are bright, and they are colorful.~~

_____ **1.** Butterflies are insects, and some butterflies' wingspans are up to ten inches, but others' are less than one-half inch.

_____ **2.** A butterfly goes through four life stages, collectively called metamorphosis.

_____ **3.** Most butterflies lay their eggs on plants, and the plants provide the offspring with food, but some other larvae eat aphids, or they consume cereals or wool clothes.

_____ **4.** Butterflies do not have stingers or other natural weapons, and many predators feed on them, but butterflies have developed other means of defending themselves.

_____ **5.** Some butterflies have bright colors, and these colors are called warning colors, and these colors scare away predators.

_____ **6.** Monarch butterfly larvae feed on the milkweed plant, and milkweed is toxic to most creatures, but the larvae store the toxins in their bodies, so predators don't like to eat monarchs.

_____ **7.** Monarch butterflies live all around the world, and there is a large population in North America, and this population migrates south, and it migrates every year.

_____ **8.** These millions of North American monarchs migrate to Mexico, where the weather is warm enough to keep them alive through the winter.

_____ **9.** Many American Indian cultures consider the butterfly to be a special creature, and the Pueblo people have a butterfly dance, and the dance welcomes the beginning of spring.

_____ **10.** The oldest known butterfly fossils are 48 million years old, and they were found in Green River shale, and the shale is in Colorado.

SENTENCES

Revising Stringy Sentences (continued)

EXERCISE B Some of the following sentences are stringy and need revision. If a numbered item needs no revision, write *C* for *correct* on the line provided. If the item is stringy, revise it by using the methods you have learned.

Example _____ **1.** ~~I am~~ very proud of my sister Jamisa, ~~and our whole family is proud of her, too, and we are proud of her talents.~~

Our whole family is (inserted) ... *and her talents.* (inserted)

_____ **11.** Jamisa is a student artist, and she paints and sculpts, and she also loves to study new art forms.

_____ **12.** She is currently working on a series of oil paintings, and she is reading about watercolors, but she wants to take a class, and the class is about welding, and she can learn how to make metal sculptures.

_____ **13.** She stays very busy with her art, and she spends a lot of time at the library and museums, and she does research, and she generates new ideas.

_____ **14.** Jamisa goes to art school in Atlanta, where she enjoys the way her instructors teach. She is interested in teaching art in the future.

_____ **15.** Jamisa has completed four sculptures and six large paintings, and she has entered them in a student art show, and the show will let her see how people like her work.

_____ **16.** Jamisa's talent impresses people who have seen her work, but she is still insecure.

_____ **17.** She is anxious about showing her latest work, but I think everyone will appreciate all the pieces, and the pieces will be in the show.

_____ **18.** She paints Monday through Friday, but she relaxes now and then, and she relaxes with a book, but she soon returns to her canvases.

_____ **19.** She also works on a book of sketches, and the sketches are done in charcoal, and she works on them whenever she has the time.

_____ **20.** Jamisa's teachers are impressed, and Jamisa's fellow students are impressed, and they are all impressed by her dedication and talent.

SENTENCES

Revising Wordy Sentences

EXERCISE A　Decide which of the following sentences are wordy and need revision. If the sentence is effective as it is, write *C* for *correct* in front of the number. If it is wordy, revise it. You can (1) replace a phrase with a word, (2) replace a clause with a phrase, or (3) take out unnecessary words.

For my research project,

Example　_____　**1.** I studied the life of Itzhak Perlman, ~~who was the topic of my research~~ ~~project.~~

_____　**1.** Itzhak Perlman is the most acclaimed and honored violinist of his generation.

_____　**2.** Born in Israel in 1945, Perlman contracted polio, which is a very serious disease, when he was four.

_____　**3.** His struggle that he had with the illness left his legs paralyzed.

_____　**4.** Within a short period of time afterward, Perlman began playing the violin.

_____　**5.** It is interesting to note that by the time he was ten, Perlman was performing with the Israel Broadcasting Orchestra.

_____　**6.** He appeared on the popular American television program *The Ed Sullivan Show* when he was thirteen.

_____　**7.** Perlman remained in the United States to attend the Juilliard School, a prestigious institution.

_____　**8.** He won the Leventritt Competition in 1964, earning engagements with major orchestras inside the borders of the United States.

_____　**9.** Since then, Perlman has appeared with every major orchestra, recorded most of the standard violin works, played on film soundtracks, and made jazz, ragtime, and contemporary recordings of music that he has played.

_____　**10.** President Ronald Reagan awarded Perlman the U.S. Medal of Freedom, which was given to Perlman in 1986.

SENTENCES

Revising Wordy Sentences (continued)

EXERCISE B Decide which of the following sentences are wordy and need revision. If the sentence is effective as it is, write *C* for *correct* in front of the number. If it is wordy, revise it. You can (1) replace a phrase with a word, (2) replace a clause with a phrase, or (3) take out unnecessary words.

Example _____ **1.** All over the ~~whole, entire~~ world, boundaries between countries often follow the course of ~~and are defined by~~ rivers.

_____ **11.** The Amur, which is the eighth longest river in the world, is almost 2,800 miles long.

_____ **12.** For some 1,100 miles of its course, the river forms the border and the boundary line between China and Russia.

_____ **13.** Each winter, the Amur is frozen close to six feet deep.

_____ **14.** Because there are few roads in the region, the frozen river serves as a route for trucks that need a place to drive.

_____ **15.** Linking Moscow to the Russian Far East, the Trans-Siberian Railroad parallels the Amur for a great stretch of its length.

_____ **16.** Although only two bridges cross the Amur at the present time, plans are being made to build one connecting the Russian town of Blagoveshchensk and the Chinese city of Heihe.

_____ **17.** The dense forests in the Amur Valley provide a habitat for the Siberian tiger, an endangered animal at risk of becoming extinct.

_____ **18.** In 1987, one of the world's largest fires burned for a month, destroying and wiping out almost 51,000 square miles of forest along the Amur.

_____ **19.** Chinese and Russians are talking of forming a joint fire commission to deal with such emergencies when the future brings them.

_____ **20.** Combined efforts by a combination of elements like this may be the only way to preserve the beauty and history of the Amur region.

Review C: **Revising Stringy and Wordy Sentences**

EXERCISE A The following paragraph is hard to read because it contains stringy and wordy sentences. Decide which sentences are stringy and wordy, and then revise them to improve the style of the paragraph.

Example In one method of juggling instruction, the first step, before you do anything else, is to

practice dropping the ball.   *In one method of juggling instruction, the first step is to*

practice dropping the ball.

    Dora developed an interest in juggling due to the fact that her friend Robyn was a skilled juggler. Dora received some juggling balls for her birthday, and she asked Robyn to teach her how to use them, and she began to practice. First, Dora learned how to juggle two balls that were in one hand. Dora mastered that, and she practiced tossing the two balls, and she tossed them from one hand to the other. She added a third ball, and a few days had gone by. Then, she learned a new way to juggle, which was switching the direction in which she was throwing the balls. Before long, she could add various different items while she juggled. She delighted the children in her neighborhood by putting on a show for them that they enjoyed very much.

_____

_____

_____

_____

_____

_____

_____

_____

_____

_____

_____

_____

_____

_____

_____

_____

SENTENCES

Review C: Revising Stringy and Wordy Sentences (continued)

EXERCISE B The following paragraph is hard to read because it contains stringy and wordy sentences. Decide which sentences are stringy and wordy, and then revise them to improve the style of the paragraph.

Example The heart signifies and is associated with love and compassion and caring about others, but its physical function is as an organ of the body. _The heart is associated with love and compassion, but its physical function is as an organ of the body._

    The human heart is a muscle, and it is roughly cone shaped, and it is about the size of a fist, and it pumps blood throughout the body. Physical exercise and working out help keep the heart healthy. Smoking and a poor diet can increase the risk of a heart attack, which is a sudden decrease in the blood supply to the heart. People with high blood pressure should receive treatment due to the fact that this condition can cause heart attacks. Problems with the heart may be treated with medication or surgery and the most extreme form of surgical correction is the heart transplant. After the first human heart transplant occurred in 1967, many surgeons began to perform this operation, and most of these early heart transplants were unsuccessful. Medical procedures and treatments have improved, and the transplant operation is still extremely risky, but the success rate is much higher now.

_____

_____

_____

_____

_____

_____

_____

_____

_____

_____

_____

_____

_____

_____

_____

_____

SENTENCES

Varying Sentence Openings and Structure

EXERCISE A   The following paragraph sounds dull because its sentences do not contain variety. Make the paragraph more interesting by revising sentence openings or by rearranging the structure of the sentence.

Example   My older sister said as the sun began to set, it was getting colder.   <u>My older sister said,</u>

<u>"As the sun begins to set, it's getting colder."</u>

    We walked along the forest trail. There was a thick mist in the air. We could hardly see twenty feet ahead of us. The sunlight barely broke through the mist. We heard a noise. We were startled. I turned around. A squirrel was running over some dry leaves. I breathed a sigh of relief. We kept walking down the narrow trail. Pine trees surrounded us. Their dark green needles looked almost pale behind the mist. A lone bird sailed across the path. Silence added to the beauty of the scenery. My stomach growled suddenly. We spotted our cabin in the distance. We looked at one another. We smiled. Our hike was nearly over. I could picture the sandwiches on the table already.

_____

_____

_____

_____

_____

_____

_____

_____

_____

_____

_____

_____

_____

_____

_____

_____

_____

_____

_____

_____

_____

SENTENCES

Varying Sentence Openings and Structure (continued)

EXERCISE B The following paragraph sounds dull because its sentences do not contain variety. Make the paragraph more interesting by revising sentence openings or by rearranging the structure of the sentence.

Example Almost everyone Anna knew would be in the audience. <u>*In the audience would be*</u>

<u>*almost everyone Anna knew.*</u>

    Anna was nervous. She stood backstage. She had never acted in a play before. She looked at the thick, red curtain in front of her. It would open in two minutes. The curtain muffled the sounds of the audience. Anna could still hear laughter through it. She could still hear conversation through it. Anna looked at the clock. She took a deep breath. She straightened the collar of her costume. Anna scanned the room backstage. The actor to her left looked calm. He wasn't wringing his hands. Mrs. Ortega was behind the wings. She was beaming. Mrs. Ortega was the director. The butterflies in Anna's stomach increased. The curtain slowly began to rise. Anna felt relieved. She remembered her first line. She was ready.

SENTENCES

Using Transitions and Parallel Structure

EXERCISE A The paragraph below does not read smoothly because its sentences do not have transitions. Rewrite the paragraph, adding transitions when necessary. The transitions you add may be words, phrases, or clauses. Write your revision on the lines provided.

Example Making major decisions can be difficult. It can also be worthwhile. *Making major deci-*

sions can be difficult, but it can also be worthwhile.

My cousin Gina, who is seventeen, has a big decision to make. She was offered a full-time summer job. A local architecture firm asked her to be their office assistant. Taking the job could be a good idea. Gina could earn her own money. She could start a savings account. She could have some money left over to buy books and CD's for herself. She would learn more about architecture. She wants to become an architect one day. Gina might prefer not to take the job. A full-time job would require her to sacrifice most of her summer's free time. She would have less time to babysit her two-year old brother Todd. She would have less time to spend with her friends. Gina would miss many of her soccer games and practices if she worked all summer. She is glad to have options.

Using Transitions and Parallel Structure (continued)

EXERCISE B   Bring balance to the following sentences by putting the ideas in parallel form. You may need to add or delete some words. If a sentence is already correct, write *C* on the line provided.

Example _____ **1.** The characters in the story hide from the dragon, concoct an escape plan,

and then fleeing from the dungeon.

_____ **1.** Four characteristics of reptiles are having scaly skin, breathing with lungs, being cold-blooded, and backbones.

_____ **2.** Uncle Han loves sports: he loves playing tennis, watching football, to referee volleyball, and to coach soccer.

_____ **3.** In the winter, many rabbits live in dens made of piles of brush, rocks, or under wood.

_____ **4.** All the volunteers enjoyed being outdoors, so they were happy to plant flowers, dig weeds, and mowing the yard.

_____ **5.** A rotary engine goes through four steps in each combustion cycle: intake, compression, expansion, and exhaust.

_____ **6.** Learning Spanish, to run track, and studying geography are my favorite parts of going to school.

_____ **7.** Martha likes the field hockey team because it allows her to stay active, meeting more friends, and be competitive.

_____ **8.** Carla, do you think that the Cyclones will shut out their opponent and win the game?

_____ **9.** Mr. Davis said that he will give us a quiz tomorrow and to study hard for it.

_____ **10.** Quanah Parker, a Comanche chief in the late nineteenth century, encouraged his people to get an education and that they should farm the land.

SENTENCES

Review D: Applying Sentence Revision Strategies

EXERCISE A Rewrite the following paragraph by combining sentences, revising sentence fragments, run-on sentences, and stringy and wordy sentences. Use proofreading symbols to make your revisions.

Example Being well versed in many of the arts and sciences, Leonardo da Vinci was one of the original, ~~early~~ Renaissance men. ~~He was well versed in many of the arts and sciences.~~

Leonardo da Vinci was born in 1452. His birth took place in Italy. Died in 1519. Leonardo was a skilled scientist, he was also a talented artist. One of his masterpieces is *The Last Supper*. He painted it on dry plaster, which is a poor surface for oil paints. The painting began to disintegrate. Its disintegration was gradual. Leonardo also painted the *Mona Lisa*. This is his most famous and well-known work. He must have liked this painting. Because he carried it with him when he traveled. Leonardo's scientific contributions are impressive as well, he was ahead of his scientific peers. He filled many notebooks with scientific theories and observations and he wrote his notes in mirror script. This writing made it difficult for other people to read his notes. He planned many devices, such as an underwater diving suit. Many of his devices were not actually created for hundreds of years. People still recognize the name of Leonardo da Vinci. They recognize it centuries after his lifetime.

SENTENCES

Review D: Applying Sentence Revision Strategies (continued)

EXERCISE B Rewrite the following paragraph by combining sentences, revising sentence fragments, run-on sentences, and stringy and wordy sentences. Write your revised paragraph on the lines provided.

Example The guitar has been around and existed longer than you may think.   *The guitar has*

existed longer than you may think.

    Modern guitars derive from the *guitarra latina*. The *guitarra latina* was an instrument used in the late Middle Ages. It was an instrument with four strings. The guitar was probably developed in Spain and it was probably developed sometime during the sixteenth century. The early guitar four courses, or rows, of strings. The three bottom courses had two strings, and the top course had one string, and before 1800 a fifth and sixth course were added. Before 1800, the double courses were replaced. They were replaced by single strings. When the nineteenth century was occurring, the guitar's body underwent changes. These changes improved the guitar's tone. The body became broader and it became shallower, the wood on the front became extremely thin. At the present time, the basic guitar has been adapted to suit different purposes and to suit different tastes. The classical guitar has three strings of nylon and three strings of metal. The classical guitar is used to perform classical music. The metal-strung guitar is popular with rock, folk, country, and jazz musicians. These musicians frequently play electric guitars as well. The guitar might be the most widely played instrument that was played in the twentieth century.

_____

_____

_____

_____

_____

_____

_____

_____

_____

_____

_____

_____

_____

_____

_____

SENTENCES

HOLT HANDBOOK | Second Course